D0055581

GOOD FRIEND, what Matter how or whence you come
To walk thefe Streets which are the Nation's Home;
Reft for a Time and—refting—read herein,
Seek from the Paft and—feeking—Wifdom win:
For if the Things you fee give you no Gain,
The LIVES of many MEN were lived in vain.

A Likeness of His Majesty, King William III, in whose
Honour the City of Williamsburg in Virginia was
named. Now newly made by E. Jones
after an ancient Engraving

A
BRIEF & TRUE REPORT
CONCERNING

Williamsburg
in VIRGINIA:

Being an Account of the most important Occurrences in that Place from its first Beginning to the present Time.

TO which is added an Appendix composed of Records and Works from which this Account is drawn; with Copies of the Acts for building the Capitol and the City of *Williamsburg*, and its Charter.

By *RUTHERFOORD GOODWIN*,
An Inhabitant *of the* Place.

A third Edition revis'd & enlarg'd by the Author. Reissued now with some small Alterations.

WILLIAMSBURG:
Printed for the *Colonial Williamsburg* Foundation, by *August* and *Charles Dietz* on their Press in *Cary* Street at *Richmond, Virginia.* MCM,LXXX.

LC No. 41-5562   ISBN 0-910412-39-1

A
PREFACE
TO THE
READER.

IT may be considered a somewhat strange Thing to write of the Present in a Fashion of the Past; yet, in a Treatise which concerns a City the chief Interest and Enterprise of which is found in the Efforts to recall and restore its Past, it would be an equally strange Thing to write of the Past in the Fashion of the Present. Especially is this true when the Fashions of the Past have so much to distinguish and commend them for the Purpose.

Moreover,

Moreover, it is no broad Assumption that Persons having Interest in this ancient City have Interest also in the Methods of those who built the Homes and Gardens of the Period now styled COLONIAL. *Similarly, it may be taken that such Visitors have Respect and Liking for the Manner of the Printers who made the ancient Books—and often stamped more Character upon their Pages than did the Authors.*

And of the History of WILLIAMSBURG *it should be immediately confessed that it cannot be fully told in any Work of this Size, nor in any Work of thrice this Size. In Consequence, it is commended to the Reader that he look upon the City itself as a great Book of History, to which this Treatise is but an Index. And if this Volume can bring the Reader to a Humour for further Contemplation or Instruction, its Hopes will have been fulfilled and its intended Service will have been performed.*

Also, the Attention of the Reader should be directed to the Fact that the History of the

the City treated is still undergoing the most exhaustive Investigation, and the Author cannot stand responsible for those Things which may appear hereafter, no Matter what their Prominence.

Yet, it is believed that the chiefest Facts of the History of this Section are known at this present Time and will remain forever unchanged, and your Author has endeavored to advance especially the Facts of this Description. When Additions to this Instruction are made and well established, it may be that they will be accommodated in yet another Edition of this Work—until which Time

FAREWELL.

R. G.

A Preface

A
PREFACE
FOR THIS
3rd EDITION.

IN offering the third Edition of this
Work, which is now much enlarged
and altered, ſome Explanation of its
preſent Nature would ſeem adviſed.

The two Editions appearing formerly
contained a general hiſtorical Outline
of the City's Paſt, ſupplemented by
a Diviſion intended for guiding the
Traveller to Buildings and Sites of
eſpecial Intereſt. In Conſequence, the
Volumes were deſigned after the Manner
of the rude Travel Books of the Period
treated. But, owing to the continued Ex-
panſion of the *Williamſburg Reſtoration*,
it

it has proved more prudent to prefent Guide Information in Publications of a lefs permanent Character.

Therefore, in this third Edition the Divifion for Guiding is omitted and, in its Stead, an Endeavor is made to expand the hiftorical Outline and to fubftantiate it. This is done in the Hope that the Outline may prove acceptable as a bafic hiftorical Pattern to thofe who in Time will treat its many Phafes in greater Detail. Moreover, it is recognized that many have greater Admiration for the Words of the Ancients than can be accorded the Opinions of their Pofterity. In Knowledge of this Truth, it is hoped that the extenfive Appendix will fatisfy fuch Minds and contribute both to their Enjoyment and the Furtherance of their Labours. And it is becaufe of thefe Afpirations that the prefent Volume is defigned to be reminifcent of fuch 18th Century Volumes as *The Hiftory of the Firft Difcovery and Settlement*

Settlement of Virginia, by *William Stith*, which was printed at *Williamſburg* by *William Parks*, in 1747.

Finally, with Regard to the Appendix, it ſhould be particularly noted that it was in the greateſt Part compiled and edited by Miſs *Mary Randolph Mordecai*, whoſe Averſion to the Prominence of the Title Page has faced the Author with the Neceſſity of thus obſcuring a Fact which ſhould appear there. Beyond this, ſpecific Acknowledgment cannot go, for they that write on hiſtorical Subjects are in-debted to thoſe who gave them birth, to thoſe who enable them to write, to thoſe under or with whom they have worked, to ſome of their Friends and moſt of their Enemies; indeed they ſhould be grateful to all who have lived upon the Earth, and more eſpecially to Him who made it —— and ſo

AGAIN FAREWELL,
R. G.

A Table

A TABLE
TO THE
CONTENTS.

CHAPTER

CHAPTER III.

THE History of *Williamsburg* from 1780 until the Year 1927. And showing the City to have subsided into a State of dignified Decline.
p. 78.

CHAPTER IV.

A Relation of Facts which will be of Interest to the Reader concerning the *Williamsburg Restoration*—from 1927 to the present Time.
p. 94.

APPENDIX.

PART I.

A List of the Sources from which this Report is drawn. Being a careful Account of the Authors and Works referred to, these appearing under Numbers which correspond with those in the printed Text.
Page 127.

PART II.

PART III.

ILLUSTRATIONS.

ILLUSTRATIONS.

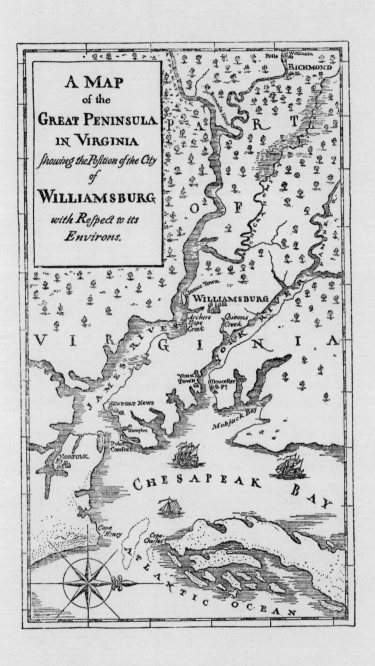

A BRIEF & TRUE REPORT

CONCERNING

WILLIAMSBURG
in VIRGINIA

CHAPTER I.

ILLIAMSBURG, which was known at its firſt Beginning as *Middle Plantation*, was born in the Year 1633 out of thoſe dreadful Miſgivings which oppreſſed the Settlers that firſt dwelt in the *Virginia* Colony.[1]

SOME Years previous to this Time, in 1622, the heathen *Indians*, doubtleſs thinking themſelves well juſtified by the Encroachment of the *Engliſh*, had contrived and perpetrated the moſt barbarous Maſſacre, wherein near one Third of all the Inhabitants of the Colony were cruelly ſlain.[2] And it was this grievous Occurrence which brought about the Raiſing of Paliſades acroſs the Peninſula between the

the Rivers *York* and *James*.[3]   The Raifing of fuch
Palifades, in itsTurn, occafioned the Eftablifhment
of a Settlement which, perhaps becaufe it centered
upon the Ridge of the Peninfula and filled the
Space that was between the newly feated Plantations on the *York* River and the older Plantations
on the *James* River, or perhaps becaufe it was
eftablifhed within the Space between two Palifades,
was called *Middle Plantation*.

From the meager Records of thofe Times it appears that the general Purpofe was this: That
Fortifications of Pales (that is of Logs planted end-
wife) fhould be built acrofs the expofed Breadth of
the Peninfula, and that between the Palifades
there fhould be a continued Succeffion of inhabited
Lands.   With this Front prefented to the *Indians*,
it was further purpofed to maintain a Guard upon
the Palifades and to exclude all *Indians* and *Indian*
Habitations from the Eaft of them, in Order that
the Settlers in the lower End of the Peninfula might
labour unguarded in their Fields, and that their
Children, their Servants, their Cattle, and their
Swine might go in fome Affurance of their Lives.[4]

Thus it was that at a Grand Affembly of the
Burgeffes and the Council " holden at *James Citty*
" [*Jameftown*] the firft Day of *February*, 1632/3,"
at which Sir *John Harvey* fat as Governor, an
Act was paffed entitled *An Act for the Seatinge of
the Middle Plantation*.   And this Act, in the Words
which follow ordered:

    " That every fortyeth Man be chofen and
                                " maynteyned

" maynteyned out of the tithable Perfons of all the
" Inhabitants, within the Compaffe of the Forreft
" conteyned betweene *Queenes* Creeke in *Charles*
" River [meaning either *York* River or *Charles*
" *River* County, afterwards the County of *York*],
" and *Archers Hope* Creeke in *James* River, with
" all the Lands included, to the Bay of *Chefepiake*,
" and it is appoynted that the fayd Men be there
" at the Plantation of Doct. *John Pott*, newlie built
" before the firft Day of *March* next, and that
" the Men be imployed in buildinge of Houfes, and
" fecuringe that Tract of Land lyinge betweene the
" fayd Creekes. And to doe fuch other Workes as
" foone as may bee, as may defray the Chardges
" of that Worke, and to be directed therein as they
" fhall be ordered by the Governor and Counfell.
" And yf any free Men fhall this Yeare before the
" firft Day of *May*, voluntarilie goe and feate
" uppon the fayd Place of the *Middle Plantation*,
" they fhall have fifty Acres of Land Inheritance,
" and be free from all Taxes and publique Chardges
" accordinge to a former Act of Affembly made the
" forth Day of *September* laft paft."[5]

AND it fhould be well obferved by the Reader
that the Plantation, ordered and encouraged by
this Act, was a Planting of Men in a Settlement,
rather than the Seating of a fingle Planter.[6] The
Reader, on the other Hand, fhould not be mifled to
picture *Middle Plantation* in his Mind, as fome
have done, as a Town to be compared with the
Towns of this prefent Day, nor even as a Town in
the Senfe that *Jameftown* was a Town in that early
Day.[7] More Truth will be found in looking upon
it as a wide-fcattered Settlement in which no Man
had

had Need to be difturbed by the Wailing of his
Neighbor's Offspring; yet which, with the Years,
converged upon a middle Point[8] until, of a Sudden,
it became a City[9]—as fhall be told in its proper
Time and Place.

🌣 🌣 🌣

THE Hiftory of the early Years of *Middle
Plantation* is, in great Part, hidden in Ob-
fcurity; for in thofe Times all Men were, to a furprifing Extent, Soldiers and Labourers in a common Caufe, even while they fought their own
Profperity and Advancement. In this Wife the
Hiftory of the Part did frequently become loft in
the Hiftory of the Whole; and the Admiffion fhould
be made that even Facts of Intereft pertaining to
the whole Country have in many Inftances been
loft in the Advance and Deftruction of Time, and
muft now be fupplied from Speculation.

YET, it would feem that as foon as 1634 the
Settlement had its Commander, one *Richard Pope-
ley*;[10] and it would appear that in 1646, after the
Indians had rifen in their fecond great Maffacre in
the Year 1644, *Middle Plantation* had become of fuch
a Confequence that Captain *Robert Higginfon* was
appointed to erect a new Pale at that Place or, it may
be, to repair the old one.[11] Nor was the Service of
God neglected there, for a Parifh was early eftablifhed, which, in 1658, was united with *Harrop*
Parifh to form *Middletowne* Parifh;[12] and this
Parifh, in its Turn, was united in 1674 with *Mar-
fton*

The Great Massacre in the Colony of VIRGINIA, in the Year 1622.
From a fine Engraving by Theodore de Bry.

ſton Pariſh to form *Bruton* Pariſh,[13] which laſt ſurvives to this preſent Day.

AND in theſe Years there were many of every Rank who patented Land in *Middle Plantation*. The firſt among them, who indeed was ſeated before the Settlement, was Doctor *John Pott*,[14] the Phyſician General of the Colony,[15] a Man in whom there was a great Conflict of Virtue and Miſchief; for, though he had ſerved as the Governor of *Virginia* in the Year 1629, yet in 1630 he was tried and convicted of ſtealing Cattle;[16] and, though he was held to be the foremoſt Phyſician of the Country and the only one that could be ſaid to be " ſkilled in Epidemical Diſeaſes,"[17] yet was he equally renowned for his Appetite for ſtrong Waters and low Company " who hung upon him while his " good Liquor laſted."[18] And, again, though he had himſelf been Governor, he was a prominent Member of the Council which, in 1635, thruſt Sir *John Harvey* out of his Governorſhip and ſent him Home to his Sovereign.[19]

AMONG the many others, leſs confuſed in their Diſpoſitions than this Doctor *Pott*, who ſettled at *Middle Plantation*, were *Edward* and *George Wyatt*, Nephews of Sir *Francis Wyatt*, who was twice Governor of *Virginia*; *Henry Tyler*, the Anceſtor to Preſident *John Tyler*; *Richard Kempe*, who was made Secretary of the Colony by Sir *John Harvey*;[20] *Robert Higginſon* of the " ancient Family of the *Higgin-* " *ſons*," known as " the Valliant Captain *Robert* " *Higginſon*. One of the firſt Command'rs that
" ſubdued

" fubdued the Country of *Virginia* from the Power
" of the Heathen ";[21] *Thomas Ludwell*, who was
alfo Secretary of the Colony; Major *Otho Thorpe*,
whofe Kinfman, *George Thorpe*, had been a great
and devoted Friend to the *Indians* and had been
killed by them in the Maffacre of 1622; Colonel
John Page, a Member of the Council; *James Bray*,
alfo a Member of the Council;[22] and many others of
like and lefs Diftinction.   Thus, it will be feen that
the Settlement, even in its firft forty Years, was not
without Standing in the Colony, nor without Influence in its Governance.

❀ ❀ ❀

BY the Year 1676, *Middle Plantation* had come
to be recognized as " the very Heart and
" Centre of the Country,"[23] and had gained an
Importance fecond only to that of *Jameftown*.
And in that Year it gained further Diftinction and
Prominence when it became, to fome Degree, the
Heart and Centre of a great Revolt of the People;[24]
which was led by *Nathaniel Bacon*, Jr., and which,
though it began as a March againft the heathen
Savages,[25] yet ended in an open War againft the
tyrannical Mifdoings of Sir *William Berkeley*, the
King's Governor.

THE Caufes of *Bacon's Rebellion* were of many
varying Sorts, and in this brief Space it can only be
recited that, on Account of the low Ebb of Tobacco
Prices, the Times were exceeding poor;[26] yet the
Taxes were daily and mightily increafed for the
Enrichment

Enrichment of the *Grandees* who furrounded the Governor,[27] for the Support of a weak and biafed Affembly which the Governor had held in Office for fome fourteen Years,[28] for the Coft of Oppofition to the Proprietorfhip into which the King had been pleafed to grant away the whole Colony,[29] and for the Erection and Maintaining of Forts which the People confidered fmall Protection.[30]   And upon a People already thus diftreffed and burdened the *Indian* Infidels fell daily with their Murderings and Maraudings in the outlying Places,[31] yet met with fmall Cenfure and lefs Oppofition from the Governor; which fome may have thought was becaufe he feared a War with them, but others faid was becaufe he loved them too well, he having a profperous private Trade with them in Beaver Skins.[32]

So it was that the People, defpairing of Protection from thofe that governed them, began without Authority to "beat up Drums for Volunteers to goe "out againft the *Indians* "[33] and to draw into Arms. And foon they had for their Leader this *Bacon*, a Gentleman of great Figure and Prominence in the Country, who, though he was a young Man, yet was born to lead other Men and to infpire their Spirit with his Words.[34]

TWICE *Bacon* led an Army againft the Savages; at the firft in Defiance of Sir *William Berkeley*, and, in the fecond Inftance, with a Commiffion as General of all the Forces in *Virginia* againft the *Indians*, which he had forced from the Governor

and

and the Affembly with a great Show of Arms. Yet
on each Occafion he and thofe that followed him
were proclaimed Rebels and Mutineers by the
Governor, who fought to raife Men to put them
down. Thus, *Bacon* was brought to fee that if he
would go out againft the *Indians*, he muft firft go
againft thofe that he fought to protect; and fo he
reverfed his March to give them Battle.

RETURNED from the Frontier, *Bacon* found
that the Governor, having been deferted by moft
of thofe he had raifed to fight the Rebels, had fled
into *Accomac* County on the eaftern Shore of the
Chefapeake.[35]　And, fo, finding himfelf embroiled
in a civil War againft the King's Regent, he
quartered his Troops at *Middle Plantation* and
fummoned all the People of the Colony " of what
"Quality foever, excepting Servants,"[36] to meet
with him there. And when a great Company of
People, including many of the principal Men of the
Country, had come together in that Place, *Bacon*
propofed an Oath to them by which, according to
one of the Times, they fhould fwear:

　" Firft, to be aideing, with their Lives and
" Eftates, the Generall, in the *Indian* War; fecond-
" ly, to oppofe Sir *William's* Defignes, if hee had
" any, to hinder the fame; and, laftly, to protect
" the Generall, Army and all that fhould fubfcribe
" to this Ingagement, againft any Power that
" fhould be fent out of *England*, till it fhould be
" granted that the Country's Complaint might be
" heard againft Sr. *William* before the King and
" Parliament."[37]

And

And in Defenfe of this Oath, which fome feared, *Bacon* argued that five Hundred *Virginians* might beat two Thoufand Red Coats,[38] and he further ftated that he would refign his Commiffion to the Affembly if the Oath fhould be refufed; and fo there were few that refufed it.[39]

Now *Bacon*, having the Support of near the whole Country, marched out a third Time againft the *Indians;* but he found his chofen Adverfaries exceeding fcarce, they having hidden themfelves in the Swamps or fled to other Parts through Fear of him.[40] And, as he purfued them, he learned that *Berkeley* had returned out of *Accomac* with a confiderable Following from that Quarter, and had taken *Jameftown* and fortified it. Then, with his cuftomary Difpatch and Boldnefs, *Bacon* marched upon *Jameftown* and laid a Siege there;[41] and, after many brave and ftrange Happenings, *Berkeley* difcovered that his Supporters were as fickle in their Loyalty as *Bacon's* Men were ftrong in theirs, and fo, with thofe that were true to him, he fled again into *Accomac*.[42] And immediately *Bacon* entered into the Town and burned it into an Heap of Afhes that " the Rogues," as he faid, " fhould harbour " no more there."[43]

At the Height of his Power, *Bacon* now moved into *Gloucefter* County,[44] and there he laid many promifing Plans for the Furthering of the *Indian* War; the Purfuit of *Berkeley* into *Accomac;* the general Ordering and Relief of the Country; and, if Need be, the Refiftance of the armed Force of a Thoufand

Thousand Red Coats that had been sent against
him out of *England*. But, as one Story of the
Times has told it, *Bacon*, having destroyed *James-*
town, was himself destroyed by *Jamestown*;[45] for a
great Fever, taken in the Swamps in the Siege of
that Place, came upon him and, Fate being stronger
than Man, he surrendered to it and died. And it
is a true Measure of the Strength and Power of the
Man that, upon his Death, the Rebellion he had
led sputtered like a Candle Flame and went out.

IN an amazing small Space of Time Sir *William*
Berkeley came again into full Control of the Government, and, in a vengeful Fury, he set about to hang
all of the principal Followers of *Bacon* that came
to his Hands. Some, including *William Drum-*
mond, who had been Governor of *North Carolina*,
he hanged at *Middle Plantation;* and yet others he
hanged at *Green Spring*, his own country Estate.[46]
And a few, among whom were *Richard Lawrence*,
Thomas Whaley, and *John Forth*, fled away into the
Forests with their Arms,[47] and were never heard of
again; though some have supposed that they made
their Way into *New England*,[48] they preferring Life
in that Climate to Death upon a Gallows. So that
when the King's Troops arrived from *England*
there was Nothing left for them to do in putting
down the Revolt; but for the three Commissioners
who came in charge of them, and to inquire into
the whole Affair, there was much to do. And when
the Commissioners set about to restore Tranquility
in the tortured Colony, *Berkeley*, who could not
bear

bear that Peace and Prosperity should be spread among his Enemies, crossed them at every Turn.[49] In the End he was recalled, and, leaving one of the Commissioners, Colonel *Herbert Jeffreys*, in his Place as Governor, he sailed for *England* in the Year 1677, and there he soon died.[50]

THUS ended *Bacon's* Rebellion. And the Cause for being so particular in the Description of these Things should be plain: For not only did *Middle Plantation* have a prominent Part in all this melancholy Business, but also out of it, in devious Ways, came many of those Conditions which brought about the Upbuilding of the City of *Williamsburg* at *Middle Plantation;* for in those Times the Soil of *Virginia* was more suited to the Growth of Tobacco than it was to the Growth of Cities,[51] and one City might grow only from the Strength and Fertility gained from Ashes of another. Nor was this Rebellion a Matter of small Concern and Consequence, as some ill-informed Persons have supposed; for though *Bacon's* Cause was lost upon the Field, yet many of its Principles and Purposes were won, and it is not beyond Reason to find in these Happenings the Planting of Seeds which were to blossom forth in later Times.

❊ ❊ ❊

WITH Peace restored to the Colony, yet with *Jamestown* lying in Ruin, *Middle Plantation* now served for a brief Space of Time as the Seat of Government. In *October*, 1677, a Grand Assembly

was

was held there at the Houfe of Captain *Otho Thorpe*, at which Aſſembly Acts were made for the Relief of the Country[52] and a Proclamation from the King was read which pardoned all thofe that were engaged in the late Diſturbance, *Bacon* himſelf being alone excepted[53] (though, by Reaſon of the previous haſty Actions of *Berkeley*, there were many who lay beyond the Aid of this Pardon, unleſs its Words were to be carved upon their Graveſtones). Alſo in this Year the King's Soldiers were quartered at *Middle Plantation*,[54] and Governor *Jeffreys* ſummoned the chief Men of all the neighboring *Indian* Nations to come to the Camp there to treat abcut a laſting Peace. And with a great Show of Ceremony it was agreed that the *Indians* ſhould live in Submiſſion to the *Engliſh* and ſhould be guaranteed good Treatment by them.[55]

About this Time certain Inhabitants of *York* County filed a Petition with the King's Commiſſioners in which they entered the following Supplication:

" . . . And if a Towne be built for the Govnor
" Councell, Aſſembly to meet and for the Generall
" Court we humbly propofe the *Middle Plantation*
" as thought the moſt fitt Place being the Center of
" the Country as alfoe within Land moſt ſafe from
" any fforeigne Enemy by Shipping, any Place upon
" a River Side being liable to the Battery of their
" greatt Guns."[56]

Yet *Jameſtown* was ſtill held in Favour and the State Houſe was ordered to be rebuilt there;[57]
though

though it is probable that the Place itfelf never again enjoyed the Size and Prominence it formerly had.

But in the Year 1693 a great Diftinction did fall to *Middle Plantation*, for at that Time, their Majefties having been pleafed to grant a Charter for the Founding of a College to be known in their Honour as the College of *William and Mary* in *Virginia*,[58] the Affembly, having inveftigated feveral likely Locations, found *Middle Plantation* to be the moft convenient and proper for that Defign.[59]   In Confequence, it was enacted:

"... That *Middle Plantation* be the Place for
" erecting the faid College of *William and Mary* in
" *Virginia* and that the faid College be at that
" Place erected and built as neare the Church now
" ftanding in *Middle Plantation* old Fields as Con-
" venience will permitt."[60]

And it fhould be mentioned that the Founding of the College grew in good Part from the Fervour and Labours of the Reverend Dr. *James Blair*, a young *Scotch* Clergyman in the Colony, who having fuggefted and furthered the Defign in *Virginia*, was fent to *England* by the Affembly to promote the Plan at Court.[61]   And there he fecured not only the Charter, but alfo a generous Endowment from the Crown; to which he added confiderable Sums raifed from private Perfons, including certain Pirates whom he found in Prifon and who were defirous of their Freedom.[62]   And fo the Foundation Bricks of the principal College Building were laid

in

in the Year 1695[63] under the Direction of Mr. *Thomas Hadley*,[64] a Mafter Builder, who had been brought from *England* to fulfill the Plans which had been prepared in that Country by Sir *Chriſtopher Wren*,[65] the Surveyor General to their Majeſties (he who drew the Plans for *St. Paul's* Cathedral in *London*).

AND there are ſome who have ſought to trace the Inſpiration of the College to the Univerſity at *Henrico* that was propoſed for *Virginia* in the Year 1618,[66] and thus to advance it as the earlieſt College in all the Colonies. Yet, ſince the Deſign for the Univerſity at *Henrico* was defeated by the great Maſſacre of 1622[67] and by the Diſſolution of the *Virginia* Company (by which Company the Univerſity was propoſed), and moreover, ſince the propoſed Univerſity was ſeated in another Place, it is more proper to ſay that the College of *William and Mary* was in Foundation and Eſtabliſhment the ſecond College in the Colonies, *Harvard* College in the *Maſſachuſetts Bay* having been founded in 1636, or thereabouts.[68] Yet, it can be ſaid in Truth that the College of *William and Mary* was the firſt College of royal Foundation in all the *Engliſh America*.[69]

❀ ❀ ❀

WHILE the College was yet building at *Middle Plantation*, in the Year 1698, a final Calamity fell upon *Jameſtown* in the Burning of the new State Houſe at that Place.[70]   And, now, the Deſire to eſtabliſh the Seat of Government in a more central and

and healthful Spot having gained great Strength, and the Plan having found the ſtrong Support of the Governor, the Hon. *Francis Nicholſon*, Eſq.,[71] *Middle Plantation* was brought forward in this Wiſe:

" . . . and foraſmuch as the Place commonly call-
" ed and knowne by the Name of yᵉ *Middleplanta-*
" *tion* hath been found by conſtᵗ Experience to be
" healthy and agreeable to the Conſtitutions of yᵉ
" Inhabitants of yᵉ His Majeſtyes Colony and Do-
" minion haveing the naturall Advantage of a
" ſerene and temperate Aire dry and champaign
" Land and plentifully ſtored with wholeſome
" Springs and the Conveniency of two navigable
" and pleaſᵗ Creeks that run out of *James* and *York*
" Rivers neceſſary for the Supplying the Place with
" Proviſions and other Things of Neceſſity . . . "[72]

So that the Thought of rebuilding the State Houſe at *Jameſtown* could not ſtand in the Face of ſo handſome a Reputation; and in the Year 1699 the Aſſembly was prevailed upon to paſs an Act en-titled *An Act directing the Building the Capitoll and the City of Williamſburgh*, which, among other Things in its great Length, directed that the City to be built at *Middle Plantation* " in Honour of our " moſt gratious & glorious King *William*, ſhall be " for ever hereafter called and known by the Name " of the City of *Williamſburgh*."[73]

THIS, then, is the Story of *Williamſburg*, and how, under the Name of *Middle Plantation*, it came about and grew through the ſeventeenth Century of our Lord's Time. And, in *Virginia*, this had been a brave and arduous Span; a Time of Maſſ-

acres

acres and Wars, of Plagues and hard Living; a
Time of little Lace and lefs fine Dancing; a frugal
Time in which free Men, with their white inden-
tured Servants (for there were then few Blacks),[74]
and even Gentlemen laboured with the Strength
and Sweat of their Bodies to gain a Hold in a favage
and virgin Wildernefs. And, further, it was a
Time in which *Englifh* Men reached out for Land,
Land for themfelves and a Dominion for their
King; fo that the People were fcattered Abroad, and
there were few Towns. But now the firft Fruits of
thefe Labours were won; and fo, as *Virginia* ftood
before the Spread of another Century, *Williamfburg* rofe up—a Metropolis in the new World.

CHAPTER II.

Chapter II.

IT has been held that the History of the chief City of a Country is, in great Measure, the History of that Country itself. And if there be any Truth in this Philosophy, it will be left to the Reader to judge how much greater would be that Truth if the chief City should also be the only City of Consequence in such a Country: For, through those Years of the eighteenth Century in which it was the Metropolis of the *Virginia* Colony, *Williamsburg* was not only the Seat of *Virginia's* Government, but also the principal Seat of its Religion, Education, Society, Commerce, and Fashion. Moreover, it enjoyed this unusual Distinction in a Colony which was then everywhere acknowledged to be the most populous, the most powerful, and the most prosperous of all *Great Britain's* Plantations in *America;* so that though *Williamsburg* was in *Virginia* what *Boston* was in *Massachusetts* and what *Philadelphia* was in *Pennsylvania*, yet, because of its unusual Importance in *Virginia* and because of *Virginia's* Ascendancy among the Colonies, it was (although smaller in Size) in many Ways more potent than even those great Places.

FROM this the Reader will plainly see that it were as simple to pour the *Chesapeake* Bay into a Thimble

Thimble or to thruft the Tower of *London* into a
Snuffbox, as to prefs the full Hiftory of *Williamfburg* between thefe Covers.   Yet, in an oppofite
Cafe, it is not furprifing that many find it moft
curious, the Hiftory of the City being fo broad and
impofing, that they have not heard more of it from
their Schools and Hiftories in the Paft.   And, as to
this, it fhould be made clear that the Hiftory of the
Colony and of this Capital City were fo clofely
bound together that Hiftorians for thefe Years
needed but to write either a Hiftory of *Williamfburg*, or a Hiftory of *Virginia;* and fo chofe the
latter.   And, having made this Choice, they fo
long affumed that the true Importance of *Williamfburg* would be remembered, that they have fome of
them forgot it themfelves.

M o r e o v e r , it fhould be well noted that *Williamfburg* has ever been a Place of great Extremes
—one which, taken from one View or another, was
both great and fmall, both rich and poor, both
populous and deferted, both magnificent and
wretched, depending upon the Mind that looked
upon it and the Rule by which it was tefted.   And
this will be fully fhown.

❀ ❀ ❀

T HE Act directing the Building of the Capitol
and the City of *Williamfburg* at *Middle Plantation*,[75] which was paffed by the Affembly (with the
Urging of his Excellency, *Francis Nicholfon*, Efq.,
the Governor) in *June*, 1699,[76] fet afide two
Hundred

Hundred eighty-three Acres, thirty-five Poles and a Half of Land for the fole Ufe of the City to be there built. Of this, two Hundred and twenty Acres were furveyed and allotted to the City proper, and the Reft was fet afide for two Ports to be known as *Queen Mary's* Port and *Princefs Anne* Port (together with Land for Roads leading to them) upon *Queen's* Creek and *Archer's Hope* or *Princefs* Creek, fo that the City's Bounds might be acceffible from the *James* and *York* Rivers, yet the City proper not fubject to Bombardment from either.[77]

AND the Portion of *Middle Plantation* thus fet afide was, defpite its fine Hiftory in the Paft, a forry Place at beft; it bordering upon the College Lands[78] and containing a Church (which was in poor Condition),[79] a Magazine[80] (which was probably in worfe), a few Stores, Mills and inhabited Dwellings, a Smiths Shop, and a Publick Houfe[81] —all of which had for a Street an old Horfeway. Yet, this was of fmall Concern to the Governor and the Affembly, and, if anything, it was an Affiftance to their Purpofe; for it was now deliberately intended to raife a new and well ordered City according to a careful and prepared Defign,[82] fuitable for the Reception of a confiderable Number and Concourfe of People.

ONE Hiftorian of the Times has faid that the Governor propofed to lay out the new City in the form of a Cipher compofed of a *W* and an *M*,[83] and others have faid that he propofed but a *W*;[84] and

it

it matters little which had the Truth of it, for the
Proposal, whatever it was, was abandoned, and the
City was laid out upon a principal Street which ran
near a Mile on a Straight, and which, in Honour of
his Highneſs *William*, Duke of *Gloucester*, was
called the *Duke of Gloucester* Street.[85]   And two
parallel Streets, one on either Side of the principal
Street, were run and were called *Francis* and *Nich-
olson* Streets in Honour of the Governor; beſides
which numerous other Streets were run at various
Times and were named for the Kingdoms of *Great
Britain* and in Honour of royal or publick Perſons.
And moſt of theſe Streets ſurvive to this preſent
Day, together with their Names; among which are
England, *Ireland*, and *Scotland* Streets, *King* and
Queen Streets, *Prince George*, *Henry*, *Naſſau*, and
Botetourt Streets, and many others.[86]

IT is likely that, for ſome Space at leaſt, the
Duke of Gloucester Street followed the old Horſe-
way, but not for its whole Length; for it was neceſſary to diſmantle four old Houſes and an Oven belonging to Mr. *John Page* (from whom much of the
Land for the Building of the City had been purchaſed) which ſtood in the Middle of the Street at
one Point.[87]   And the Street was ſet ſo that the
College, which had been completed, ſtood at its
weſtern End; and now the Aſſembly ſet aſide a
four Hundred ſeventy-five Foot Square of Land at
its eaſtern End for a Building to be known by the
Name of the *Capitol*, the Act giving the moſt
minute

minute and thoughtful Defcription of how it was to be built and adorned.[88]

THE firft Act, together with fupplemental Acts, for building the Capitol and the City appear in the Appendix of this Volume, but it fhould be mentioned here that, in addition to many of the foregoing Inftructions, they contain, befides others, the following Provifions: That his Excellency *Francis Nicholfon*, Efq., his Majefty's Lieutenant and Governor General of *Virginia; Edmund Jenings*, Efq., of his Majefty's honourable Council; *Philip Ludwell*, Efq., and *Thomas Ballard*, Gentleman, Members of the right worfhipful Houfe of Burgeffes; *Lewis Burwell, Philip Ludwell*, Jr., *John Page, Henry Tyler, James Whaley*, and *Benjamin Harrifon*, Jr., Gentlemen, be appointed the Directors for the Settlement and Encouragement of the City; that the City be laid out and proportioned into half Acre Lots, and that the whole Country have timely Notice of the Act, and an equal Liberty in the Choice of Lots; that no Perfon fhould build upon the *Duke of Gloucefter* Street a Houfe of lefs than ten Foot Pitch, and that Houfes upon this Street fhould come within fix Feet of the Street and fhould front alike; that the Building (within twenty-four Months' Time) of a Houfe of ftated Size or greater, depending upon the Location, be required for the Referving of Lots and to prevent their efcheating to the Truftees for the City's Lands; that Perfons having Lots contiguous to the great Street fhould enclofe the faid Lots with a Wall, Pales, or Poft and Rails, within fix Months after

after the Building (which the Law required) fhould
be finifhed.   And the whole Act was directed to the
Building and Ordering of a City fuitable for the
Accommodation and Entertainment of the confiderable Number of Perfons that muft, of Neceffity,
refort thither; fo that it was held that the City
would probably prove highly advantageous and
beneficial to the Succefs of his Majefty's royal
College of *William and Mary*.

And it was a fortunate Condition that the
College Building was ftanding when the Government came to *Williamfburg*, for, while the Capitol
was raifing at the oppofite End of the Street, the
Offices of the Government and the Affemblies were
feated there from 1700 to the Year 1704.[89] Befides
which, in thefe Years his Excellency, Governor
Nicholfon, had his own Offices in the College[90] for
fome Time, which lent no fmall Diftinction to the
new Inftitution. Yet, it is to be queftioned
whether his Excellency's Influence upon the
Scholars was of the beft; for, on one Occafion at the
leaft, being approached in the Halls of the College
by one feeking Money out of the publick Funds, the
Governor did fly into fuch a Rage and did curfe and
fwear fo loudly, that a Sea Captain, who lay afleep
at fome Diftance in the Building, fprang from his
Bed and, neglecting to affix his wooden Leg, came
leaping through the Halls in his Shirt, thinking the
Building to be afire again,[91] as it often was.

Yet, it would be prefumptuous to affume that
it was becaufe of fuch Things that his Excellency
                                                    Edward

Edward Nott, Efq., who fucceeded *Nicholfon* as
Governor in the Year 1705, was able in 1706 to
fecure from the Affembly the Paffage of an Act
directing the Building of a Houfe for the Governor,[92]
fuch an Act having been before this conftantly refufed by the Affembly.[93]

THIS, then, is the Manner in which *Williamfburg* commenced to be built, and grew more in fix
Years than, as *Middle Plantation*, it had grown in
fixty-fix. And it is a Credit to the Reputations of
thofe who had a Hand in thefe Affairs that the
Plan for a City which they arrived at has not required altering and meddling in for thefe two
Hundred Years and more.

❁ ❁ ❁

IN the Year 1710 Colonel *Alexander Spotfwood*,
a Man of great Vigour and many Abilities,
came out to *Virginia* as the Lieutenant-Governor[94]
and as the Succeffor to *Edmund Jenings*, the
Prefident of the Council, who had ferved as acting
Governor for four Years, fince the Death of Govern-
or *Nott* in 1706, (*Robert Hunter*, who had been commiffioned to fucceed *Nott*, having been captured
on his Way to *America*). And *Spotfwood* found the
Capitol in its full Grandeur, it having been firft
ufed by the Affembly in 1704,[95] and finally completed in the Year 1705.[96] The Governor's Houfe
he found well advanced, but the Work at a Halt,
fo that he fet himfelf to bring it to Completion;[97]
which Aim he purfued with fuch Zeal and Afpira-
tion

tion that in 1718 he was charged by the Burgeſſes
with laviſhing away the Country's Funds.[98]   And
it is of Intereſt to note that, as one Appropriation
followed upon another, the Building came to be
known as the *Palace* for the Governor, inſtead of as
the Governor's Houſe, which was intended at the
firſt; and the Name *Palace* has continued for it.

THE College, to the Sorrow of the Country,
Spotſwood found in Ruin, it having been damaged
by a Fire in 1705;[99] but now (in the Words of one
of the Times) it was rebuilt, and nicely contrived,
altered and adorned by the ingenious Direction of
the Governor.[100]   Moreover, the brick Church
which had been built at *Middle Plantation* in 1683
being now in ruinous Condition, and the Veſtry
having been for ſome Time deſirous of rebuilding
it,[101] Governor *Spotſwood* encouraged this Deſign
alſo.   On Behalf of the Aſſembly, he preſented a
Draught or Plan for the Enlargement of the Church
propoſed by the Veſtry, and offered a generous
Subſcription to it;[102] and this Church, which yet
ſtands, was in thoſe Days deſcribed as being a large,
ſtrong Piece of Brickwork in the Form of a Croſs,
nicely regular and convenient, and adorned as the
beſt Churches in *London*.[103]   And it would appear
that the Governor, through theſe Things, gained a
ſplendid Reputation for Knowledge in the Deſign
and Advancement of fine Buildings; for in the Year
1714 the Aſſembly ordered that he be impowered
and deſired to order and direct the Building of a
brick Magazine for the Arms and Ammunition of
the

the Country, at fuch a Place as he might think proper;[104] and this refulted in a handfome octagonal Structure conveniently placed in the *Market Square* (which was Mid-way of the great Street), where it ftill ftands. About the fame Time, the County Seat of *James City* County being moved from *Jameftown* to *Williamfburg*,[105] a new Court Houfe was built upon the Border of the Market Square and near the Magazine.[106] Meanwhile, many private Dwellings and Publick Houfes were raifed, and the Streets, efpecially the great Street, were much improved and levelled.[107] Befides which, about the Year 1716, one *William Levingfton* erected a Playhoufe or Theatre upon the Avenue near to the Palace, which was the firft Theatre to be built in the *Englifh American* Colonies.[108]

NOR were the Energies of Governor *Spotfwood* directed folely to the Upbuilding of the City of *Williamfburg;* for in his Time there was a fteady Increafe of Profperity in the Colony, to which the Governor endeavored to add by the Encouragement of various Manufactures.[109] And Piracy upon the Seas, which was a Hinderance to Profperity, he fought to put down by an Expedition which he fent out againft one *Edward Teach*, who was better known as *Blackbeard;* and this Expedition returned with *Blackbeard's* Head fwung upon a Bowfprit and with certain of his Followers in Irons, who were later tried at *Williamfburg* and afterwards hanged.[110] Moreover, the *French* and their *Indians* having commenced to be a Menace in the weftern Lands, *Spotf-wood,*

wood, in the Year 1716, led a Company of about fifty Gentlemen (who have fince been called the *Knights of the Golden Horfefhoe*) in a great exploratory March to the Mountains of the *Blue Ridge*, upon a Peak of which they drank King *George's* Health in a brave Affortment of Wines and Spirits; and, to affure that the Land was fairly taken, they proceeded into the fertile Plains in the Valley of the *Shenandoah* beyond, where they planted a Claim in an emptied Bottle.[111]   And it would appear that the Governor's Purpofe was to extend and fettle the *Virginia* Colony to the weftward, fo that it might become a Barrier to the *French* Line of Communication between Lake *Erie* and *Louifiana*.

IN the Year 1717 an Endeavour was made under a previous Act of Parliament to fettle the *Britifh* Poftal Syftem in *Virginia* (as it had already been fettled in fome of the northern Colonies) by the Eftablifhment of a Poft to run each Fortnight between *Williamfburg* and *Philadelphia*.[112]   And it is of Intereft to note that the *Virginians* immediately and loudly protefted that Parliament could levy no Tax (for they confidered the Rates of Poftage to be fuch) without the Confent of their General Affembly[113] (and, as to this, it fhould be explained that the Affembly itfelf, almoft from its firft Beginning in 1619, had claimed the fole Right to tax *Virginians*).[114]   Now, in 1718, Laws were paffed by the Affembly which would have defeated the new Poftal Syftem, had not the Governor refufed his Affent to them.   Thus, *Virginia* early exhibited

a

a Diſtaſte for Stamp Taxes, which, as will be ſhown,
was not a paſſing Prejudice. And the Diſlike in
which the new Syſtem was held at *Williamſburg* is
ſhown by a Letter written in 1718 by Col. *John
Cuſtis*, the Father of the firſt Huſband of Mrs.
Martha Dandridge Cuſtis Waſhington, which went
as follows:

   " Wee have a damn'd confounded, pretended
" Poſt Office here, wᶜʰ keeps Letters as long as they
" think fitt; it is a generall Grievance to yᵉ
" Country: but am not ſure of its being redreſſed.
" I deſire you to putt all my Letters in a ſmall Box;
" directed to me, and give yᵐ into yᵉ Captˢ Charge;
" and then I may bee in ſome Hopes of having yᵐ
" ſafe and not peep'd into; a Form of Land Piracy to
" practicable in *Virgᵃ* nowadays . . . "[115]

WITHIN the next few Years *Spotſwood* entered
upon ſeveral Diſagreements with the Aſſembly,
beſides which he fell at Odds about the Clergy with
the Reverend Dr. *Blair*,[116] the Preſident of the College and Commiſſary of the Biſhop of *London*, who
has been pointed to by Hiſtorians as the Rock
upon which Governors *Andros* and *Nicholſon* had
already foundered; ſo that in 1722 he was relieved
of his Commiſſion as Lieutenant-Governor.[117]
Yet, *Spotſwood* continued to live in the Colony,
and, though his Years as Governor were not un-
ſcarred by ſome Diſpute and Contention, yet was
he generally held in high Eſteem and conſidered a
Friend to *Virginia*.[118] Moreover, when, in the
Year 1724, the Reverend *Hugh Jones* prepared and
                               publiſhed

publifhed in *England* his Hiftory called *The Prefent State of Virginia*, he wrote:

> " Though they [the *Virginians*] are permitted to
> " trade to no Parts but *Great Britain* . . . yet
> " have they in many Refpects better and cheaper
> " Commodities than we in *England*, efpecially of
> " late Years; for the Country may be faid to be
> " altered and improved in Wealth and polite Liv-
> " ing within thefe few Years, fince the Beginning of
> " Col. *Spotfwood's* Government, more than in all
> " the Scores of Years before that, from its firft
> " Difcovery."[119]

Moreover, this fame and reverend Author, who was for fome Years before his Return to *England* a Citizen of *Williamfburg* (he having been Profeffor of Mathematicks at the College and the Chaplain to the Houfe of Burgeffes),[120] wrote alfo in his Work a full Defcription of the publick Buildings in *Williamfburg*, faying that they were juftly reputed the beft in all the *Englifh America* and exceeded by few of their Kind in *England*. The College and the Capitol he defcribed at great Length, the latter being ftyled the beft and moft commodious Pile of its Kind that he had feen or heard of. The Palace he difpofed of in briefer Space and in the following Manner:

> " From the Church runs a Street northward
> " called *Palace* Street; at the other End of which
> " ftands the Palace or Governor's Houfe, a mag-
> " nificent Structure, built at the publick Expence,
> " finifhed and beautified with Gates, fine Gardens,
> " Offices, Walks, a fine Canal, Orchards, &c. . . .
> " This

" This likewife has the ornamental Addition of a
" good Cupola or Lanthorn, illuminated with moft
" of the Town, upon Birth-Nights, and other
" Nights of occafional Rejoicings.

" At the Capitol, at Publick Times, may be feen
" a great Number of handfom, well-dreff'd, com-
" pleat Gentlemen.   And at the Governor's Houfe
" upon Birth-Nights, and at Balls and Affemblies,
" I have feen as fine an Appearance, as good Diver-
" fion, and as fplendid Entertainments in Governor
" *Spotfwood's* Time, as I have feen any where
" elfe."[121]

And the Capital City itfelf this fame Author
defcribed in this Fafhion:

" *Williamfburgh* is now incorporated and made a
" Market Town, and governed by a Mayor and
" Aldermen; and is well ftock'd with rich Stores, of
" all Sorts of Goods, and well furnifhed with the
" beft Provifions and Liquors.

" Here dwell feveral very good Families, and
" more refide here in their own Houfes at Publick
" Times.

"They live in the fame neat Manner, drefs after
" the fame Modes, and behave themfelves exactly
" as the Gentry in *London;* moft Families of any
" Note having a Coach, Chariot, Berlin, or Chaife.

" The Number of Artificers is here daily aug-
" mented; as are the convenient Ordinaries or Inns
" for Accommodation of Strangers.

" The Servants here, as in other Parts of the
" Country, are *Englifh*, *Scotch*, *Irifh*, or *Negroes*.

" The Town is laid out regularly in Lots or fquare
" Portions, fufficient each for a Houfe and Garden;
" fo that they don't build contiguous, whereby may
" be prevented the fpreading Danger of Fire; and
                                              "this

" this alſo affords a free Paſſage for the Air, which
" is very grateful in violent hot Weather.

" Here, as in other Parts, they build with Brick,
" but moſt commonly with Timber lined with Ciel-
" ing, and caſed with feather-edged Plank, painted
" with white Lead and Oil, covered with Shingles
" of Cedar, &c. tarr'd over at firſt; with a Paſſage
" generally through the Middle of the Houſe for
" an Air-Draught in Summer.

" Thus their Houſes are laſting, dry, and warm
" in Winter, and cool in Summer; eſpecially if there
" be Windows enough to draw the Air.

" Thus they dwell comfortably, genteely, pleaſ-
" antly, and plentifully in this delightful, health-
" ful, and (I hope) thriving City of *Williamſ-*
" *burgh*."122

And the Reverend Mr. *Jones* prayed that the College in *Williamſburg* might become a laudable Nurſery and a ſtrong Bulwark againſt the " contagious
" Diſſentions in *Virginia*," which Colony, in the moſt
glowing Terms, he deſcribed in this Wiſe:

" . . . the moſt antient and loyal, the moſt plen-
" tiful and flouriſhing, the moſt extenſive and bene-
" ficial Colony belonging to the Crown of *Great
" Britain*, upon which it is moſt directly dependant;
" . . .

" Moſt other Plantations, eſpecially they   that
" are granted away to Proprietors, are inferior to
" *Virginia*: . . . whereas *Virginia* is eſteemed
" one of the moſt valuable Gems in the Crown of
" *Great Britain*. . . .

" If *New England* be called a Receptacle of Diſ-
" ſenters, and an *Amſterdam* of Religion, *Penſylvania*
" the Nurſery of *Quakers*, *Maryland* the Retire-
" ment of *Roman Catholicks*, *North Carolina* the
                                             " Refuge

" Refuge of Run-aways, and *South Carolina* the
" Delight of Buccaneers and Pyrates, *Virginia* may
" be juftly efteemed the happy Retreat of true
" *Britons* and true Churchmen for the moft Part;
" neither foaring too high nor drooping too low,
" confequently fhould merit the greater Efteem
" and Encouragement."123

A n d thefe Things written by a Man of the Cloth
and one given to the Accuracies of Mathematicks,
who had dwelt in the Colony, yet was diftant from
it at the Time of his Writing, fhould be of Intereft
to the Reader; for it will be feen from them that
Virginia had now fuddenly left the Coarfenefs
of its pioneer Times, and had commenced to difplay the Polifh of full Eftablifhment.   And whether
Williamfburg was the Reafon of this new Era or the
firft Refult of it, would be difficult to fay; but there
can be no Queftion that it was now in full Truth
the chief City of the Colony.

❁ ❁ ❁

COLONEL *Spotfwood* was fucceeded as the
Lieutenant-Governor by the Honourable
Hugh Dryfdale in 1722;124 and, upon *Dryfdale's* dy-
ing in 1726, Colonel *Robert Carter*, the Prefident of
the Council,125 ferved as Governor for about a
Year's Time, until the Year 1727, in which the
Honourable *William Gooch*, Efq., came out to
Virginia as the Lieutenant-Governor.126

T h e twenty-two Years of Governor *Gooch's*
Adminiftration have ever been known as a Time of
great Profperity and Advancement in *Virginia;* for
that

that Gentleman was poſſeſſed of the ſcarce and happy Capacity to balance the Aſſembly on the one Hand againſt the Lords of Trade upon the other, and to ſmile with Amiableneſs upon the People beſides.[127]   So that the Laws, eſpecially thoſe that controlled the Trade in Tobacco, were vaſtly improved, to the Advantage of the Planters. The Revenues were better regulated and increaſed, to the Pleaſure of the Lords of Trade; and the Colony was extended and ſettled to the weſtward, to the Benefit of the whole Country and to the Glory of the Crown.   Thus, whereas *Spotſwood* had built Proſperity, *Gooch* built yet greater Proſperity upon it.

AND this Proſperouſneſs in the Country was re-flected upon its Capital City in the Growth and Im-portance of that Place, and, in a Senſe, it was re-flected back to the Country again; for the Influence of the fine Deſign, Character, and Craftſmanſhip diſplayed in the prominent early Buildings of *Will-iamſburg* was (and yet is) to be ſeen in many of the great Plantation Houſes which commenced to be raiſed on Gentlemen's Eſtates about this Time.

AND it may be taken that the Underſtanding between the Government and the People was, in ſome Meaſure, increaſed by the Arrival in *Will-iamſburg* of *William Parks*, one of the foremoſt Printers of thoſe Times; who opened an Office in the City about 1730 and, in the Year 1736, com-menced to print the *Virginia Gazette*,[128] which was the firſt Newſpaper in *Virginia*, and one of the
earlieſt

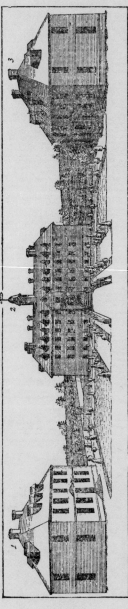

(1) THE BRAFFERTON   (2) THE COLLEGE   (3) PRESIDENT'S HOUSE

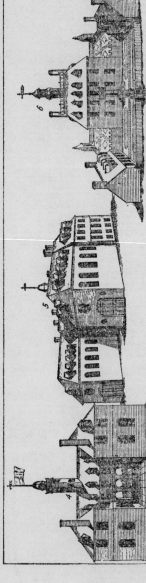

(4) THE CAPITOL   (5) THE COLLEGE (REAR)   (6) THE PALACE

From an Engraving made in the Year 1740, as thrown out, the Original of which was presented by the Bodleian Library, Oxford, to Mr. John D. Rockefeller, Jr., in 1937.

earlieft in the Colonies. Moreover, about 1744, *Parks*, with the friendly Affiftance of *Benjamin Franklin*, of *Philadelphia*, began the Manufacture of Paper in a Mill which he erected on the Out-fkirts of the City, and which he advanced as " the " firft Mill of the Kind, that ever was erected in " this Colony. " [129]

❀ ❀ ❀

THOSE who deal in Matters of Hiftory have commonly found Times of Tranquillity and Succefs to be ill-fuited to their Bufinefs; and fo it is that thofe quiet Years of Governor *Gooch's* Gov-ernment may herein be given over to a Difcuffion of the true Nature of the City of *Williamfburg*, which, for the Underftanding of the Reader, fhould now be explained:

AT the firft it fhould be made plain that, though it became a City Incorporate in the Year 1722,[130] *Williamfburg*, in the Time of Governor *Gooch*, numbered not more than one Thoufand refident Perfons (both white and black), nor more than two Hundred Houfes.[131] Moreover, it fhould be ftated that at no Time in its Hiftory as the Capital of *Virginia* did it number greatly more than two Thoufand refident Perfons, nor more than three Hundred Houfes. Yet, the Reader fhould be mindful of the Fact that thefe Figures reprefented in that Time a proportionate Part of the Population of the Colony as great as that reprefented by many Capital Cities in our prefent Day. Befides which,

it

it fhould alfo be held in Mind that the great Wealth
of *Virginia* in thofe Years fprang from Tobacco,
and Tobacco fprang from the Land; fo that even a
Thoufand Perfons gathered together in a City was
a rare Thing indeed. Thus it was that Lord *Adam
Gordon*, who vifited *Virginia* in 1764, wrote in his
Journal the following:

" They live at their own Seats and are feldom at
" *Williamfburg* but when the publick Bufinefs re-
" quires their Attendance, or that their own pri-
" vate Affairs call them there, fcarce any of the
" topping People have Houfes there of their own,
" but in the Country they live on their Eftates
" handfomely and plentifully, raifing all they
" require and depending for Nothing on the
" Market."132

Yet, if limited in Numbers, the refident Citizens of *Williamfburg* compofed an active and di-
verfe Population; for, at one Time and another, be
fides the Officials of the Government and the College, they included among them:

Actors	Carpenters	Glaziers
Apothecaries	Chandlers &	Goldfmiths &
Attorneys	Soap-boilers	Silverfmiths
Bakers	Clerks	Gunfmiths
Barbers &	Coach & Riding	Hatters
Hairdreffers	Chairmakers	Jailers
Blackfmiths &	Coopers	Jewelers
Farriers	Copperfmiths	Joiners
Bricklayers &	Cutlers	Lead Workers
Mafons	Dancing Mafters	Mantua-Makers
Butchers	Doctors	Merchants
Cabinet Makers	Gardeners	Midwives
		Millers

Millers	Sawyers	Tanners
Milliners	Servants	Tavern Keepers
Minifters	Shipmafters	Tinfmiths
Muficians	Shoemakers	Watchmakers
Plaifterers	Snuffmakers	Weavers
Poft Riders	Staymakers	Wheelwrights
Potafh Makers	Surgeon-	Wigmakers &
Printers	Dentifts	Perukers
Sadlers &	Surveyors	&c. &c. &c.
Harneffmakers	Tailors	

133

But it fhould be marked that it was not in normal Seafons of the Year, when Men went about their ufual daily Tafks and the City was concerned only with its cafual Offices as Capital and County Seat, that *Williamfburg* enjoyed its true Prominence and Power. It was during the Publick Times (ufually in the *Spring* and *Fall*) when the Affemblies were held or the Courts fat " with a " Dignity and Decorum that would become them " even in *Europe* "[134] that the City became the true Metropolis: For then the Population was increafed from one and two Thoufand Perfons to five and fix Thoufand;[135] then the Taverns, Inns, Publick Houfes, Ordinaries, private Dwellings, and nearby Plantations were filled to overflowing; then all Men of publick Office or Prominence, and even moft Perfons of private Wealth or Confequence thronged to *Williamfburg*, as did thofe who lived by their Wits and the Influence to be fought there. So that there was no publick Commotion to be feen in all *Virginia*, or elfewhere in the Colonies, which
would

would compare with *Williamſburg* at Publick
Times; for as *Virginians* lived apart, ſo they came
together, and the Iſolation of a Half-year was loſt
in a Fortnight or more of Society, Merriment,
Commerce, and Politicks, ſo long as the General
Court ſtood convened.

And of ſuch great Moment were theſe Publick
Times, that moſt Events that could be ſo adjuſted
were ſet to fall within them: So that the Fairs,
which were held in *April* and *December*, often coin-
cided with ſuch Occaſions, lending a Side-play of
Puppet Shows, Conteſts in Beauty, Fiddling,
Dancing, Foot Races from the College to the
Capitol, Cudgellings, and Chaſes for Pigs to be
caught by the Tails (which were ſoaped).[136] Moreover, the Seaſon in the Theatre reached its Height
at ſuch Times; Race Meetings for the beſt Horſes
were held upon the Mile Courſe near the City, and,
doubtleſs, Matches between the prize Cocks of different Sections were fought;[137] the Craftſmen then
diſplayed their fineſt Works, and the Merchants advanced the lateſt Faſhions out of *London;* Slave Auctions were held; the Prize-winners in Lotteries and
Raffles were announced; and the Merchants and
Men of Affairs gathered upon *The Exchange* beyond the Capitol,[138] where Debts were paid and
contracted and the Money Buſineſs of the Country
tranſacted.

The beſt People of every Section of the Colony
ſtopped in *Williamſburg* and appeared in its Streets
at Publick Times; ſo that even an ill-diſpoſed
                                        Traveller

Traveller out of *England*, who could find Nothing
confiderable in *Williamfburg* fave the Capitol, the
Palace, and the College (which he admitted to be
" no bad Piles "), wrote of his Amazement at " the
" prodigious Number of Coaches that croud the
" deep fandy Streets of this little City."[139] Thefe
were the People who were in Attendance at
the elegant Balls, Banquets, Lawn Fetes, and Difplays of Fireworks given at the Palace; fo that
Colonel *Spotfwood* fhowed fmall Concern in report-
ing that upon an official Occafion he had entertained two Hundred Guefts at his Houfe,[140] and Governor *Gooch* was later able to ftate in a Letter to
his Brother " The Gentm. and Ladies here are per-
" fectly well bred, not an ill Dancer in my
" Govmt."[141]   And the Popularity of the City
with the fine People is further fhown by Letters
fuch as the following, which would feem to have
been written by a forlorn Suitor:

" . . . I flatter'd myfelf with the Pleafure of fee-
" ing Mifs *Baffett* in *Hanover* before this Time, but
" I fuppofe fhe intends ftaying below, to partake of
" the Mirth of the Metropolis, and come to *Han*.
" to take a Refpite from Dancing, as fhe knows this
" is no Place for Jollity . . . "[142]

NOR is it remarkable, in the Light of thefe
Things, that an unufual Number of Taverns and
Publick Houfes fprang up in *Williamfburg;* of which
Number the *Raleigh* Tavern (which was built fome-
time before 1742)[143] ftood forth as the foremoft
Hoftelry

Hoſtelry for the fine People, and as a ſocial gathering Place ſecond only to the Palace itſelf.

YET, it ſhould be ſtated that Celebrations in *Williamſburg* were not entirely confined to Publick Times; for even when the Aſſembly was not convened, nor the Courts in Seſſion, ſuch Reports as the following appeared in the *Virginia Gazette:*

" Laſt *Friday* being the Anniverſary of our moſt
" gracious Sovereign's Acceſſion to the Throne, his
" Excellency the Governour gave a Ball and an
" elegant Entertainment at the Palace, to a numer-
" ous and ſplendid Company of Ladies and Gentle-
" men. The *Raleigh* Tavern likewiſe, by Direction
" of his Excellency, was opened for the Entertain-
" mentofSuch as might incline to ſpend the Evening
" there; plenty of Liquor was given to the Populace;
" and the City was handſomely illuminated."[144]

SUCH, then, was the true and twofold Nature of *Williamſburg* when it was the Seat of Government; and if one Chronicler deſcribed it as reſembling a ſmall Country Town in *England*,[145] and another ſaw it as a boiling Metropolis in the new World,[146] they both had ſome Truth upon their Sides, depending upon when they came thither.

AND if the Reader ſhould harbour Doubts in his Mind concerning theſe Things, he may find for himſelf in the Records not leſs, but more.

❀ ❀ ❀

NO Treatiſe upon the true Nature of the City of *Williamſburg* could be conſidered complete that lacked ſome Diſcuſſion of the College of *William*
iam

iam and Mary in *Virginia*, for that Inſtitution has ever been a great Ornament to the City and an Honour to the whole Country. And as the *Virginia* Colony and the City of *Williamſburg* are bound together in Hiſtory, ſo are the City and its College bound; and an Endeavor to treat the one without the other would reſult in a Diſtortion.

AT its firſt Foundation the College, in Accordance with the Supplication of the Aſſembly, was deſigned to the End that the Church of *Virginia* might be furniſhed with a Seminary of Miniſters of the Goſpel, that the Youth might be piouſly educated in good Letters and Manners, and the *Chriſtian* Faith might be propagated amongſt the Weſtern *Indians*, to the Glory of *Almighty God*. And the Charter of the College, which was granted in the Year 1693, looked toward a perpetual College for Divinity, Philoſophy, Languages, and other fine Arts and Sciences, conſiſting of one Preſident, ſix Maſters or Profeſſors, and a Hundred Scholars, more or leſs, Graduates and Non-Graduates.[147]

WITH theſe worthy Objects in view, the College grew but ſlowly at the firſt (as moſt Things of great Worth ſhould); it beginning with a Grammar School, in which were taught *Latin* and *Greek*, and a common School in which *Indians* were taught " Reading, Writing, and vulgar Arithmatick."[148] And, though a Profeſſorſhip of Natural Philoſophy and Mathematicks was added by 1711,[149] the Curriculum was not much advanced beyond this for ſome Time; ſo that the Reverend Mr. *Hugh Jones*

was

was juſtified in writing the following in his Hiſtory
as late as 1724:

" As for Education ſeveral are ſent to *England*
" for it; though the *Virginians* being naturally of
" good Parts, (as I have already hinted) neither re-
" quire nor admire as much Learning, as we do in
" *Britain*; yet more would be ſent over, were they
" not afraid of the Small-Pox, which moſt commonly
" proves fatal to them.

" But indeed when they come to *England* they
" are generally put to learn to Perſons that know
" little of their Temper, . . .

" For Grammar Learning taught after the com-
" mon round-about Way is not much beneficial nor
" delightful to them; ſo that they are noted to be
" more apt to ſpoil their School-Fellows than im-
" prove themſelves; . . .

" Thus the Youth might as well be inſtructed
" there as here by proper Methods, without the
" Expence and Danger of coming hither; eſpecially
" if they make Uſe of the great Advantage of the
" College at *Williamſburgh*, . . . "[150]

AND it would appear that the *Virginians* ſoon
thereafter began to recognize the Advantage of
their College; for by the Year 1729 its Faculty had
reached the full Complement ſpecified in its Charter, and included, beſides the Preſident, a Profeſſor
of Natural Philoſophy and Mathematicks, a Profeſſor of Moral Philoſophy, two Profeſſors of Divinity, the Maſter of the Grammar School, the Maſter
of the *Indian* School,[151] and an Uſher.   Moreover,
the *Indian* School was now eſtabliſhed in a new
Building to itſelf called the *Brafferton*, which had
been

been built in the Year 1723;[152] oppofite to which, upon the College Grounds, a handfome Houfe for the Prefident was built in the Year 1732.[153]   And thefe two Structures, together with the great College Building, ftand to this prefent Day.

B y the Year 1754 there were fixty-feven Scholars and Students boarded at the College, befides eight *Indians;*[154] and it has been conjectured that about forty other Students refided or boarded in the City.[155]   So that there were in all about one Hundred and fifteen in Attendence.   And though this Number did not greatly increafe, the Scheme of the College was changed from Time to Time as the Years advanced, the Grammar School and the *Indian* School being difcontinued, and new advanced Schools or Profefforfhips being added.[156] And in this Procefs the College accumulated an Affortment of Priorities in *American* Education, a Lifting of which would weary the Reader with its Length and Detail.

A n d it fhould be pointed to that if the College was a great Adornment to the Reputation and Life of *Williamfburg*, the City, by Way of Return, provided the College with an unfurpaffed and ready Laboratory of Society, Politicks, and Government. Thus, if the College gave to *Virginia* a Majority of thofe who fhaped its Deftinies in its Progrefs from a loyal Colony to a Leader of Rebellion, and fo to a free and independent State, it fhould be remembered that *Williamfburg* had already fchooled thefe Leaders in the Ways of good Government and

polite

polite Living before they came to the Halls of its
Capitol.   As a single Example of this Truth may
be advanced the Autobiography of *Thomas Jefferson*, who wrote of Dr. *William Small* (one of the
Professors of the College) as the man who " fixed
" the Destinies of my Life " and who " filled up the
" Measure of his Goodness to me, by procuring for
" me, from his most intimate Friend *G. Wythe*, a
" Reception as a Student of Law, under his Direc-
" tion, and introduced me to the Acquaintance and
" familiar Table of Governor *Fauquier*—the ablest
" Man who ever filled that Office."[157]

As to the Success of the College in the Field of
Divinity, a late Historian, the good Bishop *William
Meade*, bears Witness in this Wise: " The best
" Ministers in *Virginia* were those educated at the
" College and sent over to *England* for Ordination.
" The Foreigners were the great Scandal of the
" Church."[158]

And since the full and true History of the College cannot here be given, it is a happy Circum-
stance that the real Worth of a College may best
be seen in the Accomplishments of its Students:
Thus, it should be of Interest to the Reader to note
that, in addition to that Host of publick Figures
the College gave to the *Virginia* Colony, it gave to
the united Colonies sixteen Members of the Continental Congress at *Philadelphia* (including *Peyton
Randolph*, of *Williamsburg*, the first President of
that Body), and to the *Declaration of Independence*
it gave four Signatures—those of *George Wythe*,
Thomas

Thomas Jefferson, *Carter Braxton*, and *Benjamin Harrison*. To the new Nation brought about by thefe Things, the College gave four of the firft ten Prefidents—*George Washington* (who, though not a Student of the College, was commiffioned a Surveyor by the College and who was afterwards its Chancellor), *Thomas Jefferson*, *James Monroe*, and *John Tyler*. Befides which, to the Federal Government the College has given four Juftices of the Supreme Court (including *John Marshall*, the great Chief Juftice); four Secretaries of State; feventeen Senators from *Virginia* and twelve from feven other States; three Speakers of the Houfe of Reprefentatives, and fifty-eight Members of that Body; four Attorneys General, including *Edmund Randolph*, the firft Attorney General; a Secretary of War; a Secretary of the Navy; a Poftmafter General; a Secretary of the Treafury; a Secretary of the Interior; eighteen Minifters to nine foreign Countries; and a vaft Number of leffer Officials. To the individual States the College has given twenty-feven Governors, including eighteen to *Virginia* and nine to feven other States.[159] And the Reader will be fpared from more and others.

THUS, though the College did not fulfill the Hope of the Reverend *Hugh Jones* and become a " ftrong Bulwark againft the contagious Diffen- " tions in *Virginia*,"[160] ftill it would feem to have become as ftrong in an oppofite Caufe; fo that the Reverend Author and Mathematician did not mifcalculate in Strength, but in Direction.

To

TO return to the Sequence of our Narration, it fhould be ftated that upon the Departure of Sir *William Gooch* in the Year 1749 (he refigning becaufe of his Health),[161] the Office of Governor was filled for about three Years by *John Robinfon*, *Thomas Lee*, and *Lewis Burwell*, who fucceeded in due Order as Prefidents of the Council.

In their Time was commenced the Rebuilding of the Capitol;[162] it having been myfterioufly burned in the Year 1747.[163]   Moreover, the Palace having fallen into a fomewhat ruinous Condition, and it being unoccupied, Work was commenced to repair, enlarge, and adorn that Structure[164] even in Advance of its former Magnificence. Alfo, in this Time, there came a great Revival of Intereft in the Theatre and, *Levingfton's* old Playhoufe near the Palace having fometime before been given over to the City for a Town Hall,[165] a new Theatre was built beyond and near the Capitol by publick Subfcription.[166]

And it fhould be ftated here that the Rebuilding of the Capitol at *Williamfburg* was not undertaken without confiderable Difcuffion, Debate, and Illfeeling in the Affembly. There had been, in Governor *Gooch's* Time, a great Expanfion of the Colony to the weftward, this coming about both by natural Growth and by a great Influx of *Scotch-Irifh Prefbyterians* and of *Pennfylvania Germans* into the weftern Frontier. Thus, when the Capitol burned, a Majority of the Burgeffes favored a Removal of the Seat of Government to a more central

tral

tral Spot, and a Place more fuitable for direct Navigation. But, Governor *Gooch*, the Council, and certain prominent Citizens of the City having come to the Defenfe of *Williamfburg*, and they being aided by the Fact that the City was fingularly free from an Epidemic of *Small-Pox* which was raging in the Colony at that Time, their Motion was carried and *Williamfburg* continued as the Capital.[167]

❀ ❀ ❀

THE Honourable *Robert Dinwiddie*, Efq., arrived in *Williamfburg* to become the Lieutenant-Governor on *November* 21, 1751, and was inducted into Office with a great Ceremony and Celebration, which ended with an elegant Banquet at *Wetherburn's* Tavern.[168] To him the City, through its Mayor, Recorder, Aldermen, and Common Council, delivered an eloquent Addrefs in which was ftated:

" . . . His Majefty, always good and gracious to
" his People, could not more agreeably have re-
" paired the Lofs we fuftained in our late Governor
" Sir *William Gooch*, than by appointing you who
" are fo well acquainted with us, our Laws and
" Conftitutions, to be his worthy Succeffor; and we
" hope that your Adminiftration may be longer,
" and if poffible more happy, than his. . . ."[169]

BUT, though he was an able and an induftrious Gentleman, *Dinwiddie's* Government was not to be bleft as that of Governor *Gooch* had been. Moreover, though other capable royal Deputies were to

hold

hold the Governorſhip, neither were their Times to be ſo bleſt. In Governor *Dinwiddie's* Caſe, almoſt at the Start, he fell at Odds with the Aſſembly concerning a Fee for the Iſſuing of Land Patents (which Fee the Burgeſſes conſidered a Tax);[170] and ſoon after this Diſagreement came the War with the *French* and their *Indians*.[171]

At his firſt Coming, the Governor and his Family occupied a Dwelling juſt ſouth and weſt of the Palace, which Houſe the Aſſembly had purchaſed for his Uſe until the Alterations and Repairs at the Palace ſhould be completed.[172]   Yet, by the Year 1752 he was inſtalled in the Palace; for in *November* of that Year he received the Emperor and Empreſs of the *Cherokee* Nation there, they having come to the City with their Son and their chief Men to treat of Trade and Friendſhip.[173]

In the Year 1753 the *Virginia* Colony (its Bounds under its Charter of 1609[174] having been reduced by Grants to *Maryland*, the *Carolinas*, and *Pennſylvania*)[175] ſtill encompaſſed what is now the weſtern Part of *Pennſylvania* and the Territory now repreſented by the States of *Weſt Virginia*, *Kentucky*, *Ohio*, *Indiana*, *Illinois*, *Michigan*, and *Wiſconſin;* and *Williamſburg* was the Capital of all this vaſt Dominion.   Thus, when the *French* commenced to eſtabliſh Settlements upon the *Ohio* River, Governor *Dinwiddie* choſe as his Emiſſary, to warn them againſt ſuch Encroachments, one *George Waſhington*,[176] a young Man ſcarce come of

Age,

Age, who was well fitted for fo arduous a Journey by his Work as a Surveyor in the weftern Wilds.

(Here it fhould be of Intereft to the Reader to note that the major Courfes of *Wafhington's* Life were fhaped in *Williamfburg:* His active military Career commenced with his being fent out from the Palace as the Envoy of the Governor (he having been for fometime Adjutant-General and a Major in the *Virginia* Militia) and with his being fubfequently placed in Command of the *Virginia* Militia againft the *French;* all of which, in a roundabout Fafhion, grew out of the Surveyor's Commiffion which he had gained from the College of *William and Mary.* His political Career, though it was founded upon his military Fame, was juftified and ftrengthened by fome fixteen Years fpent as a Member of the Houfe of Burgeffes, and as a Delegate of that Body to the Continental Congrefs. His domeftic Life began with his Marriage (in the County of *New Kent*) to the Widow of Mr. *Daniel Parke Cuftis,* fhe being a Refident of *Williamfburg* and one of the wealthieft Women in all the Country).

In the Year 1754, it becoming apparent that the *French* would not comply with his Requeft that they vacate the *Virginia* Territory in the Weft, *Dinwiddie* again fent *Wafhington*, now a Lieutenant-Colonel, with three Hundred *Virginia* Militia to the Aid of a Garrifon in that Quarter. And this Expedition, meeting with a Party of *French*, and flaying twelve of them, and taking twenty-one

Prifoners,

Prisoners,[177] brought about the Opening of a War with *France* which was fought up and down the whole *American* Frontier, in *Canada*, and extended into *Europe* and *Asia*.

AND some Historians have held that the War with the *French* was, in large Measure, responsible for that great Revolt in the Colonies which followed after it; they claiming that it brought the Colonies for the first Time into concerted Action, that it relieved them from the Fear of Invasion by the *French*, that it taught them the Weakness of *British* Regulars in an unfamiliar Land, and that the Expense of the War brought about the Passage of the *Stamp Act*.[178] Yet, it should not be neglected that, no Matter what came of it, the War in *America* was fought by *Great Britain* in Defense of her Colonies and with the loyal Aid of those Colonies.

THE Responsibilities of the War, together with Disagreements with a determined Assembly and the usual heavy Tasks of his Office, overtaxed the Strength of *Dinwiddie;* so that, while the War was yet raging, he asked to be relieved.[179] He left the Colony in *January*, 1758, carrying with him the high Regard of the People and (the Bounds of *Williamsburg* having been increased in his Time) he carried also a Testimonial of Gratitude from the Authorities of the City.[180]

AFTER his Departure, the Honourable *John Blair*, the President of the Council and Nephew of the

the deceafed Prefident of the College, ferved for a Time as Governor.

❁ ❁ ❁

I N *June* of the Year 1758 the Honourable *Francis Fauquier*, Efq., whom *Thomas Jefferson* (as has already been noted) defcribed as the ableft Man ever to hold the Office, arrived in *Williamfburg* to be Lieutenant-Governor.[181]

I N his Time the Tide of the War with the *French* turned to the Favour of the *Englifh* and their Colonies; fo that in 1763 *Fauquier* was able to notify the Affembly of the " Conclufion of a moft " glorious and honourable Peace between his " Majefty and all his Enemies."[182]   And by the *Treaty of Paris* concluded at this Time, virtually that entire Part of the Continent of *North America* lying Eaft of the *Miffiffippi* River was affured to the *Englifh*.[183]

G O V E R N O R *Fauquier* has ever been known to the Hiftory of *Virginia* as a Man of liberal and popular Views, and as one of great fcientific Interefts and gentlemanly Purfuits in Learning.   And if his Intereft in Science led him too often to invefti-gate the Laws of Chance, and thus to eftablifh a Vogue for the Gaming Table in the Colony,[184] yet were his Sins vaftly out-weighted by his Virtues (which is the true Teft of any Man).

I T has been eftablifhed that *Fauquier* was fore-warned of the Plan to tax the Colonies after the Clofe of the War with the *French*, and that he, knowing

knowing the Temper of the Colonifts, advifed
ftrongly againft fuch Taxation.[185] Howbeit, the
Stamp Act was paffed by the Houfe of Commons on
February 27, 1765;[186] and immediately there arofe
a Storm of Difpleafure in the Colonies. Yet, this
Difpleafure had no popular Expreffion until one
Patrick Henry, a young Lawyer newly rifen to
Prominence through a Defenfe againft the *Parfon's
Caufe*, offered before the Houfe of Burgeffes of
Virginia a Series of Refolutions againft the *Stamp
Act*.[187] And thefe Refolutions, being deemed un-
wife by the more confervative Members of the
Houfe, brought on a bitter Debate, efpecially with
Regard to the fifth Refolution, in which it was pro-
tefted that the fole Right to tax *Virginians* refted
with the *Virginia* Affembly and that any Effort to
veft this Right elfewhere had a " manifeft Tend-
" ency to deftroy *Britifh* as well as *American* Free-
" dom." And it was in the Courfe of a Defenfe
of this Refolution that *Henry* cried out, " *Cæfar* had
" his *Brutus—Charles* the Firft his *Cromwell—*and
" *George* the Third— " (here, fome fay, he was
interrupted by Cries of " Treafon " from the
Houfe;[188] and another Witnefs has faid that he was
interrupted by the Speaker's rebuking the Houfe
for its Complaifance[189]) " —and *George* the Third "
Henry continued, " may profit by their Example.
" If this be Treafon—make the moft of it! "

The fifth Refolution was carried in the Houfe
of Burgeffes by a fingle Vote; though Mr. *Peyton
Randolph*, the Attorney-General and an eminent
though

though confervative Patriot, expoſtulated in the Lobby, " By *God*, I would have given five Hun-
" dred Guineas for a ſingle Vote."[190]   And though, on the following Day, *Henry's* fifth Reſolution was ordered to be expunged from the Record,[191] News of the Reſolutions and the Action of the Affembly travelled through *Virginia* and throughout the Colonies.   Thus, for thoſe that relate Cauſes and Reſults, and for thoſe ingenious Perſons who can bring themſelves to attribute the Beginning of any War to a ſingle Event, the *American Revolution* was born in the Capitol at *Williamſburg* on *May* 30, 1765.

THESE Things, quite naturally, were far too aſtoniſhing to be overlooked by even ſo liberal a Governor as *Fauquier;* and ſo the Affembly was at once diffolved.[192]   And when one *George Mercer* arrived from *England* as the Chief Diſtributor of the Stamps, *Fauquier* gave him the Protection of his own Perſon and Company[193] until Mr. *Mercer* publickly announced that he would not undertake the Diſtribution of the Stamps without the Conſent of the Affembly.[194]   Moreover, *Fauquier*, with that Wiſdom ſo characteriſtic of him, continued to prorogue the Affembly until he was able to pro-
claim to the People on *June* 9, 1766, an Act of Par-
liament which repealed the hated *Stamp Act;*[195] whereat there was great Rejoicing and Celebrating in *Williamſburg* and through the whole Country.[196]

AND though *Fauquier* fulfilled his Office as the Deputy of the Crown with the greateſt Loyalty and
Dignity,

Dignity, yet, the People and the Affembly fenfed a moft fincere Intereft and Sympathy beneath all his Actions. So that there was great Mourning in *Virginia* when the Governor died on *March* 3, 1768, and was laid at Reft in the north Aifle of *Bruton* Church;[197] while in the *Virginia Gazette* appeared Verfes fuch as the Following:

> " If ever Virtue loft a Friend fincere,
> " If ever Sorrow claim'd *Virginia's* Tear,
> " If ever Death a noble Conqueft made,
> " 'Twaswhen *Fauquier* the Debt of Nature paid."[198]

✿ ✿ ✿

IT does not lie within the Power (or Province) of any brief and true Report to trace the Development and Courfe of the Revolution, nor even to explain the important Part which *Virginia* had in this complicated Affair; for if it fought to unfold the Truth of thefe Matters, the Brevity of fuch a Report would foon depart. Yet, though it muft (under thefe Circumftances) be effected by general inftead of by detailed Difclofures, the true Significance of *Williamfburg* in Relation to thefe Things fhould be explained herein:

In fhort, the firft Caufes of the Revolution may be found in the irreconcilable Divergence between the growing Demands of *Great Britain* as an Empire and the Determination of the Colonies that their Right of Self-Government be recognized. Thus, Parliament was mindful of the Needs of the Empire in the Paffage of the *Stamp Act;* whereas the

the Colonists, on their Side, advanced the Principle
of *No Taxation without Representation*. These Differences brought on a War against what the Colonists considered to be unjust Taxation, and this Dis-
turbance soon turned into a War for Independence.

In this Cause the Colonies of *Virginia* and
Massachusetts Bay were, beyond Question, the
Leaders; and though an Effort to distinguish the
relative Importance of these two can be considered
an invidious Thing, *Virginia* may be held with
some Truth to have carried the more Weight, both
because of its Size and because of the greater
Prestige which it enjoyed in *England* and among
the other Colonies. An Indication of this last, by
Way of Example, may be seen in the Statement of
John Adams of *Massachusetts* to the Effect that he,
in commenting to *Thomas Jefferson* upon the Propriety of the latter's Authorship of the Declaration
of Independence, said, " You are a *Virginian*, and
" a *Virginian* ought to appear at the Head of this
" Business."199

Moreover, it should be pointed to that in
seeking to effect her Purpose of Taxation and also
to subdue the Opposition to this Purpose, *England*,
at the first, sent Troops to *Massachusetts*, but *Virginia* she sought to appease with Diplomacy and
Politicks. Thus, it is but natural, as it turned
out, that *Massachusetts* was the first to enter the
Field with Arms, and that *Virginia* became the
leading Force in the Field of Politicks; though it is
equally true that *Virginia* and *Massachusetts* entered

tered each into both Fields and were by no Means
the sole Occupants of either.

AND these Statements are neither intended nor
advanced as a full Discussion of a Cause which was
common to all the Colonies. They are set forth
merely to indicate the true Importance of the City
of *Williamsburg*, which is the Concern of this Report; for if *Virginia* was the most influential political Leader of the Colonies in the Revolution, the
Position of *Williamsburg*, the political Center of
Virginia, must become obvious.

✿ ✿ ✿

UPON the Passing of his Excellency, Governor
Francis Fauquier, the Honourable *John
Blair*, Esq., the President of the Council and a
strong Supporter of the popular Cause, again served
as the acting Governor of *Virginia*.[200]

IT had so happened that in the closing Years of
Fauquier's Government, *George* III had repented of
what he termed to be the fatal Compliance with the
Demands of the Colonies for the Repeal of the *Stamp
Act*. Moreover, the Chancellor of the *British* Exchequer is said to have protested, " *England* is un-
" done, if this Taxation is given up."[201]   And so
new Tax Duties were levied upon the Colonies;[202]
whereupon, just before the Death of *Fauquier*, the
House of Representatives of *Massachusetts* answered
back with a Petition to the King in which were
advanced the Rights of the Colonies.[203]

NOW, in the Time of *John Blair*, Esq., and
while

while the other Colonies waited upon its Action, *Virginia's* Houfe of Burgeffes forwarded from *Williamfburg* a Communication applauding *Maffa-chufetts'* Attention to *American* Liberty and ftating that the Steps that they, the Burgeffes, had already taken would affure *Maffachufetts* of *Virginia's* " fixed Refolution to concur with the other " Colonies in their Application for Redrefs."²⁰⁴

❄ ❄ ❄

IN the Year 1768 *Great Britain* inftituted a new Means to revive the faft failing Loyalty of the *Virginia* Colony: For fome fixty-two Years the Governors of *Virginia*, though they had en-joyed the full Powers and Privileges of the Office, had in Title and Perquifites been but Deputies of the full Governors, who refided in *England*. But now the Right Honourable *Norborne Berkeley*, *Baron de Botetourt*, was made the full Governor and was fent out to *Virginia* to refide there. He bore the Title—*His Majefty's Lieutenant, Governor-General and Commander-in-Chief*.

LORD *Botetourt* arrived in the Month of *October* aboard a Man-of-War of fome fixty Guns; and he was met with Ceremonies and Celebrations at *Williamfburg*²⁰⁵ which, if anything, exceeded the Ufual, to be in Keeping with his Station. The Honourable *William Nelfon*, Efq., (who, as Prefi-dent of the Council, was later to fucceed *Botetourt*) fpoke thus of thefe Occurrences in a Letter to a Friend in *London:*

" Lord

" Lord *Botetourt* is arrived among us, with the
" greateſt Advantages imaginable: for we had
" Time, before his Coming, to receive the moſt
" favourable Impreſſions of his Lordſhip's amiable
" Character & good Diſpoſition towards the Colony.
" He hath been received & wellcomed in a Manner,
" which gives him great Pleaſure; & I ſhould ſend
" you Copies of the ſeveral Addreſſes & his Anſwers
" to them, if I were not well aſſured that you will
" ſee them in the publick Papers before this can
" reach you. . . . Among them you will find that
" of the Merchants & Traders (*Andrew Sprowle*
" Spokeman) wch I think does Honour to that
" Body, from its Plainneſs, Elegance and Simplic-
" ity; & far out does the ſtudied Performance of
" the P. & Maſters of the College; and this Obſer-
" vation being made to *Sprowle*, he reply'd (Aye,
" Sir, the Parſons do Nothing well, unleſs they are
" paid for it). The old Fellow wears his own
" Hair, as white as old *Charles Hansford's* was,
" with a Pig Tail to it, but bald as the brave Lord
" *Granby*, and cuts as droll a Figure as ever you
" ſaw him in a ſilk Coat & two or three Holes in
" his Stockings, at the ſame Time he is a reſpect-
" able Appearance, the oldeſt among the Trade, &
" acquitted himſelf well. Indeed, my dear Friend,
" I hope we ſhall be happy under his Lordſhip's
" Government, . . . unleſs . . . when he opens his
" Budget to the Aſſembly in *May* next, Something
" may be required of them, that is too hard of Di-
" geſtion: however, I will not anticipate Misfor-
" tunes, nor of myſelf caſt a Cloud over the pleaſing
" Proſpect before us; and let the Worſt come, that
" can come, we are I believe determined to a Man
" to behave with Decency, Duty & Reſpect; and,
" our Cauſe being a good one, theſe I think are the
" Means

" Means (adding fome Firmnefs) to fucceed; for
" Liberty I truft is a good Caufe, & we may fay
" of it as of Truth, *Magna eft et prævalebit*, if we
" do not fpoil it by our own Intemperance, Vio-
" lence & Folly. Enough of Politicks . . . "[206]

FROM the Time of his firft Arriving, Governor
Botetourt gained and held the Refpect and Affection
of the People by his Gracioufnefs and Sympathy.
To the Addrefs of Welcome by the Prefident of the
College he replied:

" The College of *William and Mary* does Honour
" to this great Country, Ages unborn will feel its
" Effect, and upon this you may depend that you
" cannot oblige me more than by marking out any
" Plan by which I may be enabled to contribute to
" its Advancement and Profperity."[207]

INDEED, the Friendlinefs between the Governor and the Colonifts foon became fo pronounced
that even his Actions againft the popular Caufe
were looked upon as the Refults of unavoidable
Demands of Duty; not as Indications of perfonal
Sentiment.[208] So that there was Bowing and Smil-
ing upon the Streets of *Williamfburg* when his
Lordfhip rode forth in the handfome Coach of
State which he had brought with him from *England*, and for which he had fix fplendid white
Horfes.[209]

YET though Friendfhip exifted between the
Governor and the Affembly, that fame Sentiment
was by no Means exchanged between the Affembly
and Parliament. And, the Trouble furrounding
the

the Revenue Act having reached such Heights that certain popular Leaders in the Colonies were ordered arrested and transported to *England* for Trial, the House of Burgesses of *Virginia* on *May* 16, 1769, passed a strong Series of Resolutions.²¹⁰ In these was again protested the Right of that House to levy Taxes for *Virginia;* and the Transporting of Colonists beyond the Sea for Trial was held to be derogatory to the Rights of *British* Subjects. And Copies of these Resolutions were ordered to be transmitted to the other Colonies. At once the Governor dissolved the Assembly, saying, " I have heard of your Resolves, and augur Ill " of their Effect: You have made it my Duty to " dissolve you; and you are dissolved accord- " ingly."²¹¹ Whereupon, the Burgesses, calling themselves " the late Representatives of the " People," at once reconvened at the *Raleigh* Tavern as a Convention,²¹² and there drew up Articles of Association in a Non-Importation Agreement.²¹³

In *New England*, where these Grievances and the Pressure of them was the greater, these Things brought about Riots and Upheavals. But in *Virginia* the general Discontent continued beneath the Surface of such peaceful Scenes as the following, which was described by Miss *Anne Blair* of *Williamsburg* in a Letter written to her Sister in *August*, 1769:

" . . . Mrs. *Dawson's* Family stay'd yᵉ Evening " with us, and yᵉ Coach was at yᵉ Door to carry " them

" them Home, by ten o'Clock; but everyone appear-
" ing in great Spirits, it was propofed to fet at y^e
" Steps and Sing a few Songs wch was no fooner
" faid than done; while thus we were employ'd, a
" Candle or Lanthorn was obferved to be coming
" up Street; (except *Polly Clayton* cenfuring their
" ill Tafte, for having a Candle fuch a fine Night)
" no one took any Notice of it—till we faw, who
" ever it was, ftopt to liften to our enchanting
" Notes—each Warbler was immediately filenced;
" whereupon, the Invader to our Melody, call'd
" out in a moft rapturous Voice, 'Charming!
" Charming! proceed for *God* Sake, or I go Home
" directly'—no fooner were thofe Words uttered,
" than all as with one Confent fprung from their
" Seats, and ye Air eccho'd with 'pray, walk in my
" Lord;' No—indeed he would not, he would fet
" on the Step's too; fo after a few Ha, Ha's, and being
" told what all knew—that it was a delightfull Even-
" ing, at his defire we ftrew'd the Way over with
" Flowers &c &c till a full half Hour was elapf'd
" when all retir'd to their refpective Homes . . ."[214]

YET, defpite fuch Difplays of focial Serenity,
the political Rancour beneath them feemed to be
bringing forth the Fruits of Redrefs. For, foon
after his Diffolution of the Affembly, Lord *Botetourt*
was affured by the *Britifh* Secretary of State that
further Duties would not be levied upon the Colonifts, and, further, that thofe which had been impofed would be repealed. Thus, his Excellency
fummoned a new Affembly to announce this happy
News;[215] but, when it convened in *November* of the
Year 1769, *Botetourt* found that the Affurances
which

which had been given him were not yet fulfilled. Whereupon, his Lordſhip informed the Aſſembly of the Promiſe which was made to him and concluded in this Wiſe:

" . . . It may poſſibly be objected that, as his
" Majeſty's preſent Adminiſtration are not im-
" mortal, their Succeſſors may be inclined to at-
" tempt to undo what the preſent Miniſters ſhall
" have attempted to perform; and to that Objec-
" tion I can give but this Anſwer, that it is my
" firm Opinion that the Plan I have ſtated to you
" will certainly take Place, and that it will never
" be departed from, and ſo determined am I for-
" ever to abide by it, that I will be content to be
" declared infamous, if I do not to the laſt Hour of
" my Life, at all Times, in all Places, and upon all
" Occaſions, exert every Power with which I either
" am or ever ſhall be legally inveſted, in order to
" obtain and maintain for the Continent of *America*
" that Satisfaction which I have been authorized
" to promiſe this Day, by the confidential Ser-
" vants of our gracious Sovereign, who, to my cer-
" tain Knowledge, rates his Honour ſo high, that
" he would rather part with his Crown than pre-
" ſerve it by Deceit."²¹⁶

And it is ſaid that, the Tax upon Tea being continued, his Lordſhip propoſed to reſign his Commiſſion;²¹⁷ but was prevented by a great Illneſs which came upon him. And as to this laſt, it has been told that prior to his fatal Sickneſs, he was viſited at the Palace by *Robert Carter Nicholas*, Eſq.,

the

the Treafurer of the Colony; who remarked to him
that he, of all Men, fhould be moft unwilling to die—
he being fo focial in his Nature, fo greatly beloved,
and furrounded by fo many good Things miniftering
to his every Whim and Comfort. Remembering
thefe Words when he lay upon his Death-bed, Lord
Botetourt fummoned *Nicholas* to him, and, when
that Gentleman enquired what he defired, his Lordfhip in a calm Voice anfwered, " Nothing, but to
" let you fee that I refign thofe good Things which
" you formerly fpoke of with as much Compofure
" as I enjoyed them."[218]

Botetourt died on *October* 15, 1770,[219] and with
general Mourning and the greateft Solemnity his
Remains were laid at reft in a Vault beneath the
Chancel of the Chapel of the College,[220] which Inftitution he had ever favoured in Word and Deed.
And it is fmall Wonder that to the Honour of fuch
a Man the General Affembly of *Virginia* reared a
fplendid Statue upon the Piazza of the Capitol,[221]
which Statue, in this prefent Day, is in the poffeffion
of the College of *William and Mary*. Upon oppofite
Sides of its Pedeftal 'appear the following Infcriptions; and thefe Infcriptions, in themfelves, will
explain to Readers the otherwife ftrange Fact that
the *Virginia* Affembly appropriated Funds for the
Care and Cleaning of this Statue of his Excellency,
even in the Midft of thofe fevered Years of the War
of Revolution which were to come:[222]

DEEPLY

DEEPLY IMPRESS'D WITH THE WARMEST SENSE OF GRATITUDE FOR HIS EXCELLENCY THE RIGHT HONB^LE LORD BOTETOURT'S PRUDENT AND WISE, ADMINISTRATION, AND THAT THE REMEMBRANCE OF THOSE MANY PUBLIC AND SOCIAL VIRTUES, WHICH SO EMINENTLY ADORN'D HIS ILLUSTRIOUS CHARACTER, MIGHT BE TRANSMITTED TO LATEST POSTERITY, THE GENERAL ASSEMBLY OF VIRGINIA ON THE XX DAY OF JULY ANN: DOM: M, DCC, LXXI RESOLVED WITH ONE UNITED VOICE, TO ERECT THIS STATUE TO HIS LORDSHIP'S MEMORY.

LET WISDOM AND JUSTICE PRESIDE IN ANY COUNTRY; THE PEOPLE WILL REJOICE AND MUST BE HAPPY.

AMERICA, BEHOLD YOUR FRIEND: WHO, LEAVING HIS NATIVE COUNTRY, DECLIN'D THOSE ADDITIONAL HONOURS WHICH WERE THERE IN STORE FOR HIM, THAT HE MIGHT HEAL YOUR WOUNDS, AND RESTORE TRANQUILITY AND HAPPINESS TO THIS EXTENSIVE CONTINENT: WITH WHAT ZEAL AND ANXIETY HE PURSUED THESE GLORIOUS OBJECTS, VIRGINIA, THUS BEARS HER GRATEFULL TESTIMONY.[223]

THE Honourable *William Nelson*, Efq., (as it has already been intimated) became the Acting Governor upon the Death of Lord *Botetourt;* he being the Prefident of the Council. And he continued in this Capacity for near a Year's Time; during which Term there was Peace and Quietude in the Colony. The defpifed Revenues were now reduced

duced to a Minimum and, it has been ſaid, the whole Diſturbance might have paſſed far into the Future, had theſe Affairs continued with the Mildneſs that they now for a brief Time enjoyed. But this was not to be.[224]

❀ ❀ ❀

IN the Fall of the Year 1771, *John Murray*, Earl of *Dunmore*, arrived in *Virginia*[225] to be the full and reſident Governor. And of this Executive it were next to an impoſſible Thing to give a fair and true Appraiſal; for any Man who followed after *Dumore's* deceaſed Predeceſſor could expect only to loſe much or little by Compariſon. Moreover, at the Palace in *Williamſburg*, *Dunmore* ſucceeded a Line of Governors who, in more favourable Times, had ſhown themſelves to be Men as able, liberal, and aſſiduous as ever ruled a *Britiſh* Colony. Nor can it be denied that this new Governor faced Conditions and Events more violent and more hopeleſs than had any of his Predeceſſors. So that, if the *Virginia* Coloniſts looked upon *Dunmore* as a Man imperious and vindictive, their Judgement ſhould now be tempered with Inſight.

AT *Dunmore's* firſt Coming and for ſome Time thereafter, Things continued quietly in *Virginia*. If there was a Spirit of Refractorineſs and a Yearning for Independence, it appeared not upon the Surface, but in Signs ſuch as that diſcuſſed by the Honourable *William Nelſon* in a Letter to a Correſpondent in *London*, which went as follows:

" I

" I now wear a good Suit of Cloth of my Son's
" Wool, manufactured, as well as my Shirts in
" *Albemarle & Augufta* Counties; my Shoes, Hofe,
" Buckles, Wigg & Hat &c., of our own Country:
" and in thefe we improve every Year in Quantity
" as well as Quality."[226]

YET, if the Colonifts were now determined to
purfue a Courfe of " Decency, Duty, and Re-
" fpect "[227] in feeking their Objectives, it would
feem that his Excellency was not able thus to dif-
guife his Humour, for in *September*, 1772, the following appeared in the *South Carolina Gazette:*

" In *Virginia* their new *Scotch* Governor began
" his Government with Negligence and Difregard
" to the Duties of his Office. His Lordfhip was
" hardly ever vifited, very difficult of Accefs and
" frequently could not be fpoken with, when the
" moft urgent Bufinefs of the Public called for his
" Attendance. Thefe fpirited Colonifts could not
" bear thefe haughty Airs, but deputed one of their
" Lawyers to remonftrate againft this fupercilious
" Behavior, fo inconfiftent with the Service of the
" great Prince whom he reprefented. At firft he
" ftormed, but at laft he agreed to name Office-
" Hours, when every Perfon concerned might at-
" tend on Bufinefs. Since which Time all Things
" have gone on very peaceably, and his Lordfhip
" has become much more tractable, to the Honour
" of his Mafter, and the great Advantage of the im-
" portant Colony he prefides over. Thanks to the
" true *American* Spirit of Liberty."[228]

AND peaceably Things continued until the Affembly, which had been held prorogued for fome
Time,

THE ALTERNATIVE OF WILLIAMSBURG

Showing either the Burgesses forced by their Constituents to the signing of an Agreement of Non-Importation, or else the Loyalists forced to such an Association by the Sentiment of the aroused and angry Publick

From an Engraving done at London, 1775.

Time, convened in *March* of the Year 1773. Then, a *British* Revenue Ship having been burned by Colonists in *Rhode Island* and it being noised about that the Perpetrators of this Deed would be sent to *England* for Trial, the Spirit of Revolt rose again in the House of Burgesses at *Williamsburg*. Upon the gathering of the Assembly, *Thomas Jefferson, Patrick Henry, Richard Henry Lee, Francis Lightfoot Lee,* and *Dabney Carr* met together in a private Room of the *Raleigh* Tavern, and there they draughted Resolutions calling for the Appointment of a *Committee of Correspondence* to secure authentic Intelligencies concerning the Actions of *Great Britain* and to communicate with the sister Colonies concerning such Things. And these Resolutions were offered in the House of Burgesses by *Dabney Carr*[229] on *March* 12th,[230] and, they being passed, brought about the Formation of similar Committees in the other Colonies. This Action, being looked upon by some Historians as the first successful Step toward a Uniting of the Colonies, has been considered the most significant Advance of the revolutionary Movement since the Resolutions against the *Stamp Act*.

Lord *Dunmore* now held the Assembly prorogued for more than a Year's Time,[231] during which the *Committees of Correspondence* carried on a lively Exchange of Communications. Also during this Time occurred in *Massachusetts* that bold Rebuke to *British* Taxation which has come to be known as the " *Boston Tea Party*."[232] And *Dun-*

more

more had the Misfortune to have the *Virginia* Affembly in Seffion in *May*, 1774, when News was
received at *Williamfburg* concerning the Act of
Parliament which ordered the Sealing of the Port of
Bofton with an armed Force, the Embargo to become effective on *June* 1ft of that Year. At once
the Burgeffes paffed Refolutions protefting this
Act and fetting *June* 1ft afide to be a Day of Fafting, Humiliation, and Prayer.[233] (That this Refolve was adhered to is fhown by the Diary of
George Wafhington, who, for that Day, wrote:
" Went to Church [*Bruton*] and fafted all Day ").[234]

At this his Excellency diffolved the Affembly[235]
—but only to fee them reaffemble the following
Day (*May* 27th) at the *Raleigh* Tavern, where fome
eighty-nine Burgeffes entered into a general Affociation againft the *Eaft India* Company, and proceeded to the following important Recommendation:

" . . . We are further clearly of Opinion, that an
" Attack, made on one of our fifter Colonies, to
" compel Submiffion to arbitrary Taxes, is an At-
" tack made on all *Britifh America*, and threatens
" Ruin to the Rights of all, unlefs the united Wif-
" dom of the Whole be applied. And for this Pur-
" pofe it is recommended to the *Committee of
" Correfpondence*, that they communicate, with
" their feveral correfponding Committees, on the
" Expediency of appointing Deputies from the
" feveral Colonies of *Britifh America*, to meet in
" general Congrefs, at fuch Place annually as fhall
" be thought moft convenient; there to deliberate
                                                    " on

" on thofe general Meafures which the united
" Interefts of *America* may from Time to Time
" require."[236]

AND, it being learned that the Sentiment in
favour of a general Congrefs was fhared by feveral
other Colonies, *Virginia* took the Lead and the
Reprefentatives of the People fummoned the *Firſt*
Virginia Convention to meet at *Williamſburg* for the
Purpofe of electing Delegates to gather with thofe
of the other Colonies in fuch a general Congrefs.
This Convention appointed *Peyton Randolph*,
Richard Henry Lee, *George Waſhington*, *Patrick*
Henry, *Richard Bland*, *Benjamin Harriſon*, and
Edmund Pendleton to reprefent *Virginia*.[237] Of
thefe *Peyton Randolph*, of *Williamſburg*, was
elected the Prefident of the firſt Congrefs (which
convened at *Philadelphia* in *September*, 1774),[238] and
Patrick Henry made his great Speech, in which he
declared that *Britiſh* Oppreſſion had effaced the
Boundaries of the feveral Colonies.[239]

YET, in the Courfe of thefe Things, Life proceeded at *Williamſburg* with the greateſt Decorum
and Reſtraint. If the Citizens fent Caſh and Provifions to the beleagured City of *Boſton* in *Maſſachuſetts*,[240] they, on the other Hand, greeted the
Arrival of Lady *Dunmore* in their Midſt (ſhe and
her Children coming to join his Lordſhip) with
Bon-Fires, Illuminations and Rejoicing.[241] And,
when her Ladyſhip, who was much refpected, prefented the Governor with a new Daughter at the
Palace,

Palace, the Rejoicing was such that the Infant, in return, was named *Virginia*.[242]

❀ ❀ ❀

BY the Year 1775 the Dispute between *Great Britain* and the Colonies had come to such a Pass that an open War appeared to be inevitable. In *March* of that Year a second *Virginia* Convention was summoned, and, a *British* Man-of-War lying too close to *Williamsburg* for Conveniency, the Meetings were held in *St. John's* Church at *Richmond*. It was there (and not in *Williamsburg* as many have supposed) that *Patrick Henry*, on *March* 23rd, 1775, introduced his Bill for assembling and training the Militia.[243]   And, some Opposition arising from conservative Members, *Henry* carried his Motion with a great Oration, in the Course of which he said:

" Is Life so dear, or Peace so sweet, as to be pur-
" chased at the Price of Chains and Slavery?   For-
" bid it, Almighty *God!*   I know not what Course
" others may take, but as for me, give me Liberty
" or give me Death! "[244]

THE Action of the Convention brought about a decisive Act on the Part of the Governor, which precipitated the Outburst of Hostilities in *Virginia*. In a Letter to the *British* Secretary of State, written from *Williamsburg*, Lord *Dunmore* described this Event:

" The Series of dangerous Measures pursued by
" the People of this Colony against Government,
                                    " which

" which they have now entirely overturned, & par-
" ticularly their having come to a Refolution of
" raifing a Body of armed Men in all the Counties,
" made me think it prudent to remove fome Gun-
" powder which was in a Magazine in this Place,
" where it lay expofed to any Attempt that might
" be made to fieze it, & I had Reafon to believe the
" People intended to take that Step. I accord-
" ingly requefted of Lieut^r *Collins*, commanding his
" Majefty's armed Schooner the *Magdalen*, to con-
" vey the Powder on Board the *Fowey*, Man-of-
" War now on this Station, which that Officer,
" with a Party of his Seamen diligently executed;
" but tho' it was intended to have been done pri-
" vately, Mr *Collins* & his Party were obferved, &
" Notice was given immediately to the Inhabitants
" of this Place; Drums were then fent thro' the
" City.—The independent Company got under
" Arms. All the People affembled, & during their
" Confultation, continual Threats were brought to
" my Houfe, that it was their Refolution to fieze
" upon, or maffacre me, & every Perfon found giv-
" ing me Affiftance if I refufed to deliver the Pow-
" der immediately into their Cuftody."[245]

IT is both interefting and a fignificant Thing that
the Confifcating of the Powder at *Williamfburg*,
thus defcribed by Lord *Dunmore*, occurred on the
20th Day of *April*, 1775; which was the Day after
the Battle at *Lexington* in *Maffachufetts*. Concerning this, many have held it to be but a ftrange
Coincidence, while others have feen in it a concerted Plan by which *Great Britain* had hoped to
foreftall an Outbreak of Rebellion in both Colonies.
And, if this laft were indeed the Cafe, the Failure
of

of the Plan was tremendous; for when (in the
ſhort Space of nine Days) Word of the Affair at
Lexington and *Concord* was received at *Williamſburg* (which was already virtually in Arms), a
Broadſide was iſſued by the *Virginia Gazette* cloſing
with the Words, " The Sword is now drawn, and
"*God* knows when it will be ſheathed."[246]

Nor were the Diſturbances which followed the
Seizure of the Powder in *Virginia* confined to
Williamſburg alone. For Troops were raiſed in
various Places; and on *May* 3rd *Patrick Henry*
appeared near the City with about one Hundred
and fifty armed Men, gathered in a March from
Hanover. Theſe demanded the Return of the Powder or a Settlement for it; and the Governor found
it neceſſary to comply with a Bill of Exchange for
£330 before the Men would diſperſe.[247]

There now followed at *Williamſburg* an event-
ful Period which is impoſſible of brief Deſcription:
The publick Treaſury was held under the Guard of
the angered Citizens. The Governor and the Aſſembly exchanged Communications in which the
Sentiments of the Times were but poorly con-
cealed.[248] Diſpatches from the Governor to the
Britiſh Secretary of State (which were evidently
ſeized or intercepted) appeared in the *Virginia
Gazette*, as did ſuch Items as the following, which
furthered the unfriendly Spirit of the Times:

" A Correſpondent thinks it an odd Circum-
" ſtance, that the *Cerberus* (whom the Poets feign
" to be the three-headed Dog that guards the
                                    " Mouth

" Mouth of *Hell*) fhould be the Ship appointed to
" carry over to *America* the three Generals ap-
" pointed to tame the *Americans*."[249]

LOYALISTS began to fettle their Affairs and to
leave the Colony.[250] The Palace for fome Time had
been virtually an armed Fortrefs;[251] and now, in the
dark Hours of the Morning of *June* 8th, his Lordfhip and his Family fled from it to the Protection
of the *Fowey* Man-of-War lying in the *York*
River,[252] the Governor fearing longer to try the
Temper of the People. For a Time he fought to
control the Government from the Safety of the
Warfhip. But, failing this, and finding the Colonies to be in a State of open Rebellion (*George Wafhington* having taken Command of the Forces of the
united Colonies on *July* 2nd) he fet himfelf to making War upon the Colony he had lately governed.[253]
Then, fuffering Reverfes in this alfo, he failed for
New York[254] and thence for *England*—and with him
royal Authority departed forever from *Virginia*.[255]

❀ ❀ ❀

IN the Time of the Interregnum the Government
of *Virginia* devolved firft upon the Affembly,
and, when that Body adjourned its laft active
Seffion on *June* 24th, 1775,[256] the Powers of Government paffed to the *Virginia Convention of Delegates* and to the *Committee of Safety* appointed by
that Convention.[257] The Convention alfo made
Patrick Henry the Commander-in-Chief of all the
Virginia

Virginia Forces, and *Williamsburg* was appointed the Place for the Gathering of the Troops.[258]

Meanwhile, the House of Burgesses continued to convene in *Williamsburg* from Time to Time, but a sufficient Number of Members could never be gathered to enable the House to proceed to Business. And so it was that the Minutes of the Session called on *May* 6th, 1776, read:

> " SEVERAL Members met, but did neither pro-
> " ceed to Business, nor adjourn, as a House of
> " Burgesses.   FINIS."[259]

Thus ended the *General Assembly* of *Virginia* that was composed of a *Council* and a *House of Burgesses*.   It has since been advanced with Assurance to be the oldest representative legislative Institution in all *English America;* and by some (with devious Arguments) it has been shown to be the oldest in the World.   For one Hundred and fifty-seven Years it had made the Laws for the *Virginia* Colony; and for at least one Hundred and fifty-three Years of this Time it had claimed and defended its sole Right to levy and approve Taxes upon *Virginians*.[260]   Now, in the Victory of this Principle, it passed away.

❋ ❋ ❋

ON *May* 6th, 1776, that same Day that the House of Burgesses ceased to exist, the fifth and, perhaps, the most memorable of the *Virginia* Conventions of Delegates met in the Capitol at *Williamsburg*.[261]

It

IT so happened that a Number of Counties had now instructed their Delegates to declare for Independence (this Number including *Cumberland* County, which had directed its Delegates to " abjure any Allegiance to his *Britannick* Majesty, and " bid him a good Night forever.")²⁶² In Consequence of these Things, Resolutions were draughted, offered, and argued before a Committee of the whole House, directing the *Virginia* Delegates in the General Congress at *Philadelphia* to move that Body to declare the United Colonies to be free and independent States, and carrying the Assent of *Virginia* to such a Declaration. In these Proceedings, *Thomas Nelson*, Jr., *Patrick Henry*, *Meriwether Smith*, and *Edmund Pendleton* were conspicuous.²⁶³ The Resolutions, being presented to the Convention on *May* 15, 1776, by *Archibald Cary*, were unanimously passed.²⁶⁴ The Instructions of the Convention were fulfilled at *Philadelphia* by *Richard Henry Lee*, where they brought about the *Declaration of Independence*.

YET, *Virginia* did not wait upon the Results of her Motion in the General Congress to proceed in the Matter of Independence. For, on *June* 12th the Convention of Delegates approved a *Declaration of Rights*, which was for the most Part prepared by the Honourable *George Mason*, Esq., as a " Basis " and Foundation of Government."²⁶⁵ And, subsequently, on *June* 29th, the Convention unanimously adopted a *Plan of Government* (this also proceeding chiefly from the Pen of *George Mason*),²⁶⁶ which has

has been advanced as the firſt Conſtitution of a free
and independent State. Thus, when the *Declaration of Independence* was ſigned at *Philadelphia, Virginia* already exiſted as an Independency.   By its
Conſtitution a new General Aſſembly had been
formed, it conſiſting of a *Houſe of Delegates* and a
Senate, and this Aſſembly governs the *Commonwealth* of *Virginia* to this preſent Day.

⚙ ⚙ ⚙

UNDER the new Conſtitution *Patrick Henry*
became the firſt Governor of the Commonwealth, he being choſen by the Convention upon
its firſt Ballot.²⁶⁷   And ſoon he took up his Reſidence at the Governor's Palace,²⁶⁸ which, the
Effects of Lord *Dunmore* having been diſpoſed of
at publick Auction,²⁶⁹ was now newly fitted out for
his Uſe.²⁷⁰   And it has been told that ſome Men
of Prominence and Faſhion in that Time feared
that *Henry's* Plainneſs of Appearance would not
lend itſelf to the great Dignity of his new Office;
but, it has further been told that he who in a
former Day had ridden into *Williamſburg* upon a
lean Horſe and in poor Attire, now roſe handſomely
above all Expectations—he appearing at the Palace in a fine black Suit, a ſcarlet Cloak, and a Wig
as great as any in the Country.²⁷¹

N o w , in *Henry's* Time as Governor, the War
continued apace.   With its Succeſſes and Reverſes
the Tenour of Life in *Williamſburg* roſe and fell; ſo
that there were Times of Celebration and Times of
Grief.

Grief.   The Hoftilities, in which *Virginia* joined
with all her Strength and Refources, raged to the
North of her Boundaries and then to the South of
them.   News of the Surrender of *Burgoyne* in the
North was received at *Williamfburg* with the great-
eft Rejoicing,[272] as is indicated by the following
Letter written by *John Page* of *Williamfburg* to
General *Weedon:*

" . . . You relate the Battle with *Burgoyne*
" . . . We have had a *Feu de Joye* from our
" Troops, ringing of Bells and a grand Illumina-
" tion, and tho' it is now paft 10 at Night the
" People are fhouting and firing in Platoons about
" the Streets.   . . . I have been obliged to go down
" into the Streets and prevent a Riot and to pre-
" vail on my Neighbour *Lenox* to ceafe firing—who
" drunk as a Lord had been endeavoring to imitate
" a Cannon. . . "[273]

In the Year 1777 *Patrick Henry* and *George
Rogers Clark* laid a Plan to carry a War of *Virginia's* own into her Northweft Territory,[274] and
there to put an End to the Incurfions of the *Britifh*
under *Henry Hamilton*, the Governor of the Northweft (who, from his inciting the *Indians* againft the
Americans, was called " the Hair-Buyer.")[275]
Twice *Clark* proceeded againft Fort *Vincennes*, and,
on the fecond Occafion, in the Winter of 1779, he
captured not only the Fort, but *Hamilton* alfo, who,
being brought back to *Williamfburg*, languifhed for
fome Time in the Prifon near the Capitol.[276]   Of
his Arrival at *Williamfburg*, this unhappy Prifoner
wrote the Following in his Journal:

" About

" About Sunfet reached *Williamſburg*, wet, jaded,
" diſpirited, forming Ideas of what Sort of judicial
" Examination I was to undergo. By the Time
" we reached the Palace as it is called, the Gover-
" nor's Reſidence, our Eſcort of curious Perſons
" had become very numerous. The Officer went
" in to give Account of his Miſſion, and we re-
" mained on Horſeback before the Door expecting
" the Civilities naturally to be looked for from a
" Man in firſt Place in the Province. In half an
" Hour not finding our Expectations anſwered, I
" flung myſelf from my Horſe fatigued and morti-
" fied to be left a Spectacle to a gazing Crowd. We
" were however ſoon relieved from the painful State
" of Uncertainty by the Appearance of the Officer,
" who conducted us to the common Priſon, diſtant
" a ſmall Mile, our Attendants increaſing every
" Step. At the Jail we were received by the Jailer, a
" Character, however beneath other People's
" Notice, which ſoon called our Attention. . ."277

IN *June*, 1779, *Thomas Jefferſon* ſucceeded
Patrick Henry as the Governor of the *Virginia*
Commonwealth.278 And now, in *Jefferſon's* Time,
the Propoſal to move the Seat of *Virginia* Government to a more central Situation was again advanced,279 as it had been ſome thirty Years be-
fore.280 The Meaſure found great Favour in the
Eyes of the new Governor, who, being a Reſident
of *Albemarle*, could well underſtand the Juſtice of
the Notion.281 Moreover, *Williamſburg's* Acceſſi-
bility to the Enemy in a Time of War entered into
the Diſcuſſion; ſo that on *June* 12th, 1779, the
Aſſembly was prevailed upon to paſs an Act for
removing

removing the Seat of Government to *Richmond*[282] (the Group of small Villages which composed that Place being looked upon as a Town " more safe and " central than any other Town situated on navi- " gable Water.")[283] The Removal of the Offices of Government was effected in the opening Months of the Year 1780.[284]

THE Passing of the Seat of Government brought the Close of another Epoch in the History of *Williamsburg*. For near a Century and a Half it had now been looked upon as the " Heart and " Centre " of *Virginia*—literally at the first and figuratively at the last. In this Time other Cities and Towns had grown up in *Virginia*, and some had surpassed *Williamsburg* in Growth and Size;[285] but it is safe to say that, until the Removal of the Gov- ernment, no City in all *America* had surpassed this Capital in its Influence and Accomplishment. For, as *Jamestown* had led *Virginia* through the Perils of Conquest and Settlement, so *Williamsburg* led that Colony through Times of Establishment and Ex- pansion—and on to Liberty.

Now it was to rest from these Labours.

CHAPTER III.

Chapter III.

ILLIAMSBURG was now to rest; yet, at the first, its Quiet was but short-lived. Gone from it were the Commotions of Publick Times, the Solemnities of the high Courts, the Fire and Fervour of political Debate, and all the Display and Ceremony of Government. But, in their Stead, the War moved in to the Confines of the City; so that the Passing of the Seat of Government was near forgotten.

WITH the Beginning of the Year 1781, the *British* commenced a mass Invasion of *Virginia*,[286] that Commonwealth being known to be but poorly equipped to resist such an Attack. *Virginia's* Resources were now near Exhaustion; and her Men and Guns were scattered in the Defense of her Sister States to the North and South.[287] It has been said that the *British*, in Consequence of these Things, looked forward to an easy Campaign by which, through the Subjection of this central and important "Colony," they might break the Strength and Spirit of the Union arrayed against them.[288]

Benedict Arnold now entered *Virginia* in Command of a *British* Force,[289] and these Troops were later joined and augmented by a Force under General *Phillips*.[290] Together these two ravaged the eastern

eaſtern Parts of *Virginia* at their Leiſure; they being reſiſted at the firſt by ſmall Bands of Militia, and later by an inferior Number of *American* Regulars ſent by General *Waſhington* under the Command of the Marquis *de Lafayette*.[291] After the Death of General *Phillips* at *Peterſburg* (he dying of the Fever) the *Britiſh* Force was greatly increaſed by the Arrival of Troops from the South commanded by Lord *Cornwallis*,[292] and that General then aſſumed Command of the united Forces, which numbered about ſeven Thouſand.[293]

T H E R E now followed a Series of Maneuvers and Stratagems in which *Cornwallis* ſought to engage the vaſtly inferior Force under *Lafayette* in Battle. Failing in this, the *Britiſh* retired down the *Virginia* Peninſula, followed at ſome Diſtance by the *Americans*.[294] On *June* 25th, 1781, *Cornwallis* entered into *Williamſburg*[295] and encamped there for ten Days.[296]

N o w there was Plundering and Famine in the City; Slaves were confiſcated; the Small-pox was ſpread Abroad; and a Swarm of Flies (as denſe as the Gloom that pervaded the Place) ſettled upon *Williamſburg*. *Cornwallis* eſtabliſhed his own Headquarters in the Houſe of the Preſident of the College; leaving that Official to find Shelter elſewhere.[297] The Price of Liberty now ſeemed dear indeed.

O N *July* 4th the *Britiſh* moved out of the City[298] and, having adminiſtered a ſharp Defeat to *Lafayette* near *Jameſtown*,[299] they croſſed the River and proceeded

proceeded to their Bafe at *Portfmouth*,[300] from
whence they later moved by Water to *Yorktown*.[301]

In *September* the Scene at *Williamfburg* was altered mightily; for then had begun that great Man-
euver of the *American* and *French* Forces, together
with the *French* Fleet,[302] which brought about the
Capture and Surrender of the *Britifh* at *Yorktown*.
And as this Affair drew on, *Williamfburg* became
the Place for the Maffing of the *French* and *American* Forces,[303] while the *Britifh* lay behind their
Fortifications on the *York*.[304] The Arrival of General *Wafhington* in *Williamfburg* was defcribed by
Colonel *St. George Tucker*, a Refident of the City
and an Officer of the *Virginia* Militia, in this
Fafhion:

" I wrote you Yefterday that General *Wafhing-
" ton* had not yet arrived.   About four o'Clock in
" the Afternoon his Approach was announced.
" He had paffed our Camp, which is now in the
" Rear of the whole Army, before we had Time to
" parade the Militia.   The *French* Line had juft
" Time to form.   The *Continentals* had more Lei-
" fure.   He approached without any Pomp or
" Parade, attended only by a few Horfemen and
" his own Servants.   The Count *de Rochambeau*
" and General *Hand*, with one or two more Officers
" were with him.   I met him as I was endeavoring
" to get to Camp from Town, in order to parade
" the Brigade; but he had already paffed it.   To
" my great Surprife he recognized my Features and
" fpoke to me immediately by Name.   General
" *Nelfon*, the Marquis, etc., rode up immediately
" after.   Never was more Joy painted in any Coun-
" tenance

" tenance than theirs.   The Marquis rode up with
" Precipitation, clafped the General in his Arms,
" and embraced him with an Ardor not eafily de-
" fcribed.   The whole Army and all the Town
" were prefently in Motion.   The General, at the
" Requeft of the Marquis *de St. Simon*, rode through
" the *French* Lines.   The Troops were paraded for
" the Purpofe, and cut a moft fplendid Figure.
" He then vifited the *Continental* Line.   As he
" entered the Camp the Cannon from the Park of
" Artillery and from every Brigade announced the
" happy Event.   His Train by this Time was much
" increafed; and Men, Women and Children
" feemed to vie with each other in Demonftrations
" of Joy and Eagernefs to fee their beloved Country-
" man.   His Quarters are at Mr. *Wythe's* [*George
" Wythe's*] Houfe.   Aunt *Betty* [Mrs. *Peyton Ran-
" dolph*] has the Honor of the Count *de Rochambeau*
" to lodge at her Houfe.   We are all alive and fo
" fanguine in our Hopes that Nothing can be con-
" ceived more different than the Countenances
" of the fame Men at this Time and on the firft of
" *June*.   The Troops which were to attend the
" General are coming down the Bay—a Part, if not
" all, being already embarked at the *Head of Elk*.
" *Cornwallis* may now tremble for his Fate, for
" Nothing but fome extraordinary Interpofition of
" his Guardian Angels feems capable of faving him
" and the whole Army from Captivity."305

❀ ❀ ❀

A DESCRIPTION of the Happenings at
Yorktown belongs to the Hiftory of that
Place, and not to a Report of this Nature.   *Will-
iamfburg* faw the Gathering of the Troops and the
Planning

Planning of the Siege. It faw the allied Forces march out with their Flags waving; and it faw the Wagons return bearing the *American* Wounded to their Hofpital at the Governor's Palace,[306] and the *French* Cafualties to the Great Building of the College.[307] Following that memorable Day, *October* 19th, when the *Britifh* laid down their Arms,[308] it faw the victorious Armies march back, and there was Cheering and a Firing of Salutes. Indeed, fome of the *French* Troops were now quartered at *Williamfburg*, and wintered there.[309]

THE Peace with *Great Britain*, the provifional Articles of which were figned at *Paris* in *November*, 1782,[310] was proclaimed at *Williamfburg* on *May* 1ft, 1783,[311] with great Ceremony. The Order of the Proceffion and Celebration for that Day was announced as follows:

" 1ft Two Attendants in front, fupporting two
"   Staffs, decorated with Ribbons, &c., &c.
" 2d The Herald mounted on a Gelding neatly
"   caparifoned.
" 3d Two Attendants, as at firft.
" 4th Sergeant bearing the Mace.
" 5th Mayor, Recorder, with Charter.
" 6th Clerk, behind carrying the Plan of the City.
" 7th Aldermen, two and two.
" 8th Common Council, in the fame Order.
" 9th The Citizens in the fame Order.

    " THE Citizens to be convened on *Thurfday* at 1
" o'Clock at the Court Houfe by a Bell Man.
    " AFTER the Convention of the Citizens they
" are to make Proclamation at the C: Houfe, after
                                        " which

" which the Bells at the Church, College & Capitol
" are to ring in Peal.

" From the C' Houſe the Citizens are to proceed
" to the College, and make Proclamation at that
" Place, from whence they are to proceed to the
" Capitol and make Proclamation there; and from
" thence proceed to the *Raleigh* & paſs the Reſt of
" the Day." 312

And now the Quiet returned.

    ✿ ✿ ✿

SOME Obſervers have held that, with the Paſſing of the War, *Williamſburg* fell into a Sleep;
while Others have proteſted that it was not a Sleep,
but a Soliloquy (which is a Talking to one's Self).
The Population fell away;313 for many of the
Tradeſmen now followed the Government to *Richmond*. Yet, many of the eſtabliſhed Families continued their Reſidence; ſo that for more than a
Century Travellers have been moved to remark on
the genteel Society and the Hoſpitality of the
Place.314

The College, with brief Interruptions, had continued in Operation through the Revolution (it
had, in Fact, been made a Univerſity in the Year
1779).315 Now, with the Seat of Government removed, the Revenues from the Crown cut off, and
the Support of the *Engliſh* Church loſt to it, the
College ſtruggled on under the Guidance of its
Preſidents and Profeſſors. The Lands granted by
the Crown were yet held, and, indeed, the College
Holdings were now increaſed by the Gift of the
Palace

Palace Lands and other public Lands, prefented by the Affembly. Chiefly upon Proceeds from the Renting or Sale of thefe the College continued.[316]

The Palace no longer ftood, it having been myfterioufly burned while ferving as an Hofpital in 1781.[317]   Now the Capitol commenced to fall into Ruin, fo that in 1794 the eaftern Halfwasdemolifhed and the Materials fold to defray the Expenfes of maintaining the other Half[318] (and that remaining Half was deftroyed by a Fire in 1832).[319]

From Time to Time *Williamfburg* rofe again to Prominence upon brief Occafions; fuch, for Example, as that upon which *Lafayette* (who was in the Country as the Gueft of the Congrefs) returned to the City in the Year 1824.[320]   The great *French* General was entertained at the Refidence of Mrs. *Mary Monroe Peachy* upon the *Court Houfe Green*, where he received an Ovation from the Citizens; following which, he was banqueted at the *Raleigh* Tavern.[321]   But fuch Events became increafing Rare, and the Interludes of Peacefulnefs the longer.

In the Year 1827, a new Profeffor at the College defcribed the Poft Office at*Williamfburg* in a Letter to a Friend; and, the Poft Office being a fair Indication of the Temper of any Town in that Time, the Letter is here fet down:

" . . . I thought I was tranfported to *Noah's*
" Ark, when I firft came into this Town, fo pro-
" digious was the Quantity of Animals I met with,
" without feeing a fingle Perfon till I reached the
" Poft Office which ftands in the Center of Main St.
                                                    " It

" It is one of the Curiofities of this Place.   I wifh
" I could defcribe it to you, but fuch Thing is en-
" tirely out of my Power, and I defy *Walter Scott*
" himfelf to do it, notwithftanding his aftonifhing
" Imagination, but as to enable you to form an
" incorrect Idea of this fuperb Eftablifhment I will
" tell you that there is not Article whatever in the
" World which could not be found in it.   It is a
" Book Seller's Store in which you will find Hams
" and *French* Brandy; it is an Apothecary's Shop
" in which you can provide yourfelf with black filk
" Stockings and fhell Oyfters; it is a Poft Office in
" which you may have Glifters, chewing Tobacco
" & in a Word it is a Mufeum of natural Hiftory
" in which we meet every Afternoon to difpute
" about the Prefidential Election, and about the
" Quality of *Irifh* Potatoes. . . . "322

THE Houfes and Buildings of the City continued
to mellow with Years; and fome of the older Structures (together with thofe that were unoccupied)
commenced to fall into Ruin. From Time to
Time a Building would fall a Prey to Flames; and,
more rarely, a new Building would rife, to fhine
forth in the Manner of a frefh Patch upon a well-
worn Garment.

IN the Year 1838, *Bruton* Church became the
Prey, not of Flames, but of a Church Fair, by
which a confiderable Sum was raifed for the Repair
and Modernizing of its Interior.323 In 1859 the
Great Building of the College burned,324 and,
though it was at once rebuilt,325 it loft the Hand-
fomenefs and Dignity with which Sir *Chriftopher*
Wren and Colonel *Spotfwood* had bleffed it.   In
the

the fame Year the *Raleigh* Tavern, which in Addition to its Guefts, had for fome Years houfed
Memories perhaps more momentous than thofe of
any *American* Hoftelry, fell alfo to Flames.[326]

YET, *Williamfburg* continued in its philofophical Serenity — which fome miftook for Slumber.

❀ ❀ ❀

THE Quiet and Serenity of *Williamfburg* were
fhattered in the Year 1861 by the Outbreaking
of the *War Between the States*. And at once the
Men and Boys of the City (including the Students,
Profeffors, and the Prefident of the College) dif-
tributed themfelves to the Armies of the *Confederacy*.[327]

IT would appear that it was almoft an inevitable
Thing that the War fhould come to *Williamfburg;*
and, in the Year 1862, it came. From its firft
Foundation the City had been recognized and
noted as a ftrategic and defenfible Spot; and now
it lay between a *Federal* Stronghold (Fortrefs *Monroe*) at the Foot of the Peninfula, and the *Confederate* Capital (*Richmond*) at the Head of it.   And
fo it was that in *April*, 1862, General *George B.
McClellan* advanced up the Peninfula with a *Union*
Force numbering above a Hundred Thoufand
Men.[328]   He was met at *Yorktown* by a fmall *Confederate* Force, under Major General *J. Bankhead
Magruder*.[329]   And while the *Federals* were held in
check at *Yorktown*, *Magruder* threw a fecond Line
of Redoubts, Rifle Pits, and a Barricade of Trees
acrofs

acrofs the Peninfula on the eaftern Outfkirts of
Williamfburg, with a Fort at the commanding
Center of the Line.[330]   Then *Confederate* Reinforcements began to arrive; General *Jofeph E.
Johnfton* appeared and took Command, and Generals *Early*, *Jones*, and *Hill* came up with reinforc-
ing Divifions.[331]

ON *May* 3rd *McClellan* was ready to fight at
Yorktown, but the *Confederates* quietly fell back to
the Fortifications at *Williamfburg*.   *Johnfton* now
placed General *Longftreet* in Command of the Field
for the *Confederates*.   The Battle of *Williamfburg*
was fought on *May* 5th,[332] and the Homes,
Churches, and publick Buildings of the City were
filled with Wounded and Dying.[333]   Certain Citizens of *Williamfburg* ventured out beneath their
Umbrellas (for it was raining) to watch the Battle
at clofe Hand;[334] but, becoming involved in the
Retreat of a *Confederate* Company, they retreated
alfo.

AT Nightfall (as previoufly planned) the Southern Forces fell back in good Order towards *Richmond;* and the *Federals* took Command of the City,
refting at *Williamfburg* for feveral Days.[335]   Both
Sides claimed the Victory[336] and, the Queftion
being a clofe one, moft Hiftorians of the War have
been content to leave the Point undecided.

THE Campaign moved on to *Richmond*, where
the Affault of the *Federals* was fuccefsfully refifted.
Whereupon, many of *McClellan's* Troops marched
back through *Williamfburg;* but the City continued

in

in the Poffeffion of the *Union*, and (with the Exception of one Day)[337] ferved as an unwilling Outpoft
of the *Federal* Army throughout the remaining
Years of the War.

In *September*, 1862, a Band of *Confederate* Cavalry, under the Command of General *Wife*, recap-
tured *Williamfburg* and held it for one Day; they
captured alfo the *Federal* Provoft Marfhall,[338] who
had made himfelf fomewhat unpopular with the
Citizens. Yet, in the Evening the City (but not
the Provoft Marfhall) was retaken by the *Federals*;[339] and, in Retaliation, certain Soldiers from the
Rank and File of the 5th *Pennfylvania* Cavalry
fired the Great Building of the College.[340]

Nor was the College the only Building to fuffer
during this Period of Occupation.   For many un-
tenanted Dwellings were difmantled or torn down
for Fire-wood;[341] and the old Offices of the Palace
(which had furvived the Fire which deftroyed that
Building in 1781) were now taken down, that the
Bricks might be ufed for the Chimneys of Officers'
Huts.[342]   And through thefe Times the Citizens of
Williamfburg continued fo loyal to the Caufe of the
South that, in the Year 1863, it became neceffary
for the *Federal* Provoft Marfhall to threaten to
place outfide the Lines all thofe who would not
take an Oath of Allegiance to the *Union*.[343]   Yet,
this Threat was but partially fulfilled; for after a
Number of Citizens were marched out of the City
they were permitted to return, it becoming apparent

ent that their Determination could not be changed
by fuch Meafures.[344]

BUT thefe things paffed with the Surrender at
Appomatox on the 9th Day of *April*, 1865.[345]

❁ ❁ ❁

WITH the Ending of the War the Quiet again
refumed at *Williamfburg;* but it was a Quiet
not of Peace alone, but alfo of Poverty.   The Story
of the Days of Reconftruction in the South is a
familiar one.   The Dwellings of the colonial Times
and of the early Days of the *Republic* continued in
Ufe now, not only becaufe they were held in high
Efteem, but alfo becaufe the Funds neceffary for
their Replacement or even their Repair were rare indeed.   The Slaves (happily) were gone; but the
pleafant and fymmetrical Gardens that they had
tended now fell to Weeds and Ruin.   Yet, Fifh and
Game might ftill be taken, and fome Corn would
fpring from a Soil exhaufted by the Culture of
Tobacco; fo that the fame genteel Families lived on
at *Williamfburg*.

THOUGH the Great Building of the College was
lying in Ruins, the Inftitution refumed Exercifes on
a fomewhat limited Scale in 1865; and in 1869 it
was operating with a full Complement of Profeffors,
and with its principal Building again in Ufe.[346]
Yet, in 1881 (on Account of a Lack of Funds) its
Activities were again fufpended, and they were not
refumed until 1888,[347] when Affiftance was gained
from the Commonwealth.   In 1893, the College
was

was indemnified in Part by the *Federal* Government
for its Loffes in the *War Between the States*. Ulti-
mately (in 1906), the College paffed into the
Ownerfhip of the Commonwealth.[348]

THESE trying Times in *Williamfburg* were
recently and ably defcribed by the Honourable
George P. Coleman, a Mayor of the City, in this
Fafhion:

" . . . *Williamfburg* on a Summer Day! The ftragg-
" ling Street, Ankle deep in Duft, grateful only to
" the Chickens, ruffling their Feathers in perfect
" Safety from any Traffic Danger. The Cows taking
" Refuge from the Heat of the Sun, under the Elms
" along the Sidewalk. Our City Fathers, affembled in
" friendly Leifure, following the Shade of the old
" Court Houfe around the Clock, fipping cool Drinks
" and difcuffing the Glories of our Paft. Almoft al-
" ways our Paft! There were Men and Women who
" ftrained every Nerve, every Means in their Power,
" to help the *Williamfburg* of the prefent Day, to
" fupply the Neceffities of Life to poorer Neighbors,
" to build up the College and procure Means of Edu-
" cation for their Children, but even they fhrank
" from looking toward the Future. The Paft alone
" held for them the Brightnefs which tempted their
" Thoughts to linger happily . . ."[349]

AND in this Fafhion *Williamfburg* continued, a
quiet, thoughtful Center of Education and County
Government.   Nor did it alter greatly until a Time
well into the twentieth Century.

❀ ❀ ❀

IN

I N the Year 1903, a new Minifter, the Reverend *William Archer Rutherfoord Goodwin*, aſſumed the Rectorſhip of *Bruton Pariſh* Church. And he (becoming intereſted in the fine Hiſtory of his ancient Charge) ſet about to raiſe a conſiderable Sum of Money for the Repair of that Structure and for the Reſtoration of its interior Appearance, which (as has been already ſtated) was greatly altered in 1839. This Work was brought to Completion in the Year 1907.[350]

S O M E Years later, after a long Abſence from the City, this ſame Doctor *Goodwin* reſumed his Rectorſhip at *Bruton* Church; whereupon, in 1926, the ancient Reſidence of the Honourable *George Wythe*, Eſq. (the Teacher of *Jefferſon*, *Marſhall*, *Monroe*, and many others) was purchaſed and reſtored, it becoming the Pariſh Houſe of *Bruton* Church.[351]

B U T the Salvage and Reſtoration of a Church and a ſingle Dwelling could not ſtem the Tide which had now ſet in, nor could the ſplendid Labours of the *Aſſociation for the Preſervation of Virginia Antiquities* (which Aſſociation had now for ſome Time preſerved the Powder Magazine and protected the Site of the ancient Capitol)[352] ſtem this Tide. The World War with its fevered Activities and Reſults brought the twentieth Century to *Williamſburg* in great and generous Meaſure; for the City, becauſe of its geographical Poſition, had ever ſtood in the Path of Wars. The Peninſula now became a Center for the Concentration of the Forces of the Army and the Navy, and for the Manufacture

Manufacture and Storage of Ammunition and Supplies.[353]   In Addition to this Activity, *Williamfburg* became the Bafe of Supplies for *Penniman*, a
Town of fome fifteen Thoufand Inhabitants,[354]
which fprang up near by.   This Town, which has
fince entirely difappeared, was efpecially created
for the Making of War Munitions.   Its fudden
Growth brought about a Period of temporary Bufinefs Activity and Profperity in *Williamfburg*.
Properties changed Ownerfhip rapidly.   Enlargement of the City was contemplated and new Subdivifions were laid out.[355]

As a Refult of thefe Things the *Duke of Gloucefter* Street became a teeming Highway of Concrete; great Pofts to carry Wires and Cables were
raifed on every Hand; the empty Spaces in *Williamfburg*, which were the Sites of forgotten Buildings and Gardens, began flowly to be filled with
Shops, and Stores, and with Stations for Gafo-
line.[356]   The old Houfes and many of their Occupants refifted; but *Williamfburg*, with the Paffing
of the War, ftood upon the Brink of a poor Succefs
in a World of vaft Accomplifhment.

In the Year 1924 Dr. *Goodwin* fpoke before the
Phi Beta Kappa Society in *New York* City concern-
ing the College at *Williamfburg* and its hiftoric
Environment.   Mr. *John D. Rockefeller*, Jr., was in
Attendance at this Lecture, following which Dr.
Goodwin invited him to vifit *Williamfburg*.   This
Mr. *Rockefeller* did many Months later, in 1926,
and in the Courfe of this Vifit Dr. *Goodwin* pre-
fented

fented and explained to him the Thought which had long been in his Mind of reftoring the City to its colonial Appearance, and of preferving it both for the Future and from the Fate which then feemed imminent.357

In 1926 Mr. *Rockefeller* returned again to *Williamfburg* to attend the Dedication of a Hall memorial to the Founders of the *Phi Beta Kappa* Society at the College, and in the Courfe of this Vifit the Preparation of preliminary Reftoration Drawings was authorized. In the Year 1927 Mr. *Rockefeller* made the Decifion to undertake the Fulfillment of Dr. *Goodwin's* Plan,358 which Plan was foon defined as " an Endeavor to reftore accurately " and to preferve for all Time the moft fignificant " Portions of an hiftoric and important City of " *America's* colonial Period."359 And this Plan and Endeavor are now fulfilled; fo that the City which in the Year 1926 looked forward to a Future of little Promife has inftead moved backward into the Protection of a Paft which in the Annals of *American* Hiftory is unexcelled.

Chapter IV.

Chapter IV.

T O the Minds of Many the *Williamſburg Reſtoration* will appeal principally as a Means to an End. To ſuch Minds the Methods of the Work will be of ſmall Concern, as compared with the Reſults and their Meaning. For theſe it will be ſufficient that the *Reſtoration* is nearing material Accompliſhment and that its inſpiriting Proceſſes have begun.

To other Minds, more technical in their Intereſt, the Project will appeal not as a Means to an End alone, but alſo as an End in itſelf. And theſe will wiſh to know how the Work was done, as well as the Whys and the Wherefores of it.

T H I S Chapter, then, can be directed to neither of theſe Types; for in one Caſe no Chapter is required, and in the other the Adherents will wiſh to await the detailed Reports and Publications which the Future, of Neceſſity, muſt bring as an Explanation and a Record. The Chapter is directed, rather, to thoſe who lean neither to one Extreme nor the other; yet, in its Brevity, it is deſigned to give to thoſe that do as little Diſpleaſure as may be.

✿ ✿ ✿

THERE

THERE are thofe who hold, with little or greater Infight, that if Hiftory moves in Cycles, then Progrefs may be made along either of its Courfes—and much Effort faved by thofe who but ftand ftill.

WHEN its Reftoration was undertaken, *Williamfburg* (as has been intimated) difplayed abounding Evidence of the architectural Implications of this philofophical Confufion. In a few fhort Years it had ceafed to be an ifolated and pleafingly decayed colonial City. Outwardly it had become a Highway Town in which the Ancient and the Modern were mingled in an Effect of peculiar Aggravation.[360]

THE early Plan of the City was unchanged, and, even in its makefhift Modernity, *Williamfburg* preferved a Proportion of its colonial Buildings which, in Relation to its eighteenth Century Size, was perhaps greater than that poffeffed by any *Englifh-American* colonial City.[361] Yet, the intruding modern Buildings were fubftantial in Number, if, as in many Inftances, they were unfubftantial in aefthetic Conception.[362]

A THEATRE which now ftood upon the Site of a colonial Dwelling evidenced its Safety from Flames, if not from the Advance of Time, in its Conftruction of unpainted galvanized Iron. A Garage, alfo of corrugated Iron, difplayed on its rufted Doors a facetious Acknowledgment to Archaeology in the Form of a Sign reading "Toot-"an-kum-in"—in timely Recognition of the Opening of of the Tomb of *Tutenkhamon*, a *Pharoah* of the fourteenth Century before *Chriſt*.

SOME thirty Structures of varying Purpoſe and Deſign, ranging from a National Bank to a Pig Sty, had arisen upon the ſouthern Part of the *Market Square*, obſcuring the Power Magazine and a ſmall brick ſtructure miſnamed by tradition the Debtors' Priſon. At the Foot of the *Duke of Glouceſter* Street the original Foundations of the Capitol were outlined by a Concrete Covering in a rolling Field of Weeds. Two School Houſes, one a monſtrous Structure, ſtood at the Head of the *Palace Green*, while a Dwelling of the *Victorian* Era cloſed what had been the Viſta at its Foot. Two modern Brick Stores occupied the Site of the *Raleigh* Tavern. The Great Building of the College ſtood (after three Fires and as many Alterations) ſupported chiefly by Neceſſity and its own good Balance. On the new-columned Portico of the Court Houſe of 1770 Orange-coloured Benches bore, in large black Letters, the hoſpitable Inſcription "Reſt here in a *Garner* Suit."

HERE and there a leaning Dormer or a handſome Chimney Cap offered the only viſible identifying Features which marked Inſtances in which colonial Buildings had been ſwallowed up in ſucceſſive Renovations, Alterations, and Repairs. At Intervals appeared colonial Buildings which had been little changed or partially reſtored. Old Structures and new ſtood Side by Side in a Confuſion in which each detracted from the other. The

The Concrete Sidewalks of the *Duke of Gloucefter* Street were fhaded by Trees, but its Center was lined with heavy Poles from which Wires and Cables radiated. There was a Beauty, too, of a Kind which cannot be gained by confcious Effort; but this was available only to thofe who, looking out of half-clofed Eyes, were able to fee thofe Things which they valued, to the Exclufion of all elfe.

Such, then, was the Dilemma which the City of *Williamfburg* prefented in 1926. There was much of the Worft that was new; there was much of the Beft that was old—very old.

❀ ❀ ❀

In 1927 Mr. *Rockefeller* commiffioned Dr. *Goodwin* to purchafe the Property neceffary to the Accomplifhment of the Reftoration.[363]   In the Courfe of this buying Program, moft of the Properties which had compofed the more important colonial Areas of the City proper were acquired. Much of this Property was purchafed outright, though in certain Inftances Properties were purchafed fubject to the Life Right or Tenure of Individuals whofe Age or whofe Affociations with the Properties made fuch Procedure defirable.[364]

The Areas thus fecured were turned over to two Corporations which were now formed to carry the Undertaking forward.[365]   The *Williamfburg Holding Corporation* (later *Williamfburg Reftoration*, Incorporated) became the adminiftrative Organization

Organization in Charge of the Project and acquired Title to much of the Property which had been purchafed. *Colonial Williamfburg*, Incorporated, was formed to hold Title to Properties traded or prefented to the *Reftoration* by the City of *Williamfburg*, the *Affociation for the Prefervation of Virginia Antiquities*, and by individual Donors. This Corporation has fince held Title to and managed Properties, Buildings, and Activities devoted and reftricted to hiftorical and educational Purpofes. Colonel *Arthur Woods* was the firft Prefident of both Corporations.

MEANWHILE, the Firm of *Perry, Shaw & Hepburn*, Architects, was retained to have Charge of the architectural Development of the Plan;[366] *Arthur A. Shurcliff* to have Charge of Landfcape Reftoration and the Work of City Planning;[367] and the Firm of *Todd & Brown*, Incorporated, Engineer-Contractors,[368] to develop and control the Organization which executed the Plans developed by the Architects and Landfcape Architects, when approved by the executive Corporations.

OPERATIONS were prefaced by exhauftive Studies of the City, in Order that thofe engaged in the Work might familiarize themfelves with the practical Intricacies of the Problem before them. A complete Property, Utility, and Topographical Survey of the City was made, and a Map prepared which, fo far as poffible, recorded every Detail of Intereft.[369] Engineering Specialifts were employed to ftudy the Water Syftem, fanitary Syftem,

System,[370] and the Light and Telephone Facilities,[371] in the Knowledge that these would have to be improved, extended, and obscured. A zoning Expert was retained to prepare Recommendations for Codes and Ordinances which would assure an ordered Development.[372] Tree Surgeons were employed to protect and revive failing Vegetation.[373] A Survey of Fire Prevention and Protection was made.[374] Committees of Specialists and Authorities in many of the Fields involved were formed to aid in a critical and advisory Capacity. These included a Committee of Advisory Architects,[375] a Committee of Landscape Architects,[376] a Committee of Historians and Scholars,[377] and several Committees on Decoration and Furnishings.[378]

❀ ❀ ❀

AT its Beginning, the *Restoration* was considered to be primarily an architectural Problem. In Consequence, a Division of Decoration was formed to serve under the Architects, as was a Department of Research and Record.[379] Under the Department of Research and Record a Division of archaeological Investigation was established.

THE Properties purchased within the colonial Area of the City were at first divided, roughly, into two Areas.[380] One of these was designated for immediate Restoration, the other being looked upon at the Time as a protective Area, concerning the Restoration of which no Commitments were made. The first Endeavors were

were therefore confined to the more prominent
colonial Sections of the City, including the original
Yard and Buildings of the College, the full Length
of the *Duke of Gloucester* Street, the *Capitol Square*,
the *Market Square*, and the *Palace Green*.

WITHIN the Area thus defined, the architectural Problems were claffified under four general
Types of Work:

I.   The Removal of all modern Buildings.

II. The Reftoration of exifting and partially ex-
     ifting eighteenth Century Buildings and
     Outbuildings.

III. The Reconftruction of certain Buildings
     and Outbuildings which had difappeared.

IV. The Decoration of Buildings thus reftored
     and reconftructed, and the Furnifhing of
     thofe to be exhibited to the Publick.

❊ ❊ ❊

THE firft of thefe Divifions of the Work (the
Removal of modern Buildings, which is to
fay, thofe wholly of the nineteenth and twentieth
Centuries) has proved to be the fimpleft, though
perhaps the moft protracted and trying. At the
prefent Writing, all but a few of them have been
removed from the Area of historic Reftoration or
have been torn down.[381] Yet, throughout this Procefs, the Ideal has been that in no Inftance fhould
a Tenant be left without a Home, and that no
Bufinefs fhould be afked to vacate its Quarters
without the Offer of a new Location.

❊ ❊ ❊

                                        THE

T H E Accomplishing of the second Division of the Work (the Repair and Restoration of existing colonial Buildings) was prefaced by a comprehensive and detailed Study of existing colonial Buildings throughout *Virginia*, especially in the *Tidewater* Section surrounding *Williamsburg*, and more especially within the City itself. This Study was made in Order that original structural Features and architectural Details which had been effaced by successive Repairs and Alterations might be replaced upon the Basis of definite contemporary sectional or local colonial Precedent.[382]

A s to this, it should be pointed to that the eighteenth Century Buildings of *Williamsburg* and of its surrounding Countryside were built by a limited Number of Master Builders, Mechanics, Artisans, and their Apprentices, representing but a few Generations in Time and Tradition. Again, these Builders were to a considerable Degree limited by the Implements and Materials which were readily available. So that the judicious Use of contemporary Precedent was resorted to with more than reasonable Assurance of Authenticity.

M O R E O V E R , it should be noted that from its Findings the Research Department was frequently able to supply specific documentary and pictorial Evidences in Cases in which more tangible Indications were lacking.

B y such and similar Processes more than eighty existing

exifting or partially exifting early Buildings[383] have been reftored or extenfively repaired up to the prefent Time.

❊ ❊ ❊

WITH Regard to the third Divifion (the Reconftruction of colonial Buildings which had difappeared) the Solutions were attained through the foregoing Procefles, as outlined, but with efpecial Emphafis laid upon the Evidences contributed by the Department of Refearch and Record and by its archaeological Divifion.

Here it fhould be explained that the Department of Refearch and Record, throughout the firft Years of its Activity, was concerned primarily and principally with the Collecting of Source Data relating to the architectural, landfcape, and decorative Problems of the *Reftoration*. In feeking this Type of Information, every conceivable Source of pertinent colonial *Virginiana* was untiringly inveftigated. Governmental Archives, military Records, and commercial Accounts were carefully ftudied. The Collections and Archives of Libraries, hiftorical Societies, and Mufeums were fearched. Family Records and perfonal and publick Papers in private Hands were fought out. Early Newfpapers, old Infurance Policies, local Tax and Court Records were efpecially fruitful. Paintings, Prints, Sketches, Maps, and old Photographs were minutely ftudied. Such Inveftigations were conducted in every Section of this Country,

Country, and were purfued as affiduoufly in
England and in *France*.[384]

Thus, by Way of Example, in the Cafe of
the Governor's Palace, the Department of Refearch
and Record was able to provide a Report compofed
of more than three Hundred Pages of Source
Material relating fpecifically to the Palace, its
Grounds, Buildings, and outlying Lands. It was
alfo able to provide Prints from a provably accurate Engraving in Copperplate (located in the
Bodleian Library, *Oxford*, *England*, and afterwards
prefented by that Inftitution to Mr. *John D.
Rockefeller*, Jr.)[385] which depicted the principal
Facade of the Palace, together with its flanking
Offices and a Portion of its Gardens. This Infor-
mation was further fupplemented by a detailed
Floor-plan of the Palace proper (located in the
Collections of the *Maffachufetts Hiftorical Society*)
drawn by *Thomas Jefferfon*,[386] who once lived in
the Palace as the Governor of the *Virginia*
Commonwealth.

It fhould alfo be explained, in Connection with
the Reconftruction of Buildings, that the archaeological Divifion of the Refearch Department
located, excavated, and recorded Score upon Score
of colonial Foundations, not only eftablifhing the
Location of early Buildings and Outbuildings, but
alfo difcovering from Evidences and Indications,
and to varying Degrees, their Size, Plan, Purpofe,
and general ftructural Character.[387]   In this Work
the fo-called "*Frenchman's Map*," believed to have
been

been drawn by a *French* Army Cartographer in 1782, was of ineſtimable Aſſiſtance. This Map, the original Draught of which is preſerved in the Library of the College of *William and Mary*, preſents the Plan of the City proper and outlines, roughly, the Shapes, relative Sizes, and Poſitions of its Buildings and many of their Outbuildings as they appeared at the Cloſe of the *American* Revolution.

T h e Foundations thus located and excavated were, naturally, of primary and fundamental Importance to the Reconſtruction of Buildings which had diſappeared. Yet, it ſhould be men-tioned that, as ſucceſſive Foundations were exca-vated, Ton after Ton of Objects and Fragments of Objects were recovered from the Earth removed from within and around them. Such excavated Relics provided not only contributory ſtructural and architectural Evidences, but provided alſo, within obvious Limitations, a remarkable Record of the Life and Activities which the original Buildings had ſheltered. Viewed as a whole, the Collection, accumulated from ſo large a Number of Excavations of widely varying Types within a ſingle Community, indicates Modes, Faſhions, and general Trends, thus affording an intereſting Inſight into the ſocial, domeſtic, and economic Life of the entire City and, to a Degree, of the Times.

T o uſe the Palace again as an Example, archaeological Inveſtigation revealed the entire original Foundation and Baſement of the Palace proper,

proper, with its Stone Floor intact, and with its
Partition Walls, Chimney Bafes, Wine Bins, and
vaulted Cellars exiftent or clearly indicated.
Inveftigation alfo revealed the Foundations of its
flanking Offices, its Outbuildings, Walls, Wall
Piers, Gates, Garden Steps, Walks, Wells, arched
Drains, and many other interefting and fignificant
Indications of the early Plan of the Place.[388]

In the Seeking out of fuch fundamental
Information, loofe Objects and Fragments en-
countered in digging, or fcreened from the Earth
removed, provided a Variety of ufeful Knowledge,
including: Indications of the general Calibre and
Character of interior and exterior Hardware and
of decorative wrought Iron; invaluable Evidences
pertaining to the Defign and Material of many
Mantel-pieces, fculptured Mantel Panels, Fire-
place Facings, Under-fires, Firebacks, and Hearth
Stones; Evidences eftablifhing certain Types of
Stone Embellifhment, fuch as Caps for Wall Piers
and the Defign and Detail of Entrance Steps;
Examples of Wall Copings, Paving Tiles, Water-
table Bricks, ground or rubbed Bricks for Orna-
mentation, Gutter Bricks, Well Bricks. Even a
large Section of the original exterior Wall of the
Palace was recovered, which Section had fallen
intact and which eftablifhed the Size of the Face
Brick employed, the decorative Ufe of glazed-head
Brick as the header Bricks laid in *Flemifh* Bond,
and eftablifhed alfo the Texture of the Mortar
and the Tooling of the Mortar Joints.

Thus,

T h u s , with such extensive Information available and with, in this Case, the Assistance of both
Virginia and *English* Precedent (for the Building
was unusually pretentious for the Colonies), it was
possible for the Architects to evolve a Conception
of the Palace which, it is believed, would be
convincing to the colonial Governors themselves,
could they return to look upon it.

A n d the Palace, while it is one of the major
Accomplishments of the *Restoration*, is but one
of several hundred Buildings reconstructed on ancient Foundations in Reproduction of Structures
long or late destroyed.[389]

❀ ❀ ❀

I N the Accomplishment of the fourth Division
of the Work (the Decoration of restored and
reconstructed Buildings, and the Furnishing of
those to be exhibited to the Publick), the Architects'
Division of Decoration also had Recourse to the
voluminous documentary Records assembled, to
the specific and generalized Findings resulting from
archaeological Investigation, and to the Use of
Virginia and *English* Precedent.

T h e Question of Paint Colours for decorating
Exteriors and Interiors presented a Problem of
particular Subtilty. In the Case of existing Buildings, Information could often be had by scraping
through successive Paint Coats, with a View to
discovering the early Colours employed. A Wealth
of similar Precedent was provided by the Investigation

tion of Paint Coats on Buildings throughout the Section. Yet, if a true Appreciation was to be attained, it was neceſſary that theſe Colours be enviſaged in their original Condition and Appearance, with the Effects of Age, Decay, Soilure, and of contiguous Coats diſcounted. Again, though explicit Records exiſted concerning particular Colours employed in certain of the reſtored and reconſtructed Buildings, the Shades and Tones of theſe Colours had to be arrived at through ſtudied Conjecture. When, as in the Majority of Inſtances, ſpecific Records of Colour were lacking, the prevailing Practices of the Section and of the Period were purſued, theſe being eſtabliſhed not only by the Examination of more or leſs defaced Examples of actual Paint, but alſo through the careful Study of import Manifeſts, Merchants' Advertiſements, and the Orders for Paints, Pigments, and kindred Supplies placed by the Coloniſts with their *London* Agents.[390] Thus, in the Solution of the Problem, it was neceſſary to bring to bear a Combination of Knowledge, Reaſon, and adviſed good Taſte; for Partialities in Colour and Shade vary with Times, as they do with Peoples— and Colour, in itſelf, has been a Phenomenon which has ſorely perplexed Artiſans, Artiſts, and Philoſophers in many Ages.

I t was, perhaps, in their Bearing upon Furniture, Furniſhings, and Acceſſories that the documentary Records, as firſt aſſembled, made their moſt generous Contribution to the phyſical Reſtoration

toration of *Williamfburg*. For thefe Records contained the Enumerations of a Time when a Man's
cracked Punch-bowl, his Bolfter, Bed-feathers,
and Parcels of damaged Pewter were carefully
itemized in the Inventory of his Eftate—a Time
when a Merchant would not fpare the Mention
of a Hat-pin or a Pound of Thread in advertifing
his lateft Shipment juft imported from *London*.

T h u s, when the Furnifhing of the Palace was
undertaken, two extenfive Inventories were available, outlining not only the Belongings of two
colonial Governors (*Fauquier* and *Botetourt*), who
died while refiding in the Palace, but alfo indicating
the Diftribution of thefe Belongings within the
Building and its Offices.[391] Moreover, one of the
Inventories lifted alfo the " Standing Furniture "
in the Palace, which was owned by the Colony
and remained in the Building from one Adminiftration to another.[392]

F o r the Furnifhing of the reconftructed Capitol, the precife Records of the Affembly were to be
had from the Journals and Statutes of Government, thefe fpecifying the Furniture and Accef-
fories required for the various Rooms, and ranging
in their Detail to the Meafurements of Tables, the
Colour and Material of Table Carpets, and the
Colour of the Tape and the Type of Nails to be
ufed in upholftering the Benches in the Hall of the
Houfe of Burgeffes.[393]

I n the Cafe of the *Raleigh* Tavern, the detailed
Inventories of two of its colonial Keepers exifted,[394]
                                                    thefe

these indicating an Elegance which its unique Function and persistent Tradition demanded, and which its exacting Patronage required.

O n the Basis of such Records, contemporary Furniture and Furnishings were purchased in *Virginia*, in various other Sections of the *Atlantic* Seaboard, and in *England*, in Keeping with the Practice of the *Virginia* Colonists.   Also many valued Gifts were received. In some Instances, original *Williamsburg* Pieces were traced and purchased; and yet others have been lent by the General Assembly of *Virginia*.   In Cases in which old Pieces could not be had, careful Reproductions of contemporary Originals were made.   This last Procedure was especially indicated in the Case of the Capitol, the original Furniture of which was doubtless for the most Part destroyed in the Fire of 1747, and was of a cumbersome, institutional Type not readily come by.

A G A I N , the detailed Findings and general Conclusions resulting from archaeological Investigation were of great Assistance. It is (or should be) common Knowledge among Antiquarians that the ordinary Possessions of the People of a given Age, while generally existing in great Quantity, are often accorded little Thought and less Care— and so survive in ever diminishing Numbers among the Possessions of their Posterity. Thus, in Time, these once-common Things may even come to be looked upon as the extraordinary, if they survive at all.   On the other Hand, the unusual, the fine,
the

the unique Poffeffions of that fame Day, accorded at firft the Protection of locked Cupboards and higher Shelves and later entrufted to the Keeping of Mufeums of Art and Hiftory, come in Time to be (and therefore feem) the more ufual and reprefentative Articles of the Time. Againft fuch Diftortions the Tons of ftained and corroded Fragments recovered from the local Soil provide, for *Williamfburg*, an admirable Affurance. Here, within the Limitations of the Collection, are the Poffeffions of the Period, in Fact and in Proportion. Moreover, in the many Inftances in which fuch tangible Evidences can be applied in Conjunction with documentary Records, a high Degree of Authenticity is attained; for then the " 2 Doz. "large Plates " lifted in an Inventory affociated with a given Site become Plates of a fpecific Ware, Colour, and Defign, and fo it is with various other Types of houfehold and general Paraphernalia.

By fuch Methods, and by countlefs others too intricate and varied for Inclufion in Generalizations fuch as thefe, have the reftored and reconftructed Buildings of *Williamfburg* been decorated, and its Exhibition Buildings refurnifhed. Many Buildings are privately tenanted, and others adapted to the Reception of the confiderable Concourfe of People who again refort thither; yet thefe, more often than not, are furnifhed by their Occupants after a Manner which their Decoration and

and Defign all but demand.   And other Buildings
of every Type continue to materialize, as will be
told.

❀❀❀

THE Problem of the Landfcape Architect,
while in many Ways lefs confined and technical than that of the ftructural Architects, was
more obfcure.

As has been faid, many of the Homes and
Buildings of the colonial Period were preferved as
a Matter of practical and phyfical Neceffity
throughout that increafing economic Depreffion
which had pervaded *Williamfburg* fince the Removal of the Seat of Government in 1780, and
more efpecially fince the *War Between the States*.
On the other Hand, the Pleafure Gardens which
had furrounded fo many of thefe Buildings fell
Victims not only to the Curtailment and Neglect
commonly accorded Luxuries in fuch Times, but
alfo to their own tranfitory Nature.   Beyond this,
and again by the very Nature of them, the phyfical
Evidences for Landfcape Reftoration were neither
fo numerous nor fo clearly defined as thofe exifting
as a Bafis for ftructural Reftoration and Reconftruction.

In fome few Inftances major Evidences and
Indications of colonial Gardens had furvived.
More often, their Re-creation was of Neceffity
bafed upon documentary References or Defcrip-
tions, upon Precedents and Prints, and upon fuch
                                            Evidences

Evidences as buried Brick Walks, long-used Paths, and the general Arrangement of the older Trees, surviving Shrubbery, and indicative Difturbances of the Terrain. And fuch Indications had, of courfe, to be inter-related with the Arrangement of furviving Buildings and ancient Foundations.

I N View of this Situation, and in Order that a Wealth of Precedent and a thorough Underftanding of the Feeling of the Period might be developed, an extenfive Survey was made of the diftinguifhing colonial Features furviving in the Defign of the Gardens of the South and of Characteriftics in the Defign of *Englifh* Gardens continuing from the eighteenth Century.[395]　A particularly intenfive Study was made of contemporary Pictures, Plans, and Maps.

I N the Matter of Plantings, another careful Study was made of the Hiftory of native Trees, Shrubs, and Flowers, and of Records pertaining to the Importation of foreign Seeds, Plants, and Cuttings. Fortunately, the Writings and Records of both profeffional and occafional Botanifts and Horticulturifts were voluminous, and the Exchange of Information between them habitual. So that it can be ftated with Confidence that there are today no Plantings in the reftored and re-created Gardens of *Williamfburg* which might not have exifted in the colonial Gardens which they reprefent.

T H E Queftion of City Planning confronted the Landfcape Architect with the Problem of preferving

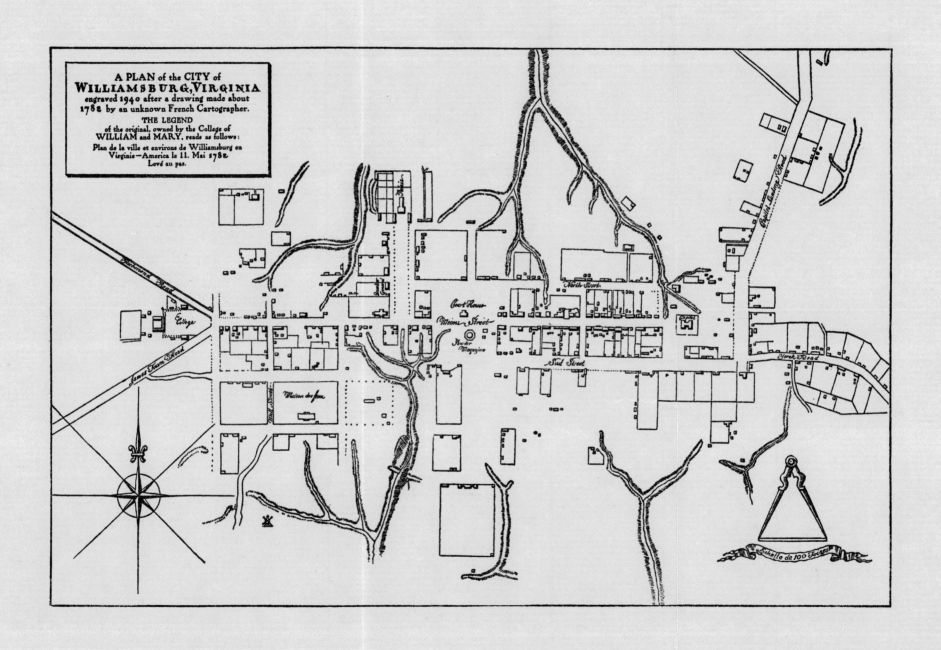

A PLAN of the CITY of
WILLIAMSBURG, VIRGINIA
engraved 1940 after a drawing made about
1782 by an unknown French Cartographer.

THE LEGEND
of the original, owned by the College of
WILLIAM and MARY, reads as follows:

Plan de la ville et environs de Williamsburg en
Virginie—America le 11. Mai 1782
Levé au pas.

ing the early Plan of the City (which had furvived with but few Alterations), while meeting the Requirements of prefent-day Traffic.[396] With the Cooperation of the Federal, State, and City Governments, new Routes, Roads, and Streets have been provided outfide and underneath the reftored Area in a Profufion which, though it may perplex the Uninitiated, will ferve the increafed Demands and Purpofes of the Publick.

T H E Landfcape Architect and the ftructural Architects collaborated in the Removal of the outward or exterior Evidences of Modernity, and in the Replacing of them with the Appurtenances of colonial Times. Thus, again on the Bafis of contemporary Records and Precedent, the Lamp-pofts, Fences, Brick Walks, Street Surfaces, and other exterior Features of the colonial City have reappeared; though, in certain Inftances, thefe have been adapted to the Demands of the prefent Age and to the Convenience and Conveyances of its People.

※ ※ ※

A N D of the foregoing major Types and Divifions of the Work of Reftoration, planned and fupervifed by Architects, Engineers, Land-fcape Architects, Decorators, and Experts in many Fields, working under the Direction of the admin-iftrative Corporations, it fhould be noted that the phyfical Execution of it has been and is being accomplifhed, in generous Part, by an Organization of of fkilled Mechanics and Artifans, trained to the Methods of colonial Builders and verfed in the peculiar and exacting Demands of Reftoration Work. And though the Labourer, as the Scripture holds, is worthy of his Hire; yet, they that work in Advance of the normal Skills and Demands of their Crafts are worthy alfo of Admiration and Efteem.   ❀ ❀ ❀

AT the Clofe of the Year 1934, after eight Years of intenfive Work and the Expenditure of many Millions of Dollars, the *Williamfburg Reftoration* was confidered and announced to be formally complete. Over four Hundred modern Buildings had been demolifhed and one Hundred and fifty early Buildings had been reftored or reconftructed.[397] A new Bufinefs Diftrict, defigned to be in Keeping with the reftored Areas, had been provided. Wires had been placed Underground and Streets refurfaced. Four Exhibition Buildings, the Capitol,[398] the Governor's Palace,[399] the *Raleigh* Tavern,[400] and the Court Houfe of 1770 (containing the *Williamfburg Reftoration Archaeological Exhibit*),[401] had been opened to the Publick; and the Opening of the *Ludwell-Paradife* Houfe[402] (containing Mrs. *John D. Rockefeller*, Junior's, Collection of *American* Folk Art) was pending. In *October* of that Year the Prefident of the *United States*, in Company with the Governor of *Virginia*, officiated at the formal Opening of the *Duke of Gloucefter* Street[403] and the Areas adjoining it.

YET,

YET, in the Paſſage of Time, it has turned out that ſuch Announcements and Ceremonies marked not the Completion of the Reſtoration, but marked, rather, the Beginning of a new Conception of it and of new Advances toward the Fulfillment of that broadened Conception.

As firſt projected, the Intention of the *Reſtoration* had been to reſtore certain of the ancient and hiſtoric Buildings ſurviving in *Williamſburg* (thus ſaving them from impending Deſtruction or Decay), to reconſtruct certain other Buildings of eſpecial hiſtorical Intereſt, to landſcape the Grounds and Areas thus involved, and, with the more modern and anachroniſtic Buildings removed, to preſerve and preſent a Memorial indicative (or, at leaſt, reminiſcent) of the *Engliſh-American* colonial Period.[404] Thus, in the Minds of Moſt, the ultimate Reſult was at firſt viſualized as an hiſtorical Center in which a generous Scattering of reſtored and reconſtructed Buildings, interſperſed with Gardens and landſcaped Areas, would exemplify the various architectural and ſtructural Types which had exiſted in *Williamſburg*, and which would be generally remindful (though not fully repreſentative) of the local colonial Scene.

As to this, and of theſe Years, the Following has been written of the Architects of the *Reſtoration:*

    " Approaching the Work in a Belief that
" perhaps it might require Buildings and
                " Gardens

" Gardens freely defigned in the old Manner,
" the Architects, as the Soil and the old Records
" commenced to give up their Secrets, became
" paffionate hiftorical Students, happy to fub-
" ordinate their creative Abilities to a loyal
" Interpretation of the ample Evidence dif-
" covered."405

SIMILARLY, on the Part of Mr. *Rockefeller* and the adminiftrative Corporations, it can be faid that, as the Work advanced, countlefs new Actualities, Potentialities, and Poffibilities for the Project as a whole became increafingly apparent; and that only out of the Experience and Knowledge gained from thefe opening Years could a broader Conception of the Reftoration have developed.

IT is often difficult to date Proceffes of Thought and Decifions developing out of Experience. Let it fuffice, then, to fay that after a Period of Contemplation, in which the Revealments of its opening Years were weighed, the *Reftoration* moved forward toward a Fulfillment more complete than could have been envifioned at the firft.

❀ ❀ ❀

IN 1935, Mr. *Kenneth Chorley* became the Prefident of *Williamfburg Reftoration*, Incorporated, and *Colonial Williamfburg*, Incorporated. Long the Vice-Prefident of both Corporations, and for fome Time their acting Prefident, he fucceeded Colonel *Woods*, who became Chairman of the Boards and who fubfequently retired becaufe of ill Health.
Colonel

Colonel *Woods* was fucceeded as Chairman of the Boards by Mr. *John D. Rockefeller, III.*

WITH an enlarged and extended Program decided upon, the various Divifions of the Work were at this Time integrated to center in a fingle Organization, operating under the immediate Direction of the adminiftrative Corporations. The Architects and certain other Experts were retained in an advifory Capacity. But now the feveral Departments which had been continued, taken over, or formed for the Maintenance and Interpretation of the Project, became alfo the active Agencies for the Development and Supervifion of its added Endeavors.

SUBSEQUENT to thefe Alterations of Plan and Organization, a Number of the wide Spaces which exifted between the reftored or reconftructed Buildings of the firft Period of Reftoration have gradually filled with yet other Buildings, thus offering a more complete Reprefentation of a colonial Metropolis. Alfo new Areas have been added to thofe originally chofen for Reftoration, and additional Properties have been purchafed or have become available within them all.

SINCE 1934, feven major Exhibition Buildings, all Survivors of colonial Times, have joined thofe already open to the Publick: in the Year 1936, the Publick Gaol,[406] in 1940, the *George Wythe* Houfe,[407] in 1952, the *Brufh-Everard* Houfe,[408] and in 1968, the *James Geddy* Houfe, the *Peyton Randolph* Houfe,

Houfe, and *Wetherburn's* Tavern, as well as feveral
refurnifhed Rooms in the Sir *Chriftopher Wren*
Building of the College of *William and Mary.*[409]
Through the Years, alfo, a Number of Shops of
Artificers and Tradefmen have been added, *viz.*,
Apothecary, Baker, Barber & Peruke-maker, Baf-
ketmaker, Blackfmith, Boot & Shoemaker, Cabi-
netmaker, Cooper, Jeweler & Clockmaker, En-
graver, Gunfmith, Harnefs-maker, Metal Founder, Miller, Milliner, Printer & Bookbinder, Silver-
fmith, Spinner & Weaver, and Mufick Teacher.[410]

A N D , though they are not owned by the
Colonial Williamfburg Foundation, it fhould alfo
be noted that the complete Reftorations of *Bruton
Parifh* Church[411] and of the Powder Magazine[412]
(owned by the *Affociation for the Prefervation of
Virginia Antiquities*) were accomplifhed in this
Period, the Work for the moft Part being contributed by Mr. *Rockefeller*, even as the *Wren* Building, the Prefident's Houfe, and *Brafferton* Hall
were reftored for the College in the opening Years
of the *Reftoration.*[413]

M O R E O V E R , new Buildings have been added
in the Bufinefs Area of the City; and great
Advances have been made in the Provifion of
Accommodations for the Vifitors from every Section of the Country and from all Parts of the
World who are attracted to *Williamfburg* in ever-
increafing Numbers. Two large Hotels and a 314-
unit Motor Hotel have been erected on the Border
of the Reftoration Area, and a Number of reftored

or

or reconftructed Taverns, Ordinaries, and Dwelling
Houfes have been affociated with thefe in the Reception and Entertainment of Guefts. Thefe leffer
Buildings, for the moft Part, are thus returned
to the Purpofes which they ferved originally
when, during colonial Publick Times, the City was
no lefs crowded than at the Prefent.

ALSO, in this Period, the *Reftoration* has
entered upon a Programme for the Promotion of
Crafts,[414] through which it hopes to extend the
Influences of its Buildings and their Furnifhings,
as well as thofe of the Period and Civilization
reprefented. In this Endeavor carefully felected
and accredited Manufactories, working under the
Supervifion of *Reftoration* Experts, are reproducing
countlefs Selections from the Collections and
decorative Materials of the *Reftoration*, and are
making thefe available for Publick Purchafe both
in *Williamfburg* and throughout the Country.

To promote the Study of early *American* Hiftory
through Refearch, Publication, and Teaching,
Colonial Williamfburg and the College of *William
and Mary* founded in 1943 the *Inftitute of Early
American Hiftory and Culture*, [415] eftablifhing a
cooperative Program on behalf of hiftorical Scholar-
fhip which reaches beyond the Locality in its
Contribution to Learning and attracts Scholars to
Williamfburg. Seeking to create Conditions
favourable to Underftanding through Exhibits and
a new motion Picture—*"Williamfburg:* The Story
of a Patriot"—*Colonial Williamfburg* opened in
1957

1957 a new, $12,000,000 *Information Center* [416]
featuring twin 250-Seat Theatres utilizing the
lateſt and moſt advanced audio-viſual Techniques.
Earlier the ſame year, the *Abby Aldrich Rockefeller
Folk Art Collection* [417] was moved from the *Ludwell-
Paradiſe* Houſe to a ſpecially conſtructed two-
ſtory brick Building containing nine Galleries
ſuggeſting interiors of the nineteenth Century
when moſt *American* folk Art was produced.
The new Building, made poſſible by a Gift from
Mr. *John D. Rockefeller*, Jr., permits the exhibition of the Collection in its entirety for the firſt
Time.

M o r e recently, as the *Reſtoration* has begun
to approach its enlarged and final Form, new and
added Emphaſis has been placed upon the Means
and Methods of its Interpretation. Endeavors
in hiſtorical Reſearch, at firſt directed principally
to the Proviſion of Information requiſite for
phyſical Reſtoration, have been broadened to
permit extenſive Studies in the general Field of
Engliſh-American colonial Hiſtory and its ſocial,
political, economic, and religious Pertinences—
with particular Emphaſis laid upon the Hiſtory
of *Virginia* and of *Williamſburg*. [418] Nor are
ſuch Endeavors confined wholly to *Reſtoration*
Agencies, for in late Months a limited Number of
Fellowſhips have been granted to certain well-
qualified Scholars deſiring to purſue and publiſh
Studies concerning *Williamſburg* in the eighteenth
Century, and the Origin, Development, and Expan-
ſion

fion of the Civilization of which the City was the Center.[419] It is intended that the publifhed Refults of fuch Studies will fupplement the more extenfive Endeavors of the feveral Departments of the *Reftoration* and the Publications iffued by them. And the Information thus attained will in Time become diffufed in the common Knowledge, to the End that *Williamfburg* (which has been advanced herein as a City which, through a ftrange Coincidence of Hiftory, was all but forgotten) will refume its rightful Place in the Hiftory of *Virginia* and, thence, in the Hiftory of the Country at large.

S o it is, then, that the *Reftoration* faces the Future at the Time of this Writing. And, though the Future is not the proper Province of an hiftorical Report, it may be faid with confiderable Affurance that fo, with flowly changing Emphafis, it will continue. A further Number of Buildings of the eighteenth Century will likely be reftored or reconftructed, Plans having been completed for several fuch Additions, and Plans for yet Others being in Preparation. As the ftructural Part of the *Reftoration* has approached its attainable Limits, Activities of an educational and interpretive Nature have increased and multiplied. Undoubtedly they will continue to do fo. It is the Purpofe and Defire of *Colonial Williamfburg* that a fair Reprefentation of the early domeftic, institutional, commercial, and induftrial Life of the Community be rendered againft its authentic and enhancing Background,

Background, ſo that the Importance of *Williamſ-burg's* Heritage for twentieth-Century America can be clearly and widely underſtood.

I n carrying out the current Duties as well as the future Planning of the *Reſtoration*, ſome three thouſand Perſons are now employed. In Place of the two Corporations earlier charged with the Work, a ſingle Organization, chartered on *July* 1, 1971, and called *The Colonial Williamſburg Foundation*, holds Title to all Properties of the *Reſtoration*, and is reſponſible for all of its Activities.

T h i s Account would be ſorely lacking, both in Completeneſs and in Propriety, did it not record in Sorrow that on the 7th Day of *September* in the Year of our Lord 1939, the Reverend *W. A. R. Goodwin* departed this Life, as did Mr. *John D. Rockefeller*, Junior, on the 11th Day of *May*, in the Year of our Lord 1960. To Dr. *Goodwin* and Mr. *Rockefeller*, the true Founder and principal Benefactor of the Reſtoration of colonial *Williamſburg*, thoſe who follow, be they Reſidents of the City, Members of the *Foundation* Staſſ, or Viſitors from a Diſtance, owe a Debt of Gratitude none can repay.

Colonial *Williamſburg* is fortunate to have grown from the Viſion, Dedication, and Support of Men like Dr. *Goodwin* and Mr. *Rockefeller*. Up to the time of his Death in 1960, Mr. *Rockefeller* and his Family provided financial Support for the purchaſe and reſtoration of hiſtoric Properties, the conſtruction of ſupport Facilities, and the preſentation of the

the mufeum and educational Programs. Complementing Mr. *Rockefeller's* intereft was that of his fon, Mr. *John D. Rockefeller* 3rd, who ferved as Chairman of the Colonial Williamfburg Board of Truftees from 1939 to 1953. Following his Retirement, Mr. *Winthrop Rockefeller* ferved as Chairman of the Board from 1953 until his Death in 1973.

Subfequently, it became clear that *Colonial Williamfburg* could no longer be underwritten by any one Perfon or Family. The Officers and Truftees of the *Reftoration* determined that if colonial *Williamfburg* was to be preferved for future Generations, the *Foundation* would have to broaden its bafe of philanthropic Support and appeal to all Americans who cherifh their Hiftory and Heritage, and it accordingly initiated its firft Financial Development Program in 1976. An immediate Priority was to build a broad bafe of Donors making unreftricted Gifts to fupport the mufeum and educational Programs of the *Foundation*, for Admiffions provide only about fifty percent of the Funds needed to meet the operating Cofts of the *Hiftoric Area.* Another important Goal has been to fecure major Gifts for fpecific mufeum and educational Capital Projects.

Colonial Williamfburg is proud of the private gift Support it receives from its many Friends who believe in this educational Inftitution. The philanthropic Support begun in *Williamfburg* more than a half-century ago is carried on today by more than 7,000 Individuals, Corporations, and Foundations.

Foundations. From 1976 through 1979, more than $22 Million has been received or pledged to the *Foundation* in the form of Caſh, Tangible Objects, Securities, and Real Property.

The Leſſons of *Williamſburg's* eighteenth-century Hiſtory which moved Mr. *Rockefeller* are ſtill important. As one Contributor wrote, "No thinking American can deny that *Colonial Williamſburg* is a ſtirring Inſpiration for all Americans. It is only fair that all Inſtitutions acroſs our Country be aſked to aſſume a ſhare of the Coſts. Truly the future of *Colonial Williamſburg* reſts with the American People."

F I N I S.

APPENDIX.

APPENDIX.

PART I.

A Lift of the ancient Sources from which this Report is drawn. Being a careful Account of the Authors and Works confulted, lifted by Numbers which correfpond with thofe appearing in the Text.

PART II.

1. The Acts directing the Building the Capitol and the City of *Williamfburg*.
2. The Charter of the City.

WILLIAMSBURG:

Printed for the *Colonial Williamfburg* Foundation, by *Auguft* and *Charles Dietz*, on their Prefs in *Cary* Street at *Richmond*, *Virginia*,
MCM,LXXX.

APPENDIX.

PART I.

A Lift of the ancient Sources from which this Report is drawn. Being a careful Account of Authors and Works confulted, lifted by Numbers which correfpond with thofe in the Text.

NOTE: The quoted Materials in thefe Notes are believed to be true Copies of the Originals in every Refpect fave that of Typography—which laft is univerfally adapted to the typographic Style of this Volume. Thus, the uniform Capitalizing of Nouns, the Italicizing of proper Names, and the Ufe of ancient printing Characters follows the general Style of Williamfburg's *colonial Printers, rather than that of the Materials quoted.*

[1]

William Waller Hening, THE STATUTES AT LARGE (New York: R. & W. & G. Bartow, 1823), Vol. I. pp. 208-209. 1632/3 " An Act for the Seatinge of the Middle " Plantation."

This Act appears in full on Pages 2-3 of this Volume.

[2]

This Statement is bafed upon two Records as follows:—

Sufan M. Kingfbury, ed., THE RECORDS OF THE VIRGINIA

VIRGINIA COMPANY OF LONDON (Wafhington: Government Printing Office, 1935), Vol. IV, p. 158.

" 2ˡʸ By the laſt Muſter Rowle of the People there taken the laſt
" Sumer much about the Tyme of the Maſſacre there were in all
" of Men Women & Children in *Virginia* but 1240: . . . "

Captaine John Smith, THE GENERALL HISTORIE
OF VIRGINIA, NEW-ENGLAND, AND THE
SUMMER ILES (*London:* 1629. Reprinted *Richmond, Va.: Franklin Preſs*, 1819), Vol. II, pp. 75-76.

" The Number that was ſlaine in thoſe ſeuerall Plantations . . .
" The whole Number—347. "

[3]

It would appear that the *Middle Plantation* Paliſade
was preceded by a Paliſade between *Martin's Hundred*
and *Kiſkyacke*. The Purpoſe of the latter is deſcribed
in the following Report, and it may be aſſumed that
the Purpoſe of the *Middle Plantation* Paliſade was
ſimilar:

Angus W. McDonald, TRANSCRIPTS—MISCEL-
LANEOUS, 1619-1626 [*Ms.* Tranſcripts from the
Britiſh Public Record Office] *Virginia State Library*
Archives, *Richmond*, Vol. I, pp. 297-298. Governor
Francis Wyatt to the Privy Council, *May* 17, 1626.

" We have found by Experience ſince the Maſſacre as wee
" alſoe did then foreſee and advertize, that being ſeated in the
" Courſe wee now are in ſmale Bodies, neither is it poſſible to pre-
" vent the ſuddaine Incurſions of the Salvages, ncr ſecure any
" Range for Cattle, which is a generall Diſcouragement to the
" Planter . . . for Redreſs of which Inconveniences wee knowe
" no other Courſe, then to ſecure the Forreſt by running a Palli-
" zado from *Marttins Hundred* to *Kiſkyack*, which is not above ſix
" Miles over, and placeing Houſes at convenient Diſtance, with
" ſufficient Gard of Men to ſecure the Necke wherby wee ſhall
" gaine free from Poſſibillity of any Annoyance by the Salvages,
" a rich Ceramite of Ground contayneing litle leſſe the 300,000
" Acres of Land, which will feed ſuch Nombers of People, with
" plentifull

" plentifull Range for Cattle as may bee able to defend the Plan-
" tacon againſt any Enimy whatſoever.

   " The readieſt and certaineſt Way for Accompliſhment thereof,
" is to agree in Certainety with ſome experienced in the Country,
" for undertaking it, which wilbe £1200 in readie Mony, for the
" Building of the Pallizado and Houſes, and £100 yearly for
" mainetayneing them; and becauſe untill this Worke bee
" effected all the Reſt is to litle Purpoſe, wee have reduced the
" Agreement to a Certainety, which wee here incloſed ſend your
" Lordſhipps, humbly deſiring an Anſwere by the firſt Shipping:"

Alſo:

ASPINWALL PAPERS, Yonge's Voyage Ms., p. 3,
[*Virginia State Library* Archives. Alſo printed in
Collections of the Maſſachuſetts Hiſtorical Society,
(Fourth Series) Vol. IX, pp. 108-111.] Letter of
Captain *Thomas Yonge* to Sir *Tobie Matthew* " From
" *James Towne Cittie* this 13th of July " 1634.

   " While I ſtay heere at *James Towne* where now I am I meet
" dayly wᵗʰ ſeverall of the beſt and moſt underſtanding Sort of
" the Inhabitants of this Place by whome I enforme my ſelf as
" much as I can of the State of this Countrey and I find really
" that the preſent Governor hath caried himſelfe heere with very
" great Prudence hath been extraordinary dilligent in advancing
" and furthering the Colony, . . .

   " When the Governor [Sir *John Harvey*] came firſt hither he
" found *James* River only inhabited and one other Plantation on
" the eaſtern Side of the Bay, but now he hath ſettled divers good
" Plantations upon another River, which lieth northerly from
" *James* River and hath cauſed a ſtrong Palliſadoe to be builded
" upon a Streight betweene both Rivers and cauſed Houſes to
" be built in ſeverall Places upon the ſame, and hath placed a
" ſufficient Force of Men for Defence of the ſame, whereby all
" the lower Part of *Virginia* have a Range for their Cattle neere
" fortie Miles in Length and in moſt Places twelve Miles broade.
" The Palliſadoe is very neer ſix Miles long bounded in by two
" large Creekes. He hath an Intention in this Manner to take
" alſo in all the Ground betweene thoſe two Rivers & ſo utterly
" exclude the *Indians* from thence, wᶜʰ Work is conceaved to be
" of extraordinary Benefitt to yᵉ Country, and of no extreame
" Difficultie . . ."

[4]

See Note 3

[5]

See Note 1

[6]

H. R. McIlwaine, ed., *MINUTES OF THE COUNCIL AND GENERAL COURT OF COLONIAL VIRGINIA, 1622-1676 (Richmond: 1924)*, pp. 104-106.

" A Courte held the 7ᵗʰ & 8ᵗʰ Dayes of *Awguſte* 1626 . . .

" 1 *Yt is ordered* yᵗ no Planter ſhall remoue from yᵉ Plantatione
" wherone he is ſeated, to ſeat himſelfe vppon any other wᵗʰowt
" ſpecyall Order from the Governor and ſome Pte of yᵉ Councell
" vppon Penaltie and Forfeeture of 300ˡⁱ Waight of Tobacco to be
" paide into the publique Treaſury, . . .

" And that no Pſone vppon any Ptext or Couler of his owne
" privat Occaſiones ſhall abſent him ſelf from his Plantatione
" wᵗʰowt Conſent and Approbatione of the Comander of the
" Plantatione vppon Paine and Forfeeture of 25ˡⁱ of Tobacco for
" every 24 Howers Abſence.

. . .

"5 *Yt is ordered* that the Gouernor wᵗʰ his beſt Conveniency ſhall
" give Comiſſione to ſome ſufficyent Man in every Plantatione
" for the Comande and Gouerment therof.

. . .

"16 *Yt is ordered* accordinge to the ſaid Generall Aſſembly that
" the Comander of every Plantatione, take Care that there be
" ſufficyent of Powder and Munitione wᵗʰin yᵉ Plantatione vnder
" his Comande and theire Peeces fixt and theire Armes com
" pleate. "

[7]

See Note 1

[8]

LIBRARY OF CONGRESS, Diviſion of Manuſcripts.
[Photo-films from the *Society for the Propagation of the Goſpel in Foreign Parts, London*—Miſcellaneous, p. 90.] A Speech delivered by a Student at the College of *William and Mary* on *May* 1, 1699.

" 6.

" 6. Here [at *Middle Plantation*] is good Neighbourhood of as
" many fubftantial Houfekeepers that could give great Help
" towards the Supplying and Maintaining of a conftant Market,
" as is to be found again in the whole Country.

" 7. Here are great Helps and Advances made already towards
" the Beginning of a Town, a Church, an Ordinary, feveral
" Stores, two Mills, a Smiths Shop a Grammar School, and
" above all the Colledge: . . . "

[9]

See the *Acts directing the Building the Capitol and the
City of Williamfburg* which appear in full in the
APPENDIX, Part II, of this Report.

[10]

*VIRGINIA MAGAZINE OF HISTORY AND BI-
OGRAPHY*, Vol. IX (1902), p. 57. [From *Ms.* Copy
of Acts of *Virginia* Affembly of 1741, in Poffeffion of
Virginia Hiftorical Society.]

" Concerninge Acts Repealed. . . . That one Act *Ano* 1634
" comandinge Left. *Popely* to make good the *Middle Plantation;*
" . . . bee from henceforth repealed."

[11]

YORK COUNTY RECORDS, Wills & Deeds. No. 2,
1645-1649, pp. 142, 188-189.

[*June* 16th 1646] " The Difference depending between Capt.
" *Robert Higginfon* Plantiffe and *John Wetherford* is referred to
" be determined on the firft Day of *July* Court next in Regard ye
" Daingeroufneffe of the Tyme will not permitt to leave the
" Charge & Care of his Undertakinge at the *Midle Plantation*
" Pale ye prefent Court. "

[*Nov.* 26th 1646] " Whereas there was divers Men liveing at the
" lower End of *Yorke* Pfh who weare delinquent in fending upp
" a Man to ye *Midle Plantation* for that generall Work in putting
" upp a Pale yere according to former Order whereby Capt. *Robert*
" *Higgenfon* was firft to put a Man in his Rome. The Court doe
" yerefore order that the fd Men foe delinquent fhall upon demand
" pay to ye fd Capt. *Robert Higinfon* the Sumye of forrty-five [?]
" Poundes of Tobacco per Pole for Satisfacon of the Hire of a
" Man in yt Rome. . . . "

[12]

H. R. McIlwaine, ed., *JOURNALS OF THE HOUSE OF BURGESSES OF VIRGINIA, 1619-1659 (Richmond:* 1915), p. 109.

Alſo:

William Waller Hening, THE STATUTES AT LARGE (*New York: R. & W. & G. Bartow*, 1823), Vol. I, p. 498.

" *April* the firſt, 1658
   " VPON the Petition of the Inhabitants of *Middle Plantation*
" and *Harrop* Pariſhes, *It is ordered*, That both of them be
" henceforth incorporated into one Pariſh which is to be called
" the Pariſh of *Middletowne* and the Bounds of the ſame to be
" thoſe already includeing both the aforeſaid former Pariſhes."

[13]

THE CHURCH REVIEW, AND ECCLESIASTICAL REGISTER, Vol. VIII (1856), p. 591.
   " *Sketches of* Bruton *Pariſh*, Williamſburg, Virginia,"
   by the Rev. *John C. McCabe*.

" . . . The firſt Entry in the Veſtry Book bears Date '*April* yᵉ 18ᵗʰ,
" 1674,' and on that Day, at a Meeting of the Veſtry, we find
" preſent, 'The Honourable Coll. *Danl. Parke*, Mr. *Rowland*
" *Jones*, Miniſter, Mr. *John Page*, Mr. *James Bɩſouth*, Mr. *Robert*
" *Cobb* and Mr. *Bray*.,— Capt. *Cheſley*, and Mr. *Aylett*, Church
" Wardens. Mr. *John Owens*, Sideſman. . . . ' "

[*Note:* The firſt Veſtry Book of *Bruton* Pariſh, from which the Rev. *John C. McCabe* gives Excerpts, has diſappeared, and Mr. *McCabe's* Treatiſe is the only known Source for this Material.]

[14]

See Note 1

[15]

Suſan M. Kingſbury, ed., *THE RECORDS OF THE VIRGINIA COMPANY OF LONDON (Waſhington: Government Printing Office*, 1906), Vol. I, pp. 515-516.
                                                              "*July*

" *July* 16, 1621

" For fo much as the Phificons Place to the Company was now
" become voyde by Reafon of the vntimely Death of Doctor
" *Bohune* [Phyfician General, *ibid.*, p. 431] flaine in the Fight with
" two *Spanifh* Ships of Warr the 19ᵗʰ of *March* laft; Doctor *Gul-*
" *ftone* did now take Occafion to recomend vnto the Company for
" the faid Place one Mʳ *Pottes* a Mʳ of Artes and as hee afirmed
" well practifed in Chirurgerie and Phifique, and expert allfo in
" Diftillinge of Waters and that hee had many other ingenious
" Devices foe as hee fuppofed his Service would be of great Vfe
" vnto the Colony in *Virginia*, . . . "

Alfo:

William Stith, THE HISTORY OF THE FIRST
DISCOVERY AND SETTLEMENT OF VIR-
GINIA *(Williamfburg: William Parks,* 1747), p. 188.

" . . . Mr. *John Pot* was elected, by the Company, Phyfician-
" General to the Colony. He was recommended by Dr. *Gulftone,*
" an eminent Member of their Society, as a Mafter of Arts, well
" practiced in Chirurgery and Phyfic, and expert in Chymical
" Proceffes and other ingenious Parts of his Profeffion; whofe
" Service, he therefore conceived, would be of great Ufe to the
" Colony. He was accordingly fent, upon the fame Foot, as Dr.
" *Bohun;* and was allowed his own, his Wife's, and two Servants
" Paffages."

[16]

William Waller Hening, THE STATUTES AT
LARGE *(New York: R. & W. & G. Bartow,* 1823),
Vol. I, pp. 145-146.

" *July* the 9th, 1630.—Dr. *John Pott,* late Governor, indicted,
" arraigned and found guilty of ftealing Cattle, 13 Jurors 3
" whereof Councellors. This Day wholly fpent in pleading; next
" Day, in unneceffary Difputation: *Pott* endeavouring to prove
" Mr. *Kingfmell* (one of the Witneffes againft him) an Hypo-
" crite, by a Story of *Gufman* of *Alfrach* the Rogue. In Regard of
" his Quality and Practice, Judgment refpited till the King's
" Pleafure known; and all the Councel became his Security. "

[17]

W. Noel Sainfbury, ed., CALENDAR OF STATE
PAPERS, COLONIAL SERIES, *1574-1660 (Lon-*
don:

don: Longman, Green, Longman & Roberts, 1860), p.
118.

[*July* 16, 1630] " (98) Governor *Harvey* to Sec. *Dorchefter*. Sends
" Petition to the King in Favour of Dr. *John Pott*, who he found
" Governor, the only Phyfician in the Colony fkilled in Epedemi-
" cal Difeafes . . . "

[18]

*Edward D. Neill, VIRGINIA VETUSTA, DURING
THE REIGN OF JAMES THE FIRST (Albany,
N. Y.: Joel Munfell's Sons, 1885), pp. 122-127.*

Letter from *George Sandys* to *Samuel Wrote*, a Member of the *London Company*, written from " *James
" Cittie*, 28 *Martii*, 1623. "

"   . . .and what a pittifull Councellour have wee of yoᵣ Doc-
" tour [Doctor *John Pott*] I have given from Time to Time the
" beft Councell I am able, at the firft he kept Companie too much
" with his Inferiours who hung upon him while his good Liquor
" lafted. After he conforted with Captaine *Whitacres* (a Man of
" no good Example) with whom he is gone into *Kicotan* yet where-
" foever he bee he fhall not bee without the Reach of my Oare, nor for
" Want of anie Thing that I or my Credit can procure him, . . . "

[19]

*Angus W. McDonald, TRANSCRIPTS-MISCELL-
ANEOUS, 1627-1640. [Ms. Tranfcripts from Britifh
Public Record Office.] Virginia State Library Archives.
Vol. II, pp. 191-199. " Declaration of Sir John Harvey
" concerning the Mutiny in Virginia. July 1635. "*

" . . . And that upon the 28. Day of *Aprill* laft which was the
" Time when they were to meet for his Majefties faid Service, the
" faid *Mathewes, Utye, Farrer, Pearce, Perry, Mineur,* and *John
" Pott* came all armed and brought with them about 50 Mufket-
" eers, and befett mee in my owne Houfe, which was the Place that
" I appointed for our Meeting
" That I and Mᵣ *Kemp* (his Majefties Secretary there) were
" then fitting together expecting the Councell when the faid
" mutinous Company entred the Place, and *John Utye* in the
" Prefence of the Reft, gave mee a very greate and violent
" Stroake upon the Shoulder, and fayd with a loud Voyce, ' I
" arreft

" arreſt you for Treaſon; '. . . and all of them ſayd to me; ' You
" muſt prepare yourſelf to goe for *England*, for you muſt and
" ſhall goe, to anſwere the Complainte that are againſt you. '

" That upon this Uproare *John Pott* (who by the ſaid Com-
" pany was placed at the Doore of the ſaid Houſe) with his Hand
" gave a Signe and imediately the Muſketeers which before that
" Time lay hid, came preſently running with their Peeces preſented
" towards my Houſe: . . . and when they were come neare to
" him, he ſayd to the Muſketeers: ' Stay there untill there be uſe
" of you; ' and there upon they retired again.

" . . . And the ſaid Councellors then choſe Mr *John Weſt* for
" Governor, who thereupon tooke the Place and Title of Governor
" upon him, and gave Orders and Directions as Governor. . ."

[20]

Records aſſociating theſe Names with Property
Ownerſhip in *Middle Plantation* may be found in the
following Sources:

YORK COUNTY RECORDS, Deeds, Orders, Wills.

VIRGINIA LAND OFFICE, Richmond, Virginia. Patent Books 1-5.

[21]

THE VIRGINIA MAGAZINE OF HISTORY AND BIOGRAPHY, Vol. IV (1897), p. 207.

" Captain *Robert Higginſon* . . . ſeems to have been promi-
" nent as an *Indian* Fighter. In 1646 and earlier he commanded
" at the *Middle Plantation*, a paliſaded Settlement. . . . The
" Epitaph of his Daughter *Lucy* (who died *Nov.* 6, 1675,) on her
" Tomb in the *Burwell* Graveyard at ' *Carter's Creek*, ' *Gloucester*,
" only ſtates that . . . ' She was deſcended from the ancient
" Family of the *Higginſons*. She was ye only Daughter of the
" Valliant Capt. *Robert Higginſon*. One of the firſt Command'rs
" that ſubdued the Country of *Virginia* from the Power of the
" Heathen. ' "

[22]

See Note 20

[23]

F. A. Winder, VIRGINIA MANUSCRIPTS FROM THE

THE BRITISH PUBLIC RECORD OFFICE &c.,
Vol. II, *Bacon's Rebellion.* [*Virginia State Library*
Archives, *Richmond*], p. 482.

" *A True Narrative of the Rise, Progresse, and Cessation of the*
" *late Rebellion in* Virginia *most humbly and impartially reported*
" *by his Majestyes Commissioners appointed to enquire into the*
" *Affaires of the said Colony.*"

" . . . foe leading his Men to *Middle-Plantacion* (the very
" Heart and Centre of the Country) hee [*Bacon*] there for fome
" Tyme quarters them. . . . "

[24]

Ibid., p. 482.

" Then iffues forth Proclamation, inviting the Gentlemen of
" *Virginia* to come in and confult with him [at *Middle Plantation*]
" for the prefent Settlement of that his Ma^tyes diftracted Colony
" to Preferve its future Peace, and advance the effectual Profe-
" cuting of the *Indian* Warr. . . . "

[25]

Ibid., pp. 462-467.

" The Affembly mett to confult for the Safety and Defence of
" the Country ag^t the Incurfions and Deftructions of the *Indians,*
" dayly comitted upon the Inhabitants of *Virginia,* there having
" beene within the Space of about 12 Monethes before, neer 300
" *Chriftian* Perfons murder'd by the *Indians* Enemy.
" What Care the Affembly tooke to prevent thefe barbarous
" Mafacres, was onely to build Forts at the Heads of each River
" and on the Frontiers and Confines of the Country; for erecting
" of wch and mainteining Guards on them a heavie Leavy was
" laid by Act of Affembly on the People; throughout the Country
" univerfally difliked before the Name of that Impofture *Bacon*
" was heard of, as being a Matter from which was expected great
" Charge and little or noe Security to the Inhabitants, . . .
" Thus the Senfe of this Oppreffion, and the Dread of a comon,
" approaching Calamity made the giddy-headed Multitude madd,
" and precipitated them upon that rafh Overture of runing out
" upon the *Indians* themfelves, at their owne voluntary Charge,
" and Hazard of their Lives and Fortunes, onely they firft by Pe-
" tition humbly craved Leave or Comiffion to be ledd by any
" Comander or Comanders as the Governour fhould pleafe to ap-
" point over them to be their Chieftaine or Generall.

" But

"But inftead of granting this Peticion ye Governor by Procla-
" mation under great Penalty forbad the like Petitioning for
" the Future.

" This made the People jealous that the Governor for the
" Lucre of the Beaver and Otter Trade &c wth ye *Indians*, rather
" fought to Protect the *Indians* than them, fince after publick
" Proclamation prohibiting all Trade with the *Indians* (they com-
" plaine) hee privately gave Comiffion to fome of his Friendes to
" truck with them, and that thofe Perfons furnifhed the *Indians*
" with Powder, Shott &c. foe that they were better provided
" than his Majeftyes Subjects.

" The People of *Charles-City*-County (neere *Merchants-Hope*)
" being denyed a Commiffion by the Governor, (although he was
" truly informed (as by a Letter of his to his Matie he confeffeth)
" of feverall formidable Bodies of *Indians* coming downe on the
" Heads of *James* River within 50 or 60 Miles of the *English* Plan-
" tations, and knew not where the Storme would light) they begin
" to beat up Drums for Volunteers to goe out againft the *Indians*
" and foe continued fundry Dayes drawing into Armes; the Mag-
" iftrates being either foe remife, or of the fame Faction, that
" they fuffered this Diforder, w^thout Contradiction, or endeavour-
" ing to prevent foe dangerous a Begining, & going on.

" The Rout being got together, now wanted nor waited for
" Nothing but one to head and lead them out on their Defigne.

" It foe happen'd that one *Nathaniel Bacon* Junr a Perfon
" whofe loft and defperate Fortunes had throwne him into that
" remote Part of the World about 14 Moneths before, and fram'd
" him fitt for fuch a Purpofe, as by the Sequel will appeare, which
" may make a fhort Character of him noe impertinent Digreffion.

" Hee was a Perfon whofe erratique Fortune had carryed and
" fhewne him many forraigne Parts, and of no obfcure Family;
" upon his firft comming into *Virginia* hee was made one of the
" Councill, the Reafon of that Advancement (all on a Suddain)
" being beft knowne to the Governour . . .

" Hee was faid to be about four or ffive and thirtie Yeares of
" Age indifferent tall but flender black hair'd and of an ominous,
" penfive, melancholly Afpect, of a peftilent & prevalent logical
" Difcourfe tending to Athifme in moft Companyes, not given to
" much Talke, or to make fuddain Replyes, of a moft imperious
" and dangerous hidden Pride of Heart, . . . and arogant. But
" all thefe Things lay hidd in him till after hee was a Councellor,
" and untill he became powerfull and popular.

" Now this Man being in Company with one *Crews* [Capt.
" *James*

" *James Crews*, of *Turkey Ifland*, *Henrico* County] *Ifham* [*Henry*
" *Ifham*, Sr.] *& Bird* [*William Byrd* the firft of *Weftover*] who
" growing to a Highth of Drinking, and making the Sadneffe of
" the Times their Difcourfe, and the Fear they all lived in be-
" caufe of the *Sufquahanocks* who had fettled a little above the
" Falls of *James* River and comitted many Murders upon yᵐ
" among whome *Bacon's* Overfeer happen'd to be one, *Crews* and
" the Reft perfwaded Mʳ *Bacon* to goe over and fee the Soldiers
" on the other Side *James* River, and to take a Quantity of Rum
" with them to give the Men to drinke, which they did, and (as
" *Crews &c* had before laid the Plot wᵗʰ the Soldiers) they all at
" once in Field fhouted and cry'd out ' a *Bacon!* a *Bacon!* a
" *Bacon!* ' wᶜʰ taking Fire with his Ambition, and Spirit of
" Faction & Popularity, eafily prevail'd on him to refolve to head
" them, his Friends endeavouring to fix him the ffafter to his
" Refolves by telling him that they would alfo goe along with
" him to take Revenge upon the *Indians*, and drunk Damnation
" to their Soules to be true to him, and if hee could not obtaine a
" Comiffion, they would affift him as well, and as much as if hee
" had one, to which *Bacon* agreed.
       " This Forwardneffe of *Bacons* greatly cheer'd and animated
" the People, who looked upon him as the onely Patron of the
" Country and Preferver of their Lives and Fortunes. "

[26]

Sir *William Keith*, Bart., *THE HISTORY OF THE
BRITISH PLANTATIONS IN AMERICA* (*Lon-
don:* Printed at the Expence of the *Society for the
Encouragement of Learning*, by *S. Richardfon*, 1738),
p. 155.

       " 2. About this Time the Act of the twenty-fifth of *Charles* the
" Second, for better fecuring the Plantation-Trade, was paffed
" in *England;* whereby feveral Duties were laid on the Trade
" from one Colony to another, and appropriated to Ufes quite
" foreign to the People, from whom they were raifed; and whether
" it was the Confequence of fuch fevere Impofitions on the Trade
" of the Plantations, or the too artful and partial Conduct of the
" Merchants in *England*, who enjoy'd confiderable Profits by
" being Factors for the Tobacco Planters in *Virginia*, or partly
" from both, we cannot prefume to determine; but certain it
" was, that the Price of Tobacco then was fo low, that the Bal-
" ance due to the Planter on his Account of Sales from *England*,
                                                              " amounted

amounted to Little or Nothing, nay, often brought him in Debt
" to the Factor; fo that they really had not Wherewithal, out of
" their laborious Toil, to cloathe themfelves, and their poor
" Families. "

Alfo:

[*John Oldmixon*], *THE BRITISH EMPIRE IN AMERICA* (*London:* Printed for *J. Brotherton, J. Clarke* in *Duck-Lane*, 1741), Vol. I, p. 382.

" Before we come to the Facts, it will be proper to let the
" Reader into the Caufes of the Peoples Murmurs and Refent-
" ments, of which thefe four were the chief:
" 1. The low Price of Tobacco in *England*, and the high Prices
" of all Goods exported thence to *Virginia*.
" 2. The Grants made by King *Charles*, of feveral Parts of
" their Country to Noblemen in *England*, in fome of which fev-
" eral of their Plantations were included.
" 3. The Burdens laid upon them by the Parliament in *Eng-*
" *land*, and Taxes by the Affembly in *Virginia*.
" 4. The Difturbances given them by the *Indians*. "

Alfo:

F. A. Winder, VIRGINIA MANUSCRIPTS FROM THE BRITISH PUBLIC RECORD OFFICE &c., Vol. II, *Bacon's Rebellion.* [*Virginia State Library* Archives, *Richmond*.] pp. 84-90, 153-255.

[Grievances of fundry Counties in *Virginia* as re-ported to the Commiffioners appointed to enquire into the Affairs of the Colony.]

[27]

See Note 25

[28]

Ibid., p. 160.

" *The Greevances of* Surry *County*.

" 1. That ye laft Affembly continued many Yeares and by
" their ffrequent Meeting being once every Yeare hath been a
" continuall Charge and Burthen to the poore Inhabitants of this
" Collony; and that the Burgeffes of the faid fd Affembly had
" 150ᵗʰ Tobacco *p* Day for each Member they ufually continue-
" ing

" ing three or 4 Weekes togither did arrife to a great Some And
" that the faid Affembly did give to feverall Gentlemen (for what
" Service wee know not) great Somes of Tobacco, . . . "

Alfo:

*VIRGINIA MAGAZINE OF HISTORY AND BI-
OGRAPHY*, Vol. I (1894), p. 170. Letter of *William
Sherwood* to Sir *Jofeph Williamfon*, written from
James City, *June* 28, 1676.

" . . . But Mr. *Nath^{ll} Bacon*, Junr diffuading ye People from
" theire Subjection to ye Laws, giveing out he would do ftrange
" Matters & eafe y^m of their Levies, the Rabble rife, exclameing
" ag't the P'ceedeings of the Affembly and feeme weary of it,
" in y^t itt was of 14 Y'rs Continuance; . . . "

[29]

William Waller Hening, THE STATUTES AT
LARGE (*New York: R. & W. & G. Bartow*, 1823),
Vol. II, pp. 518-528.

" References to Papers relating to the Grant to Lords *Arling-*
" *ton* and *Culpeper*, of the whole Colony of *Virginia*, for 31 Years,
" and the Miffion to *England* for the Purpofe of obtaining a Revo-
" cation of that Grant, and a new and more perfect Charter for
" *Virginia*. . . . "

Alfo:

Sir *William Keith*, Bart., THE HISTORY OF THE
BRITISH PLANTATIONS IN AMERICA (*London: S. Richardfon*, 1738), pp. 154-155.

" 1. King *Charles* the Second, to gratify fome Noblemen about
" his Perfon, had made two large Grants, which were diftin-
" guifh'd by the Names of the Northern and Southern Grants of
" *Virginia*, altho' the fame Men were concern'd in both. Thefe
" Grants happen'd unfortunately to include within their Limits
" feveral improved Plantations, which had been feated for many
" Years before, and poffeffed under the legal unqueftionable
" Title of Patents from the Crown. When thefe latter Grants
" therefore, which had lain dormant until the Year 1674, came to
" be known and claimed, it created fo much Uneafinefs in the
" Country, that the Affembly drew up an humble Addrefs to his
" Majefty, complaining of the Injuftice of the faid Grants, and
" befeeching

" befeeching the King to recall them, as being highly derogatory
" of thofe Rights granted to the People of that Colony, by his
" Royal Progenitors; and tho' this Addrefs was fent over, and
" folicited by particular Agents, for many Months together, at a
" great Expence to *Virginia*, which was heavily taxed by the
" Affembly for that Purpofe, yet it never had any Effect. "

[30]

See Note 25

[31]

See Note 25

[32]

See Note 25

Alfo:

THE ENQUIRER (*Richmond, Va.*, Publifhed by
Ritchie & Worfley,) Volume I, No. 37, *Wednefday*
Morning, *September*, 12, 1804. [Letter of Mrs. *An.
Cotton* of *Queen's Creek* in *Virginia*, to Mr. *C. H.* at
Yardly in *Northamptonfhire*, written in 1676. Alfo
printed in *Peter Force, Tracts and Other Papers*,
(*Wafhington:* 1836), Vol. I.]

" . . . hee [*Bacon*] upbrades fom in Authorety with the Meane-
" nefs of there Parts, others now rich with the Meanenefs of there
" Eftates, when they came in to the Countrey, and queftions by
" what juft Ways they have obtaned there Welth; whether they
" have not bin the Spunges that hath fuck'd up the publick
" Trefury: . . . fath Sumthing againft ye Governour concern-
" ing the Beaver Trade, as not in his Power to difpofe of to his
" owne Proffit, it being a Monopeley of the Crowne; queftions
" whether the Traders at the Heads of the Rivers being his Fac-
" ters, do not buy and fell the Blood of there Bretheren and
" Country Men, by furnifhing the *Indians* with Pouder, Shott
" and Fire Arms, contrary to the Laws of the Collony: . . . "

[33]

See Note 25

[34]

[34]
See Note 25

Alfo:

Sir *William Keith*, Bart., THE HISTORY OF THE
BRITISH PLANTATIONS IN AMERICA (*London: S. Richardfon*, 1738), pp. 156-157.

" There was at this Time one *Nathanael Bacon*, a young Gen-
" tleman of a very comely Afpect, who having had his Education
" at the Inns of Court in *England*, and being indued with the
" Talent of an eafy and engaging Elocution, had been lately pro-
" moted to be a Member of the Council; and was not only very
" much efteem'd at that Board, but looked on by every Body as a
" Man of elegant fine Parts.
" This giddy-headed Youth, who had already conceived but
" too well of his own Perfections, was every-where careffed by
" thefe Mobs, whom he often harangued, aggravating the Mif-
" chiefs that were daily committed by the *Indians* on the Fron-
" tier Settlements; . . . and offering his Service to lead them
" againft the *Indians*, and to rectify all their Grievances.
" The unthinking Multitude were fo charm'd with his Oratory,
" that they unanimoufly elected Mr. *Bacon* their General; . . . "

[35]

F. A. Winder, VIRGINIA MANUSCRIPTS FROM
THE BRITISH PUBLIC RECORD OFFICE &c.,
Vol. II, *Bacon's Rebellion*. [*Virginia State Library
Archives, Richmond*]. pp. 468-483.

" *A True Narrative of the Rife, Progreffe, and Ceffation
" of the late Rebellion in* Virginia, . . . "

" *Bacon* having gott about 300 Men together in Armes pre-
" pared to goe out againft the *Indians:* The Governour and his
" Friends endeavour to divert his Defignes, but cannot.
" Hee proclames *Bacon*, and his Followers Rebells and Mu-
" tineers for going forth againft the *Indians* without a Commif-
" fion. And (getting a Company of Gentlemen together) the
" Governor marcheth up to the Falls of the *James* River to
" purfue and take *Bacon*, or to feife him at his Returne, but all
" in vaine, ffor *Bacon* had got over the River with his Forces,
" and

" and haftning away into the Woods went directly and fell upon
" the *Indians* . . .

" While the Governour was in the upper Parts to wait
" *Bacons* Returne the People below began to draw into Armes,
" and to declare againft the Forts.

" Hee, to appeafe the Comotions of the People leaves off that
" Defigne and comes immediately back to his own Houfe, and
" caufed at his Returne the *Surry* and other Forts to be forth-
" with difmantled, and diffolving the Affembly that enacted
" them, gave the Country a free new Election, which new Affem-
" bly were to be for the Settlement of the then diftracted Con-
" dicion of *Virginia*.

" At this new Election (fuch was the Prevalency of *Bacons*
" Party) that they chofe inftead of Freeholders, Free-men that
" had but lately crept out of the Condicion of Servants . . . for
" their Burgeffes, . . .

" The Affembly being mett, *Bacon* comes downe in a Sloope to
" *James-Towne*, but the People being very fond of him, would
" not truft his Perfon without a Guard, fearing fome Violence
" fhould be offered him by the Governour, . . . foe fent fforty
" armed Men along in the Sloope with *Bacon*.

" Coming fomewhat neerer to Towne than *Swann's Point* dropt
" Anchor, and fent (as 'tis faid) on Shore to the Governour, to
" know if he might in Safety come on Shore, and fitt as a Mem-
" ber *&c.* What Anfwer was return'd we have not heard onely
" what the Governor caufed to be given him from the great Guns
" that fired at the Sloope from the Towne-Fort, foe that having
" gott his Sloope out of Gun-fhott, he lay higher up the River,
" and in the Night Tyme with a Party of his Men ventured on
" Shore, and having had fome Conference (at *Lawrance's* Houfe)
" with *Lawrance & Drumond* came off againe undifcovered.

" Severall Propofitions were made, and fome Boats fent off to
" apprehend him but could effect Nothing; *Bacon* endeavours to
" make his Efcape up the River. In this Juncture Capt *Thomas*
" *Gardner* Mafter of the Ship *Adam and Eve* being at Towne, hav-
" ing an Order from the Governor to purfue and feize him imedi-
" ately got on Board his Ship and as *Bacon* returned up the River
" comanded his Sloope in by ffiring at him from on Board, and
" foe tooke him and all his Men Prifoners and brought them
" away to the Governor at Towne.

" *Bacon* being delivered up Prifoner to the Governor by
" Capt *Gardner*, the Governor lifting up his Handes and Eyes,
" faid in the Hearing of many People, ' Now I behold the greateft
" Rebell

" Rebell that ever was in *Virginia* ' who (with a dejected Look)
" made noe Reply, till after a ſhort Pauſe the Governour aſk'd
" *Bacon* theſe Words, ' Sir, doe you continue to be a Gentleman,
" and may I take your Word? If ſoe you are at Liberty upon yoͬ
" owne Parrol. '

" *Bacon* feignes a moſt deep Senſe of Shame and Sorrow for his
" Guilt, and expreſſes the greateſt kind of Obligacion to Grati-
" tude towards the Governour imaginable.

" And to make it looke the more reall and ſincere drew up an
" humble Submiſſion for, and Acknowledgemͭ of his ſoe late
" Crimes and Diſobedience, imploring thereby the Governors
" Pardon, and Favor, . . .

" After a ſhort While hee was ſent for in againe and had his
" Pardon confirmed to him.

" Is reſtor'd into Favor and readmitted into the Councell, to
" the Wonder of all Men.

" Now Capͭ *Gardner* inſtead of a Reward for the Service hee
" performed in taking, and bringing away *Bacon* Priſoner was ſuf-
" fered to be ffined 70ͥᵇ Damage for ſeiſing him and the Sloope . . .

" However ſoe powerfull (it ſeemes) was *Bacons* Intereſt in this
" new Aſſembly that he procured a publick Order to paſſe agͭ
" *Gardner* for the Payment of the 70ͥᵇ whereupon he threw *Gard-*
" *ner* into Goale till he found Security for his Enlargement. . . .

" But when they underſtood that the Governor had not onely
" ſett him ffree, but readmitted him into the Councill, with
" Promiſe alſo of a Commiſſion to be given him to goe out againſt
" the *Indians* the People were ſoe well pacified for the pͬſent as
" that every Man wͭʰ great Gladneſſe return'd to his owne Home.

" *Bacon* attending at Towne for a Comiſſion (wᶜʰ the Governor
" is ſaid to have promiſed him) *&* being delayed or putt off; was
" ſecretly whiſpered to by ſome of his Friendes, that thoſe De-
" layes would endanger his Life, and that . . . there was a Con-
" ſpiracy to Murder him on ſuch a Night: Upon wᶜʰ hee privately
" leaves the Towne; . . .

" Hee no ſooner was come to the upper Parts of *James* River,
" but the impatient People run to him to aſk how Affairs ſtood,
" . . . and underſtanding he had or could not obtaine any [Com-
" miſſion], they began to ſett up their Throats in one comon Key
" of Othes and Curſes, and cry'd out aloud, that they would
" either have a Comiſſion for *Bacon* that they might ſerve under
" his Conduct or elſe they would pull downe the Towne or doe
" worſe to ſome if they had it not. And if *Bacon* would goe but
" with them they would gett him a Commiſſion.

" Thus

" Thus the raging Tumult came downe to Towne (fitting the
" Affembly) and *Bacon* at the Head of them, having entred the
" Towne, hee feifes and fecures the principal Places and Avenues,
" fetts Sentinells and fends forth Scouts, fo that noe Place could
" bee more fecurely guarded.

" Having foe done, hee drawes up all his Men in Armes againft
" the State-houfe where the Governor Councill and Burgeffes
" were then affembled . . . and fends in to the Affembly to
" know if now they would grant him a Commiffion, which Sʳ
" *William Berkeley* utterly refufed, and rifing from his Chair of
" Judicature came downe to *Bacon*, and told him to his Face and
" before all his Men that hee was a Rebell and a Traytor *&c.* and
" fhould have noe Commiffion, and uncovering his naked Bofome
" before him, required that fome of his Men might fhoot him,
" before ever he would be drawne to figne or confent to a Comif-
" fion for fuch a Rebell as *Bacon*, ' Noe ' (faid the Governor)
" ' lett us firft try and end the Difference fingly betweene our-
" felves ,' and offer'd to meafure Swords with him; all the
" anfwer *Bacon* gave the Governor was ' Sir, I came not, nor in-
" tend to hurt a Haire of yoʳ Honors Head, and for yoʳ Sword
" yoʳ Honor may pleafe to putt it up, it fhall ruft in the Scabbard
" before ever I fhall defire you to drawe it. I come for a Com-
" miffion againft the Heathen who dayly inhumanely murder us
" and fpill our Brethrens Blood, and noe Care is taken to prevent
" it '; adding ' *God* damne my Blood I came for a Commiffion,
" a nd a Commiffion I will have before I goe, ' and turning to his
" *S*oldiers, faid ' Make ready and prefent, ' which they all did.

" Some ot the Burgeffes looking out at the Windows and feeing
" the Soldiers in that Pofture of firing cry'd out to them, ' For
" *Gods* Sake hold your Handes and forbear a little, and you fhall
" have what you pleafe .' Much Hurrying, Solicitation and Im-
" portunity is ufed on all Sides to the Governor to grant *Bacon* a
" Commiffion.

" At laft the Governor confents, a Commiffion is drawne up
" and fent him, he diflikes it, they pray him to draw or direct one
" himfelf and the Governor fhould figne it: Whereupon *Bacon*
" drawes up the Contents of a Commiffion according to his owne
" Mind, and returns it to the Clerke, . . .

" After the Governor had figned the principall Comiffion to
" *Bacon*, hee is alfo pleaf'd to figne 30 Comiffions more . . . for
" Officers that were to ferve under him. . . .

" The Affembly alfo paffe Orders to raife or preffe 1000 Men, and
" to raife Provifions *&c* for this intended Service agᵗ the *Indians* . . .
" Severall

" Severall Voluntiers and Reformadoes come in to lift them-
" felves under *Bacon*, and many were preff'd into this Service, till
" at laft having his Complement of Men, and all Things elfe
" being in Readyneffe according as the Affembly had provided for
" this Expedition.

" *July* 15ᵗʰ. A generall Rendezvous is appointed by *Bacon* at the
" Falls of *James* River, where all Things being well appointed for
" the March, *Bacon* makes a Speech to his Men, . . .

" And finally before them all tooke the Oath of Allegiance and
" Supremacy, willing his Soldiers alfo to doe the like, which hav-
" ing freely comply'd with. Hee drew up an Oath of Fidelity to
" himfelfe, which hee (as their Head & Generall) required them
" to take, . . .

" Juft now (even on the very Night before their going out on
" the intended March agᵗ the *Indians*) a Meffanger comes Poft
" from *Glofter* Countyes bringing Intelligence to *Bacon*, that the
" Governor was there, endeavouring to raife Forces to come and
" furprize him and his Men, and that hee was refolved by Force to
" take his extorted Commiffion away from him, for that the whole
" County had petition'd agᵗ him as a Rebell and a Traytor &c

" This amufing Meffage was noe fooner brought to *Bacon*, but
" immediately he caufes the Drums to beat and Trumpett to
" found for calling his Men together, to whom he fpake after this
" Manner.

" ' Gentlemen and Fellow Soldiers.

" ' The Newes juft now brought mee, may not a little ftartle
" as you well as myfelfe, but feeing it is not altogether unexpedted,
" wee may the better beare it and provide our Remedies.

" ' The Governour is now in *Glofter* County endeavouring to
" raife Forces againft us, having declared us Rebells and Tray-
" tors: . . . It is Revenge that hurryes them on without Re-
" gard to the Peoples Safety, and had rather wee fhould be
" murder'd and our Ghofts fent to our flaughter'd Country-men
" by their Adtings, than wee live to hinder them of their Intereft
" with the Heathen, and preferve the remaining Part of our
" ffellow Subjects from their Crueltyes. Now then wee muft bee
" forced to turne our Swords to our owne Defence, or expofe our-
" felves to their Mercyes, or Fortune of ye Woodes, whileft his
" Majeftyes Country here lyes in Bloode and wafting (like a
" Candle) at both Ends . . .

" ' Therefore while wee are found at Heart, unwearyed and
" not receiving Damage by the Fate of Warr, lett us defcend to
" know the Reafons why fuch Proceedings are ufed againft us. . . . '

" Now

" Now in vaine the Governor attempts raifing a Force againft
" *Bacon*, and although the Induftry & Endeavors hee ufed to
" effect it was great, yet at this Juncture it was impoffible: for
" *Bacon* at this Tyme was as much the Hopes and Darling of the
" People that the Governors Intereft prov'd but weake, and his
" Friends foe very few that he grew fick of the Effay, and with
" very Griefe and Sadneffe of Spirit for foe bad Succeffe (as is
" faid) ffainted away on Horfeback in the Field. And hearing of
" *Bacon's* being on his March to *Glofter*, hee was feigne to fly
" thence to *Accomack*, leaving now the Seat of the Government
" lyable to the Ufurpation of that Rebell, who had then alfo the
" Militia of the Country in his Hands . . .

" Where being arrived with his Forces, hee findes the Gover-
" nour fled, and (without more adoe) the Field his owne; foe lead-
" ing his Men to *Middle-Plantacion* (the very Heart and Centre of
" the Country) hee there for fome Tyme quarters them.

" Then iffues forth Proclamation, inviting the Gentlemen of
" *Virginia* to come in and confult with him for the prefent Settle-
" ment of that his Ma^tyes diftracted Colony to preferve its future
" Peace, and advance the effectual Profecuting of the *Indian* Warr.

" Severall Gentlemen, appearing on this Summons of *Bacons*
" at *Middle-Plantation*, mett him at one Capt *Thorps*, where
" (under a great Guard) were feverall Perfons confin'd. After a
" long Debate, pro & con a mifchievous Writing was drawne
" up and produced by *Bacon*; . . . The Tenor of the Oath is
" as followes:

" 1. You are to oppofe what Forces fhall be fent out of *Eng-
" land* by his Majefty againft mee, till fuch Tyme I have ac-
" quainted the King with the State of this Country, and have
" had an Anfwer.

" 2. You fhall fweare that what the Governor and Councill
" have acted is illegal and deftructive to the Country, and what I
" have done is according to the Lawes of *England*.

" 3. You fhall fweare from your Hearts that my Comiffion is
" lawfull and legally obtained.

" 4. You fhall fweare to divulge what you fhall heare at any
" Time fpoken againft mee.

" 5. You fhall keepe my Secrets, and not difcover them to any
" Perfon.

" Copyes of this Oath are fent to all, or moft of the Countyes
" of *Virginia*, and by the Magiftrates and others of the refpective
" Precincts adminiftered to the People, which none (or very
" few) for Feare or Force durft, or did refufe. . . . "

[36]

THE ENQUIRER (*Richmond*, *Va.:* Publiſhed by
Ritchie & Worſley), Volume I, Number 37, *Wedneſ-
day* Morning, *September* 12, 1804. [Letter of Mrs. *An.
Cotton* of *Queen's Creek*, 1676.]

" *Bacon* being ſate down with his Army at the *Middle Planta-
" tion*, ſends out an Invitation unto all the prime Gent:men in
" theſe Parts, to give him a Meeting in his Quarters, there to
" conſult how the *Indians* were to be proceeded againſt, and him-
" ſelf and Army protected againſt the Deſines of Sʳ *W. B.* . . .

" To comply with the Generalls Invetation, . . . there was a
" grate Convention of the People met him in his Quarters; the
" Reſult of whoſe Meeting was an Ingagement, for the People (of
" what Qullety ſoever, excepting Servants) to ſubſcribe to con-
" ſiſting of 3 Heads.

" Firſt, to be aideing, with there Lives and Eſtates, the Gen-
' erall, in the *Indian* War; . . . " [See Page 8 of Text.]

[37]

See Note 36

[38]

PUBLIC RECORD OFFICE, *London*. *Colonial Office*
5/1371, Fols. 232-240. [Photoſtat, *Colonial Williamſburg* Foundation.]

" A Dialogue between the Rebel *Bacon* and one *Good* as it was
" preſented to the Rᵗ Honᵇˡᵉ Sʳ *Wᵐ Berkley*—Governor of *Vir-
" ginia.*

" Honᵇˡᵉ Sʳ

" In obedient Submiſſion to yᵗ Honoᵣˢ Comand direᵭed to
" me by Capᵗ *Wᵐ Bird* I have written the full Subſtance of a
" Diſcourſe *Nath: Bacon* deceaſed propoſ'd to me on or about
" the 2ᵈ Day of *Septʳ* laſt, both in Ordᵣ and Words as followeth:
" *B:* ' There is a Report Sʳ *Wᵐ Berkeley* hath ſent to the King for
" 2000: Red Coates, and I doe believe it may bee true, tell me
" your Opinion, may not 500: *Virginians* beat them, wee
" having the ſame Advantages againſt them, the *Indians* have
" agᵗ us. '
" *G:* ' I rather conceive 500: Red Coates may either ſubjeᵭ
" or ruine *Virginia.*'

" *B:*

" *B:*   ' You talk ſtrangely, are not wee acquainted with the
" Country, can lay Ambuſcadoes, and take Trees and putt
" them by the Uſe of their Diſcipline, and are doubtleſſe as
" good or better ſhott then they. '

"*G:*   ' But they can accompliſh what I have ſayd without Haz-
" zard or Coming into ſuch Diſadvantages, by taking Oppor-
" tunities of Landing where there ſhall bee noe Oppoſition,
" firing our Houſes and Fences, deſtroying our Stocks, and
" preventing all Trade and Supplies to the Country. '

" *B:*   ' There may bee ſuch Prevention that they ſhall not bee
" able to make any great Progreſſe in ſuch Miſcheifes, and
" the Country or Clime not agreeing wth their Conſtitutions,
" great Mortality will happen amongſt them, in their Seaſon-
" ing wch will weare and weary them out. '

"   . . .

" *Jan^{ry}* ye 30th 1676

John Goode "

[39]

THE ENQUIRER (*Richmond, Va.:* Publiſhed by
Ritchie & Worſley), Vol. I, Number 37, *Wedneſday*
Morning, *September* 12, 1804. [Letter of Mrs. *An.
Cotton* of *Queen's Creek*, 1676.]

" . . . Theſe 3 Heads being methodized, and put in to Form,
" . . . and redd unto the People, held a Deſpute, from allmoſt
" Noone, till Midnight, pro and con, whether the ſame might, in
" the laſt Article eſpecially, be with out Danger taken. The Gen-
" erall, and ſom others, of the cheife Men was reſalute in the
" Affirmative, aſſerting its Innoſſcency, & proteſting, without it,
" he would ſurrender up his Commiſſion to the Aſſembly, and lett
" them finde other Servants, to do the Countreys Worke: this,
" and the Newſe, that the *Indians* were fallen downe in to
" *Gloſter* County, and had kill'd ſom People, a bout *Carters
" Creeke;* made the People willing to take the Ingagement. "

[40]

*F. A. Winder, VIRGINIA MANUSCRIPTS FROM
THE BRITISH PUBLIC RECORD OFFICE &c.,*
Vol. II, *Bacon's Rebellion.* [*Virginia State Library*
Archives], pp. 484-492.

[41]

[41]

Ibid., pp. 492-494.

" *A true Narrative of the Rife, Progreffe, and Ceffation
of the late Rebellion in* Virginia . . . "

" The Governor having regain'd this Ship, goes on Board and
" in Company with the Ship *Adam & Eve* Capt *Gardner* Coman-
" der 16 or 17 Sloopes and about 600 Men in Armes goes up to
" *James Towne*, which hee ffortifies as well as he could, and again
" proclames *Bacon* and his Party Rebells and Traytors, threat-
" ning them with the utmoft Severityes of Law.

" Upon this *Bacon* calls his few Men together which upon a
" Mufter made a little after the laft Skirmifh with the *Indians*
" . . . were but 136. tyr'd Men, and told them how the Gov-
" ernor intended to proceed againft him and them.

" But this rather animated and provoked new Courage in them
" than anywife daunted them, foe that among other cheerfull
" Expreffions they cry'd out they would ftand by him their
" Generall to the laft. . . .

" *Bacon* in moft incenf'd Manner threatens to be revenged on
" the Governor and his Party fwearing his Soldiers to give noe
" Quarter . . . and foe in great Fury marches on towards *James*
" *Towne*, onely halting a while about *New Kent* to gaine fome
" ffrefh Forces, . . .

" Having increafed his Number to about 300 in all, hee pro-
" ceeds directly to Towne, as hee marcheth the People on the
" High Wayes coming forth praying for his Happinefs and railing
" ag^t the Governour and his Party . . . the Women telling him
" if hee wanted Affiftance they would come themfelves after
" him.

" Intelligence coming to *Bacon* that the Governour had good
" in Towne a 1000 Men, well arm'd & refolute ' I fhall fee
" that ' faith hee, ' for I am now going to try them. ' "

[42]

Ibid., pp. 494-496.

" Having planted his Great-Guns, hee [*Bacon*] takes the Wives
" and female Relations of fuch Gentlemen as were now in the
" Governors Service againft him (whome hee had caufed to be
" brought to the Workes) and Places them in the Face of his
" Enemy, as Bulworkes for their Battery, by which Policy hee
" Promifed himfelf (and doubtleffe had) a goode Advantage. Yet
" had

" had the Governors Party by much the Odds in Number befides
" the Advantage of Tyme and Place.

"   " But foe great was the Cowerdize and Bafeneffe of the Gener-
" ality of Sʳ *William Berkeley's* Party (being moſt of them Men
" intent onely upon Plunder or compell'd and hired into his Ser-
" vice) that of all at laſt there were onely fome 20. Gentlemen
" willing to ſtand by him, the Reſt (whome the Hopes or Promife
" of Plunder brought thither) being now all in haſt to be gone
" to fecure what they had gott; foe that Sʳ *Wᵐ Berkeley* himfelfe,
" who undoubtedly would rather have dyed on the Place than
" thus defferted it, what with importunate and refiſtleffe Solici-
" tations of all was at laſt overperfwaded, nay hurryed away
" againſt his owne Will to *Accomack* and forced to leave the
" Towne to the Mercy of the Enemy. "

[43]

THE ENQUIRER (*Richmond*, *Va.*: Publiſhed by
Ritchie & Worſley), Vol. I, No. 36, *Saturday* Morn-
ing, *September* 8, 1804. *The Beginning Progreſs and
Concluſion of* Bacon's *Rebellion in* Virginia, *in the
Years 1675 & 1676.* By T[*homas*] M[*athews*] 1705.
[Printed alfo in *Peter Force*, *Tracts and Other Papers*
(*Waſhington*: 1836), Vol. I.]

"   " . . . finding a Bank not a flight Shot long, caſt up thwart the
" Neck of the Peninfula there in *Jameſtown*, he [*Bacon*] ſtormed
" it, and took the Town, . . . but the Govern'r with moſt of his
" Followers fled back, down the River in their Veſſells.

"   " Here reſting a few Daies they concerted the Burning of the
" Towne, wherein Mr. *Laurence* and Mr. *Drumond* owning the
" two beſt Houfes fave one, fet fire each to his own Houfe, which
" Example the Souldiers following laid the whole Town (with
" Church and Statehoufe) in Afhes, faying, the Rogues fhould har-
" bour no more there. . . . "

[44]

Peter Force, TRACTS AND OTHER PAPERS
(*Waſhington*, *D. C.*: Printed by *Peter Force*, 1836),
Vol. I. " *A Narrative of the* Indian *and Civil Wars*
" *in* Virginia *in the Years 1675 and 1676*, " pp. 26-29.
[The manufcript Copy of this Narrative was found
among

among the Papers of Capt. *Nathaniel Burwell* of *King William* County. Its Author is unknown.]

". . . he [*Bacon*] wafts his Soulders over the River at *Tindells* Point, into *Glocefter* County: takeing up his Head Quarters at Collonell *Warners;* from whence hee fends out his Mandates, through the wholl County, to give him a Meeting at the Court- howfe; there to take the Ingagement, that was firft promoted at the *Midle Plantation:* for as yet, in this County, it was not admitted. While he was feduoufly contriving this Affaire, one Capt. *Potter* arives in Poft Hafte from *Rapahanock*, with Newes that Coll: *Brent* was advancing faft upon him (with a Refolu- tion to fight him) at the Head of 1000 Men, . . . Hee had no fooner red the Letter, but hee commands the Drums to beate for the Gathering his Soulders under their Collours; which being don he acquaints them with *Brents* Numbers and Refolutions to fight, and then demands theirs; which was cherefully anfw- ered in the Affirmative, with Showtes and Acclemations, while the Drums thunders a March to meet the promifed Conflict: The Soulders with Abundance of Cherefullnefs difburthening themfelves of all Impediments to Expedition, Order, and good Difciplining, excepting their Oathes, and Wenches. . . .

" This Bufinefs of *Brents* haveing (like the Hoggs the Devill fheared) produced more Noyfe than Wooll, *Bacon*, according to Summons, meets the *Glofter* Men at the Court Howfe: where appeared fom 6 or 7 Hundred Horfs and Foot, with their Arms. After that *Bacon*, in a long Harange, had tendered them the In- gagement . . . one Mr. *Cole* offered the Sence of all the *Glofter* Men there prefent: which was fumed up in their Defires, not to have the Oath impofed upon them, but to be indulged the Benefitt of Neutralitie: But this he would not grant, telling of them that in this their Requeft they appeared like the worft of Sinners, who had a Defire to be faved with the Righteous, and yet would do Nothing whereby they might obtaine there Salvation; and fo offering to go away, one Coll: *Gouge* (of his Party) calls to him and told him, that he had onely fpoke to the Horfs (meaning the Troopers) and not to the Foote. *Bacon*, in fom Paffion, replide, he had fpoke to the Men, and not to the Horfs; having left that Servis for him to do, becaufe one Beaft beft would underftand the Meaneing of another . . . "

[45]

F. A. *Winder*, *VIRGINIA MANUSCRIPTS FROM THE*

THE BRITISH PUBLIC RECORD OFFICE &c.,
Vol. II, *Bacon's Rebellion.* [*Virginia State Library*
Archives], pp. 502-508. " *A True Narrative of the Rife,*
" *Progreffe, and Ceffation of the late Rebellion in*
" Virginia . . . "

" . . . foe that S⋅ *Wᵐ Berkeley* himfelfe, who undoubtedly would
" rather have dyed on the Place than thus defferted it, . . .
" was at laft overperfwaded, nay hurryed away againft his owne
" Will to *Accomack* and forced to leave the Towne [*Jameftown*]
" to the Mercy of the Enemy.

" Soe ffearfull of Difcovery they are, that for Secrecy they im-
" barque and weigh Anchor in the Night and filently fall downe
" the River, thus flying from the Face of an Enemy that during
" this Siege (which lafted one whole Weeke) lay expofed to much
" more Hardfhip, Want and Inaccomodation than themfelves,
" befides the Fatigue of a long March at their firft Coming to
" Towne, for this very Service was fuppofed to be the Death of *Ba-*
" *con,* who by lying in a wett Seafon in his Trenches before Towne
" contracted the Difeafe whereof hee not long after dyed. . . .

" This profperous Rebell, concluding now the Day his owne,
" marcheth with his Army into *Glofter* County, intending to vifit
" all the northerne Parts of *Virginia* to underftand the State of
" them, and to fettle Affairs after his owne Meafures, . . .

" But before he could arrive to the Perfeċtion of his Defignes
" (wᶜʰ none but the Eye of Omnifcience could penetrate) Provi-
" dence did that which noe other Hand durft (or at leaft did) doe,
" and cut him off. . . .

" . . . Hee dyed much diffatisfied in Minde enquiring ever and
" anon after the Arrivall of the Friggats & Forces from *England,*
" and afking if his Guards were ftrong about the Houfe. . . . "

[46]

THE ENQUIRER, (*Richmond, Va.* Publifhed by
Ritchie & Worfley), Vol. I, No. 37. *Wednefday* Morn-
ing, *September* 12, 1804. [Letter of Mrs. *An. Cotton* of
Queen's Creek, 1676.]

" Sr *William* no fooner had News that *Bacon* was dead but he
" fends over a Party, in a Sloope to *Yorke* who fnap'd Collonell
" *Hansford,* and others with him, that kep a negilent Gard at
" Coll. *Reades* Howfe under his Command: When *Hansford* came
" to *Acomuck,* he had the Honour to be the firft *Verginian* born
" that

" that ever was hang'd; . . . Capt. *Carver*, Capt. *Wilford*, Capt.
" *Farloe*, with 5 or 6 others of lefs Note, taken at other Places,
" ending there Days as *Hansford* did; . . .

" This Execution being over . . . Sr. *William* fhips himfelf
" and Soulder for *York* River, cafting Ancor at *Tindells* Point;
" from whence he fends up a Hundred and 20 Men to furprize a
" Gard, of about, 30 Men and Boys, kept at Coll. *Bacons* Howfe,
" under the Command of Major *Whaly;* . . . *Ingram* himfelf,
" and all under his Command, with in a few Days after, being
" reduced to his Duty, . . . which put a Period to the War, and
" brought the Governour a Shoare at Coll. *Bacons*, where he was
" prefented with Mr. *Drumond;* taken the Day before in *Cheeka-*
" *nonimy* Swomp, half famifhed, as him felf related to my Huf-
" band. From Coll. *Bacons*, the next Day, he was convayed, in
" Irons to Mr. *Brays* (whither the Governour was removed) to
" his Tryall, where he was condemn'd with in halfe an Hower
" after his coming to Efqr. *Brays*, to be hanged at the *Midle*
" *Plantation*, within 4 Howers after Condemnation; where he was
" accordingly, executed, with a pittifull *French* Man. Which don,
" the Governour removes to his owne Howfe, to fettle his and
" the Countryes Repofe, after his many Troubles; which he
" effected by the Advice of his Councel and an Affembly con-
" vein'd at the *Greene Spring;* where feverall were condemned to
" be executed, prime Actors in ye Rebellion; . . . enough (they fay
" in all) to out number thofe flane in the wholl War; on both
" Sides: it being obfervable that the Sword was more favourable
" then the Halter, as there was a grater Liberty taken to run from
" the Sharpnefs of the one, then would be alowed to fhun the dull
" Imbraces of the other: the Hangman being more dredfull to
" the *Baconians*, then there Generall was to the *Indians*; as it is
" counted more honourable, and lefs terable, to dye like a Soul-
" der, then to be hang'd like a Dogg. "

[47]

*William Waller Hening, THE STATUTES AT
LARGE (New York: R. & W. & G. Bartow, 1823),
Vol. II, p. 370.*

" . . . *Richard Lawrence, Thomas Whaley* and *John Forth*, who
" were principall Actors in the faid Rebellion, and are ffled from
" Juftice, . . . "

Alfo:

THE ENQUIRER, (Richmond, Va. Publifhed by
Ritchie

Ritchie & Worſley), Vol. I, No. 36. *Saturday* Morning, *September* 8, 1804. " *The Beginning Progreſs and* " *Concluſion* of Bacons *Rebellion in* Virginia *in the* " *Years 1675 and 1676.* " [By *T. M.*]

" The laſt Account of Mr. *Laurence* was from an uppermoſt " Plantation, whence he and ffour others Deſperado's with " Horſes Piſtolls etc. march'd away in a Snow Ancle deep, who " were thought to have caſt themſelves into a Branch of ſome " River, rather than to be treated like *Drumond.* "

[48]

In recent Years ſeveral Students of *Virginia* Hiſtory have unſucceſsfully endeavored to aſſociate theſe Men (notably *Thomas Whaley*) with Perſons of the ſame Name reſiding in *New England* ſubſequent to the Time of their Departure from *Virginia.*

[49]

PUBLIC RECORD OFFICE, London.   Colonial Office 5/1371, pp. 152-156. [Photoſtat in *Diviſion of Manu-ſcripts, Library of Congreſs.*]

Letter from the Commiſſioners to inquire into the Affairs of the Colony of *Virginia* to " Mʳ Secrʸ " *Williamſon.*" From " *Swanns Point*, 27ᵗʰ *March* " 1677."

Alſo:

Ibid., pp. 132-147, 182-187.

Letters from the Commiſſioners to " Mʳ Secretary " *Coventry*," from *Swanns Point, March* 27, 1677, and *April* 5, 1677.

[50]

THE ENQUIRER, (*Richmond, Va.* Publiſhed by *Ritchie & Worſley*), Vol. I, No. 36. *Saturday* Morning, *September 8,* 1804. " *The Beginning Progreſs and* " *Concluſion* of Bacons *Rebellion in* Virginia *in the* " *Years 1675 and 1676.* " [By *T. M.*]

" Near

" Near this Time arrived a fmall Fleet with a Regiment from
" *England* S'r *John Berry* Admirall, Col. *Herbert Jefferies*, Com-
" ander of the Land Forces and Col. *Morrifon* who had one Year
" been a former Govern'r there, all three joined in Comiffion with
" or to S'r *William Barclay* . . .

" The Govern'r went in the Fleet to *London* (whether by Com-
" and from his Majefty or fpontaneous I did not hear) leaving
" Col. *Jefferyes* in his Place, and by next Shipping came back a
" Perfon who waited on his Hono'r in his Voyage, and untill his
" Death, from whom a Report was whifper'd about, that the
" King did fay that old Fool has hang'd more Men in that
" naked Country, then he had done for the Murther of his
" Father, whereof the Govern'r hearing dyed foon after without
" having feen his Majefty; which fhuts up this Tragedy. "

[51]

Angus W. McDonald, TRANSCRIPTS-MISCEL-
LANEOUS, *1627-1640*. [*Ms.* Tranfcripts from
Britifh Public Record Office], *Virginia State Library*
Archives, Vol. II, pp. 249-250. Letter from Governor
John Harvey and Council of *Virginia* to Privy Coun-
cil, written from " *James Cittie* the 18th of *January*
" 1639. "

" Wee are required to indeavour to reduce and drive the
" People into Townes, which as yet is by noe other Meanes and
" Wayes to be effected then by confining the Trade to one Place
" which will draw Merchants and Tradefmen to build and in-
" habit together. In Purfuance of which his Majefties Inftruc-
" tions, wee did the laft Yeare propound to the Affembly and an
" Act did accordingly paffe.

" That a convenient Oportion of Ground for a Houfe and a Gar-
" den Plott fhould be alotted to every Perfon that would under-
" take to build upon the fame Land . . .

" Since which Order there are twelve Houfes and Stores built
" in the Towne [*Jameftown*], one of Brick by the Secretarye, the
" faireft that ever was knowen in this Countrey for Subftance
" and Uniformitye; by whofe Example others have undertaken
" to build framed Houfes to beautifye the Place; confonant to
" his Majefties Inftructions that wee fhould not fuffer Men to
" build flight Cottages as heretofore. "

Alfo:

Alſo:

William Waller Hening, THE STATUTES AT LARGE (New York: R. & W. & G. Bartow, 1823), Vol. II, pp. 471-478.

[*June*, 1680] " *An Act for Cohabitation and Encourage-*
" *ment of Trade and Manufacture. . . .* "

[52]

Ibid., Vol. II, pp. 407-423. Acts and Orders paſſed by the General Aſſembly of 1677.

[53]

Ibid., Vol. II, pp. 423-424.

" Att a Grand Aſſembly, begunne at *Middle Plantation* att the
" Houſe of Capt. *Otho Thorpe* the 10th Day of *October*, . . . 1677 . . .
" CHARLES the Second by the Grace of *God*, of *England*,
" *Scotland*, *France* and *Ireland*, . . . to our truſty and well be-
" loved Sir *William Berkeley*, Knt. our Governour of our Planta-
" tion of *Virginia*, Greeting: WHEREAS *Nathaniell Bacon* the
" younger, and diverſe ill diſpoſed Perſons, his Complices and
" Adherents have raiſed a Rebellion and levyed Warre againſt us
" in our ſaid Plantation, wee being gratiouſly inclined and willing
" to extend our royall Compaſſions to ſuch our Subjects as have
" acted in, and been guilty of, or ſhall act in, or be guilty of the
" ſaid Warre and Rebellion, who being ſenſible and repenting of
" their Diſloyalty and Diſobedience to us and our Government,
" ſhall humbly implore our Grace and Mercy, and ſhall returne
" to their due Obedience and Duty, have thought fitt to give and
" grant, and doe by theſe Preſents give and grant full Power and
" Authority to you our ſaid Governour for us and in our Name
" to pardon releaſe and forgive unto all ſuch our Subjects (other
" than the ſaid *Nathaniell Bacon*) as you ſhall thinke fitt and con-
" venient for our Service, all Treaſons, Fellonyes and other Crimes
" and Miſdemeanors by them or any of them, acted, done or
" comitted, or which ſhalbe acted, done or comitted by them or
" any of them, during and relateing to this preſent Warre and
" Rebellion, with full Reſtitution to the Perſons ſoe by you to be
" pardoned, their Heires, Executors and Adminiſtrators of their
" Eſtates, as well reall as perſonall, . . . "

[54]

[54]

PUBLIC RECORD OFFICE, London.   Colonial Office
5/1371, pp. 182-187. [Photoftat, *Divifion of Manufcripts, Library of Congrefs.*]

Letter from the Commiffioners to " Mr Secretary
" *Coventry,*" dated "*Swanns Point, April* 5th 1677."

[55]

*THE VIRGINIA MAGAZINE OF HISTORY AND
BIOGRAPHY*, Vol. XIV (1907), pp. 289-296.

" Articles of Peace between the moft mighty Prince & our
" dread Soveraigne Lord *Charles* the II . . . And the feverall
" *Indian* Kings and Queens &c Affentors and Subfcribers here-
" unto made and concluded at the Camp of *Middle Plantacon,*
" the 29th Day of *May:* 1677; being the Day of the moft happy
" Birth & Reftauration of our f'd Soveraigne Lord, and in the
" XXIX Yeare of his faid Ma'ties Reigne. . . .

" It is hereby concluded, confented to & mutally agreed as
" followeth:

" I. That the refpective *Indian* Kings and Queens doe from
" henceforth acknowledge to have their imediate Dependancy
" on, and own all Subjection to the great King of *England* . . .
" his Heires and Succeffors, when they pay their Tribute to the
" Right Hon'ble his Ma'ties Govern'r for the Time being.

" II. That thereupon the faid *Indian* Kings & Queens and
" their Subjects fhall hold their Lands, and have the fame con-
" firmed to them and their Pofterity by Patent under the Seale of
" this his Majefties Colony, without any Fee Gratuity or Reward
" for ye fame, . . . and in as free and firme Manner as others his
" Majefties liege Subjects, have and enjoye their Lands, and
" Poffeffions, paying onely yearly for, and in Liew of a Quitrent
" or Acknowledgement for the fame three *Indian* Arrowes.

" III. That all *Indians* who are in Amity with us, & have not
" Land fiffitient to plant up, be upon Information forthwith pro-
" vided for, and Land laid out, and confirmed to them as afforef'd
" never to be difturbed therein, or taken from them, foe long as
" they owne keep and maintaine the due Obedience & Subjection
" to his Majeftie his Govern'r and Government; & Amity &
" Friendfhip towards the *Englifh.* . . .

" V. That the faid *Indians* be well fecured & defended in theire
" Perfons Goods and Properties againft all Hurts and Injuries of
" the *Englifh,* . . . "

[56]

[56]

F. A. *Winder*, *VIRGINIA MANUSCRIPTS FROM BRITISH PUBLIC RECORD OFFICE, &c.*, Vol. II, *Bacon's Rebellion*. [*Virginia State Library* Archives], pp. 84-85.

Alſo:

Ibid., p. 88.

The Petition to the King's Commiſſioners (quoted on Page 12 of this Volume) was anſwered by them as follows:

" That the Town now burnt ſhould be removed to the *Midle*
" *Plantation* wᶜʰ is noe other than if *Midleſex* ſhould have
" deſired, that *London* might have beene new built on *Highgat*
" Hill, and removed from the grand River that brings them in
" their Trade. "

[57]

H. R. *McIlwaine*, ed., *JOURNALS OF THE HOUSE OF BURGESSES OF VIRGINIA, 1659/60-1693* (*Richmond:* 1914), pp. 205-206, 244-245.

Alſo:

H. R. *McIlwaine*, ed., *LEGISLATIVE JOURNALS OF THE COUNCIL OF COLONIAL VIRGINIA* (*Richmond:* 1918), Vol. I, p. 86.

[58]

THE CHARTER, AND STATUTES OF THE COLLEGE OF WILLIAM AND MARY, IN VIRGINIA (*Williamſburg: William Parks*, 1736).

[The Charter is alſo printed in *THE HISTORY OF THE COLLEGE OF WILLIAM AND MARY* (*Richmond: J. W. Randolph & Engliſh*, 1874), pp. 3-16.]

[59]

H. R. *McIlwaine*, ed., *JOURNALS OF THE HOUSE OF BURGESSES OF VIRGINIA, 1659/60-1693* (*Richmond:* 1914), p. 466.

" Thurſday

" *Thurſday October* the 26ᵗʰ 1693. "

" Then according to yᵉ Order of Yeſterday the Houſe reſumed
" yᵉ adjourned Debate about a Place for the Colledge & yᵉ Rector
" & divers of the Governors of the Colledge who attended alſo
" according to Order, were called into the Houſe where yᵉ ſᵈ
" Rector having given a ſhort Accoᵗ of yᵉ Reaſons, why Libertie
" was left to the Aſſembly in their Majᵗˢ Charter to make Choice
" of another Place if they thought fit, & read & preſented a Me-
" moriall concerning four Places vizᵗ *Middle Plantation*, *Yorke*
" *Towne*, *Yorke Old Fields*, & *Greens* Land in *Glocester* County as
" proper Places for ſuch an Uſe with a Narratiue of yᵉ Conveni-
" ences & Inconveniences of each they ſeverally wᵗʰ drew and
" the Houſe tooke yᵉ whole Matter under Conſideracon, & there-
" in having ſpent ſome Time. . . .

" *Reſolued* yᵗ it is the Opinion of the Houſe that *Middleplanta-*
" *tion* is the moſt convenient & fit Place to erect the Colledge
" upon & that a Byll be prepared for erecting the ſame at that
" Place, as near the Church as Convenience will permit. "

[60]

William   Waller   Hening, THE   STATUTES   AT
LARGE (*Philadelphia: Thomas Deſilver*, 1823), Vol.
III, p. 122.

" *An Act Aſcertaining the Place for erecting the College*
" *of* William and Mary *in* Virginia. "

[61]

H. R. McIlwaine, ed., *JOURNALS OF THE HOUSE
OF   BURGESSES   OF   VIRGINIA*,   *1659/60-1693*
(*Richmond:* 1914), p. 368.

" *Wedneſday May* yᵉ 20ᵗʰ 1691. "

" To their moſt Excellᵗ Maᵗⁱᵉˢ *Wᵐ & Mary*| by yᵉ Grace of *God*
" of *England, Scotland, France, Ireland,* & *Virgᵃ* . . .
" The humble Supplication of yᵉ Generall Aſſembly of *Virgᵃ*
" Wee the Lᵗ Governʳ Councill & Burgeſſes of this General Aſ-
" ſembly which is the firſt ſince your Maᵗⁱᵉˢ moſt gracious & happy
" Reigne over us being encouraged by yoʳ princely Zeall for pro-
" motingReligion & Vertue, and incited by yᵉ urgent Neceſſities
" of this yoʳ Maᵗⁱᵉˢ Dominion, where our Youth is deprived of the
" Benefitt of a liberal & vertuous Education, and many of our
" Pariſhes of that Inſtruction & Comfort which might be expected
" from

" from a pious & learned Miniftry have unanimoufly refolved as
" the beft Remedy for thofe great Evills, and as the moft fuitable
" Expreffion wee can make of our hearty Concurrence with your
" Maties in fupporting the *Proteftant* Religion, & the Church of
" *England*, humbly to fupplicate yor Maties for your royall Grant
" & Charter to erect & endow a free Schoole & Colledge within
" this yor Maties Dominion, as to the Perticulars relateing to the
" f^d Defygne wee have given our Inftructions to the Reverend
" Mr *James Blayre* whome wee have appointed to prefent this our
" humble Supplication, & to attend & receive your Maties Com-
" ands thereupon, but fince wee defygne that our intended free
" Schoole & Colledge together with Learning and Vertue may
" convey to future Generations the Memory of our Obligacons to
" your Maties . . . wee humbly pray that the faid Schoole &
" Colledge may tranfmitt to our Pofterity thofe Names which are
" fo deare & aufpicious to us, and may accordingly be called the
" Colledge of King *William* and Queen *Mary*, . . ."

[62]

*WILLIAM AND MARY COLLEGE QUARTERLY
HISTORICAL MAGAZINE, Firft Series*, Vol. VII
(1899), p. 165.

" At the Court at *Whitehall* the
" 10 of *March* 1691/2 . . .

" Upon reading the Peticon of *Edwd Davies*, *John Hinfon*
" and *Lionel Delawafer*, . . . and it appearing by the Report of
" the Right Hono^{ble} the Lords Comm^rs of the Treafury that y^e
" Pet^rs by writing under their Hands had own'd themfelves to be
" Pirats & had claim'd the Benefitt of a Proclamacon iffued by
" the late King *James* for the Suppreffion of Pirats and Privateers
" in *America*, by Force or Affurance of Pardon but had not
" ftrictly comply'd with the Conditions of the faid Proclamacon
" and the Pet^rs being willing that the Sum or Value of three
" Hundred Pounds of the Goods belonging unto them and now
" lying in their Maties Warehoufe together with the fourth Part of
" w^t fhall be recovered belonging to the Pet^rs from the faid Capt
" *Rowe* or his Execut^rs fhall be employ'd towards the Erecting a
" Colledg or free Schoole in *Virginia*. . . ."

Alfo:

Ibid., *Firft Series*, Vol. VIII (1900), pp. 169-170.
[Building Account. Board of Trade, *Virginia*, Vol.
6. 1694-1697.]

" By

" By their Maj⋅ Guift, . . . [£] 1983 : 14 : 10 . . .
" By Money obtained of the Privateers [£] 300 : 00 : 00."

[63]

*H. R. McIlwaine, ed., EXECUTIVE JOURNALS
OF THE COUNCIL OF COLONIAL VIRGINIA
(Richmond: 1925), Vol. I, p. 334.*

" *July* the 25ᵗʰ 1695."

" His Excellency was pleafed to acquaint the Councill that
" Capt *Miles Cary* Rector of the College of *William and Mary*
" did inform him that the Comittee had appointed *Thurfday*
" the eight of *Auguft* next for the Laying the Foundation of the
" faid College and prayed his Excellencys Company at that
" Time, . . . "

[64]

*William Stevens Perry, PAPERS RELATING TO
THE HISTORY OF THE CHURCH IN VIR-
GINIA, A. D. 1650-1776 (Privately printed: 1870),
pp. 55-56.*

[65]

*Hugh Jones, THE PRESENT STATE OF VIRGINIA
(London: J. Clarke, 1724), p. 26.*

" The Buiiding is beautiful and commodious, being firft
" modeled by Sir *Chriftopher Wren*, adapted to the Nature of
" the Country by the Gentlemen there; . . . "

[66]

*VIRGINIA MAGAZINE OF HISTORY & BI-
OGRAPHY,* Vol. II (1895), pp. 158-159. Inftructions
to Governor *Yeardley*, 1618.

" The Treafurer and Company of Adventurers and Planters
" of the City of *London* for the firft Colony in *Virginia*. To Cap-
" tain *George Yeardley* Elect Governor of *Virginia* and to the
" Council of State therein being or to be Greeting.
" . . . And whereas by a fpecial Grant and Licenfe from his
" Majefty a general Contribution over this Realm hath been
" made for the Building and Planting of a College for the Training
" up of the Children of thofe Infidels in true Religion moral
" Virtue

" Virtue and Civility and for other Godly Uſes.   We do therefore
" according to a former Grant and Order hereby ratify, confirm
" and ordain that a convenient Place be choſen and ſet out for
" the Planting of a Univerſity at the ſaid *Henrico* in Time to
" come, and that in the mean Time Preparation be there made
" for the Building the ſaid College for the Children of the Infidels
" according to ſuch Inſtructions as we ſhall deliver.   And we
" will and ordain that ten Thouſand Acres partly of the Lands
" they impaled and partly of other Land within the Territory of
" the ſaid *Henrico* be allotted and ſet out for the Endowing of the
" ſaid Univerſity and College with ſufficient Poſſeſſons."

Alſo:

Suſan M. Kingſbury, ed., *THE RECORDS OF THE
    VIRGINIA COMPANY OF LONDON (Waſhing-
    ton: Government Printing Office*, 1906), Vol. I, pp. 220-
    221, 234.

Alſo:

Captaine *John Smith, THE GENERALL HISTORIE
    OF VIRGINIA, NEW-ENGLAND, AND THE
    SUMMER ILES (London:* 1629.   Reprinted *Rich-
    mond, Va.: The Franklin Preſs*, 1819), Vol. II, pp.
    39, 40, 60 and 75.

[67]

*William Stith, THE HISTORY OF THE FIRST
    DISCOVERY AND SETTLEMENT OF VIR-
    GINIA (Williamſburg: William Parks*, 1747), pp.
    211, 217.

[p. 217].   " . . . The College People alſo received a great and deadly
" Slaughter in the Maſſacre; which, together with the Death of
" Mr. *Thorpe*, their grand Principle of Life and Action, cauſed
" them to abandon the College Lands, and to retire lower down
" the River, to ſuch Places as were more defenſible againſt the
" ſudden Aſſaults and Inroads of the *Indians*, becauſe of the
" greater Numbers of People, and the nearer Situation, and more
" ready Aſſiſtance, of other Plantations.   Thus did that brutiſh
" and unhappy People tear up, as it were, with their own Hands,
" the Foundations, which had been laid, for their Converſion to
" *Chriſtianity* and Civility of Life.   For altho' the Company, in
" *London*, did afterwards frequently enter upon ſerious Conſulta-
                                                                    " tion

" tion, about reftoring again and fetting forward this charitable
" Work, yet by Reafon of their own Troubles, and of the Factions
" and Difcords among themfelves, Nothing therein was ever
" brought to Effect. So that, from this Time, there was no publick
" Attempt, nor any School or Inftitution, purpofely defigned for
" their Education and Converfion, before the Benefaction of the
" late Honourable *Robert Boyle*, Efq; which fhall be fully related,
" in its proper Time and Place. "

[68]

Nathaniel B. Shurtleff, ed., *RECORDS OF THE
GOVERNOR AND COMPANY OF THE MASSA-
CHUSETTS BAY IN NEW ENGLAND* (*Bofton:
William White*, 1853), Vol. I, pp. 183, 208, 253.

[*October* 28th 1636.] " The Court agreed to give 400l towards a
" Schoale or Colledge, whearof 200l to bee paid the next Yeare,
" & 200l when the Worke is finifhed, & the next Court to appoint
" wheare & wt Building. "
[*November* 15th 1637.] " The Colledg is ordered to bee at *New-
" towne* [later called *Cambridge*.] "
[*March* 13, 1638/9.] " It is ordered, that the College agreed
" vpon formerly to bee built at *Cambridge* fhalbe called *Harvard*
" Colledge."

[69]

*WILLIAM & MARY COLLEGE QUARTERLY
HISTORICAL MAGAZINE, Firft Series*, Vol. XXV
(1917), p. 165.

[70]

H. R. McIlwaine, ed., *EXECUTIVE JOURNALS
OF THE COUNCIL OF COLONIAL VIRGINIA*
(*Richmond:* 1925), Vol. I, pp. 392-393.

" At a Councill held at *James City* the 20th *October* 1698.
" His Excellency takeing into ferious Confideration the un-
" fortunate Accident which this Day happened to the State
" Houfe by being burnt down & the publick Records & Papers
" of this Countrey (there kept) which were forced to be hurryed
" out & thrown into Heaps & defireing the Opinion of the Coun-
" cill what prefent Care fhould be taken thereof likewife called
" into the Councill Chamber fuch of the noted Gentlemen of this
" Countrey as were prefent in Town . . . "

[71]

[71]

H. R. McIlwaine, ed., *JOURNALS OF THE HOUSE OF BURGESSES OF VIRGINIA, 1695-1702 (Richmond:* 1913), pp. 166-167.

" *Thurſday May* 18th 1699. "

" A Meſſage from his Excellency [Governor *Francis Nicholſon*] in
" writeing by Mr *Harriſon* was read at the Table as followeth . . .
    " ' You having deſired me to continue my Favour in generall to
" this his Majeſties Colony and Dominion of *Virginia* but par-
" ticularly to the Colledge is another very great Obligation vpon
" me for my Vſeing all lawfull Wayes and Meanes for the Pro-
" moteing and Supporting the Good of them, and therefore I do
" now cordially recomend to you the Placeing of yor publick
" Building (weh *God* willing you are deſigned to have) ſomewhere
" at *Middle Plantation* nigh his Majeſties Royall Colledg of *Wil-*
" *liam and Mary* which I think will tend to *Gods* Glory, his
" Majeſties Service, and the Welfare and Proſperity of yor Coun-
" try in generall and of the Colledge in particular . . . ' "

Alſo:

[*Robert Beverley*], *THE HISTORY OF THE PRESENT STATE OF VIRGINIA (London: R. Parker,* 1705), Part I, p. 98.

" 147. Soon after his [*Francis Nicholſon's*] Acceſſion to the
" Government, he cauſed the Aſſembly, and Courts of Judica-
" ture, to be remov'd from *James-Town*, where there were good
" Accommodations for People, to *Middle-Plantation*, where
" there were none. . . . "

[72]

" An Act directing the Building the Capitoll and the
" City of *Williamſburgh.* "

This Act is given in full on pp. 335-343.

[73]

See Appendix, Page 338.

[74]

William Waller Hening, *THE STATUTES AT LARGE (New York: R. & W. & G. Bartow,* 1823), Vol. II, p. 515.

" ' Enquiries

"' Enquiries to the Governor of *Virginia*' fubmitted by the
" Lords Commiffioners of Foreign Plantations. [Thefe Enquiries
" were propounded in the Year 1670, and received their Anfwers
" in 1671, while Sir *William Berkeley* was Governor of *Virginia*.]
" . . .

" 15. What Number of Planters, Servants and Slaves; and
" how many Parifhes are there in your Plantation?

" *Anfwer.* We fuppofe, and I am very fure we do not much
" mifcount, that there is in *Virginia* above forty Thoufand Per-
" fons, Men, Women and Children, and of which there are two
" Thoufand black Slaves, fix Thoufand Chriftian Servants, . . ."

Alfo:

W. Noel Sainfbury, ABSTRACTS [of *Virginia* Manufcripts in *Britifh Public Record Office, &c.*] *Virginia
State Library* Archives, *Richmond*. Vol. V, p. 302.

[75]
See Appendix, Pages 335-343.

[76]
H. R. McIlwaine, ed., *JOURNALS OF THE HOUSE
OF BURGESSES OF VIRGINIA, 1695-1702 (Rich-
mond:* 1913), pp. 168, 170.

[*Note:* After fome Difcuffion and feveral Amendments
thereto, the Bill directing the Building the Capitol
and the City of *Williamfburg* was paffed by the
Houfe of Burgeffes and the Council on *Wednefday,
June* 7th, 1699.]

[77]
See Petition of Inhabitants of *York* County, Page 12.

Alfo:

LIBRARY OF CONGRESS, Divifion of Manufcripts,
[Photo-films from the *Society for the Propagation of
the Gofpel in Foreign Parts, London.* Mifcellaneous,
p. 87.] A Speech delivered by a Student at the College
of *William and Mary*, on *May* 1, 1699.

" 2.

" 2. Here [*Middle Plantation*] is the greateſt Conveniency of
" eaſy Acceſs for great Numbers of People both by Land and
" Water of any in the whole Country. Firſt, I ſay, by Land, ffor
" all People will own it to be already the greateſt Thorough-fair
" in *Virginia*, Nature having ſo contriv'd it that by Reaſon of
" two deep unfordable Creeks, which extend themſelves from
" *James* and *York* Rivers, and almoſt meet at this Place, all
" Paſſengers in going up or down this moſt populous Part of the
" Country muſt travell through this Paſs, and the Roads leading
" to it from all Points of the Compaſs, are ſo good and level that
" Coaches and Waggons of the greateſt Burden have an eaſy and
" delightſome Paſſage.   Then by Water where is there ever an-
" other Place in the whole Country that opens ſo conveniently to
" two ſuch great Rivers, the moſt populous, the moſt rich, and
" the moſt frequented by Shipping in the whole Country.

" But before I have done with this Subject of the Water Con-
" veniency, I muſt deſire leave to take Notice of one Objeċtion,
" which I am ſenſible is in many Mens Minds and Mouths
" againſt the Place on this very Account.   It's true, ſay they, if
" thoſe two great Rivers came up with a due Depth & Boldneſs
" of Water, ſo as to bring Ships of the greateſt Burthen to the two
" Sides of a City here built, then indeed ye might boaſt of its op-
" ening it ſelf to two ſuch noble Rivers; but when all this Opening
" is reduced to two Creeks, navigable only by ſmall Craft that
" draw 6 or 7 Foot Water, it is no ſuch mighty Conveniency to
" boaſt of.   I think I have fairly ſtated the Objection and ſhall
" indeavour to give it as fair an Anſwer, by propoſing a few
" Things to your Conſideration. 1. That by removing two or
" three Bars of Sand, the Creeks can be made much deeper than
" they are. 2. That thoſe Creeks are really ſo deep & bold
" already that all the great and urgent Occaſions of any City may
" be very well ſerved by Veſſels that can ſail in them. For can't
" Proviſions, Fewal, and all other Commodities of the Country
" that are to be there expended, be as eaſily brought in Sloops &
" Shallops as in great Ships. . . . Sure I am that if Veſſells of
" the greateſt Burthen could come to the very Town, the Advan-
" tage would not countervail the Hazard & Diſadvantage of it;
" ffor ſuch a Town if once it became a Place of Wealth and Riches,
" would ly open to the great Gunns and Bombs of any Enemies
" Men of War, and ſo to be fired or torne in Pieces by theſe In-
" ſtruments of Deſolation and Miſery, as the wealthy City of
" *Genoa* was ruined in this Manner not many Years agoe by the
" *French.* "

[78]

WILLIAM & MARY COLLEGE QUARTERLY HISTORICAL MAGAZINE, Firſt Series, Vol. X (1902), pp. 75-77.

[A Defcription of the firſt Survey of *Willamſburg* made by *Theodorick Bland* in 1699. A photoſtatic Copy of the Survey itſelf, from the Original in the *Public Record Office, London*, is in the *Reſearch Department, Colonial Williamſburg*, Incorporated, and an Engraving made from it appears oppoſite Page 16 of this Volume.]

[79]

THE CHURCH REVIEW, AND ECCLESIASTICAL REGISTER, Vol. VIII (1856), p. 597.

" *Sketches of* Bruton *Pariſh*, Williamſburg, Virginia," by the Rev. *John C. McCabe.* [See Note 13].
" . . . in 1699, the Church again ſtands in Need of Repairs, " which are ordered. . ."

[8c]

H. R. McIlwaine, ed., *JOURNALS OF THE HOUSE OF BURGESSES OF VIRGINIA, 1659-93 (Richmond:* 1914), p. 73.

" [1676] It is ordered that . . . the Armes and Ammunicon . . .
" remayne in the publique Magazine, att the *Middle Planticon*,
" vntill the next Aſſembly, . . ."

[81]

See Note 8

[82]

See Appendix Pages 338-343.

[83]

Hugh Jones, THE PRESENT STATE OF VIRGINIA (*London:* Printed for *J. Clarke*, 1724), p. 25.

" . . . When

" . . . When the State Houſe and Priſon were burnt down, Gov-
" ernor *Nicholſon* removed the Reſidence of the Governor, with
" the Meeting of General Courts and General Aſſemblies to *Mid-*
" *dle Plantation*, ſeven Miles from *James Town*, in a healthier and
" more convenient Place, and freer from the Annoyance of Muſ-
" kettoes.

" Here he laid out the City of *Williamſburgh* (in the Form of a
" Cypher, made of *W*. and *M*.) on a Ridge at the Head Springs of
" two great Creeks, one running into *James*, and the other into
" *York* River, which are each navigable for Sloops, within a Mile
" of the Town; . . . "

[84]

[*Robert Beverley*], *THE HISTORY AND PRESENT
STATE OF VIRGINIA* (*London:* Printed for *R.
Parker*, 1705), Part I, pp. 98-99.

" 147.   Soon after his [Governor *Nicholſon's*] Acceſſion to the
" Government, he cauſed the Aſſembly, and Courts of Judica-
" ture, to be remov'd from *James-Town*, where there were good
" Accommodations for People, to *Middle-Plantation*, where there
" were none.   There he flatter'd himſelf with the fond Imagina-
" tion, of being the Founder of a new City.   He mark'd out the
" Streets in many Places, ſo as that they might repreſent the
" Figure of a *W*, in Memory of his late Majeſty King *William*,
" after whoſe Name the Town was call'd *Williamſburg*.   There
" he procur'd a ſtately Fabrick to be erected, which he placed
" oppoſite to the College, and graced it with the magnificent
" Name of the Capitol. "

Alſo:

[*John Oldmixon*], *THE BRITISH EMPIRE IN
AMERICA* (*London:* Printed for *J. Brotherton*, 1741,
Second Edition), Vol. I, p. 407.

" . . . Here . . . Col. *Nicholſon* . . . cauſed a State-houſe or
" Capital to be erected, and ſeveral Streets to be laid out in the
" Form of a *W*; but we do not find that a *V*, or one Angle of it
" is yet finiſh'd, or ever likely to be ſo."

[85]

See APPENDIX Page 339.

Alſo:

Alſo:

Hugh Jones, THE PRESENT STATE OF VIRGINIA
(*London:* Printed for *J. Clarke*, 1724), p. 28.

[86]

See APPENDIX Page 339.

Alſo:

Plat of the City of *Williamſburg*, circa 1800.　Original
in *William & Mary* College Library, *Williamſburg*.

[87]

H. R. McIlwaine, ed., *JOURNALS OF THE HOUSE
OF BURGESSES OF VIRGINIA, 1702-1712* (*Richmond:* 1912), pp. 55, 61, 69.

[p. 55]　　　　　　　　　" *Thurſday April* 27ᵗʰ 1704."

" A written Meſſage from his Exᶜʸ [Governor *Nicholſon*] . . .
" I recommend to you to give Directions that the old Houſe
" belonging to Mʳ *John Page* ſtanding in the Middle of *Glouceſter*
" Street be pulled downe that the Proſpect of the Street between
" the Capitol and Colledge may be cleer and that you take Care
" to pay what you ſhall judge thoſe Houſes to be worth."

[p. 69]　　　　　　　　　" *Fryday May* the 5ᵗʰ 1704."

" *Ordered* That the Sume of three Pounds be paid to Mʳ *John*
" *Page* out of the Money in Mʳ Treaſurers Hands from the late
" Impoſitions on Liquors Servants and Slaves—
" *Ordered* That Mʳ *Henry Cary* forthwith ſett the Labourers
" imployed about the Building the Capitol to pull down the four
" old Houſes and Oven belonging to Mʳ *John Page* which ſtand
" in *Glouceſter* Street and have been appraiſed and that they lay
" the Bricks out of the Street on the Lott of the ſaid *John Page.*"

[88]

See APPENDIX Pages 336-338.

[89]

H. R. McIlwaine, ed., *EXECUTIVE JOURNALS
OF THE COUNCIL OF COLONIAL VIRGINIA*
(*Richmond:* 1927), Vol. II, p. 61.

" At

" At *James Citty April* 24 1700. . . .

" The Truſtees and Governours of the Colledge of *William and*
" *Mary* in *Virginia* having made an Offer to his Excellency and
" the Councill of whatſoever Roomes within the ſaid Colledge
" ſhall be wanted for the Uſe of the Country to hold their gen-
" erall Meetings and Aſſemblyes till the Capitoll be built and
" fitted for that Purpoſe, it is thereupon reſolved and accord-
" ingly ordered, that the preſent Generall Court (at the End
" thereof) ſhall be adjourned to ſitt at the ſaid Clledge in
" *October* next. "

Alſo:

The General Aſſembly met in the College of *William
and Mary* from *December* 5, 1700 until *April* 21, 1704,
when the Aſſembly met for the firſt Time in the new
Capitol at *Williamſburg.* (See *The Journals of the
Houſe of Burgeſſes of Virginia* and the *Legiſlative
Journals of the Council of Colonial Virginia.*)

[90]

William Stevens Perry, PAPERS RELATING TO
THE HISTORY OF THE CHURCH IN VIR-
GINIA, A. D. 1650-1776 (Privately printed: 1870),
p. 134. " *The further Affidavit of* James Blair, *Clerk,*
" *concerning Gov* Nicholſon's *mal-Adminiſtration,* . . .
" *May* 1ſt 1704 . . .

" . . . I have heard him [*Nicholſon*] ſwear that he would ſeize
" the College for the King's Uſe & he crowded into it, the Secre-
" tary's Office, the Clerk of the Council's Office, the Clerk of the
" Houſe of Burgeſſes' Office & all their Lodgings, with himſelf & all
" the Committees, & had all his public Treats in their Hall to the
" great Diſturbance of the College Buſineſs. As to the Finiſhing
" Part of the College, he did ſo exceſſively hurry it on for thoſe
" ſeveral Uſes, that partly by the Plank & Timber being green
" & unſeaſoned & partly by employing a great Number of
" unſkillful Workmen to comply with his Haſte, it was ſhame-
" fully ſpoilt, . . . "

[91]

PUBLIC RECORD OFFICE, London, C. O. 5/1314.

[Photoſtatic

[Photoftatic Copy in *Refearch Department, Colonial Williamfburg* Foundation.]

" This Depo^t further faith that about the Midle of *July* 1702
" he this Depo^t with Cap^{tn} *Dove, Roffey, Midleton*, the Captains
" of the Convoys then there, with our Officers was fent for by the
" Governour [*Nicholfon*], to come to *Williamfburgh* to the Procla-
" mation of her Maj^{tie} where was moft of the principale People
" of the Country. This Depo^t faith that next Morning affter the
" Proclamation, the Governour and he walking in fome of the
" uper Appartments of the Colledge, this Depo^t defired the Gov-
" ernour to order the Money to be paid for Carreening the Ship
" as he had promifed this Depo^t in Regard the Fleet was to faile
" for *England*, . . . But before this Depo^t could make an End
" of Speaking, the Governour flew out into fuch a Paffion againft
" the Comiff^{rs} of the Navy calling them all the bafeft Names that
" the Tongue of Man could exprefs, & with fuch a Noife, that the
" People downe in the lower Roomes caime running up Stairs, &
" likewife Capt *Dove, Roffey & Midleton*, who lay in a Roome
" fome Diftance, caime running out of their Beds in their Shirts,
" the latter with out his wooden Leg holding himfelfe by the Wall
" beleiveing that ye Colledge had been on Fire a gaine as it had
" been two Nights before, but upon Enquirey of the Ocafion,
" could but admire at the Folly & Paffion of the Governour,
" faying *Bedlam* was the fitteft Place for fuch a Man, . . . "

[92]

William Waller Hening, THE STATUTES AT
LARGE *(Philadelphia: Thomas Defilver*, 1823), Vol.
III, pp. 285-287. " *An Act directing the Building an*
" *Houfe for the Governor of this Colony and Dominion.*"

[This Act was paffed on *June* 22^d, 1706. See *Journals
   of the Houfe of Burgeffes of Virginia, 1702-1712*, p.
   234.]

" WE, her Majeftys moft dutifull and loyall Subjects, the
" Burgeffes now affembled, having taken into our ferious Con-
" fideration her Majefty's Commands concerning the Building of
" an Houfe for the Governor of this her Majeftys Colony and Do-
" minion, and how neceffary it is that fuch an Houfe be built
" without any further Delay, have cheerfully and unanimoufly
" given and granted unto her moft excellent Majefty, the Sum of
                                                              " three

" three Thoufand Pounds, to be employed, made ufe of and
" expended according to the Directions of this Act hereafter
" mentioned, and do humbly pray your Excellency it may be
" enacted,

"*And be it enacted by the Governor, Council and Burgeffes, of*
" *this prefent General Affembly, and it is hereby enacted, by the*
" *Authority of the fame*, That an Houfe for the Refidence of
" the Governor of this Colony and Dominion, be with all conveni-
" ent Expedition erected, built, and finifhed upon the Land bought
" of *Henry Tyler*, joyning to the City of *Williamfburgh*, or upon fo
" many of the next adjacent Lotts laid out for the City of *Wil-*
" *liamfburg*, as to the Directors of the faid City fhall feem moft
" fitt and convenient, or upon either or both of them, and that
" the faid Land containing fixty-three Acres, and lying on the north
" Side of the faid City, together with the forementioned Lotts,
" and the faid Houfe, and all and fingular the Appurtenances,
" fhall from Time to Time, and at all Times hereafter, be held
" and enjoyed by the Governor or Commander in Chief of this
" Dominion, for the Time being, for ever to his own proper Ufe
" and Behoof, and fhall not be applyed to any other Ufe what-
" foever.

" And that the faid Houfe be built of Brick, fifty-four Foot
" in Length, and forty-eight Foot in Breadth, from Infide to In-
" fide, two Story high, with convenient Cellars underneath, and
" one Vault, Safh Windows, of Safh, Glafs and a Covering of
" Stone Slate, and that in all other Refpects the faid Houfe be
" built and finifhed according to the Difcretion of the Overfeer,
" which fhall be employed by Virtue of this Act to take care of
" the fame, under the Direction of the Governor and Councill.

" *And be it further enacted*, That a Kitchen and Stable, fuit-
" able for fuch an Houfe be likewife built upon the Land before
" mentioned, according to the Difcretion of the faid Overfeer,
" and by the Direction aforefaid.

" *And be it further enacted*, That for the more eafy and better
" Building and Finifhing the aforefaid Houfe and out Houfes, the
" faid Overfeer have full Power to fend for *England* for Iron Work,
" Glafs, Lead, Stone, Slate, or any other Neceffarys to be made
" ufe of in or about the faid Buildings, and that the fame be im-
" ported at the Rifque of the Country, and alfo on the like
" Rifque to buy fuch and fo many Slaves, Horfes, Carts, and
" other Materials as in his Difcretion he fhall think fitt, for the
" more expeditious and cheap Carrying on the faid Work. . . .

" *And be it further enacted*, That *Henry Cary* be appointed,
" . . . an

" . . . an Overfeer to infpect, overfee, and provide for the Build-
" ing aforefaid, with full Power to begin, carry on, and finifh the
" fame, according to the Directions of this Act, . . . "

[93]

H. R. McIlwaine, ed., *LEGISLATIVE JOURNALS OF THE COUNCIL OF COLONIAL VIRGINIA* (*Richmond:* 1918), Vol. I, pp. 73-74, 81, 83, 85, 447, 448.

Alfo:

H. R. McIlwaine, ed., *JOURNALS OF THE HOUSE OF BURGESSES OF VIRGINIA, 1695-1702* (*Richmond:* 1913), pp. 146, 174-175; *1702-1712* (*Richmond:* 1912), pp. 130, 177, 180.

[94]

H. R. McIlwaine, ed., *EXECUTIVE JOURNALS OF THE COUNCIL OF COLONIAL VIRGINIA,* 1705-1721 (*Richmond:* 1928), Vol. III, p. 247.

" At a Council held at the Capitol the 23ᵈ Day of *June* 1710
" *Prefent* The Honᵇˡᵉ *Alexander Spotfwood* Efqʳ her Majeftys
" Lieutenant Governor . . .
" Her Majeftys Commiffion under the Great Seal of *Great*
" *Brittain* conftituting & appointing the Right Honᵇˡᵉ *George* Earl
" of *Orkney* her Majeftys Lieutenant and Governor General of
" this her Colony and Dominion of *Virginia* together with her
" Majeftys Commiffion under her Royal Sign Manual and Signett
" dated the 18ᵗʰ of *February* 1709/10 conftituting and appoint-
" ing the Honᵇˡᵉ *Alexander Spotfwood* Efqʳ Lieutenant Govern-
" or of this her Majeftys faid Colony were this Day opened in
" Council. . ."

[95]

H. R. McIlwaine, ed., *JOURNALS OF THE HOUSE OF BURGESSES OF VIRGINIA, 1702-1712* (*Richmond:* 1912), pp. 43-44.

" *Fryday April* 21ᵗʰ 1704
" Mr. Speaker and thirty three Burgeffes being mett at the
" Capitoll in a Room appointed for the Burgeffes to fit in . . .
" A

" A Meſſage from his Excelly by Mr *Robertſon* . . .

" His Excelly commands the imediate Attendance of this " Houſe upon him in the Council Chamber.

" And accordingly the Houſe went to attend his Excelly . . . " his Excelly was pleaſed to make a Speech . . . as followeth.

" ' Honble Gentl.

" ' *God* Almighty I hope will be gratiouſly pleaſed ſo to direct " guide, and enable us, as that we may to all Intents and " Purpoſes anſwer her Majeſts Writt by which this Aſſembly " was called and by Prorogation is now mett. in this her " Majeſty Queen *Anne* her Royall Capitol. . . ' "

[96]

Ibid., pp. 174-175.

" *Thurſday November* the 29th 1705. "

" *Reſolved* That Mr *Henry Cary* the Overſeer of the Building " of the Capitol and the ſeveral Workmen employed about the " ſame be on *Wedneſday* next diſcharged. . . .

" *Reſolved* That the four Maſter Keys to the Locks of the " Capitol in the Hands of Mr *Henry Cary* Mr *William Robertſon* " and Mr *Charles Chiſwell* be called in & deſtroyed. "

[97]

Ibid., p. 240.

" *Thurſday October* 26th 1710. "

" . . . the Governor [*Spotſwood*] was pleaſed to make a " Speech, . . . as follows

" ' Gentlemen . . . I am comand[ed] to put you in Mind of ap- " propriating a farther Sume of Mony for the ſpeedy perfecting " the Governors Houſe. This is a Matter in which your own " Honour is now ſo far engaged, that I no Ways doubt of your " ready Complyance, the ſame Reaſons which prevailed for the " Beginning, do now doubly plead for the Finiſhing of it and as " you deſigned it for an honourable Reception, ſo I hope you no " leſs intend to make it a comodious one. ' "

Alſo:

William Waller Hening, THE STATUTES AT LARGE (*Philadelphia: Thomas Deſilver*, 1823), Vol. III, pp. 482-486. " *An Act for finiſhing a Houſe for* " *the Governor of this Colony and Dominion.* "

[Act

[Act paffed *December* 9, 1710. See *Journals of the House of Burgeffes, 1702-1712*, p. 298.]

" WHEREAS by an Act of Affembly, made at a General
" Affembly, begun at the Capitol the twenty-third Day of *Octo-*
" *ber*, in the fourth Year of the Reign of our Sovereign Lady
" *Anne*, Queen of *Great-Britain*, *France* and *Ireland*, and in the
" Year of our Lord 1705, intituled *An Act directing the Building a*
" *Houfe for the Governor of this Colony and Dominion*, a Houfe ac-
" cording to the Dimenfions, Difcriptions and Directions, in
" the faid Act mentioned and given, together with a Kitchen
" and Stable, fuitable to the faid Houfe, for the Refidence of the
" Governor of this Colony and Dominion, was directed to be built
" and finifhed on the Land therein mentioned; which faid Houfe,
" Kitchen and Stable not being finifhed according to the Direc-
" tions of the faid Act;

" Wee, her Majefties moft dutiful and loyal Subjects, the Bur-
" geffes, now affembled, having ferioufly confidered the Necef-
" fity of finifhing the faid Houfe and the great Delay that hath
" happened in perfecting the fame, have chearfully and unani-
" moufly given and granted unto her moft gracious Majeftie the
" Sum of fifteen Hundred and fixty Pounds, to be employed, made
" ufe of and expended in finifhing and compleating the faid
" Houfe, Kitchen and Stable, according to the Directions in the
" faid Act given, and do humbly pray your Honour it may be
" enacted.

" *And be it enacted by the Lieut. Governor, Council and Burgeffes*
" *of this General Affembly, and it is hereby enacted by the Author-*
" *ity of the fame,* That the faid Houfe, Kitchen and Stable be
" finifhed and compleated according to the Directions laid down
" and given in the faid Act of Affembly, with all convenient Ex-
" pedition for the Ufes and Purpofes therein mentioned.

" And whereas, for rendering the faid Houfe more compleat
" and commodious for the Reception of the Governor ot this
" antient Colony and Dominion, feverall Buildings, Gardens
" and other Ornaments and Things are further neceffary and
" convenient to be made and done; therefore we, the Burgeffes
" aforefaid, taking the fame into our ferious Confideration, have
" freely and unanimoufly given and granted unto her moft gra-
" cious Majeftie the further Sum of fix Hundred thirty-five
" Pounds, to be employed, laid out and made ufe of according to
" the Directions in this Act, hereafter mentioned, and do humbly
" pray your Honour it may be enacted.

" *And*

" *And be it enacted by the Authority aforesaid*, That a Court-
" yard, of Dimentions proportionable to the said House, be laid
" out, levelled and encompassed with a Brick Wall four Foot high,
" with Balluftrades of Wood thereupon, on the said Land, and
" that a Garden of the Length of two Hundred fifty-four Foot
" and of the Breadth of one Hundred forty-four Foot from out
" to out, adjoining to the said House, be laid out and levelled and
" enclosed with a Brick Wall, four Foot high, with Balluftrades of
" Wood upon the said Wall, and that handsome Gates be made
" to the said Court-yard and Garden, and that a convenient
" Kitchen Garden be laid out on the said Land and be enclosed
" with Pailes, and that an Orchard and Pafture Ground be made
" on the said Land and be enclosed with a good Ditch and Fence,
" and also that a House of Wood be built and finished for houfeing
" Cattle, and that a House of Wood for Poultry be built and
" finished, with a Yard thereto enclosed, on the said Land.

" *And be it further enacted*, That out of the Sume of six Hundred
" thirty-five Pounds, hereby given and granted to her Maj-
" eftie, the Sume of two Hundred and fifty Pounds shall be ex-
" pended and laid out in buying neceffary standing and orna-
" mentall Furniture for the said House, which Furniture shall be
" provided in this Country or sent for from *Great-Britain* by the
" Overfeer, hereinafter named, by the Direction and Appointment
" of the Lt. Governor or Commander in Chief of this Colony, for
" the Time being, and shall forever hereafter belong to and is
" hereby appropriated to the said House.

" *And be it further enacted*, That for a Supply of Money to begin,
" carry on and finish the aforesaid House, Stable, Kitchen, Court-
" yard, Garden, Orchard, Out-houses, and all other the Work
" herein directed to be made and done, and also to buy the Fur-
" niture aforesaid, the said Overfeer shall, from Time to Time, as
" Occafion shall require, make Application to his Honour the
" Lieut. Governor, or the Governor, or Commander in Chief of
" this Colony and Dominion, for the Time being, who, upon such
" Application, is hereby desired to iffue his Warrant upon the
" Admr. of the Eftate of the late Treafurer, & upon the prefent
" Treafurer of this Dominion, for so much Money as may be
" wanted untill the full Sum of fifteen Hundred and sixty Pounds
" and of six Hundred thirty-five Pounds shall be employed, made
" ufe of and expended in finishing the said House, Kitchen and
" Stable, and in making and finishing the Court-yard, Garden,
" Orchard, Out-houses, aforesaid, and all the Work herein before
" mentioned and directed to be made and done, and in buying
" the

" the faid Furniture, and the Charges thereupon accruing, and
" to and for no other Ufe or Ufes whatfoever.

" And for the more eafy, expeditious and cheap Carrying on
" the Building and Work aforefaid;

" *Be it enacted*, That the faid Overfeer have full Power to fend
" to *Great Brittain* for Iron-work, Glafs, Lead, or any other necef-
" fary Materials to be made ufe of in and about the faid Houfe
" and Work, and that the fame be imported at the Rifque of the
" Country, and on the like publick Rifque, to buy fuch and fo
" many Slaves, Horfes, Carts and other Neceffaries for Carrying
" on the faid Work as he, by and with the Approbation of the
" Lieut. Governor or Commander in Chief of this Colony and
" Dominion, for the Time being, and Council fhall think fitt.

" *And be it further enacted*, That *Henry Cary* be appointed, and
" is hereby appointed Overfeer to infpect, overfee and provide
" for the Building and all and fingular the Work and Things
" hereby directed to be made and done, with full Power to begin,
" carry on and finifh the fame, under and with the Direction of
" the Lieut. Governor or Commander in Chief of this Colony
" and Dominion, for the Time being and Council, . . . "

[98]

H. R. McIlwaine, ed., *JOURNALS OF THE HOUSE
OF BURGESSES OF VIRGINIA, 1712-1726 (Richmond:* 1912), p. 230.

" *Friday November* the 21ᵗ 1718."

" The Houfe refumed the adjourned Debate on the Inftruc-
" tions to *William Byrd* Agent for this Colony

" The faid Inftructions containing Articles againft the Lieu-
" tenant Governor were read in the Words following . . .

" 3 His Conftruction of the Law for finifhing the Governor's
" Houfe, whereby he lavifhes away the Country's Money con-
" trary to the Intent of the Law, and even beyond what the
" Words of the Law will bear, and hath hitherto refufed any
" Redrefs therein. . . . "

Alfo:

*PUBLIC RECORD OFFICE, LONDON. Colonial
Office* 5/1318. [Photoftatic Copy in *Refearch Department, Colonial Williamfburg* Foundation.]

" Copy of Colᵒ *Spotfwood's* Anfwer to the four Articles
" exhibited

" exhibited by the Burgeffes of *Virginia* in Maintenance
" of their Complaint againft him, contained in their late
" Addrefs to His Majefty *Anno* 1718."

[99]

H. R. McIlwaine, ed., *JOURNALS OF THE HOUSE
OF BURGESSES OF VIRGINIA, 1702-1712 (Richmond:* 1912), p. 139.

" *Wednefday October* y⁰ 31ˢᵗ 1705 "

" His Excly having with great Concern reprefented to the
" Council how neceffary it is that an Examination be made into
" the Occafion of that fad and deplorable Accident (which hap-
" pened the other Night) of burning *William and Mary* Colledge;
" the Council think fitt to appoint fix of their Members to take
" Examinations concerning that unhappy Difafter, . . . "

Alfo:

R. A. Brock, ed., *THE OFFICIAL LETTERS OF
ALEXANDER SPOTSWOOD (Richmond:* Pub-
lifhed by the *Virginia Hiftorical Society*, 1882), Vol.
I, pp. 17-18. Letter from Governor *Spotfwood* to
Mr. *Blathwayt, October* 23, 1710.

" . . . I muft, however, intreat you will be pleafed to ufe your
" Intereft that no new Draughts be made on the Quitt-rents of
" this Colony till her Maj'ftie's gracious Intentions for re-build-
" ing the College fhall be accomplifhed, . . . "

Ibid., Vol. II, p. 63. Letter from Governor *Spotfwood*
to the Bifhop of *London, March* 13, 1713.

" . . . We have in this Country a Colledge, founded by ye
" Bounty of their late Maj't's, King *William* and Queen *Mary*,
" and lately raif'd out of the Afhes by the Pity of our prefent
" Soveraign; but as fuch Undertakings, efpecially in new Coun-
" trys, wants many Affiftances to bring them to Perfection, fo
" this Work is yet far from being compleated. The Building
" ftill unfinifhed, and the Revenue too fmall to fupport the Num-
" ber of Mafters requifite for carrying Youth through a Courfe
" of Univerfity Studys. "

[100]

*Hugh Jones, THE PRESENT STATE OF VIRGINIA
(London: J. Clarke,* 1724), p. 26.

" The

" The Building is beautiful and commodious, being firſt
" modelled by Sir *Chriſtopher Wren*, adapted to the Nature of the
" Country by the Gentlemen there; and ſince it was burnt down,
" it has been rebuilt, and nicely contrived, altered and adorned
" by the ingenious Direction of Governor *Spotſwood;* and is not
" altogether unlike *Chelſea Hoſpital.* "

[101]

THE CHURCH REVIEW, AND ECCLESIASTICAL REGISTER, Vol. VIII (1856), p. 604. [See Note 13.]

" Att a Veſtry held the ffirſt Day of *October*, 1706.

" The Veſtry conſidering ye great Charge ye Pariſh hath been
" at for ye Repairing of ye Church, and how bad a Condition it
" is ſtill in,—Ordered, that twenty Thouſand Pounds of To-
" bacco be levied this Year for and towards building of a new
" Church. "

Alſo:

William P. Palmer, ed., *CALENDAR OF VIRGINIA STATE PAPERS*, *1652-1781* (Richmond: R. F. Walker, 1875), Vol. I, pp. 145-146.

[*November* 21ſt, 1710.] " To the Honble her Majties Lieut:

" Governr, the Honble Councill & Houſe of Burgeſſes.

" The Veſtry of the Pariſh of *Bruton*, humbly repreſents,

" That the preſent Pariſh Church now in the City of *Williamſ-*
" *burgh*, becoming ruinous, the Veſtry have reſolved to build a
" new one of the like Dimentions, wch is ſufficient for the Conveni-
" ency of the Pariſhionrs & have raiſed Money & intend to begin
" thereon accordingly.

" That 'tis very apparent the Pariſhionrs are very much
" ſtraightened & often outed of their Places & Seats, by diſpenc-
" ing with & allowing Room for the frequent Reſort of Strangers,
" & more perticularly at the Meetings of the Generall Aſſem-
" blies: Courts: Councells: & other publick Occaſions:

" . . . there is not Room, nor can they [the Veſtry] appropri-
" ate decent & fitting Places or Pews in the intended Church for
" the Reception of the Genll Aſſembly, and ſuch as have Occaſion
" to attend the public Services of the Country. Therefore, the
" Veſtry, before they proceed to build the intended Church take
" this Opportunity humbly to repreſent the ſame to this Honbl
" Aſſembly (if they pleaſe) for their generous Contribution to-
" wards the ſame: & that they will conſider of ſuch a Building
" as

" as in their Wifdoms fhall be thought proper for yᵉ faid Occa-
" fions, & to give Directions that a Draught thereof be laid before
" yoʳ Honoʳ dureing this Affembly: The Veftry on their Parts
" being willing to advance towards ye fame, what may be
" thought neceffary for the Building a fuitable Church for theiɪ
" Parifh. "

[102]

H. R. McIlwaine, ed., LEGISLATIVE JOURNALS OF THE COUNCIL OF COLONIAL VIRGINIA (Richmond: 1918), Vol. I, p. 508.

" *Tuefaay December* the 5ᵗʰ 1710 "

" A Meffage to the Governor . . . that the Houfe had refolved
" to give two Hundred Pounds, towards rebuilding the Parifh
" Church of *Bruton* in the City of *Williamfburgh* and prayed the
" Favour of his Honʳ to take the fᵈ Sum into his Hands, and to
" take the Trouble of laying it out for enlarging the fᵈ Church
" and building Pews for the Governor Council and Burgeffes, to
" which the Governor [*Spotfwood*] was pleafed to anfwer that he
" thanked the Houfe for the Confidence they had in him, that
" tho he had never been concerned in Bufinefs of this Nature, he
" would ufe his beft Endeavours to have yᵉ Money laid out to
" anfwer their Intentions "

Alfo:

THE CHURCH REVIEW, AND ECCLESIASTICAL REGISTER, Vol. VIII (1856), p. 608. [See Note 13.]

" At a Meeting of the Veftry, held for ye Parifh of *Bruton*,
" *March* 1ft, 1711, . . .
" Upon ye Information of *James Blair*, Clerk, that he had
" received from the Honble. *Alexr. Spotfwood*, a Platt or Draught
" of a Church, (whofe Length 75 Foot, and Bredth 28 Foot in the
" Clear, with two Wings, on each Side, whofe Width is 22 Foot,)
" which he laid before the Veftry for Approbation—Adding fur-
" ther, that ye Honble ye Governor propofed to the Veftry to
" build only 53 of the 75 Foot, and that he would take care for the
" remaining Part.
" The Veftry proceeded to the immediate Confideration of the
" Commodioufnefs and Conveniency of the faid Platt or Draught:
" which is approved of. "

[103]

[103]

Hugh Jones, THE PRESENT STATE OF VIRGINIA (London: J. Clarke, 1724), p. 30.

" Near the Middle ſtands the Church, which is a large ſtrong
" Piece of Brickwork in the Form of a Croſs, nicely regular and
" convenient, and adorned as the beſt Churches in *London*. This
" from the Pariſh is called *Bruton* Church, where I had the Fa-
" vour of being Lecturer. "

[104]

*William Waller Hening, THE STATUTES AT
LARGE (Richmond: Franklin Preſs, 1820), Vol. IV,
pp. 55-57. " An Act for erecting a Magazine "*
[1714] " I. WHEREAS our late Sovereign Lady Queen *Anne*,
" of her Grace and Bounty, was pleaſed to beſtow a conſiderable
" Quantity of Arms and Ammunition, for the Service of this
" Colony, which are in Danger to be imbezzled and ſpoilt, for
" Want of a convenient and proper Place to keep them in.
     " II. *Be it therefore enacted, by the Lieut. Governor, Council,*
" *and Burgeſſes, of this preſent General Aſſembly, ana it is*
" *hereby enactea by the Authority of the ſame,* That as ſoon as
" conveniently it may be done, there ſhall be erected and finiſhed
" one good ſubſtantial Houſe of Brick, which ſhall be called the
" Magazine, at ſuch Place as the Lieutenant-Governor ſhall think
" proper: In which Magazine, all the Arms, Gun-powder, and
" Ammunition, now in this Colony, belonging to the King, or
" which ſhall at any Time hereafter be, belonging to his Majeſty,
" his Heirs or Succeſſors, in this Colony, may be lodged and kept.
" For the Building and Finiſhing which Magazine, there ſhall be
" laid out and expended any Sum or Sums of Money, not exceed-
" ing two Hundred Pounds; to be levied and paid out of the
" Monies ariſing by the Duty on Liquors & Slaves, after the
" Monies already appropriated and ordered to be paid out of the
" ſaid Duty, are fully ſatisfied and paid: And the honourable
" the Lieutenant-Governor is hereby impowered and deſired to
" order and direct the Building the ſaid Magazine, . . . "

[105]

*H. R. McIlwaine, ed., JOURNALS OF THE HOUSE
OF BURGESSES OF VIRGINIA, 1712-1726 (Richmond: 1912), pp. 146, 151-152.*

[p. 151]

[p. 151]   " *Friday Auguſt* the 26th 1715."

" To the Honoᵇˡᵉ *Alexander Spotſwood* . . .
" The humble Addreſs of the Houſe of Burgeſſes

" May it pleaſe yoʳ Honoʳ

" We his Majeſtys moſt dutiful and loyal Subjeⱥs yᵉ Burgeſſes
" now aſſembled humbly beg Leave to repreſent to your Honour
" that we having conſidered the Grievance preſented to this
" Houſe from ſeveral of the Inhabitants of the County of *James*
" *City* that by Application of ffour of the Juſtices of the ſaid
" County the Court for the ſaid County is lately removed from
" *James City* to *Williamſburgh* which laſt mentioned Place being
" ſcituate at almoſt the extream End of the ſaid County is very
" inconvenient to the greateſt Number of the Inhabitants thereof
" whoſe Buſineſs requires their frequent Attendance at the ſaid
" Court more eſpecially to thoſe who reſide on the weſtern Side of
" the River *Chiccohominy* and divers of the ſaid Inhabitants hav-
" ing propoſed to this Houſe to ereⱥ a Court Houſe together with
" all other Buildings by Law required to be built as incident there-
" to at their own proper Coſt and Charge without burthening the
" People with a Levy for that Occaſion: If your Honour will be
" pleaſed to permitt the ſaid Court to be held at ſome other Place
" more convenient to the Inhabitants of the ſaid County than
" the City of *Williamſburgh*. . . . "

" *Saturday Auguſt* 27th 1715 "

" . . . his Honour was pleaſed to give this Anſwer *Vizt.*

" . . . To remove a County Court upon the Application of its
" Juſtices (as I have done) is expreſly according to the Law of
" this Colony, and I am not inclinable to do extraordinary Aⱥs
" meerly to gratify the Humour of ſome Perſons who make it
" their greateſt Meritt with the People to oppoſe whatever may
" be for the Intereſt and Dignity of this his Majeſtys Govern-
" ment. "

[106]

*Hugh Jones, THE PRESENT STATE OF VIRGINIA
(London: J. Clarke, 1724), pp. 30-31.*

[1724] " Near this [*Bruton* Church] is a large oⱥagon Tower,
" which is the Magazine or Repoſitory of Arms and Ammunition,
" ſtanding far from any Houſe except *James Town Court-Houſe;*
" for the Town is half in *James Town* County, and half in *York*
" County. "

[107]

[107]

H. R. McIlwaine, ed., *JOURNALS OF THE HOUSE OF BURGESSES OF VIRGINIA, 1712-1726* (*Richmond:* 1912), p. 283.

" *Monday November* the 28ᵗʰ 1720. "

" On Confideration of the Petition of the Inhabitants of the
" City of *Williamfburgh* complaining of the Irregularitys of their
" principal Street . . .
" *Refolved* That the Sum of one Hundred and fifty Pounds be
" given towards making Bridges and Caufeways in the main
" Street . . . "

[108]

On *November* 4 and 5, 1716, by Inftruments of Leafe and Releafe, *William Levingflon* obtained from the Truftees for the City of *Williamfburg* three Lots of Land " defigned in yᵉ Plott of yᵉ fᵈ City by thefe " Figures 163: 164 & 169," with the cuftomary Stipulation that "one good Dwelling Houfe or Houfes" be built upon each Lot within the Space of twenty-four Months, or the Land would revert to the Truftees for the City. (See *York County Records, Deeds, Bonds*, Book III, pages 204-206.) This Property did not revert to the Truftees for the City; for in 1721 there was a Deed of Mortgage between *William Levingflon* and *Archibald Blair* for Lots 163, 164, 169, 176 and 177 " together with yᵉ Bowl- " ing Green yᵉ Dwelling Houfe Kitchen & Play- " houfe & all yᵉ other Houfes Outhoufes & Stables " &c thereon. " (See *York County Records, Orders, Wills*, Book XV.) The following Agreement between *William Levingflon* and *Charles* and *Mary Stagg*, dated *July* 11, 1716, eftablifhes *Levingflon's* Intention of erecting a Playhoufe " with all con- " venient Speed ":

YORK COUNTY RECORDS, Orders, Wills, &c. Book XV (1716-1720), pp. 52-54.

" Articles

" Articles of Agreem^t indented, concluded & made ye elev-
" enth Day of *July* in ye Year of our Lord one Thousand seven
" Hundred & sixteen between *Wm Levingstone* of ye County of
" *New Kent* Merch^t of ye one Part & *Chas. Stagg* of ye same Coun-
" ty Dancing Master & *Mary* his Wife of ye other Part Whereas
" ye s^d *Charles Stagg* & *Mary* his Wife by two severall Indentures
" bearing Date ye twenty-third & twenty-fourth Days of *Septem^r*
" one Thousand seven Hundred & fifteen were bound to ye s^d
" *Wm Levingstone* to serve him in ye Colony of *Virg^a* in ye Arts,
" Professions & for ye Time in ye s^d Indentures mentioned & y^e
" s^d *Charles Stagg* having for his Advancement & greater Profit
" requested for himself & his s^d Wife to be free of ye Service
" mentioned in ye s^d Indentures. These Presents wittness that y^e
" s^d *Wm Levingstone* hath released & acquitted & doth hereby
" release & acquit ye s^d *Charles Stagg* & *Mary* his Wife of all
" Service, Claimes on Demand, which he ye s^d *Wm Levingstone* was
" or is any Ways intituled to by Virtue of ye s^d Indentures. . . .
" And it is further covenanted & agreed between ye s^d Parties
" in Manner & Form following, that is to say, that ye s^d *W^m*
" *Levingstone* & *Charles Stagg* shall with all convenient Speed after
" ye ensealing of these Presents use their best Endeavours to ob-
" tain a Patent or a Lycence from ye Governour of *Virg^a* for y^e
" sole Priviledge of acting Comedies, Drolls or other Kind of Stage
" Plays within any Part of ye s^d Colony not only for ye three
" Years next ensueing ye Date hereof but for as much longer
" Time as ye s^d Governour shall be pleased to grant ye same for y^e
" joint Benefit of ye s^d *Wm Levingstone* or *Charles Stagg* or their
" Assigns & neither of ye s^d Parties shall accept of or use such
" Lycence without assuming ye other as Partner in Manner aforesd.
" And ye s^d *Charles Stagg* & *Mary* his Wife do hereby covenant &
" promise that they ye s^d *Charles Stagg* & *Mary* shall not only act
" in ye s^d Stage Plays (Sickness & other reasonable Accidents ex-
" cepted) but shall also use their best Endeavours to teach & in-
" struct others in ye Way & Manner of acting according to ye best
" of their Skill. . . And ye s^d *Wm Levingstone* doth further covenent
" & agree with all convenient Speed to cause to be erected & built
" at his own proper Costs and Charge in ye City of *W^msburgh* one
" good substentiall House commodious for acting such Plays as
" shall be thought fitt to be acted there And it is further
" covenanted & agreed by & between ye s^d Parties that ye s^d
" *Wm Levingstone* & *Charles Stagg* shall bear an equall Share in
" all Charges of Cloaths Musick & other Necessaries required
" for acting ye s^d Plays (ye Rent of ye Play House at *W^msburgh* only
" excepted

" excepted which is declared as aforef⁴ to be yᵉ proper Charge
" of yᵉ fᵈ *Wᵐ Levingſtone*) & ſhall alſo have, receive & enjoy an
" equall Share of yᵉ Profits ariſing thereby.   And for as much
" as yᵉ fᵈ *Wᵐ Levingſtone* hath at his own proper Coſt & Charge
" ſent to *England* for Actors & Muſicians for yᵉ better Perform-
" ance of yᵉ fᵈ Plays, it is hereby covenanted & agreed by & be-
" tween yᵉ fᵈ Parties to theſe Preſents, that yᵉ Money ariſing by
" yᵉ fᵈ Plays yᵉ ſame Allowance ſhall be made both for yᵉ Muſi-
" cians & Actors as others equally qualifyed hired here in *Virgᵉ*
" ſhall or ought to receive by yᵉ Day or other Ways. . . .
"
"   *Cha. Stagg* [Seal]
"   *Mary Stagg* [Seal] "
" At a Court held for *York* County
" 19ᵗʰ Novʳ 1716. "

[109]

Hugh Jones, THE PRESENT STATE OF VIRGINIA
(*London: J. Clarke*, 1724). pp. ii-iii.

" . . . and this Country [*Virginia*] is altered wonder-
" fully, and far more advanced and improved in all Reſpects of
" late Years, ſince the Beginning of Colonel *Spotſwood's* Lieuten-
" ancy, than in the whole Century before his Government, which
" he may be eſteemed to have diſcharged with a commendable,
" juſt, and prudent Adminiſtration; a proſperous Adminiſtration,
" glorious for himſelf, and advantageous both for the Crown and
" the Plantation; whilſt he was Lieutenant-Governor of that
" Colony; whilſt that Colony was honoured with ſuch an excel-
" lent Governor; whilſt that Governor was happy in ſuch a
" flouriſhing, large, and fertile Colony.

" And as this Country has made ſuch a conſiderable Progreſs,
" under the Management of the late Governor *Spotſwood;* ſo
" have we all imaginable Proſpect that it will in the ſame regular
" Courſe proceed towards its greateſt Perfection, under the Care
" and Conduct of the preſent Governor Colonel *Dryſdale.* "

[110]

Captain *Charles Johnſon, A GENERAL HISTORY
OF THE PYRATES* (*London: T. Warner*, 1724,
Second Edition, with conſiderable Additions), pp.
70-90.

p. 70]   " *Edward Teach* was a *Briſtol* Man born, but had ſailed
" ſome Time out of *Jamaica* in Privateers, in the late *French* War;
"   " yet

" yet tho' he had often diftinguifhed himfelf for his uncommon
" Boldnefs and perfonal Courage, he was never raifed to any
" Command, till he went a-pyrating, which I think was at the
" latter End of the Year 1716, . . .

p. 75] " Teach goes up to the Governor of North-Carolina, with
" about twenty of his Men, furrender to his Majefty's Proclama-
" tion, and receive Certificates thereof, from his Excellency; but
" it did not appear that their Submitting to this Pardon was from
" any Reformation of Manners, but only to wait a more favour-
" able Opportunity to play the fame Game over again; which he
" foon after effected, with greater Security to himfelf and with
" much better Profpect of Succefs, having in this Time cultivated
" a very good Underftanding with Charles Eden, Efq; the Gov-
" ernor above mentioned.

" The firft Piece of Service this kind Governor did to Black-
" Beard was, to give him a Right to the Veffel which he had taken,
" when he was a pyrating in the great Ship called the Queen
" Ann's Revenge; for which Purpofe, a Court of Vice-Admiralty
" was held at Bath-Town; and, tho' Teach had never any Com-
" miffion in his Life, and the Sloop belonging to the Englifh Mer-
" chants, and taken in Time of Peace; yet was fhe condemned as
" a Prize taken from the Spaniards, by the faid Teach. Thefe Pro-
" ceedings fhew that Governors are but Men. "

p. 77] " Captain Teach, alias Black-beard, paffed three or four
" Months in the River, fometimes lying at Anchor in the Coves,
" at other Times failing from one Inlet to another, trading with
" fuch Sloops as he met, for the Plunder he had taken, and would
" often give them Prefents for Stores and Provifions took from
" them; that is, when he happened to be in a giving Humour; at
" other Times he made bold with them, and took what he liked,
" without faying, by your Leave. . . . He often diverted him-
" felf with going afhore among the Planters, where he revelled
" Night and Day: By thefe he was well received, but whether
" out of Love or Fear, I cannot fay; fometimes he ufed them
" courteoufly enough, and made them Prefents of Rum and
" Sugar, in Recompence of what he took from them; but, as for
" Liberties (which 'tis faid) he and his Companions often took
" with the Wives and Daughters of the Planters, I cannot take
" upon me to fay, whether he paid them ad Valorem, or no. . . .

" The Sloops trading up and down this River, being fo fre-
" quently pillaged by Black-beard, confulted with the Traders,
" and fome of the beft of the Planters, what Courfe to take; they
" faw plainly it would be in vain to make any Application to the
" Governor

" Governor of *North-Carolina*, to whom it properly belonged to
" find fome Redrefs; fo that if they could not be relieved from
" fome other Quarter, *Black-beard* would be like to reign with
" Impunity, therefore, with as much Secrecy as poffible, they
" fent a Deputation to *Virginia*, to lay the Affair before the
" Governor of that Colony, and to folicit an armed Force from
" the Men of War lying there, to take or deftroy this Pyrate.

" This Governor [*Spotfwood*] confulted with the Captains of the
" two Men of War, *viz.* the *Pearl* and *Lime*, who had lain in St.
" *James's* River, about ten Months. It was agreed that the
" Governor fhould hire a couple of fmall Sloops, and the Men of
" War fhould man them; this was accordingly done, and the
" Command of them given to Mr. *Robert Maynard*, firft Lieutenant
" of the *Pearl*, an experienced Officer, and a Gentleman of great
" Bravery and Refolution, as will appear by his gallant Behav-
" iour in this Expedition. The Sloops were well mann'd and fur-
" nifhed with Ammunition and fmall Arms, but had no Guns
" mounted.

" About the Time of their going out, the Governor [*Spotfwood*]
" called an Affembly, in which it was refolved to publifh a Procla-
" mation, offering certain Rewards to any Perfon or Perfons,
" who, within a Year after that Time, fhould take or deftroy
" any Pyrate: . . .

p. 80-1] " The 17th of *November*, 1718, the Lieutenant fail'd
" from *Kicquetan*, in *James* River in *Virginia*, and, the 21ft in
" the Evening, came to the Mouth of *Okerecock* Inlet, where he
" got Sight of the Pyrate. This Expedition was made with all
" imaginable Secrecy, and the Officer manag'd with all the
" Prudence that was neceffary, . . . but notwithftanding this
" Caution, *Black-beard* had Information of the Defign, from his
" Excellency of the Province; and his Secretary, Mr. *Knight*,
" wrote him a Letter, particularly concerning it, . . .

" *Black-beard* had heard feveral Reports, which happened not
" to be true, and fo gave the lefs Credit to this, nor was he con-
" vinced till he faw the Sloops: Whereupon he put his Veffel in a
" Pofture of Defence; he had no more than twenty five Men on
" Board, tho' he gave out to all the Veffels he fpoke with, that he
" had 40. When he had prepared for Battle, he fet down and
" fpent the Night in drinking with the Mafter of a trading Sloop,
" who, 'twas thought, had more Bufinefs with *Teach*, than he
" fhould have had. . . .

p. 84] " They were now clofely and warmly engaged, the Lieu-
" tenant and twelve Men, againft *Black-beard* and fourteen, till
" the

" the Sea was tinctur'd with Blood round the Veſſel; *Black-beard*
" received a Shot into his Body from the Piſtol that Lieutenant
" *Maynard* diſcharg'd, yet he ſtood his Ground, and fought with
" great Fury, till he received five and twenty Wounds, and five
" of them by Shot.   At length, as he was cocking another Piſtol,
" having fired ſeveral before, he fell down dead; by which Time
" eight more out of the fourteen dropp'd, and all the Reſt, much
" wounded, jump'd over-board, and call'd out for Quarters,
" which was granted, tho' it was only prolonging their Lives for
" a few Days. . . .

p. 85] " The Lieutenant cauſed *Black-beard's* Head to be ſev-
" ered from his Body, and hung up at the Bolt-ſprit End, then
" he ſailed to *Bath-Town*, to get Relief for his wounded Men.

   " It muſt be obſerved, that in rummaging the Pyrate's Sloop,
" they found ſeveral Letters and written Papers, which diſ-
" covered the Correſpondence betwixt Governor *Eden*, the Secre-
" tary and Collector, and alſo ſome Traders at *New-York*, and
" *Black-beard*. . . .

p. 86] " After the wounded Men were pretty well recover'd, the
" Lieutenant ſailed back to the Men of War in *James* River, in
" *Virginia*, with *Black-beard's* Head ſtill hanging at the Bolt-
" ſprit End, and fifteen Priſoners, thirteen of whom were hanged.
" It appearing upon Tryal, that one of them, *viz. Samuel Odell*,
" was taken out of the trading Sloop, but the Night before the
" Engagement . . . The other Perſon that eſcaped the Gallows,
" was one *Iſrael Hands*, the Maſter of *Black-beard's* Sloop, . . . "

Alſo:

H. R. McIlwaine, ed., *EXECUTIVE JOURNALS OF
THE COUNCIL OF COLONIAL VIRGINIA, 1705
1721*, Vol. III (*Richmond:* 1928), pp. 495-496, 501.

[111]

*Hugh Jones, THE PRESENT STATE OF VIRGINIA
(London: J. Clarke*, 1724), p. 13-14.

   " The *French*, that are ſeated upon the River of St. *Laurence*
" and the *Meſſiſippi*, and the Lakes between them in *Canada* and
" *Louiſiana*, which extend behind all the *Engliſh* Plantations
" along the Heart of *North America* a vaſt Way, . . . are nu-
" merous, and through the Policy of their late King intermarry
" with the *Indians;* by which Means being united with them, they
                                                           " often

" often fet them on to deftroy the *Englifh*, which may prove dan-
" gerous in Cafe of a War with *France*.

" But to prevent more Mifchiefs of this Kind, Providence has
" fecured us from them by a continued Ridge of vaft high Hills,
" called the *Apelachian* Mountains, running nearly under the
" *Meridian*, as being paffable but in very few Places; which
" Mountains through the Care and Conduct of the Honourable
" Colonel *Spotfwood* are fecured for his Majefty, tho' not guarded
" as yet; which might eafily be done to the great Safety and En-
" couragement of back Settlements in a vaft rich Country
" weftward of the Settlements of *Virginia*, . . .

" Governor *Spotfwood*, when he undertook the great Difcovery
" of the Paffage over the Mountains, attended with a fufficient
" Guard and Pioneers and Gentlemen, with a fufficient Stock of
" Provifion, with abundant Fatigue paffed thefe Mountains, and
" cut his Majefty's Name in a Rock upon the higheft of them,
" naming it *Mount George;* and in Complaifance the Gentlemen
" from the Governor's Name, called the Mountain next in
" Height, *Mount Alexander.*

" For this Expedition they were obliged to provide a great
" Quantity of Horfe-Shoes; (Things feldom ufed in the lower
" Parts of the Country, where there are few Stones:) Upon which
" Account the Governor upon their Return prefented each of his
" Companions with a golden Horfe-Shoe, (fome of which I have
" feen ftudded with valuable Stones refembling the Heads of
" Nails) with this Infcription on the one Side: *Sic juvat tranfcen-*
" *dere Montes:* And on the other is written the Tramontane Order.

" This he inftituted to encourage Gentlemen to venture back-
" wards, and make Difcoveries and new Settlements; any Gen-
" tleman being entitled to wear this golden Shoe that can prove
" his having drank His Majefty's Health, upon *Mount George.* "

Alfo:

Ann Maury, MEMOIRS OF A HUGUENOT FAM-
ILY (*New York:* Reprinted from the original Edi-
tion of 1852 by *G. P. Putnam's* Sons), pp. 245-310.
The Journal of John Fontaine, 1710-1718.

p. 281] " *Williamfburg*, 20th *Auguft*, 1716.—In the Morning
" got my Horfes ready, and what Baggage was neceffary, and I
" waited on the Governor [*Spotfwood*], who was in Readinefs for
" an Expedition over the *Appalachian* Mountains. We break-
" fafted, and about ten got on Horfeback, and at four came to
                                                          " the

" the Brick-houſe, upon *York* River, where we croſſed the Ferry,
" and at ſix we came to Mr. *Auſtin Moor's* Houſe, upon *Matta-*
" *pony* River, in *King William* County; here we lay all Night
" and were well entertained. . . ."

" [*September*] 5th.—A fair Day. At nine we were mounted;
" we were obliged to have Axe-men to clear the Way in ſome
" Places. We followed the Windings of *James* River, obſerving
" that it came from the very Top of the Mountains. We killed
" two Rattleſnakes during our Aſcent. In ſome Places it was
" very ſteep, in others, it was ſo that we could ride up. About
" one of the Clock we got to the Top of the Mountain; about four
" Miles and a half, and we came to the very head Spring of *James*
" River, where it runs no bigger than a Man's Arm, from under a
" large Stone. We drank King *George's* Health, and all the
" Royal Family's, at the very Top of the *Appalachian* Moun-
" tains. About a Muſket-ſhot from the Spring there is another,
" which riſes and runs down on the other Side; it goes weſtward,
" and we thought we could go down that Way, but we met with
" ſuch prodigious Precipices, that we were obliged to return to
" the Top again. We found ſome Trees which had been formerly
" marked, I ſuppoſe, by the northern *Indians*, and following
" theſe Trees, we found a good, ſafe Deſcent. . . .

" 6th.—We croſſed the River, which we called *Euphrates* . . .
" We drank ſome Healths on the other Side, and returned; after
" which I went a ſwimming in it. . . . I got ſome Graſſhoppers
" and fiſhed; and another and I, we catched a Diſh of Fiſh, ſome
" Perch, and a Fiſh they call Chub. The others went a hunting,
" and killed Deer and Turkeys. The Governor had graving
" Irons, but could not grave any Thing, the Stones were ſo hard.
" I graved my Name on a Tree by the River Side; and the Gov-
" ernor buried a Bottle with a Paper incloſed, on which he writ
" that he took poſſeſſion of this Place in the Name and for King
" *George* the Firſt of *England.* We had a good Dinner, and after
" it we got the Men together, and loaded all their Arms, and we
" drank the King's Health in Champagne, and fired a Volley—
" the Princeſs's Health in Burgundy, and fired a Volley, and all
" the Reſt of the Royal Family in Claret, and a Volley. We
" drank the Governor's Health and fired another Volley. We
" had ſeveral Sorts of Liquors, *viz., Virginia* Red Wine and White
" Wine, *Iriſh* Uſqebaugh, Brandy, Shrub, two Sorts of Rum,
" Champagne, Canary, Cherry, Punch, Water, Cider, *&c.*
"   I ſent two of the Rangers to look for my Gun, which I
" dropped in the Mountains; they found it, and brought it to me
                                                          "at

" at Night, and I gave them a Piftole for their Trouble. We
" called the higheft Mountain *Mount George*, and the one we
" croffed over *Mount Spotfwood.* "

[112]

R. A. Brock, ed., *THE OFFICIAL LETTERS OF
ALEXANDER SPOTSWOOD* (*Richmond:* Pub-
lifhed by the *Virginia Hiftorical Society*, 1885), Vol.
II, pp. 280-281. [Letter to the Board of Trade, dated
June 24, 1718.]

" . . . Some Time laft Fall the Poft M'r Gen'll of *America*, having
" thought himfelf obliged to endeavour the Settling a Poft
" through *Virginia* and *Maryland*, in ye fame Manner as they
" are fettled in the other northern Plantations, purfu't to the
" Act of Parliament of the 9th of Queen *Anne*, gave out Com-
" miffions for that Purpofe, and a Poft was accordingly eftab-
" lifhed once a Fortnight from *W'mfburg* to *Philadelphia*, and for
" the Conveyance of Letters bro't hither by Sea through the
" feveral Countys. In Order to this, the Poft M'r fet up printed
" Placards, (fuch as were fent in by the Poft M'r Gen'll of *Great*
" *Britain*,) at all the Pofts, requiring the Delivery of all Letters
" not excepted by the Act of Parliament to be delivered to his
" Deputys there. No fooner was this noifed about but a great
" Clamour was raifed againft it. The People were made to be-
" lieve that the Parl't could not levy any Tax, (for fo they call ye
" Rates of Poftage,) here without the confent of the General Af-
" fembly. That, befides, all their Laws were exempted, becaufe
" fcarce any came in here but what fome Way or other concern'd
" Trade; that tho' M'rs fhould, for the Reward of a Penny a
" Letter, deliver them, the Poft M'r could demand no Poftage
" for the Conveyance of them, and Abundance more to the fame
" Purpofe, as rediculous as arrogant. This gave a Handle for
" framing fome Grievances to the Affembly againft this new
" Office; and, thereupon, a Bill is prepared and paffed both Coun-
" cil and Burg'f's, w'ch, tho' it acknowledges the Act of Parliam't
" to be in Force here, does effectually prevent its being ever put
" in Execution. The firft Claufe of that Bill impofes an Obliga-
" tion on the Poft Mafter to w'ch he is no Ways liable by the Act
" of Parliament. The fecond Claufe lays a Penalty of no lefs
" than £ 5 for every Letter he demands or takes from a board
" any Ships that ftand decreed to be excepted by the Act of Par-
" liament; and the laft Claufe appoints ye Stages and the Time
" of

" of Conveyance of all Letters under an extravagant Penalty.
" As it is impoſſible for the Poſt Maſter to know whether the
" Letters he receives be excepted or not, and y't, according to the
" Interpreters, our Judges of the Act of Parl't, all Letters ſent
" from any Merch't, whether the ſame relate to Merchandize on
" Board or not, are within the Exception of the Law, the Poſt
" M'r muſt meddle w'th no Letters at all, or run the Hazard of
" being ruin'd. . . . From whence yo'r Lop's may judge how
" well affected the major Part of our Aſſembly Men are towards
" ye Collecting this Branch of the King's Revenue, and w'll there-
" fore be pleaſ'd to acquitt me of any Cenſure of refuſing Aſſent
" to ſuch a Bill."

[Note: The Act does not appear in *Hening's* Statutes but there
are two imperfect Ms. Copies of it in the Archives of the *Virginia Hiſtorical Society*.]

[113]

See Note 112.

[114]

*William Waller Hening, THE STATUTES AT
LARGE (New York: R. & W. & G. Bartow, 1823),
Vol. I, p. 124.*

[1623/4]

" 8. That the Governor ſhall not lay any Taxes or Ympoſitions
" upon the Colony their Lands or Comodities other Way than by
" the Authority of the General Aſſembly, to be levyed and
" ymployed as the ſaid Aſſembly ſhall appoynt. "

Alſo:

Ibid., pp. 171, 364; Vol. II, p. 525.

[115]

*LIBRARY OF CONGRESS, Diviſion of Manuſcripts—
John Cuſtis Letter Book, 1717-1741. Letter from John
Cuſtis to Perry, Lane & Perry, dated Williamſburg,
1718.*

[116]

*William Stevens Perry, PAPERS RELATING TO
THE HISTORY OF THE CHURCH IN VIR-
GINIA,*

GINIA, 1650-1776 (Privately Printed: 1870), pp. 199-247.

Alfo:

R. A. *Brock*, ed., *THE OFFICIAL LETTERS OF ALEXANDER SPOTSWOOD (Richmond:* Publifhed by the *Virginia Hiftorical Society*, 1885), Vol. II, pp. 275-286, 320-326. Letters to the Lords of Trade, dated "*June* 24th 1718" and "*May* ye 26th, " 1719."

[117]

H. R. McIlwaine, ed., *EXECUTIVE JOURNALS OF THE COUNCIL OF COLONIAL VIRGINIA (Richmond:* 1930), Vol. IV, pp. 19-20.

" At a Council held at the Capitol *September* 27th 1722 "
" His Majefties Commiffion to the Right Honble *George* Earl of
" *Orkney*, and alfo a Commiffion under his Majtys Signet and
" Sign Manual bearing Date the third Day of *April* 1722 confti-
" tuting the Honble *Hugh Dryfdale* his Majefties Lieut Governor
" of this Colony and Dominion in the Room of Colo *Spotfwood*,
" being read publickly in the General Court Houfe, the faid
" Lieut Governor with the Council went from thence to the
" Council Chamber, where his Honr took the Oaths appointed
" by Act of Parliament. . ."

[118]

Sir *William Keith*, Bart., *THE HISTORY OF THE BRITISH PLANTATIONS IN AMERICA (London: S. Richardfon*, 1738), pp. 173-174.

" . . . and indeed he [Governor *Spotfwood*] was ever employed
" in fome public Defign for the Intereft and Advantage of *Vir-
" ginia;* neverthelefs by the factious Arts of fome intriguing Men
" in the Council of that Province, who had neither Ability nor
" Courage openly to contend with him, his Intereft in *England*
" was at length fo far undermined, that after he had governed
" there to the almoft univerfal Content of all the Country, for
" the Space of thirteen Years, without any Manner of Complaint
" having ever been publickly exhibited againft his Adminiftra-
" tion, he was fuperfeded . . . by Major *Drifdale*, . . ."

[119]

[119]

*Hugh Jones, THE PRESENT STATE OF VIRGINIA
(London: J. Clarke,* 1724), p. 53.

[120]

Ibid., p. 152.

   " . . . *Hugh Jones,* A.M., lately Mathematical Profeſſor at the
   " College of *William and Mary* at *Williamſburgh* in *Virginia,* and
   " Chaplain to the Honourable the Aſſembly of that Colony. "

Alſo:

H. R. McIlwaine, ed., *THE JOURNALS OF THE
HOUSE OF BURGESSES OF VIRGINIA, 1712-
1726 (Richmond:* 1912), pp. 175, 221, 251.

[121]

*Hugh Jones, THE PRESENT STATE OF VIRGINIA
(London: J. Clarke,* 1724), p. 31.

[122]

Ibid., p. 32.

[123]

Ibid., pp. 47-48.

[124]

See Note 117.

[125]

H. R. McIlwaine, ed., *EXECUTIVE JOURNALS OF
THE COUNCIL OF COLONIAL VIRGINIA
(Richmond:* 1930), Vol. IV, p. 113.

   " At a Council held at the Capitol the 1ſt day of *Auguſt* 1726. . .
      " *Robert Carter* Eſqr acquainted the Board that upon the Death
   " of the late Lieut Governor [*Dryſdale*] he had thought it neceſ-
   " ſary to call this Council in Order to his Taking upon him the
   " Adminiſtration of this Government, which he conceives is de-
   " volved on him by the Suſpenſion of Colo *Jenings,* he being now
   " the firſt named in his Maties Inſtructions to whom the Power
   " of executing the Kings Commiſſion in Caſe of the Death or Ab-
                                                               " ſence

" fence of the Governor & Lieut Governor is committed, and
" defired the Opinion of the Council whether he is not fully
" authorized to act as Prefident of the Council.

   " Whereupon the Board having read and confidered the Min-
" utes of laft Council whereby *Edm⁴ Jenings* Efq⁺ is for Inca-
" pacity fufpended from being any longer a Member of his
" Matⁱᵉˢ Council, are unanimoufly of Opinion that the faid
" *Robert Carter* is thereby become the firft named in his Matⁱᵉˢ
" Inftructions and is duly authorized to take upon him the
" Governm⁺ . . . "

[126]

Ibid., p. 145.

   " At a Council held at the Capitol *September* the 11th 1727 . . .
   " Alfo a Commiffion under the Signet and Sign Manual of his
" faid late Majefty [King *George* the Firft] bearing Date at the
" Court at *St. James's* the 23ᵈ Day of *January* 1726/7 . . . con-
" ftituting and appointing the Honourable *William Gooch* Efq⁺
" (in Cafe of the Death or Abfence of the faid Earl of *Orkney*) to
" be Lieut Governor of the faid Colony . . . "

[127]

H. R. McIlwaine, ed., *JOURNALS OF THE HOUSE
OF BURGESSES OF VIRGINIA, 1727-1740 (Richmond:* 1910), *p. 242. Addrefs of Sir John Randolph,
Speaker of the Houfe of Burgeffes, to Governor William Gooch*.

" *Friday, Auguft* 6, 1736 "

   " We have long experienced your Love and good Will to the
" People of this Country; and obferve with what Readinefs
" you exert it upon all Occafions.

   " The Art of Governing well, is thought to be the moft ab-
" ftrufe, as well as the ufefuleft Science in the World; and when
" it is learnt to fome Degree of Perfection, it is very difficult to
" put it in Practice, being often oppofed by the Pride and Intereft
" of the Perfon that governs. But you have fhew'd how eafy it
" is to give univerfal Satisfaction to the People under your Gov-
" ernment: You have met them, and heard their Grievances in
" frequent Affemblies, and have had the Pleafure of feeing none
" of them proceed from your Adminiftration: You have not been
" intoxicated with the Power committed to you by His Majefty;
" but have ufed it, like a faithful Truftee, for the public Good,
                                                          " and

" and with proper Cautions: Raifed no Debates about what it
" might be able to do of itfelf; but, on all important Occafions,
" have fuffer'd it to unite with that of the other Parts of the
" Legiflature: You never propofe Matters, without fuppoing
" your Opinion fubject to the Examination of others; nor ftrove
" to make other Mens Reafon blindly and implicitly obedient
" to yours; but have always calmly acquiefced in the contrary
" Opinion: And laftly, you have extirpated all Factions from
" among us, by difcountenancing public Animofities; and plainly
" prov'd, that none can arife, or be lafting, but from the Counte-
" nance and Encouragement of a Governor. *Hinc illæ Artes.* . . ."

[128]

On *February* 27, 1727, the Council referred to the
Houfe of Burgeffes of *Virginia* a Petition and Propofals
of *William Parks* for printing " a complete Body of the
" Laws of this Colony now in Force, " and a Committee was appointed to agree with the faid *Parks* for
the Printing thereof. (See *Journals of the Houfe of
Burgeffes of Virginia, 1727-1740*.)   At this Time, *Parks*
was operating a Printing Office at *Annapolis*, where he
publifhed *The Maryland Gazette*.   It would appear that
by 1730 he had opened a Printing Office at *Williamfburg*,
for in *The Maryland Gazette* for *November* 24-*December* 1,
1730, and in fubfequent Iffues, he advertifed certain
Books for Sale as being printed in *Williamfburg*.   *Parks*
conducted Printing Offices in both Colonies for feveral
Years, before abandoning his *Maryland* Office.

The firft known exifting Copy of *The Virginia
Gazette*, " Numb. 6, " printed in *Williamfburg* by
William Parks, is dated " From *Friday, September* 3 to
" *Friday, September* 10, 1736. "

[129]

*THE VIRGINIA MAGAZINE OF HISTORY AND
BIOGRAPHY*, Vol. VII (1900), pp. 442-444.

" THE PAPER MILL.   Infcrib'd to Mr. *Parks*.

" *In nova, fert Animis, mutates dicere formas, Corpora.*—Ovid.

" (From

" (From the *Virginia Gazette*, *July* 26, 1744.)

" Tho' fage Philofophers have faid,
  " *Of Nothing, can be Nothing made:*
" Yet *much* thy Mill, O *Parks*, brings forth
" From what we reckon *Nothing worth*.
" Hail kind *Machine!*—The Mufe fhall praife
" Thy Labours, that receive her Lays.
" Soon as the *Learn'd* denounce the War
" From pratling Box, or wrangling Bar,
" Straight, Pen and Paper range the Fight;
" They meet, they clofe, in Black & White.
" The Subftances of what we think,
" Tho' born in *Thought*, muft live in *Ink*.
" Whilft willing *Mem'ry* lends her Aid,
" She finds herfelf by *Time* betray'd.
" Nor can thy Name, Dear *Molly*, live
" Without thofe Helps the Mill muft give;
" The Sheet now haftens to declare,
" How lovely Thou, and—my Defpair.
  " Unwitting Youths, whofe Eyes or Breaft,
" Involve in Sighs, and fpoil of Reft;
" Unfkill'd to fay their piteous Cafe,
" But mifs the Girl for want of *Brafs*,
" May paint their Anguifh on the Sheet;
" For Paper cannot blufh, I weet.
" And *Phillis* (for Biffextile Year
" Does only once in four appear,
" When Maids, in dread to lie alone
" Have Leave to bid the Men *come on*),
" Each Day may write to lure the Youth
" She longs to wed, or fool, or—both.
  " Ye *Brave*, whofe Deeds fhall vie with Time,
" Whilft Mill can turn, or Poet rhime
" Your Tatters hoard for future Quires;
" So Need demands, so *Parks* defires.
" (And long that gen'rous Patriot live
" Who for foft Rags, hard Cafh will give!)
" The Shirt, Cravat, the Cap, again
" Shall meet your Hands, with *Mails* from *Spain;*
" The *Surplice*, which, when whole or new,
" With Pride the Sexton's Wife could view,
" Tho' worn by Time and gone to rack,
" It quits its Rev'rend Mafter's Back;

                            " The

" The fame again the Prieſt may ſee
" Bound up in ſacred Liturgy.
  " Ye *Fair*, renown'd in *Cupid's* Field,
" Who fain would tell what Hearts you've killed;
" Each Shift decay'd, lay by with Care;
" Or Apron rubb'd to bits at—Pray'r,
" One Shift ten Sonnets may contain,
" To gild your Charms, and make you vain;
" One Cap, a *Billet-doux* may ſhape,
" As full of Whim, as when a Cap,
" And modeſt 'Kerchiefs ſacred held
" May ſing the Breaſts they once *conceal'd*.
  " Nice *Delia's* Smock, which, neat and whole,
" No Man durſt finger for his Soul;
" Turn'd to *Gazette*, now all the Town,
" May take it up, or ſmooth it down.
" Whilſt *Delia* may with it diſpence,
" And no Affront to Innocence.
  " The Bards, beſure, their Aids will lend;
" The Printer is the Poet's Friend;
" Both cram the News, and ſtuff the Mills,
" For Bards have Rags, and—little elſe.

" Your humble Servant,

" *J. Dumbleton*."

Alſo:

Rutherfoord Goodwin, THE WILLIAM PARKS PAPER MILL AT WILLIAMSBURG, (Lexington, Va.; Journaliſm Laboratory Preſs, 1939), pp. 14-15.

[An Advertiſement for Rags for Papermaking which appeared on the Outſide Back Cover of *The Virginia Almanack, for the Year 1749,* printed in *Williamſburg* by *William Parks*. From Almanack in Poſſeſſion of the *Huntington Library, San Marino, California*.]

" THE Printer hereof; having a Paper-mill, now at work near
" this City, deſires all Perſons to ſave their old *Linen Rags*, for
" making Paper.   All Sorts are uſeful, from the coarſeſt Crocus
" or Sail-cloth, to the fineſt Holland or Cambrick; and he will
" give a Price in Proportion to the Fineneſs, from a Half-penny
" to

" to Three-half-pence, or Two-pence, per Pound. Old Thread
" Stockings, which can be ufed no other Way, will make good
" Paper. As this is the firft Mill of the Kind, that ever was
" erected in this Colony, and has coft a very confiderable Sum of
" Money, he hopes to meet with Encouragement fuitable to fo
" ufeful an Undertaking. . . . "

[130]

See APPENDIX, Pages 350-357, for complete Copy
of the Charter of the City of *Williamſburg*, dated *July*
28, 1722.

[131]

Rev. *Andrew Burnaby*, TRAVELS THROUGH THE
MIDDLE SETTLEMENTS IN NORTH AMER-
ICA IN THE YEARS 1759 TO 1760 (*London*: T.
Payne, 1775).

[*July* 5, 1759] *"Williamſburg* is the Capital of *Virginia*: . . .
" It confifts of about two Hundred Houfes, does not contain
" more than one Thoufand Souls, Whites and Negroes; . . . "

[132]

LIBRARY OF CONGRESS, Divifion of Manuſcripts.
Lord *Adam Gordon*, JOURNAL OF AN OFFICER
IN THE WEST INDIES, 1764-5. [Tranfcript
from *Britiſh Muſeum, King's* Ms. No. 213. ff. 54-b-
60.]

[133]

From a " Table of Occupations " compiled by the
Reſearch Department of *Colonial Williamſburg* Founda-
tion, from *York County Records* and the *Virginia
Gazette*.

[134]

*WILLIAM AND MARY COLLEGE QUARTERLY
HISTORICAL MAGAZINE, Firſt Series*, Vol. XV
(1907), p. 223. " *Obſervations in ſeveral Voyages and*
" *Travels in* America *in the Year 1736.* "

" *Williamſburgh* is a moft wretched contriv'd Affair for the
" Capital

" Capital of a Country, being near three Miles from the Sea,
" is a bad Situation. There is Nothing confiderable in it, but the
" College, the Governor's Houfe, and one or two more, which are
" no bad Piles; and the prodigious Number of Coaches that croud
" the deep, fandy Streets of this little City. It's very furprizing
" to me, that this fhould be preferr'd to *James-Town*, *Hampton*,
" or fome other Situations I could mention. Here the Courts of
" Juftice are held, and with a Dignity and Decorum, that would
" become them even in *Europe*. The prefent Lieut. Governor
" *Gooch* is much beloved by every one, and by his mild agreeable
" Difpofition, diffufes Content every where around. "

[135]

A FRENCH TRAVELLER IN THE COLONIES, 1765. [Original in *Paris, Service Hydrographique de la Marine*, Vol. 76, No. 2. Photoftatic Copy in *Refearch Department, Colonial Williamfburg* Foundation. Alfo printed in the *American Hiftorical Review*, Vol. XXVI, No. 4.]

" *Aipril* the 28th [1765] I have been here [*Williamfburg*] three
" Days and am heartily fick of it. This Morning hired a Chair
" and took a ride to *Jamefes City* formerly the Capital of the
" Province . . . it confifts of about 70 Houfes, the Seat of
" Government was here formely but was caryed to *Williamfburg*
" on Account of the Unhealthynefs of this Place, fome Ships
" anchor of the Town. After Dinner we came back to *Williams-*
" *burg;* there was a great Number of People from all Parts of the
" Province and alfo the adjoining Provinces, for this is Time for
" carying on Bufinefs and fetling Maters with Correfpondents.
" I fupofe there might be 5 or 6000 People here, dureing the
" Courts . . . Never was a more difagreeable Place than this at
" Prefent. In the Day Time People hurying back and forwards
" from the Capitoll to the Taverns, and at Night, caroufing and
" drinking in one Chamber and Box and Dice in another, which
" continues till Morning commonly . . . "

[136]

THE VIRGINIA GAZETTE (*Williamfburg:* Printed by *William Parks*), Numb. 175. From *Friday, November* 30, to *Friday, December* 7, 1739.

" *Williamfburg, December* 7 [1739].

" WHEREAS

" WHEREAS two FAIRS are appointed to be held in this
" City yearly, *viz.* on the 23d of *April*, and on the 12th of *De-*
" *cember*, out of a laudable Defign to encourage the Trade
" thereof, and to be a Means of promoting a general Commerce
" or Traffick among Perfons that want to buy or fell, either the
" Product or Manufactures of the Country, or any other Sorts of
" Goods, Wares, or Merchandizes: But as this Intention, like
" many others that are new and uncommon, has not met with
" the defired Succefs, for want of fufficient Tryal and Experi-
" ment; it has been taken into Confideration, by the Gentlemen
" and other Inhabitants of the faid City; and they have, by a
" voluntary Contribution, raifed a Sum of Money to be appro-
" priated in fuch Manner, and to fuch Ufes, as fhall feem moft
" conducive to the defired End,

" It is therefore agreed upon, and ordered, that the following
" Sums of Money fhall be given as Bounties, at the next FAIR,
" to be held at *Williamfburg*, on the 12th Inftant, *viz.*

" To the Perfon that brings moft Horfes to the faid FAIR, and
" there offers them to publick Sale, at a reafonable Price, there
" fhall be paid him, as a Bounty, (whether he fells them, or not,)
" a Piftole.

" To the Perfon that brings the beft draught Horfe for Sale,
" as aforefaid, a good Horfe-whip fhall be given.

" To the Perfon that brings moft Cows, Steers, or other horned
" Cattle, and there offers them for Sale, as aforefaid, a Piftole
" fhall be given. . . .

" AND for the Entertainment and Diverfion of all Gentlemen
" and others, that fhall refort thereto, the following PRIZES
" are given to be contended for, at the Fair, *viz.*

" A good Hat to be cudgell'd for; and to be given to the Per-
" fon that fairly wins it, by the common Rules of Play.

" A Saddle of 40s. Value, to be run for, once round the Mile
" Courfe, adjacent to this City, by any Horfe, Mare or Gelding,
" carrying Horfeman's Weight, and allowing Weight for Inches.
" A handfome Bridle to be given to the Horfe that comes in
" fecond.   And a good Whip to the Horfe that comes in third.

" A Pair of Silver Buckles, Value 20s. to be run for by Men.
" from the College to the Capitol.   A Pair of Shoes to be given
" to him that comes in fecond.   And a Pair of Gloves to the
" third.

" A Pair of Pumps to be danc'd for by Men.

" A handfome Firelock to be exercif'd for; and given to the
" Perfon that performs the Manual Exercife beft.

" A

" A Pig, with his Tail foap'd, to be run after; and to be given
" to the Perfon that catches him, and lifts him off the Ground
" fairly by the Tail.

" There will be feveral other Prizes given: And as the Fair is
" to hold three Days, there will be Horfe-racing, and a Variety
" of Diverfions every Day; and the Prizes not here particularly
" mentioned, (for Want of Room) will be then publickly declared,
" and appropriated in the beft Manner. "

[137]

"Cock-matches" between Gentlemen of different Sections were frequently announced in the *Virginia
Gazette*, the Gentlemen of " *James* River " being
prominent in thefe Liftings. The Following, though
written from *Culpepper* County, would eftablifh
the Frequency of fuch Matches at Places of publick
Gathering:

*WILLIAM AND MARY COLLEGE QUARTERLY
HISTORICAL MAGAZINE*, Firft Series, Vol. VIII
(1900), p. 89. Letter of *George Hume* to his Brother,
Capt *Jno. Hume*, who was in the *Britifh* Navy,
written from " *Culpepper* Co., *Virg^a*, *Aug.* 22nd,
" 1754. "

" Our Affembly are foon fitting. . . I have no oy^r News
" to tell you—Money is fo fcarce it is a rare Thing to fee a
" Dollar, and at publick Places where great monied Men will bet
" on Cock Fights, Horfe Races, etc., ye Noife is not now as it ufed
" to be—one Piftol to 2 or 3 Piftoles to one—it is now common
" Cry 2 Cows and Calves to one or 3 to one or fometimes 4
" Hogfheads Tob^o to one and y^t gives no Price, fo I do not
" know how we fhall maintain a War, y^e *French* very much y
" Advantage of us. "

[138]

PUBLIC RECORD OFFICE, *London*.   *Colonial Office*
/1331, p. 139.   Letter from Governor *Fauquier* to
Lords of Trade. [Photoftat in *Refearch Department*,
Colonial Williamfburg Foundation.]

" *W^{m}fburgh Nov^r* 3^d 1765.

" . . . I

" . . . I then thought proper to go to the Coffee Houfe (where
" I occafionally fometimes go) which is fituated in that Part of
" the Town which is call'd the Exchange tho' an open Street,
" where all Money Bufinefs is tranfacted . . . "

[139]

See Note 134

[140]

*PUBLIC RECORD OFFICE, London. Board of Trade
& Plantations*, p. 209. Copy of Col° *Spotfwood's*
Anfwer to the four Articles exhibited againft him by
the Burgeffes of *Virginia*—Received *May* 18, 1719.
[Photoftat in *Divifion of Manufcripts, Library of
Congrefs.*]

" *Nov.* 15th [1718] . . . Thefe may ferve for Inftances of pure
" ill Nature, confidering the trivial Caufe that the Burgeffes had
" to be difturbed. . . . And the Ufe I had made of fome of the
" Capitol Chairs, had happened only on the Kings Birthday,
" when at the Celebration thereof I have had 200 Perfons to
" entertain at my Houfe. "

[141]

LETTERS OF WILLIAM GOOCH [Manufcript Copy
in Poffeffion of the *Refearch Department, Colonial
Williamfburg* Foundation.] Letter of *William Gooch*
to his Brother, *Thomas*, who later became Bifhop of
Norwich, dated " *Williamfburgh*, 28th *Xber* 1727. "

[142]

*LIBRARY OF CONGRESS, Divifion of Manufcripts.
Dawfon Papers*, 1754-1775.

Letter from —— [?] *Donald* to Mrs. *Dawfon*, written
from " *Han: Town* 7th *January* 1768. "

[143]

YORK COUNTY RECORDS, Book V—Deeds, pp.
30, 493.

Alfo:

Alſo:

THE VIRGINIA GAZETTE (*Williamſburg:* Printed by *William Parks*), Numb. 511, *Thurſday, May* 8 to *Thurſday, May* 15, 1746.

The firſt Reference from the *York Records* noted above, (*i. e.* Book V, Page 30) refers to the Sale of a Building owned by *John Blair* and tenanted by *Henry Wetherburn*, Ordinary Keeper, to a Company of Merchants in 1742. The ſecond Reference (Book V, Page 493) refers to the Sale of the Property "commonly called and known by the "Name of *Raleigh Tavern*," (which *Alexander Finnie* had purchaſed of the Company of Merchants on *June* 15, 1749,) by *Alexander Finnie* to *John Chiſwell* and *George Gilmer* in 1752. The *Virginia Gazette* Reference merely eſtabliſhes the Name, "*Raleigh Tavern*" to have been in Uſe in 1746, which is the earlieſt ſpecific. Reference to that Name known at this Time.

[144]

THE VIRGINIA GAZETTE (*Williamſburg:* Printed by *Alex. Purdie & John Dixon*), No. 1057. *October* 31, 1771.

[145]

LIBRARY OF CONGRESS, Diviſion of Manuſcripts. Lord *Adam Gordon, JOURNAL OF AN OFFICER IN THE WEST INDIES, 1764-5.* [*King's* Ms. No. 213. Tranſcript from *Britiſh Muſeum* ff. 54-b-60.]

"After you croſs the *James* River the Land mends, and is
"good all the Way to *Williamſburg*, which is the Seat of Govern-
"ment and much reſembles a good Country Town in *England:*
"here is a very handſome State-Houſe, commodious for all the
"Courts, and both the Houſes of Council and Aſſembly, a very
"large and handſome College—probably eighty Students, . . .
                                                        "There

" There are many good Houfes in Town, where the Courts
" meet twice a Year, in *April* and *October* . . .
" The People are well-bred, polite and extremely civil to
" Strangers . . . the Governor's Houfe is handfome and commodi-
" ous, and he himfelf very happy, and the People fo in him. . . "

[146]

See Note 135

Alfo:

*Hugh Jones, THE PRESENT STATE OF VIRGINIA
(London: J. Clarke, 1724), pp. 25-34.*

[147]

*[Henry] Hartwell, [James] Blair, & [Edward] Chilton,
THE PRESENT STATE OF VIRGINIA, AND
THE COLLEGE (London: Printed for John Wyat,
1727), pp. 67-95.*

Alfo:

*THE CHARTER, AND STATUTES OF THE COL-
LEGE OF WILLIAM AND MARY IN VIR-
GINIA (Williamfburg: William Parks, 1736)*

[148]

Ibid., p. 98. " The Statutes of the College of *William*
" *and Mary* . . .
" The *Indian* School.

" There is but one Mafter in this School, who is to teach the
" *Indian* Boys to read, and write, and vulgar Arithmetick.   And
" efpecially he is to teach them thoroughly the Catechifm and
" the Principles of *Chriftian* Religion . . . "

[149]

R. A. Brock, ed., *THE OFFICIAL LETTERS OF
ALEXANDER SPOTSWOOD (Richmond:* Pub-
lifhed by the *Virginia Hiftorical Society*, 1882), Vol. I,
p. 103.

Governor *Spotfwood* to Mr. *Blathwayt.*

" *Virginia, July* 28th, 1711.

" I

"I have not had the Honour of any from you since my laſt,
"but having ſeen a Letter you writt to Collo. *Diggs* in Behalf of
"Mr. *Le Fevre*, I very gladly embraced the Opportunity of doing
"Hon'r to your Recommendation by getting the Governor of the
"College to receive him as Mathematick Profeſſor, with the Sal-
"lary of eighty Pounds per Annum.   I thought they could do
"no leſs to teſtify their Reſpect to ſo good a Benefactor as you
"have been to that Foundation, and of whoſe Friendſhip they
"will yet have further Occaſion in Obtaining her Ma'ty's future
"Bounty for perfecting that Work."

[150]

*Hugh Jones, THE PRESENT STATE OF VIRGINIA
(London: J. Clarke, 1724), pp. 45-46.*

[151]

*THE HISTORY OF THE COLLEGE OF WILLIAM
AND MARY (Richmond: J. W. Randolph & Engliſh, 1874), pp. 16-33. " The Transfer of the College
" of William and Mary, in Virginia." [February 27,
1729.]*

"[p. 24] . . . And whereas the ſaid ſurviving Truſtees, pur-
"ſuant to the Truſt in them repoſed, have eſtabliſhed in the ſaid
"College one School of ſacred Theology, and one other School of
"Philoſophy, beſides the Grammar School aforeſaid, and have
"appointed certain Maſters or Profeſſors in each of the ſaid
"Schools; that is to ſay, two Maſters in the Theology School,
"two other Maſters in the Philoſophy School, and one in the
"Grammar School; . . . and . . . [p. 29] have appointed a
"Maſter who is called the *Indian* Maſter, and ſhall hereafter be
"deemed the ſixth Maſter or Profeſſor of the ſaid College, . . ."

Alſo:

*COLLEGE OF WILLIAM AND MARY—Faculty
Minutes, 1729-1784, pp. 1, 4.*

[152]

*Hugh Jones, THE PRESENT STATE OF VIRGINIA
(London: J. Clarke, 1724), p. 91.*

[1724] "The *Indians* who are upon Mr. *Boyle's* Foundation
"have now a handſom Apartment for themſelves and their Maſ-
"ter,

" ter, built near the College, which uſeful Contrivance ought to
" be carried on to the utmoſt Advantage in the real Education
" and Converſion of the Infidels; . . . "

Alſo:

*WILLIAM AND MARY COLLEGE QUARTERLY
HISTORICAL MAGAZINE, Firſt Series, (Richmond: 1892), Vol. I, p. 186.*

" [fn.] Carved in a Brick near a Door of this Building [*Brafferton*]
" are the Figures 1723, ſuppoſed to repreſent the Date of
" Foundation. "

[153]

*COLLEGE OF WILLIAM AND MARY—Faculty
Minutes, 1729-1784, p. 8.*

" *July* 31, 1732. The Foundation of the Preſident's Houſe at
" the College was laid, the Preſident [*James Blair*], Mr. *Dawſon*,
" Mr. *Fry*, Mr. *Stith* and Mr. *Fox* laying the firſt five Bricks in
" Order, one after another. The Reaſon of the Foundations
" being laid that Day was, that M⁼ *Henry Cary*, the Undertaker
" had appointed his Bricklayers to be ready that Day, and that
" they could not Proceed till the Foundation was laid. "

[154]

*COLLEGE OF WILLIAM AND MARY—Burſar's
Book, 1753-1770.*

" *Due at Lady-Day 1754.* "
[Account liſts 52 Students, 15 Scholars, and *8
Indians.*]

[155]

*WILLIAM AND MARY COLLEGE QUARTERLY
HISTORICAL MAGAZINE, Firſt Series, Vol. VI
(1898), pp. 187-188. " Students in 1754 at William
" and Mary College. "*

[156]

*Paul Leiceſter Ford, ed., THE WORKS OF THOMAS
JEFFERSON (New York: G. P. Putnam's Sons,
1904), Vol. I, p. 78. Autobiography 1743-1790.*

" On

" On the 1ft of *June* 1779.   I was appointed Governor of the
" Commonwealth and retired from the Legiflature. Being elected
" alfo one of the Vifitors of *Wm. & Mary* College a felf-elect-
" ing Body, I effected, during my Refidence in *Williamfburg* that
" Year, a Change in the Organization of that Inftitution by abol-
" ifhing the Grammar School, and the two Profefforfhips of
" Divinity and Oriental Languages, and fubftituting a Profeffor-
" fhip of Law & Police, one of Anatomy Medicine and Chemiftry,
" and one of Modern Languages; and the Charter confining us to
" fix Profefforfhips, we added the Law of Nature & Nations, &
" the Fine Arts to the Duties of the Moral Profeffor, and Natural
" Hiftory to thofe of the Profeffor of Mathematics and Natural
" Philofophy. "

[157]

Ibid., p. 6.

[158]

Bifhop [*William*] *Meade*, OLD CHURCHES, MIN-
ISTERS AND FAMILIES OF VIRGINIA
(*Philadelphia: J. B. Lippincott & Co.*, 1857), Vol. I,
p. 167.

[159]

The following Publications lift diftinguifhed Alumni
of the College of *William and Mary*. It fhould be
noted, however, that a complete Record of Students at
the College has never been prepared, as the College
Records themfelves are incomplete.

WILLIAM AND MARY COLLEGE QUARTERLY
HISTORICAL MAGAZINE, Firft Series, Vol. VII
(1899), pp. 2-9.

A ROLL OF FAME, [Pamphlet publifhed by the College of *William and Mary*, n.d.]

THE ROMANCE AND RENAISSANCE OF THE
COLLEGE OF WILLIAM AND MARY, Pamph-
let. (*Richmond: Whittet & Shepperfon*, n.d.)

[160]

[160]

*Hugh Jones, THE PRESENT STATE OF VIRGINIA
(London: J. Clarke, 1724), p. 47.*

[161]

*H. R. McIlwaine, ed., JOURNALS OF THE HOUSE
OF BURGESSES OF VIRGINIA, 1742-1749 (Richmond: 1909), pp. 406-407.* Speech of *William Gooch*
to the Council and the Houſe of Burgeſſes, on *May*
11, 1749.

" . . . I am grown old and infirm, and the Leave his Majeſty has
" been gracioufly pleaſed to grant me, of going Home for the Re-
" covery of my Health, was, I muſt confeſs, on my humble Appli-
" cation; yet, be aſſured, tho' ſupported by the comfortable
" Hopes of Relief, I ſhall not, without great Reluctance, depart
" from a Country, to which, by the ſincereſt Affection, a long
" Reſidence, and the Changes and Chances of this mortal Life, I
" am ſo nearly allied. "

Alſo:

*WILLIAM AND MARY COLLEGE QUARTERLY
HISTORICAL MAGAZINE, Firſt Series, Vol. XX
(1912), p. 16.* From Manuſcript in Handwriting of
John Randolph of *Roanoke.*

" . . . Sir *Wᵐ Gooch* ſailed *Augᵗ* 24 [1749]; his Succeſſor . . .
" The Hon: *Jno Robinſon* Preſdᵗ of his My's Council died on
" *Monday* Night at the Houſe of the Hon. *Wᵐ Nelſon* at *York.* "

[162]

*William Waller Hening, THE STATUTES AT
LARGE (Richmond: Franklin Preſs, 1819), Vol. VI,
pp. 197-198. " An Act for Re-building the Capitol in
" the City of Williamſburg. "*
[This Act was finally paſſed on *December* 17, 1748.
See the *Journals of the Houſe of Burgeſſes, 1742-49,*
p. 328.]

Alſo:

*VIRGINIA HISTORICAL SOCIETY, Richmond.
Diary*

Diary of John Blair. [Ms. Diary kept in *The* Virginia *Almanack for the Year of Our Lord God 1751*.]

" *April 1* [1751]   Clear & cool.   N. W.ᵣ   Mʳˢ *Blair* fett off before
" 7 this Aftᵣnoon.   I laid a Foundᵃ Brick at Capitol.   . . .
" *May* 18.   Kiln fired at Capⁱ, Wind Weftˡʸ.   . . .
" [*June*] 4.   Col. *Wᵐ Randolph* & his Lady in Town.   He vifited
" the Works at the Capitol.   . . .
" [*September*] 14.   Found the Capitol as I left it the 3ᵈ, & as it
" had been for fome Time before; not at all advanced.   . . .
" [*December*] 12 . . .   This Afternoon I laid the laft top Brick
" on the Capitol Wall, & fo it is now ready to receive the Roof,
" & fome of the Wall Plates were raifᵈ & laid on this Day.   I had
" laid a Foundation Brick, at the firft Buildᵍ of the Capitol above
" 50 Years ago, & another Foundation Brick in *April* laft, the
" firft in Mortar towards the Rebuilding, and now the laft as
" above. "

[163]

H. R. McIlwaine, ed., *THE JOURNALS OF THE HOUSE OF BURGESSES OF VIRGINIA, 1742-1749 (Richmond:* 1909), pp. 235-236. Speech of the Governor to the Council and Houfe of Burgeffes on *March* 30, 1747.

Alfo:

THE PENNSYLVANIA GAZETTE (Philadelphia: Printed by *B. Franklin*) No. 955, *April* 2, 1747.

" *Williamfburg Feb.* 5 [1747].

" Laft *Friday*, [*January* 30] the fatal and ever memorable Day
" of the Martyrdom of King *Charles* the Firft, a moft extraordi-
" nary Misfortune befel this Place, by the Deftruction of our fine
" Capitol.   Between 7 and 8 o'Clock in the Morning, the Inhabi-
" tants of the City were furprized with the Sight of a Cloud of
" Smoak, iffuing from the upper Part of the Capitol; but no Fire
" appeared on the Outfide.   Soon after fome of the Shingles be-
" gan to kindle on Fire from within, and immediately a Blaze
" burft out, which prefently reached the Cupola, and thence
" communicated the Fire to the Covering of the whole Fabrick.
" The Cupola was foon burnt, the two Bells that were in it were
" melted, and, together with the Clock, fell down, and were de-
" ftroyed; and the whole Covering and Roof foon followed: Then
" the upper Floor of the feveral Rooms took Fire, foon burnt
" thro',

" thro', and defcended to the fecond Floor, and fo to the Bottom,
" till the whole Timber and Wood-work was deftroyed, and the
" naked Brick Walls only left ftanding, which, however, feem
" good, except one or two fmall Cracks in the Semi-circles.
" During this Confternation and Hurry, all the Records depofited
" in the Capitol, except a few loofe, ufelefs Papers, were . . .
" happily preferved; as were alfo the Pictures of the Royal
" Family, and feveral other Things . . . "

[164]

PUBLIC RECORD OFFICE, London. Colonial Office
5/1423. Journals of the Council, 1740-1752.

[p. 402]   " At a Council held *September* the fourth 1749.

" The Council having taken under their Confideration the ru-
" inous Condition of the Governor's Houfe thought proper that
" it fhould be furveyed by fome fkilful Perfons and an Eftimate
" made by them of the Charge of putting it in good Repair, and
" were pleafed to appoint Mr. *James Wray* and Mr. *Richard*
" *Taliaferro* for that Purpofe . . . "

[p. 407]   " At a Council held *November* the fecond 1749

" The Council this Day having taken a View of the Govern-
" or's Houfe, and confidered the bad State in which they found
" it, were of Opinion, that it fhould be generally and thoroughly
" repaired. "

Alfo:

VIRGINIA HISTORICAL SOCIETY, Richmond.
GOOCH PAPERS, TRANSCRIPTS. Vol. III,
p. 1015. Letter of *Thomas Lee,* acting Governor of *Vir-*
ginia, to Lords Commiffioners of Trade & Plantations.

" W^mfburg Nov. 7, 1749.

" . . . The Governor's Houfe, Gardens, etc., has been viewed
" and examined by our moft fkillful Architect and he reports that
" the neceffary Repairs will coft £1259.6, Curt Money, which
" being Matter of Revenue, the Expenfe of thofe Repairs, I have
" acquainted the Lords of His Majefty's Treafury with it, . . . "

[165]

THE VIRGINIA GAZETTE (Williamfburg: Printed
by *William Parks*), No. 490. From *Thurfday,*
December 12, to *Thurfday, December* 19, 1745.

" The

"The Play-Houſe in *Williamſburg*, being, by Order of the
"Common-Hall of the ſaid City, to be fitted up for a Court-
"Houſe, with the neceſſary Alterations and Repairs; that is to
"ſay, to be new ſhingled, weatherboarded, painted, five large Saſh
"Windows, Door, Flooring, Plaiſtering, and proper Workmanſhip
"within: Notice is hereby given, to all ſuch as are willing to
"undertake the doing thereof, That they offer their Propoſals to
"the Mayor, who will inform them more particularly what is to
"be done."

Alſo:

YORK COUNTY RECORDS, Book V, Deeds, pp. 153-155.

[166]

THE VIRGINIA GAZETTE (*Williamſburg:* Printed by *William Hunter*), No. 35. *Auguſt* 29, 1751.

"*Williamſburg, Auguſt* 27, 1751.

"By Permiſſion of His Honour the Preſident,

"Whereas the *Company of Comedians* that are in *New-York*
"intend performing in this City; but there being no Room ſuit-
"able for a Play-Houſe, 'tis propoſ'd that a Theatre ſhall be
"built by Way of Subſcription: each Subſcriber, advancing a
"Piſtole, to be entitled to a Box Ticket, for the firſt Night's Di-
"verſion.

"Thoſe Gentlemen and Ladies who are kind enough to favour
"this Undertaking, are deſired to ſend their Subſcription Money
"to Mr. *Finnie's*, at the *Raleigh*, where Tickets may be had.

"N.B. The Houſe to be completed by *October* Court."

Alſo:

Ibid., No. 43, *October* 24, 1751.

[167]

H. R. McIlwaine, ed., *JOURNALS OF THE HOUSE OF BURGESSES OF VIRGINIA, 1742-1749* (*Richmond:* 1909), pp. 235-236, 239, 242-243, 244, 245, 250-251, 256-257, 263, 266, 284-285, 290-291, 294, 296, 301, 328.

[The above Page References are to the Diſpute between the Governor, Council, and Burgeſſes regarding

ing the Removal of the Capital, and the final Deciſion to rebuild the Capitol in *Williamſburg*.]

[168]

THE VIRGINIA GAZETTE (*Williamſburg*: Printed by *William Hunter*), No. 47, *November* 21, 1751.

" *Williamſburg, November* 22.

" On *Wedneſday* the Honourable *Robert Dinwiddie* Eſq; our
" Governor, arrived ſafe at *York* with his Lady and Family, on
" board the *Martha*, Capt. *Cappes*, and the next Day came up
" to Town.   At his Entrance he was met by the Mayor, Record-
" er, Aldermen and Common Council, who congratulated him
" on his ſafe Arrival, and welcom'd him to the City.   After meet-
" ing the Council and qualifying himſelf by taking the Oaths, *&c.*
" his Honour was invited to an Entertainment prepared by the
" Gentlemen of the Corporation, and the loyal Healths drank,
" under a Diſcharge of the Cannon.   In the Evening he returned
" to *York*, and is expected back again this Day. "

Alſo:

VIRGINIA HISTORICAL SOCIETY, Richmond. *The Diary of* John Blair. [Ms. Diary kept in *The* Virginia *Almanack for the Year of Our Lord God* 1751.]

" [*November* 21, 1751.] Mr Commiſſy, Col. *Ludwell &* my ſelf
" went out to meet the Governor, and with Col. *Fairfax*, Mr
" *Nelſon &* the Secretary, (who came up with him from *York*)
" attended him to his Houſe.   At the Entrance of the Town he
" was complimented by the Mayor *&* Aldermen, who (wth the
" Gentn) were got together to welcome him, and invited him *&*
" the Council to a Dinner they had prepared at *Wetherburns*,
" where we all dined.   At the Govrs Houſe he produced his Com-
" miſſion wth a handſome Speech declaring his Purpoſe of ſtudy-
" ing the Welfare of the Country, relying on the Aſſiſtance of the
" Council, as his Majeſty had vouchſafed to appoint him to this
" Care.   Col. *Fairfax*, Mr *Nelſon* and my ſelf adminiſter'd the
" Oaths to the Govr . . .
" [*November*] 22.   The Govr went back to *York* Yeſterday, *&* re-
" turn'd this Evening wth his Lady *&* Daughters to ye Attorney's.
" [*November*] 23.   Mrs *Blair* and I dined wth them there by Invi-
" tatn *&* many Ladies *&* Gentn viſited them in the Afternoon,
" and were highly pleaſd wth them. "

[169]

[169]

THE VIRGINIA GAZETTE (Williamſburg: Printed
by *William Hunter),* No. 48, *November* 28, 1751.

[170]

H. R. *McIlwaine,* ed., *JOURNALS OF THE HOUSE
OF BURGESSES OF VIRGINIA, 1752-1758 (Rich-
mond:* 1909), pp. xvi-xviii, 121, 129, 132, 136, 140-141,
143-144, 154, 156, 166-167.

[The above Pages are concerned with the Diſpute
between Governor *Dinwiddie* and the Burgeſſes
over the Tax of a Piſtole, as a Fee for the Uſe of
the Public Seal.]

Alſo:

R. A. *Brock,* ed; *THE OFFICIAL RECORDS OF
ROBERT DINWIDDIE (Richmond:* Publiſhed by
the *Virginia Hiſtorical Society,* 1883), Vol. I, pp. 44,
45-48, 100, 103, 118, 153-154, 156, 208, 210, 306-307,
362-364, 370-371, 373-374, 376.

[171]

Ibid., pp. 39-40, 48-*et ſeq.*

[172]

PUBLIC RECORD OFFICE, London.   Colonial Office
5/1423.   *Journals of the Council, 1740-1752.*

" At a Council held *October* 29th, 1751.

" The Council having taken into Conſideration the Neceſſity
" of providing a Houſe for the Reception of the Governor It is
" ordered that *John Blair* and *Philip Ludwell* Eſqrs be impower'd
" to treat with any Perſon upon the Hiring of a Houſe for the
" Purpoſe. "

...   " At a Council held *November* 21ſt 1751

" *John Blair* and *Philip Ludwell* Eſqrs. are directed and im-
" power'd to treat and agree with Doctor *McKenzie* of *Williamſ-
" burgh* upon the Purchaſe of his Houſe for the Uſe and Accommo-
" dation of the Governor. "

[173]

[173]

THE VIRGINIA GAZETTE (Williamſburg: Printed
by *William Hunter*), Numb. 96, *November* 10, 1752.

" [*Williamſburg*] This Week arriv'd in Town the Emperor of
" the *Cherokee* Nation, with his Empreſs, to renew the Treaty
" of Friendſhip with this Government."

Ibid., Numb. 97, *November* 17, 1752.

" *Friday* laſt, being the Anniverſary of his Majeſty's Birth-
" Day, in the Evening, the whole City was illuminated. There
" was a Ball, and a very elegant Entertainment, at the Palace,
" where were preſent, the Emperor and Empreſs of the *Cherokee*
" Nation, with their Son the young Prince, and a brilliant Ap-
" pearance of Ladies and Gentlemen; ſeveral beautiful Fireworks
" were exhibited in *Palace* Street, by Mr. *Hallam,* Manager of
" the Theatre in this City, and the Evening concluded with
" every Demonſtration of our Zeal and Loyalty. "

[174]

William Stith, THE HISTORY OF THE FIRST
DISCOVERY AND SETTLEMENT OF VIR-
GINIA *(Williamſburg: William Parks,* 1747), Appendix, pp. 8-22. " *King* James *the I.'s ſecond Charter*
" *to the Treaſurer and Company for* Virginia, *erecting*
" *them into a Corporation and Body Politick, and for*
" *the further Enlargement and Explanation of the Priv-*
" *ileges of the ſaid Company and firſt Colony of* Vir-
" *ginia. Dated* May 23, 1609. . . .

" VI: And we do alſo, of our ſpecial Grace, certain Knowledge,
" and mere Motion, give, grant, and confirm, unto the ſaid
" Treaſurer and Company, and their Succeſſors, under the Reſ-
" ervations, Limitations, and Declarations, hereafter expreſſed,
" all thoſe Lands, Countries, and Territories, ſituate, lying, and
" being, in that Part of *America* called *Virginia,* from the Point
" of Land, called *Cape* or *Point Comfort,* all along the Sea Coaſt,
" to the northward two Hundred Miles, and from the ſaid *Point*
" of *Cape Comfort,* all along the Sea Coaſt, to the ſouthward two
" Hundred Miles, and all that Space and Circuit of Land, lying
" from the Sea Coaſt of the Precinct aforeſaid, up into the Land,
" throughout from Sea to Sea, Weſt, and Northweſt; and alſo all
" the

" the Iflands, lying within one Hundred Miles, along the Coaft
" of both Seas of the Precinct aforefaid; . . ."

[175]

William Maxwell, ed., *THE VIRGINIA HISTORI-
CAL REGISTER*, Vol. I (1848), No. 1, pp. 12-18.

" *The Limits of* Virginia." *by Littleton W. Tazewell.*

" . . . Thus the new Boundaries given to *Virginia* by the
" Charter of *May* 23, 1609, were, in Fact, thefe: On the North,
" the Parallel of 40°; on the South, the Parallel of 34°: on the
" Eaft, the *Atlantic* Ocean, between thefe Parallels; and on the
" Weft, the *Pacific* Ocean, between the fame Parallels.

" Thefe wide Limits were very much contracted in after Time,
" in many different Ways: 1ft. By the Grant of *Maryland*, to
" *Caecilius Calvert*, Baron of *Baltimore* in *Ireland*, made by
" *Charles* the Firft, on the 20th of *June*, 1632. 2d. By the
" Grant of *North Carolina* to the Earl of *Clarendon* and others,
" Proprietaries of that Province, made by *Charles* the Second,
" *June* 30, 1665. 3d. By the Grant of *Pennfylvania* to *William*
" *Penn*, made by *Charles* the Second, *March* 4, 1681. 4th. By
" the Treaty made between *Great Britain* and *France*, (commonly
" called the *Treaty of Paris*, becaufe it was concluded at *Paris*,)
" on the 10th of *February*, 1763; and 5th. By the Conftitution of
" *Virginia* herfelf, adopted *June* 29, 1776. . . ."

[176]

Jared Sparks, *THE WRITINGS OF GEORGE WASH-
INGTON* (*Bofton: Hilliard, Gray and Co.*, 1834),
Vol. II, Appendix, pp. 428-429. Governor *Robert Dinwiddie's* Inftructions to *George Wafhington*, regarding his Trip to the *Ohio* River, dated "*Williamfburg,
30 October*, 1753."

Alfo:

Ibid., pp. 432-447. " *Major* Wafhington's *Journal of a*
" *Tour over the* Alleghany *Mountains.*"

Alfo:

H. R. McIlwaine, ed., *JOURNALS OF THE HOUSE
OF BURGESSES OF VIRGINIA, 1752-1758* (*Richmond:* 1909), pp. 175-176.

[177]

[177]

R. A. Brock, ed., *THE OFFICIAL RECORDS OF ROBERT DINWIDDIE . . . 1751-1758 (Richmond:* Publifhed by the *Virginia Hiftorical Society*, 1883), Vol. I, pp. 208-210. Letter from Governor *Dinwiddie* to the Earl of *Albemarle*, *June* 18, 1754.

" . . . I fent Y'r L'ds. Acc't of Mr. *Wafhington's* Meffage to the
" *French* Com'd't, and his Anfwer. In Obedience to His M'y's
" Com'ds, in *Feb'ry* laft I fent from this a Compa. of Men to the
" *Ohio* to build a Fort . . . in the Mo. of *Apr.* the *French* came
" down that River in 300 Canoes, with near 1,000 Men; they
" imediately march'd up to the Fort I ordered to be built, and
" fumoned them to deliver the Fort to them; as it was not
" finifhed and but few Men, they were obliged to furrender, and
" thereon returned to the Inhabitants. I then had 300 Men on
" their march to join thofe that were building the Fort, and were
" within 75 Miles of them w'n they furrendered. A Detachm't
" of 150 marched out within 35 Miles of the Fort, where they
" entrench'd themfelves. On the 26th of *May* the *French* fent
" out a Party of about 40 Men to reconnoitre and difcover our
" Strength; one of the Chiefs of the *Ind's* fent to our fmall Camp
" an Acc't of the *French* Party, and faid if they w'd join the *Ind's*
" with him they c'd cut them off. Colo. *Wafhington*, with forty
" Men, march'd out that Night, and about fix next Morning
" joined the *Ind's* and march'd out. One of the *Ind'n* Runners
" tract the Feet of the *French* and came up to their Lodgment
" about nine. The *French* feeing our People, got under Arms,
" a Skirmifh enfued, w'n we loft one Man and had two wounded;
" the *French* had 12 killed on the Spot and 21 taken Prifoners,
" w'ch I have in Prifon in this City [*Williamfburg*]. After they
" were taken Prifoners, they pretended they were fent Ambaffa-
" dors from the Com'd'r to the *Englifh* Camp, w'ch muft appear
" an idle Story, from their hankering round our fmall Camp for
" three or four Daies, and their Intentions will appear more plain
" from their Inftruct's from their Com'd'r, w'ch I have in my
" Hands, . . . "

[178]

William Gordon, THE HISTORY OF THE RISE, PROGRESS, AND ESTABLISHMENT, OF THE INDEPENDENCE OF THE UNITED STATES OF

OF AMERICA (*London:* Printed for the Author; and fold by *Charles Dilly,* in the *Poultry;* 1788), Vol. I, p. 136.

" . . . toward the Clofe of 1759, or the Beginning of 1760, Mr.
" *Pitt* wrote to *Francis Fauquier* Efq; Lieutenant Governor of
" *Virginia,* and mentioned in his Letter, that though they had
" made Grants to the Colonies, yet, when the War was over,
" they fhould tax them in order to raife a Revenue from them.
" Mr. *Fauquier,* in his Anfwer, expreffed his Apprehenfion, that
" the Meafure would occafion great Difturbance . . . "

Alfo:

THE VIRGINIA MAGAZINE OF HISTORY AND BIOGRAPHY , Vol. XII (1905), pp. 8-14.

Letter to Mr. *Montagu,* Agent for the Colony in *London,* from the *Virginia* Committee of Correfpondence, written from "*Williamfburg,* 28th *July,* 1764."

" We have been very uneafy at an Attempt made in Par-
" liament to lay a Duty on the feveral Commodities mentioned
" in their Votes, of which you were pleafed to favour us with a
" Copy; the Tax upon *Madeira* Wine will be very inconvenient
" to us, & we had it in our Intention to furnifh you with fuch
" Reafons ag't it as we thought might have fome Weight, but
" finding from the public Prints that an Act, impofing this Duty,
" has already paff'd, it is become unneceffary for us to fay any
" Thing farther upon that Head. The Propofal to lay a Stamp
" Duty upon Paper & Leather is truly alarming; fhould it take
" place, the immediate Effects of an additional, heavy Burthen
" impofed upon a People already laden with Debts, contracted
" chiefly in Defence of the common Caufe & neceffarily to con-
" tinue by exprefs Stipulation for a Number of Years to come,
" will be feverely felt by us & our Children; but what makes the
" approaching Storm appear ftill more gloomy & difmal is, that,
" if it fhould be fuffer'd to break upon our Heads, not only we &
" our Children, but our lateft Pofterity may & will probably be
" involved in its fatal Confequences. It may, perhaps, be
" thought prefumptious in us to attempt or even to defire any
" Thing which may look like a Reftraint upon the controlling
" Power of Parliament; we only wifh that our juft Liberties &
" Privileges as free born *Britifh* Subjects were once properly de-
" fin'd, & we think that we may venture to fay that the People
" of

"of *Virginia*, however they may have been mirepreiented,
"would never entertain the moſt diſtant Inclination to tranſgreſs
"their juſt Limits.   That no Subjeɛts of the King of *Great Brit-*
"*ain* can be juſtly made ſubſervient to Laws without either their
"perſonal Conſent, or their Conſent by their Repreſentatives we
"take to be the moſt vital Principle of the *Britiſh* Conſtitution;
"it cannot be denied that the Parliament has from Time to
"Time, where the Trade of the Colonies with other Parts was
"likely to interfere with that of the Mother Country, made ſuch
"Laws as were thought ſufficient to reſtrain ſuch Trade to what
"was judg'd its proper Channel, neither can it be denied that,
"the Parliament, out of the ſame Plentitude of its Power, has
"gone a little Step farther & impoſed ſome Duties upon our
"Exports; but to fix a Tax upon ſuch Part of our Trade & Con-
"cerns as are merely internal, appears to us to be taking a long
"& haſty Stride & we believe may truly be ſaid to be of the firſt
"Importance.   Nothing is farther from our Thoughts than to
"ſhew the leaſt Diſpoſition to any Sort of Rudeneſs, but we hope
"it cannot be taken amiſs that we, apprehending ourſelves ſo
"nearly concern'd, ſhould, at leaſt whilſt the Matter is in Suſ-
"pence, humbly repreſent againſt it, & take every Meaſure
"which the Principles & Laws of our Conſtitution appear
"clearly to juſtify, to avert a Storm ſo very replete with the
"moſt dangerous Conſequences.   We cannot but conſider the
"Attempts which have been made, the more extraordinary when
"we reflect upon the Part we have taken in the late *American* War,
"& that we have always with the greateſt Chearfulneſs ſub-
"mitted to & comply'd with every Requiſition which has been
"made of us with the leaſt Colour of Reaſon or Pretence of Ne-
"ceſſity.   We would therefore have you Sir, & do moſt earneſtly
"recommend to you, as the greateſt Objeɛt of our preſent Con-
"cern, the exerting your whole Weight & Influence ſo far as
"Decency will allow in oppoſing this & every other Meaſure of
"the Sort; and ſince we find, upon other Occaſions, that you
"have met with a ready Diſpoſition in the Agents of the other
"Colonies to cooperate with you, whenever the general Intereſt
"of the Continent of *America* ſeems to have been concern'd, we
"are of Opinion that their Aid & Aſſiſtance, in all Probability
"can never, upon any Occaſion whatever, be more ſeaſonably
"aſk'd than in the preſent Conjunɛture, . . . "

Alſo:

John Pendleton Kennedy, ed., *JOURNALS OF THE
HOUSE*

HOUSE OF BURGESSES OF VIRGINIA, 1761-1765 (Richmond: 1907), Preface, pp. lix-lxiv.

[The Stamp Act was paſſed by the Houſe of Commons on *February* 27, 1765, paſſed the Houſe of Lords, *March* 8, 1765, without a ſingle diſſenting Voice, and royal Aſſent was ſecured on *March* 22, 1765. It did not go into effect, however, until *November* 1, 1765.]

[179]

R. A. Brock, ed., *THE OFFICIAL RECORDS OF ROBERT DINWIDDIE . . . 1751-1758 (Richmond:* Publiſhed by the *Virginia Hiſtorical Society*, 1884), Vol. II, p. 599. Letter of Governor *Dinwiddie* to Hon. *William Pitt.*

" *Philadelphia, Mar.* 22d, 1757.

" R't Hon.:

" The Earl of *Loudoun* having deſir'd the Southern Governors " on this Cont't to attend him in this City to concert proper " Meaſures for the Protect'n of theſe Colonies, at the Time he is " executing the Plan of Operations to the no'w'd, I have accord- " ingly been here 6 Weeks attend'g his L'd'p's Comands. . . .

" I begg leave to inform you that my Health is greatly im- " pair'd, to ſuch a Degree that makes me incapable of diſcharg- " ing the Duties of my Apointm't in ſuch Manner as H. M'ty's " Service and my Inclinat'n requires, on w'ch I've deſir'd L'd " *Loudoun's* Approbat'n to write Home for Leave of Abſence " from my Governm't, and I now moſt humbly intreat you will " procure his M'ty's gracious Permiſſion for me to return to " *Great Britain* for the Recovery of my Health, being of Opinion " that a ſhort Time at *Bath* may be of great [Service]. . . . "

Alſo:

H. R. McIlwaine, ed., *JOURNALS OF THE HOUSE OF BURGESSES OF VIRGINIA, 1752-1758 (Rich-mond:* 1909), p. 414.

[180]

R. A. Brock, ed., *THE OFFICIAL LETTERS OF ROBERT DINWIDDIE (Richmond:* Publiſhed by the

the *Virginia Hiftorical Society*, 1884), Vol. II, pp.
724-725. " Addrefs of the Corporation of *Williamf-*
" *burg* to Governor *Dinwiddie . . . [January*, 1758.] "

[181]

*THE VIRGINIA MAGAZINE OF HISTORY AND
BIOGRAPHY*, Vol. XVI (1908), p. 209. [Notes from
colonial *Virginia* Newfpapers, made by *John Randolph*
of *Roanoke.* Moft of the Papers cited are not now, fo
far as is known, in Exiftence.]

" Lt. Gov. *Fauquier* ar. the firft Week in *June*, 1758, his Com'n
" as Lieutenant Governor is dated *Feb.* 10, 1758. After Gov'r
" *Dinwiddie's* Departure & until Governor *F's* Arrival the Hon.
" *John Blair* was Com'r in Chief of the Colony as P. of the Coun-
" cil. Gov'r *D.* failed *Jan.* 12, 1758. P. *Blair's* Proclam'n
" fame Date. "

[182]

John Pendleton Kennedy, ed., *JOURNALS OF THE
HOUSE OF BURGESSES OF VIRGINIA, 1761-
1765 (Richmond:* 1907), p. 172. Speech of Governor
Fauquier to the Council and Houfe of Burgeffes,
Thurfday, the 19th of *May*, 1763.

" . . . I fhall quit this unpleafing Subject, to enter upon one
" which muft communicate Joy to all true Lovers of their Coun-
" try, I mean the Conclufion of a moft glorious and honourable
" Peace between his Majefty and all his Enemies, of which
" happy Event I take this Opportunity to congratulate with you.
" The Care his Majefty has taken of his *American* Colonies is a
" further Proof of his Attention to their Intereft and Security,
" and demands the ftrongeft Returns of Loyalty, Obedience and
" Affection, from us.

" Mr. Speaker, and Gentlemen of the Houfe of Burgeffes,
" This glorious Profpect of a folid and lafting Peace will afford
" you an Opportunity of particularly attending to the Finances
" of this Colony, and of putting them on a Footing which may
" tend to the Advancement of the Trade and Credit of the Col-
" ony, and the Security and Satisfaction of the Merchants
" trading to it, . . . "

[183]

[183]

William Waller Hening, THE STATUTES AT LARGE (Richmond: The *Franklin Preſs,* 1820), Vol. VII, pp. 663-669. [The Royal Proclamation of 1763, regarding Acquiſitions in *America,* ſecured by the *Treaty of Paris.*]

[184]

John Bukre, THE HISTORY OF VIRGINIA, FROM ITS FIRST SETTLEMENT TO THE PRESENT DAY (Peterſburg: Dickſon & Peſcud, 1805), Vol. III, p. 401.

" The Arrival of *Fauquier* gave a decided Determination to
" the Literature of *Virginia.* Elegant in his Manners, correct
" and claſſical in his Converſation and Writing, the Patron of
" Learning and learned Men, he was regarded by *Virginia* as a
" Model of the Scholar and fine Gentleman, and his Example
" was everywhere the Object of humble Imitation. Profeſſor
" *Small,* whoſe mathematical Skill has been already noticed, with
" many others of Merit, felt the Ray of his Patronage and
" Bounty. It had been well if the Governor had in other Re-
" ſpects exhibited himſelf as a Model equally worthy of Imita-
" tion. His Rage for Play introduced it more generally amongſt
" the People than his more uſeful and eſtimable Qualities, and
" this execrable Vice appeared to be ſanctioned by the Example
" of . . . the moſt elegant Gentlemen in the Country. "

Alſo:

A FRENCH TRAVELLER IN THE COLONIES, 1765. [Original Ms. in *Paris, Service Hydrographique de la Marine,* Vol. 76, No. 2. Photoſtatic Copy in *Reſearch Department, Colonial Williamſburg* Foundation.]

" *Aipril* the 25ᵗʰ [1765] . . . On our Arival [in *Williamſburg*]
" we had great Difficulty to get Lodgings but thanks to Mʳ
" *Sprowl* I got a Room at Mʳˢ *Vaubes's* Tavern, where all the
" beſt People reſorted. I ſoon got acquainted with ſeveral of
" them, but particularly with Colonel *Burd* [Col. *William Byrd*
" the Third], Sir *Peton Skiper* [Sir *Peyton Skipwith*], Capt.
" *Ruſſel,* Capᵗ *le Foré,* and others, which I ſoon, was like to have
" had

" had Reafon to repent, for they are all profeffed Gamefters, ef-
" pecially Colonel *Burd*, who is never happy but when he has y[e]
" Box and Dices in Hand, this Gentleman from a Man of the
" greateft Property of any in *America* has reduced himfelf to that
" Degree by Gameing, that few or nobody will credit him for
" ever fo fmall a Summ of Money, he was obliged to fel 400
" fine Negroes a few Days before my Arival: There were many
" Sets made at me to get me in for the Box but I had the good
" Look [Luck] to keep clear of it, but could not avoid playing
" fome Rubers at Whift notwithftanding my Averfion to it. . . .
" *Aipril* the 28th. . . . This Morning hired a Chair and took a
" Ride to *Jamefes City* formerly the Capital of the Province, . . .
" after Dinner we came back to *Williamfburg;* . . . Never was
" a more difagreable Place than this at Prefent. In the Day
" Time People hurying back and forwards from the Capitoll to
" the Taverns, and at Night, caroufing and drinking in one
" Chamber and Box and Dice in another, which continues till
" Morning commonly, there is not a publick Houfe in *Vir-*
" *ginia* but have their Tables all baterd with y[e] Boxes which
" fhews the extravagant Difpofition of the Planters; there are
" many of them who have very great Eftates, but are moftely at
" lofs for Cafh, . . ."

[185]

See Note 178

[186]

John Pendleton Kennedy, ed., *JOURNALS OF THE HOUSE OF BURGESSES OF VIRGINIA, 1761-1765 (Richmond:* 1907), Preface, lviii-lxiv.

[187]

William Wirt, SKETCHES OF THE LIFE AND CHARACTER OF PATRICK HENRY (Hartford: S. Andrus & Son, 1847, 10th edition), pp. 74-75.

" . . . After his [*Patrick Henry's*] Death, there was found
" among his Papers one fealed, and thus endorfed: ' Enclofed
" are the Refolutions of the *Virginia* Affembly in 1765, concern-
" ing the Stamp Act. Let my Executors open this Paper. '
" Within was found the following Copy of the Refolutions, in
" Mr. *Henry's* Handwriting:—

" *Refolved*, That the firft Adventurers and Settlers of this, his
" Majefty's

" Majefty's Colony and Dominion, brought with them, and
" tranfmitted to their Pofterity, and all other his Majefty's Sub-
" jects, fince inhabiting in this, his Majefty's faid Colony, all the
" Privileges, Franchifes, and Immunities, that have at any Time
" been held, enjoyed, and poffeffed by the People of *Great*
" *Britain*.

" *Refolved*, That by two royal Charters, granted by King
" *James* the Firft, the Colonifts, aforefaid, are declared entitled
" to all the Privileges, Liberties, and Immunities of Denizens
" and natural-born Subjects, to all Intents and Purpofes, as if
" they had been abiding and born within the Realm of *England*.

" *Refolved*, That the Taxation of the People by themfelves,
" or by Perfons chofen by themfelves to reprefent them, who can
" only know what Taxes the People are able to bear, and the
" eafieft Mode of raifing them, and are equally affected by fuch
" Taxes themfelves, is the diftinguifhing Characteriftic of *Britifh*
" Freedom, and without which the ancient Conftitution cannot
" fubfift.

" *Refolved*, That his Majefty's liege People of this moft ancient
" Colony, have uninterruptedly enjoyed the Right of being thus
" governed by their own Affembly, in the Article of their Taxes
" and internal Police, and that the fame hath never been for-
" feited, or any other Way given up, but hath been conftantly
" recognifed by the King and People of *Great Britain*.

" *Refolved*, therefore, That the General Affembly of this Col-
" ony have the fole Right and Power to lay Taxes and Impofi-
" tions upon the Inhabitants of this Colony; and that every
" Attempt to veft fuch Power in any Perfon or Perfons whatfo-
" ever, other than the General Affembly aforefaid, has a mani-
" feft Tendency to deftroy *Britifh* as well as *American* Freedom. "

Alfo:

John Pendleton Kennedy, ed., *JOURNALS OF THE
HOUSE OF BURGESSES OF VIRGINIA, 1761-
1765 (Richmond:* 1907), pp. 359-360.

" *Thurfday*, the 30th of *May*, 5 *Geo*. III. 1765. "

" M.r Attorney, from the Committee of the whole Houfe,
" reported, according to Order, that the Committee had con-
" fidered of the Steps neceffary to be taken in Confequence of
" the Refolutions of the Houfe of Commons of *Great Britain* rel-
" ative to the Charging Stamp Duties in the Colonies and Plan-
" tations in *America*, and that they had come to feveral Refolu-
" tions

" tions thereon; which he read in his Place, and then delivered
" in at the Table, where they were again twice read, and agreed
" to by the Houſe, with ſome Amendments, and are as follow: ..."

[Here are given the firſt four Reſolutions as above
preſented, the fifth Reſolution having been expunged
(ſee Note 191) from the Journals.]

[188]

William Wirt, SKETCHES OF THE LIFE AND
CHARACTER OF PATRICK HENRY *(Hartford:
S. Andrus & Son,* 1847, 10th Edition), pp. 83-84.

" It was in the Midſt of this magnificent Debate, while he
" [*Patrick Henry*] was deſcanting on the Tyranny of the obnoxi-
" ous Act, that he exclaimed in a Voice of Thunder, and with the
" look of a God: ' *Ceſar* had his *Brutus*—*Charles* the Firſt, his
" *Cromwell*—and *George* the Third '—('Treaſon! ' cried the
" Speaker—' Treaſon, Treaſon! ' echoed from every Part of the
" Houſe. It was one of thoſe trying Moments which is deciſive
" of Character. *Henry* faltered not for an Inſtant; but riſing to
" a loftier Attitude, and fixing on the Speaker an Eye of the moſt
" determined Fire, he finiſhed his Sentence with the firmeſt Em-
" phaſis)—' may profit by their Example. If this be Treaſon,
" make the moſt of it.' " *

[*Wirt's* Footnote] " I had frequently heard the above Anec-
" dote of the Cry of Treaſon, but with ſuch Variations of the con-
" cluding Words, that I began to doubt whether the whole might
" not be Fiction. With a View to aſcertain the Truth, therefore,
" I ſubmitted it to Mr. *Jefferſon*, as it had been given to me by
" Judge *Tyler*, and this is his Anſwer: ' I well remember the
" Cry of Treaſon, the Pauſe of Mr. *Henry* at the Name of *George*
" III., and the Preſence of Mind with which he cloſed his Sen-
" tence, and baffled the Charge vociferated. ' The Incident,
" therefore, becomes authentic Hiſtory. "

[189]

A FRENCH TRAVELLER IN THE COLONIES,
1765. [Original in *Paris, Service Hydrographique de
la Marine,* Vol. 76, No. 2. Photoſtatic Copy in
Reſearch Department, Colonial Williamſburg Foundation.]

" May

" *May* the 30ᵗʰ [1765] . . . arived at *Williamſburg* at 12.
" where I ſaw three Negroes hanging at the Galous for haveing
" robed Mʳ *Waltho* [*Nathaniel Walthoe*, Clerk of the Council] of
" 300 pˢ. I went imediately to the Aſſembly which was ſeting,
" where I was entertained with very ſtrong Debates concerning
" Dutys that the Parlement wants to lay on the *American*
" Colonys, which they call or ſtile Stamp Dutys. Shortly after
" I came in one of the Members ſtood up and ſaid he had read
" that in former Times *Tarquin* and *Julus*, had their *Brutus*.
" *Charles* had his *Cromwell*, and he did not doubt but ſome good
" *American* would ſtand up, in Favour of his Country but (ſays
" he) in a more moderate Manner. And was going to continue,
" when the Speaker of the Houſe roſe and ſaid, he, the laſt that
" ſtood up, had ſpoke Traiſon, and was ſorey to ſee that not one
" of the Members of the Houſe was loyal enough to ſtop him, before
" he had gone ſo far. Upon which the ſame Member ſtood up
" again, (his Name is *Henery*) and ſaid that if he had afronted
" the Speaker, or the Houſe, he was ready to aſk Pardon. And he
" would ſhew his Loyalty to his Majeſty King G. the Third, at
" the Expence of the laſt Drop of his Blood. But what he had ſaid
" muſt be atributed to the Intereſt of his Countrys dying Liberty
" which he had at Heart, and the Heat of Paſſion might have
" lead him to have ſaid ſomething more than he intended, but,
" again, if he ſaid any Thing wrong, he beged the Speaker and
" the Houſes Pardon; ſome other Members ſtood up and backed
" him on which that Afaire was droped. "

[190]

Paul Leiceſter Ford, ed., *THE WORKS OF THOMAS
JEFFERSON* (*New York: G. P. Putnam's* Sons,
1905), Vol. XI, pp. 400-410. Letter from *Thomas
Jefferſon* to *William Wirt*, *Auguſt* 14, 1814.

" . . . I proceed now to the Reſolution of 1765. . . . I was
" ſtanding at the Door of Communication between the Houſe and
" Lobby during the Debates and Vote, and well remember, that
" after the Numbers on the Diviſion were told, and declared
" from the Chair, *Peyton Randolph* (then Attorney General)
" came out at the Door where I was ſtanding, and exclaimed,
" ' By *God*, I would have given one Hundred Guineas for a ſingle
" Vote. ' For one Vote would have divided the Houſe, and
" *Robinſon* was in the Chair, who he knew would have negatived
" the Reſolution. . . . "

Alſo:

Alſo:

The ſeeming Inconſiſtency in the Poſition of *Peyton Randolph* and the other conſervative Patriots who looked with Disfavor on *Patrick Henry's* Reſolutions, yet adhered to the Principles involved, may be explained by *Jefferſon's* Statement, as follows:

Thomas Jefferſon Randolph, MEMOIR, CORRESPONDENCE, AND MISCELLANIES, FROM THE PAPERS OF THOMAS JEFFERSON (Boſton: Gray and Bowen, 1830), Vol. I, pp. 92-93. " *Notes for the Biography of* George Wythe, " prepared by *Jefferſon*, in 1820.

" In 1774 [1764], he [*George Wythe*] was a Member of a
" Committee of the Houſe of Burgeſſes, appointed to prepare
" a Petition to the King, a Memorial to the Houſe of Lords, and a
" Remonſtrance to the Houſe of Commons, on the Subject of the
" propoſed *Stamp Act*. He was made Draughtſman of the laſt,
" and, following his own Principles, he ſo far overwent the timid
" Heſitations of his Colleagues, that his Draught was ſubjected
" by them to material Modifications; and, when the famous
" Reſolutions of Mr. *Henry*, in 1775 [1765], were propoſed, it
" was not on any Difference of Principle that they were oppoſed
" by *Wythe, Randolph, Pendleton, Nicholas, Bland*, and other
" Worthies, who had long been the habitual Leaders of the
" Houſe; but becauſe thoſe Papers of the preceding Seſſion had
" already expreſſed the ſame Sentiments and Aſſertions of Right,
" and that an Anſwer to them was yet to be expected."

[191]

Paul Leiceſter Ford, ed., *THE WORKS OF THOMAS JEFFERSON (New York: G. P. Putnam's Sons, 1905), Vol. XI, p. 404.*

" . . . Mr. *Henry* left Town that Evening, or the next Morning;
" and Colonel *Peter Randolph*, then a Member of the Council,
" came to the Houſe of Burgeſſes about ten o'Clock of the Fore-
" noon, and ſat at the Clerk's Table till the Houſe-bell rang,
" thumbing over the Volumes of Journals to find a Precedent of
" expunging a Vote of the Houſe, which he ſaid had taken Place
" while he was a Member or Clerk of the Houſe, I do not
" recollect

" recollect which. I ftood by him at the End of the Table a
" confiderable Part of the Time, looking on as he turned over
" the Leaves, but I do not recollect whether he found the
" Erafure. In the meantime, fome of the timid Members, who
" had voted for the ftrongeft Refolution, had become alarmed,
" and as foon as the Houfe met, a Motion was made, and
" carried, to expunge it from the Journals. "

[192]

A FRENCH TRAVELLER IN THE COLONIES, 1765, [Original in *Paris, Service Hydrographique de la Marine*, Vol. 76, No. 2. Photoftatic Copy in *Refearch Department, Colonial Williamfburg* Foundation.]

" *May* the 31ᵗ [1765] I returned to the Affembly today, and
" heard very hot Debates ftil about the Stamp Dutys, the whole
" Houfe was for entering Refolves in the Records but they dif-
" fered much with Regard the Contents or Purport therof, fome
" were for fhewing their Refentment to the higheft. One of the
" Refolves that thefe propofed, was that, any Perfon that would
" offer to fuftain that the Parlement of *Englᵈ* had a Right to im-
" pofe or lay any Tax or Dutys whatfʳ on the *American* Colonys,
" without the Confent of the Inhabitants therof, fhould be
" looked upon as a Traitor, and deemed an Enemy to his Coun-
" try. There were fome others to the fame Purpofe, and the
" Majority was for entring thefe Refolves. Upon which the Gov-
" ernor difolved the Affembly. Which hindered their proceeding.

" The Kings Berth Night which was on the *Tuefday* follow'g
" was given by the Lieutenant Governor Mʳ *Faquier*, I went
" there in Expectation of feeing a great Deal of Company, but
" was difapointed for there was not above a dozen of People.
" I came away before Super. "

Alfo:

John Pendleton Kennedy, ed., *JOURNALS OF THE HOUSE OF BURGESSES OF VIRGINIA, 1761-1765 (Richmond:* 1907), p. 364.

[193]

PUBLIC RECORD OFFICE, London. *Colonial Office*, 1331. Letter of Governor *Fauquier* to Board of Trade.

Trade. [Photoftatic Copy in *Refearch Department, Colonial Williamfburg* Foundation.]

"*W^mfburgh Nov^r* 3^d 1765.

" My Lords,

" The prefent unhappy State of this Colony will, to my great
" Concern, oblige me to trouble your Lordfhips with a long and
" very difagreeable Letter. We were for fome Time, in almoft
" daily Expectations of the Arrival of Colonel *Mercer* with the
" Stamps for the Ufe of this Colony. And Rumours were induftri-
" oufly thrown out, that at the Time of the General Court,
" Parties would come down from moft Parts of the Country to
" feize on, and deftroy all ftamp'd Papers. . . .

" Very unluckily Colonel *Mercer* arrived at the Time this
" Town was the fulleft of Strangers. On *Wednefday* the 30th
" *October* he came up to Town. I then thought proper to go to
" the Coffee Houfe (where I occafionally fometimes go) which is
" fituated in that Part of the Town which is call'd the Exchange
" tho' an open Street, where all Money Bufinefs is tranfacted.
" My particular Reafon for going then was, that I might be an
" Eye Witnefs of what did really pafs, and not receive it by Re-
" lation from others. The mercantile People were all affembled
" as ufual. The firft Word I heard was ' One and all. ' Upon
" which as at a Word agreed on before between themfelves, they
" all quitted the Place to find Colonel *Mercer* at his Fathers
" Lodgings where it was known he was. This Concourfe of
" People I fhould call a Mob, did I not know that it was chiefly
" if not altogether compofed, of, Gentlemen of Property in the
" Colony fome of them at the Head of their refpective Counties,
" and the Merchants of the Country, whether *Englifh Scotch*, or
" *Virginian*, for few abfented themfelves. They met Colonel
" *Mercer* on the Way juft at the Capitol. There they ftop'd and
" demanded of him an Anfwer whether he would refign or act in
" his Office as Diftributor of the Stamps. He faid it was an
" Affair of great Moment to him, he muft confult his Friends,
" and promifed to give them an Anfwer at 10 o'Clock on *Friday*
" Morning at that Place. This did not fatisfy them, and they
" followed him to the Coffee Houfe, in the Porch of which I had
" feated myfelf with many of the Council and the Speaker who
" had pofted himfelf between the Crowd and myfelf. We all
" received him with the greateft Marks of Welcome; with wch if
" one may be allowed to judge by their Countenances they were
" not well pleafed, tho' they remained quiet and were filent.

" Now

" Now and then a Voice was heard from the Crowd, that *Friday*
" was too late, the Act would take Place, they would have an
" Anfwer tomorrow. Several Meffages were brought to M^r
" *Mercer* by the leading Men of the Crowd, to whom he conftantly
" anfwered he had already given an Anfwer and he would have
" no other extorted from him. After fome little Time, a Cry
" was heard ' Let us rufh in. ' Upon this we, that were at the
" Top of the Steps knowing the Advantage our Situation gave us
" to repell thofe who fhould attempt to mount them, advanced
" to the Edge of the Steps, of which Number I was one.   I imme-
" diately heard a Cry, ' See the Governor take care of him. '
" Thofe who before were pufhing up the Steps immediately fell
" back and left a fmall Space between me and them. If your
" Lordfhips will not accufe me of Vanity I would fay that I be-
" lieve this to be partly owing to the Refpect they bore to my
" Character, and partly to the Love they bore to my Perfon.
" After much Entreaty of fome of his Friends, Mr *Mercer* was
" againft his own Inclination prevailed upon to promife them an
" Anfwer at the Capitol the next Evening at five.   The Crowd
" did not yet difperfe, it was growing dark and I did not think
" it fafe to leave Mr *Mercer* behind me, fo I again advanced to
" the Edge of the Steps, and faid aloud I believed no Man there
" would do me any Hurt, and turned to Mr *Mercer* & told him if
" he would walk with me through the People I believed I could
" conduct him fafe to my Houfe, and we accordingly walked
" Side by Side through the thickeft of the People who did not
" moleft us, tho' there was fome little Murmurs. By my thus
" taking him under my Protection I believe I faved him from
" being infulted at leaft.   When we got Home we had much Dif-
" courfe on the Subject.   He afked me what he fhould do; in re-
" turn I afked him whether he was afraid for his Life, if he was,
" it was too tender a Point for me to advife him; if not, his Honor
" and Intereft both demanded he fhould hold the Office: and if
" that fhould be his Refolution he muft not regard the Reafonings
" of his Father and Brother two Lawyers attending the Court who
" were both frighted out of their Senfes for him.   He left me
" that Night in a State of Uncertainty what Part he fhould
" act. . . . "

[194]

THE VIRGINIA GAZETTE-SUPPLEMENT
(*Williamfburg:* Printed by *J. Royle*), October 25, 1765.

" *Williamfburg, October* 31

" . . . And

" . . . And accordingly he [Mr. *George Mercer*] was met this
" Evening at the Capitol, the Place agreed on, by a vaſt Number
" of Gentlemen, among them all the principal trading People in
" the Colony; . . . Mr. *Mercer* then addreſſed himſelf to the
" Company in the following Manner:

" ' Gentlemen,

" ' I now have met you agreeable to Yeſterday's Promiſe, to
" give my Country ſome Aſſurances which I would have been
" glad I could with any tolerable Propriety have done ſooner.

" ' I flatter myſelf no judicious Man can blame me for accept-
" ing an Office under an Authority that was never diſputed by
" any from whom I could be adviſed of the Propriety or Weight
" of the Objections. I do acknowledge that ſome little Time
" before I left *England* I heard of, and ſaw, ſome Reſolves which
" were ſaid to be made by the Houſe of Burgeſſes of *Virginia;*
" but as the Authenticity of them was diſputed, they never ap-
" pearing but in private Hands, and ſo often and differently
" repreſented and explained to me, I determined to know the
" real Sentiments of my Countrymen from themſelves. And
" I am concerned to ſay that thoſe Sentiments were ſo ſuddenly
" and unexpectedly communicated to me that I was altogether
" unprepared to give an immediate Anſwer upon ſo important
" a Point; for in however unpopular a Light I may lately have
" been viewed, . . . yet I ſtill flatter myſelf that Time will juſ-
" tify me, and that my Conduct may not be condemned after
" being coolly inquired into.

" ' The Commiſſion ſo very diſagreeable to my Countrymen
" was ſolely obtained by the genteel Recommendation of their
" Repreſentatives in General Aſſembly, unaſked for; and though
" this is contradictory to publick Report, which I am told
" charges me with aſſiſting the Paſſage of the Stamp Act, upon
" the Promiſe of the Commiſſion in this Colony, yet I hope it will
" meet with Credit, when I aſſure you I was ſo far from aſſiſting
" it, or having any previous Promiſe from the Miniſtry, that I
" did not know of my Appointment until ſometime after my Re-
" turn from *Ireland,* where I was at the Commencement of the
" Seſſion of Parliament, and for a long Time after the Act had
" paſſed.

" ' Thus, Gentlemen, am I circumſtanced. I ſhould be glad to
" act now in ſuch a Manner as would juſtify me to my Friends
" and Countrymen here, and the Authority which appointed me;
" but the Time you have allotted me for my Anſwer is ſo very
" Short that I have not yet been able to diſcover that happy
" Medium,

" Medium, therefore muſt intreat you to be referred to my future
" Conduct, with this Aſſurance in the mean Time that I will not,
" directly or indirectly, by myſelf or Deputies, proceed in the
" Execution of the Act until I receive further Orders from *Eng-
" land*, and not then without the Aſſent of the General Aſſembly
" of this Colony; and that no Man can more ardently and ſin-
" cerely wiſh the Proſperity thereof, or is more deſirous of ſecur-
" ing all its juſt Rights and Privileges, than Gentlemen, Your
" ſincere Friend, . . . *George Mercer.* ' "

[195]

John Pendleton Kennedy, ed., *JOURNALS OF THE
HOUSE OF BURGESSES OF VIRGINIA, 1761-
1765 (Richmond:* 1907), Preface, lxxv.

" A Proclamation

" *Virginia*, to wit:
" Whereas, his Majeſty has been graciouſly pleaſed to give his
" Aſſent to an Act of Parliament (a Copy of which is now in this
" Colony) entitled An Act to repeal an Act made in the laſt
" Seſſion of Parliament, entitled An Act for granting and apply-
" ing certain Stamp Duties, and other Duties, in the *Britiſh*
" Colonies and Plantations in *America*, towards further defray-
" ing the Expenſe of defending, protecting, and ſecuring the
" ſame and for amending ſuch Parts of the ſeveral Acts of Parlia-
" ment, relating to the Trade and Revenue of the ſaid Colonies
" and Plantations, as direct the Manner of determining and re-
" covering the Penalties and Forfeitures therein mentioned: I
" have thought proper, by and with the Advice of his Majeſty's
" Council, to iſſue this Proclamation, hereby notifying the ſame; ...
" Given under my Hand, and the Seal of the Colony, at *Wil-
" liamſburg*, this 9th Day of *June* 1766, and the 6th Year of his
" Majeſty's Reign.

Francis Fauquier. "

[196]

THE VIRGINIA GAZETTE (Williamſburg: Printed
by *Alex. Purdie & John Dixon*), No. 787. *June* 20,
1766.

" *Williamſburg, June* 20.
" On *Friday* laſt, a good deal of Company being in Town at
" the Oyer and Terminer Court, our Gratitude and Thankful-
" neſs upon the joyful Occaſion of the Repeal of the Stamp Act,
" and

" and the univerfal Pleafure and Satisfaction it gives that all
" Differences between the Mother Country and her Colonies are
" fo happily terminated, was manifefted here by general Illumi-
" nations, and a Ball and elegant Entertainment at the Capitol,
" at which was prefent his Honour the Governour, many of the
" Members of his Majefty's Council, and a large and genteel
" Company of Ladies and Gentlemen, who fpent the Evening
" with much Mirth and Decorum, and drank all the loyal and
" patriotick Toafts. "

[197]

THE VIRGINIA GAZETTE (*Williamfburg:* Printed
by *William Rind*), No. 95, *March* 3, 1768.

" *Williamfburg, March* 3, 1768.

" This Morning, at 2 o'Clock, the Hon. *Francis Fauquier*, Efq;
" Lieutenant-Governor and Commander in Chief of this Domin-
" ion, fubmitted to the relentlefs Hand of Death, and was re-
" lieved from thofe numerous Infirmities which imbittered the
" latter Part of his Exiftence. The many good Qualities which
" united in this Gentleman, render the Tribute of Reverence
" juftly due to his Memory. As a faithful Reprefentative of his
" Sovereign; he was vigilant in Government, moderate in Power,
" exemplary in Religion, and merciful where the Rigour of Juf-
" tice could by any Means be difpenfed with.

" In the Exercife of his lefs public Virtues; he was warm in his
" Attachments, punctual in his Engagements, munificient to
" Indigence, and in his domeftick Connexions truly paternal.
" Though his End was accompanied with uncommon Anguifh,
" yet no Sigh or Complaint iffued from his Bofom, no Pain inter-
" rupted the Serenity of his Mind. His Life was a Pattern
" worthy of Imitation. Let his Succeffors therefore walk in his
" Paths: Let his Survivors take Heed to his Ways. The Tafk
" is not Difficult, when they have before them fo ftrongly im-
" preffed the Footfteps of this upright Man. "

Alfo:

Ibid., No. 96. *March* 10, 1768.

" *Williamfburg, March* 10.

" Laft *Tuefday* the Remains of our late Governor, the Hon.
" *Francis Fauquier*, Efq; were interred in the north Ifle of the
" Church in this City. The Hon. the Prefident, and fuch
" Members of his Majefty's Council as lived convenient, the
" Hon.

" Hon. Mr. Speaker, the Treafurer, his Majefty's Attorney
" General, and all the principal Gentlemen of this Place and
" Neighbourhood, affifted in paying the laft Offices to the De-
" ceafed, fincerely lamenting the Lofs of a Ruler who had en-
" deared himfelf to them. The Militia of this City alfo attended,
" and paid the Honours due to his Memory upon this melan-
" choly Occafion. "

[198]

Ibid., No. 96. *Thurfday, March* 10, 1768.

[199]

*Paul Leicefter Ford, THE WORKS OF THOMAS
JEFFERSON (New York & London: G. P. Putnam's
Sons,* 1904), *Vol. I, pp.* 29-30. *Letter of John Adams
to Timothy Pickering, Auguft* 22, 1822.

" You inquire why fo young a Man as Mr. *Jefferfon* was
" placed at the Head of the Committee for preparing a Declara-
" tion of Independence? I anfwer: it was the *Frankfort* Advice,
" to place *Virginia* at the Head of every Thing. . . .
" The Sub-committee met. *Jefferfon* propofed to me to make
" the Draft. I faid: ' I will not. ' ' You fhould do it. ' ' Oh!
" no. ' . . . ' Why? ' ' Reafons enough. ' ' What can be
" your Reafons? ' ' Reafon firft—You are a *Virginian*, and a
" *Virginian* ought to appear at the Head of this Bufinefs.
" Reafon fecond—I am obnoxious, fufpected, and unpopular.
" You are very much otherwife. Reafon third—You can write
" ten Times better than I can. ' ' Well, ' faid *Jefferfon*, ' If you
" are decided, I will do as well as I can. ' "

[200]

John Pendleton Kennedy, ed., *JOURNALS OF THE
HOUSE OF BURGESSES OF VIRGINIA,* 1766-
1769 *(Richmond:* 1906), *pp.* 140-142. [A Proclamation iffued by " the Honourable *John Blair*, Efq;
" Prefident of his Majefty's Council, and Commander
" in Chief of the faid Colony and Dominion " ordering the General Affembly to meet on *March* 31, 1768.
Alfo *John Blair's* Speech at the Opening of the
Affembly.]

[201]

Ibid., Preface, p. ix.   " . . . The

" . . . The Effect of the Repeal of the Stamp Act, however,
" foon caufed George III to repent of his Action; he regarding
" it as a ' fatal Compliance with popular Demand, ' and de-
" termined to hold abfolute Authority in the Colonies. *Charles*
" *Townſhend*, Chancellor of the Exchequer, advanced a Method
" by which a Revenue might be drawn from *America* without
" Offence. He ftated that he was a ' firm Advocate of the Stamp
" Act, for its Principle and for Duty itfelf; . . . I laugh at the
" abfurd Diftinction between internal and external Taxes. I
" know of no fuch Diftinction. It is a Diftinction without a
" Difference; it is perfect Nonfenfe; if we have a Right to impofe
" the one, we have a Right to impofe the other; . . . ' Then laying
" his Hand on the Table in front of him, he added, ' *England*
" is undone, if this Taxation is given up. ' "

Alſo:

Mary A. M. Marks, ENGLAND AND AMERICA
(*London: Brown, Langham &* Co. Ltd., 1907), Vol.
I. pp. 86-87.

" *Townſhend* rofe. . . . He fhould bring into the Houfe fome
" Propofitions which he hoped might tend in Time to relieve
" the People of *England*, and yet not to be heavy on the Col-
" onies. ' I know the Mode by which a Revenue may be drawn
" from *America* without Offence. ' . . . ' I am ftill for the
" Stamp Act, ' . . . ' It was only the Heats that made it im-
" proper at the Time. I laugh at the Diftinction between in-
" ternal and external Taxation! ' Then looking up to where
" the colonial Agents ufed to fit, he continued: ' I fpeak this
" aloud, that you who are in the Galleries may hear me; and
" after this, I do not expect to have my Statue erected in
" *America!* ' Then, as he fat down, he added, laying his Hand
" on the Table in Front of him, ' *England* is undone if this
" Taxation of *America* is given up! ' "

[202]

William Gordon, THE HISTORY OF THE RISE,
PROGRESS, AND ESTABLISHMENT, OF THE
INDEPENDENCE OF THE UNITED STATES
OF AMERICA (*London:* Printed for the Author, and
fold by *Charles Dilly*, in the *Poultry*, 1788), Vol. I,
p. 214.

" [*May*

" [*May* 13, 1767] The Chancellor of the Exchequer [*Charles
" Townſhend*] moved for Leave to bring in Bills, for granting a
" Duty upon Paper, Glaſs, Painters Colours, *&c.* in the *Britiſh
" American* Colonies; for ſettling Salaries on the Governors, Judges,
" *&c.* in *North America;* and for taking off the Duty on Teas ex-
" ported to *America,* and granting a Duty of three-pence a Pound
" on the Importation in *America.* Two Bills were at length framed,
" the one for granting Duties in the *Britiſh* Colonies in *America,*
" on Paper, Glaſs, Painters Colours, Tea, *&c.* the other for tak-
" ing off the Duty of a Shilling a Pound on all black and *Singlo*
" Tea, and for granting a Drawback on Teas exported to *Ireland*
" and *America.* The firſt received the royal Aſſent *June* the
" twenty-ninth [1767]; the laſt *July* the ſecond. The Preamble
" to the firſt Act expreſſes, that the Duties are laid, ' for the better
" Support of Government, and the Adminiſtration of the Colo-
" nies. ' The Coloniſts deemed it unneceſſary, unjuſt, and dan-
" gerous to their moſt important Rights. There is a Clauſe in
" it, enabling the Crown, by Sign Manual, to eſtabliſh a General
" Civil Liſt, throughout every Province in *North America,* to any
" indefinite Extent, with any Salaries Penſions or Appointments,
" to any unlimited Amount, even to the Produce of the laſt
" Farthing of the *American* Revenue. The Point was now car-
" ried, which had been the Object of every Miniſter ſince the
" Reign of *Charles* II. *viz.* the Eſtabliſhment of a Civil Liſt in
" *America* independent of the Aſſemblies. . . . "

[203]

*JOURNAL OF THE HONOURABLE HOUSE OF
REPRESENTATIVES, OF HIS MAJESTY'S
PROVINCE OF THE MASSACHUSETTS-BAY
. . . 1767* (*Boſton, New-England:* Printed by *Green &
Ruſſell,* 1767), Appendix, pp. 1-3.

" Agreable to a Vote of the Honorable Houſe of Repreſen-
" tatives of the Province of the *Maſſachuſetts-Bay,* the follow-
" ing humble, dutiful and loyal Petition to the King, ſigned by
" the Speaker, by their Order of the 20ᵗʰ *January* 1768; together
" with the Repreſentations of the Houſe to his Majeſty's Min-
" iſters, their Letter to their Agent, *&c.* are here inſerted. . . . "

[204]

John Pendleton Kennedy, ed., *JOURNALS OF THE
HOUSE*

HOUSE OF BURGESSES OF VIRGINIA, 1766-1769 (Richmond: 1906), *p.* 174.

" *Friday*, the 15th of *April*, 8 *Geo.* III. 1768. "

" *Refolved, Nemine Contradicente* that Mr Speaker be directed
" to write to the Speaker of the Honorable Houfe of Reprefenta-
" tives of the Province of the *Maffachufetts Bay* to defire he
" would inform that Houfe that his Letter of *February* 11th,
" 1768 written by their Direction and in their Name had been
" confidered by this Houfe that we could not but applaud them
" for their Attention to *American* Liberty and that the Steps we
" had taken thereon would convince them of our Opinion of the
" fatal Tendency of the Acts of Parliament complained of and of
" our fixed Refolution to concur with the other Colonies in their
" Application for Redrefs. . . . "

[205]

THE VIRGINIA GAZETTE (Williamfburg: Printed
by *Alex. Purdie* and *John Dixon*), No. 910, *October*
27, 1768.

" *Williamfburg, October* 27 [1768]

" Laft *Tuefday* Evening arrived in *Hampton Road*, in eight
" Weeks from *Portfmouth*, the *Rippon* Man of War of 60 Guns,
" *Samuel Thompfon*, Efq; Commander, having on Board his Ex-
" cellency the Right Hon. *Norborne* Baron *de Botetourt*, his
" Majefty's Lieutenant and Governour General of this Colony
" and Dominion.   Next Morning his Excellency landed at *Little*
" *England*, and was faluted with a Difcharge of the Cannon
" there.   After tarrying a few Hours, and taking a Repaft, his
" Excellency fet out about Noon for this City, where he arrived
" about Sunfet.   His Excellency ftopped at the Capitol, and was
" received at the Gate by his Majefty's Council, the Hon. the
" Speaker, the Attorney General, the Treafurer, and many other
" Gentlemen of Diftinction; after which being conducted to the
" Council Chamber, and having his Commiffions read, was quali-
" fied to exercife his high Office, by taking the ufual Oaths.   His
" Excellency then fwore in the Members of his Majefty's Council,
" after which he proceeded to the *Raleigh Tavern*, and fupped
" there with his Majefty's Council.   His Excellency retired
" about ten, and took up his Lodgings at the Palace, which had
" been put in order for his Reception.   Immediately upon his
" Excellency's Arrival the City was illuminated, and all Ranks
" of

" of People vied with each other in teſtifying their Gratitude and
" Joy that a Nobleman of ſuch diſtinguiſhed Merit and Abilities
" is appointed to preſide over, and live among, them. "

Alſo:

PUBLIC RECORD OFFICE, London.   Colonial Office
5/ 1372. [Photoſtatic Copy in *Reſearch Department, Colonial Williamſburg* Foundation.] Letter
of Lord *Botetourt* deſcribing his Arrival, written from
Williamſburg, November 1, 1768.

" . . . Colonel *Cary* finding me eagerly bent upon being at
" *Williamſburg* that Night, immediately order'd his Chariot and
" Convey'd me within four Miles of the City, where I was met
" by Mr Secretary *Nelſon* and his Brother; at the Capitol we
" found the Council and all the Gentlemen of *Williamſburg* aſ-
" ſembled to receive us.   . . .   I have been aſked every Day to
" Dinner by the principal Gentlemen, and am at preſent upon
" the very beſt Terms with all.   I like their Stile exceedingly
" and augur well of Everything that is to happen.   My Houſe is
" admirable, the Ground behind it is much broke well planted
" and watered by beautifull Rills, and the whole in every Reſpect
" juſt as I could wiſh.   . . . "

[206]

*LETTER BOOK OF WILLIAM NELSON OF
YORKTOWN,* pp. 99-100. [Ms. Volume in *Vir-
ginia State Library* Archives, *Richmond.*] Letter of
William Nelſon to Mr. *John Norton* in *London,* dated
Virginia " *Nover.* 14th, 1768. "

[207]

THE VIRGINIA GAZETTE (Williamſburg: Printed
by *Alex. Purdie* and *John Dixon*), No. 911, *November*
3, 1768. Lord *Botetourt's* Anſwer to the " humble
" Addreſs of the Preſident and Profeſſors of *William
" and Mary* College. "

[208]

*LETTER BOOK OF WILLIAM NELSON OF
YORKTOWN,*

YORKTOWN, pp. 112, 114, 138. [Ms. Volume in
Virginia State Library Archives, *Richmond*.]

p. 138. Letter from *William Nelſon* to *Francis Fauquier*, Son of the deceaſed Governor, dated
September 16, 1769.

" Lord *Botetourt* is the moſt amiable Man in the World to the
" *Virginians;* tho he was obliged to diſſolve the Aſſembly, they
" conſider him as acting under Inſtructions . . . "

[209]

*WILLIAM AND MARY COLLEGE QUARTERLY
HISTORICAL MAGAZINE, Firſt Series*, Vol. XIII
(1904), p. 87. [Autobiography of *David Meade*, born
1744.]

" . . . When his Lordſhip [*Botetourt*] went down to meet the
" Aſſembly it was in much greater ſtate than any Governor of
" *Virginia* had ever before diſplayed. The Chariot he rode in
" was a ſuperbly finiſhed one, preſented to him by *William*, Duke
" of *Cumberland*, Uncle to *George* Third, and was intended for
" his ſtate Carriage, the *Virginia* Arms being ſubſtituted for the
" royal *Engliſh*. "

Alſo:

*John Daly Burke, THE HISTORY OF VIRGINIA,
FROM ITS FIRST SETTLEMENT TO THE
PRESENT DAY (Peterſburg: Dickſon & Peſcud,
1805), Vol. III, p. 363.*

" *Botetourt* began his Adminiſtration with great Parade; he
" met the Aſſembly in a ſtate Coach, and in imitation of his
" Sovereign this Equipage was drawn by ſix white Horſes, which
" ſlowly drew him from the Palace to the Capitol. "

[210]

John Pendleton Kennedy, ed., *JOURNALS OF THE
HOUSE OF BURGESSES OF VIRGINIA, 1766-
1769 (Richmond:* 1906), p. 214.

" *Tueſday*, the 16th of *May*, 9 *Geo*. III. 1769.

" M*r* *Blair* r eported, from the Committee, that they had come
" to ſeveral Reſolutions; which he read in his Place, and after-
" wards

" wards delivered in at the Clerk's Table, where the same were
" read, and are as followeth, *viz.*

" *Resolved*, That it is the Opinion of this Committee, that the
" sole Right of imposing Taxes on the Inhabitants of this his
" Majesty's Colony and Dominion of *Virginia*, is now, and ever
" hath been, legally and constitutionally vested in the House of
" Burgesses, lawfully convened according to the ancient and
" established Practice, with the Consent of the Council, and of his
" Majesty, the King of *Great-Britain*, or his Governor, for the
" Time being.

" *Resolved*, That it is the Opinion of this Committee, that it
" is the undoubted Privilege of the Inhabitants of this Colony,
" to petition their Sovereign for Redress of Grievances; and that
" it is lawful and expedient to procure the concurrence of his
" Majesty's other Colonies, in dutiful Addresses, praying the
" royal Interposition in Favour of the violated Rights of *America*.

" *Resolved*, That it is the Opinion of this Committee, that all
" Trials for Treason, Misprison of Treason, or for any Felony or
" Crime whatsoever, committed and done in this his Majesty's
" said Colony and Dominion, by any Person or Persons residing
" therein, ought of Right to be had, and conducted in and before
" his Majesty's Courts, held within the said Colony, according to
" the fixed and known Course of Proceeding; and that the seizing
" any Person or Persons, residing in this Colony, suspected of any
" Crime whatsoever, committed therein, and sending such Per-
" son, or Persons, to Places beyond the Sea, to be tried, is highly
" derogatory of the Rights of *British* Subjects; as thereby the
" inestimable Privilege of being tried by a Jury from the Vicin-
" age, as well as the Liberty of summoning and producing Wit-
" nesses on such Trial, will be taken away from the Party
" accused.

" *Resolved*, That it is the Opinion of this Committee, that an
" humble, dutiful, and loyal Address, be presented to his Majesty,
" to assure him of our inviolable Attachment to his sacred Person
" and Government; and to beseech his royal Interposition, as the
" Father of all his People, however remote from the Seat of his
" Empire, to quiet the Minds of his loyal Subjects of this Colony,
" and to avert from them, those Dangers and Miseries which will
" ensue, from the Seizing and Carrying beyond Sea, any Persons
" residing in *America*, suspected of any Crime whatsoever, to be
" tried in any other Manner, than by the ancient and long
" established Course of Proceeding.

" The said Resolutions being severally read a second Time:
                                             " *Resolved*,

" *Refolved, Nemine Contradicente*, That this Houfe doth agree
" with the Committee in the faid Refolutions. . . .
" *Ordered*, That the Speaker of this Houfe do tranfmit, without
" Delay, to the Speakers of the feveral Houfes of Affembly, on
" this Continent, a Copy of the Refolutions now agreed to by
" this Houfe, requefting their Concurrence therein. "

[211]

Ibid., p. 218.

" *Wednefday*, the 17th of *May*, 9 *Geo*. III. 1769. "
" . . . Mr Speaker, with the Houfe, went up to attend the
" Governor in the Council Chamber; where his Excellency was
" pleafed to fay to them:
" ' Mr Speaker, and Gentlemen of the Houfe of Burgeffes,
" ' I have heard of your Refolves, and augur ill of their Effect:
" You have made it my Duty to diffolve you; and you are dif-
" folved accordingly. ' "

[212]

Ibid., pp. xxxix-xliii.

[The Minutes of this Meeting do not appear in the
Journals of the Houfe of Burgeffes, but have been
printed in the Preface to the above Volume.]

Alfo:

THE VIRGINIA GAZETTE (*Williamfburg:* Printed
by *Alex. Purdie & John Dixon*), No. 939, *May* 18,
1769.

" *Williamfburg, May* 18 [1769]. "

" The late Reprefentatives of the People then judging it
" neceffary that fome Meafures fhould be taken, in their diftreffed
" Situation, for preferving the true and effential Interefts of the
" Colony, refolved upon a Meeting for that very falutary Purpofe;
" and therefore immediately, with the greateft Order and De-
" corum, repaired to the Houfe of Mr. *Anthony Hay*, in this City,
" where being affembled it was firft propofed, for the more decent
" and regular Difcuffion of fuch important Matters as might be
" taken into Confideration, that a Moderator fhould be ap-
" pointed, and on the Queftion being put, *Peyton Randolph*, Efq;
" late Speaker of the Houfe of Burgeffes, was unanimoufly
" elected.

" The true State of the Colony being then opened, and fully
" explained,

" explained, and it being propofed that a regular Affociation
" fhould be formed, a Committee was appointed to prepare the
" neceffary and moft proper Regulations for that Purpofe, and
" they were ordered to make their Report to the general Meeting,
" the next Day at 10 o'Clock. "

[213]

Ibid., No. 940, *May* 25, 1769.

[A Copy of the Affociation is printed in full in this
  Number of the *Gazette*. It alfo appears in the Minutes of the Meeting which have been printed
  in the Preface of the *Journals of the Houfe of
  Burgeffes of Virginia*, 1766-1769 (*Richmond:* 1906),
  pp. xl-xliii.]

[214]

*WILLIAM AND MARY COLLEGE QUARTERLY
HISTORICAL MAGAZINE, Firft Series,* Vol. XVI
(1908), pp. 174-180. Letter of *Anne Blair* to *Martha
Braxton, Auguft* 21, 1769.

[215]

John Pendleton Kennedy, ed., *JOURNALS OF THE
HOUSE OF BURGESSES OF VIRGINIA, 1766-
1769 (Richmond:* 1906), pp. 226-227. Speech of Governor *Botetourt* to the General Affembly, *November*
7, 1769.

" I think myfelf peculiarly fortunate to be able to inform
" you that in a Letter dated *May* the 13th, I have been affured
" by the Earl of *Hillfborough,* that his Majefty's prefent Admini-
" ftration have at no Time entertained a Defign to propofe to
" Parliament to lay any further Taxes upon *America* for the Pur-
" pofe of raifing a Revenue, and that it is their Intention to pro-
" pofe in the next Seffion of Parliament, to take off the Duties
" upon Glafs, Paper, and Colours, upon Confideration of fuch
" Duties having been laid contrary to the true Principles of
" Commerce.
    " It may poffibly be objected that, as his Majefty's prefent
" Adminiftration are not immortal, . . . " [See Page 60 of Text.]

[216]

[216]

See Note 215.

[217]

WILLIAM AND MARY COLLEGE QUARTERLY HISTORICAL MAGAZINE, Firſt Series, Vol. XIII (1904), p. 88. [Autobiography of *David Meade*, born 1744.]

" . . . the Subjeƈt of this Sketch heard ſome Time after the
" Diſſolution of the Aſſembly, at Mr. Treaſurer *Nicholas'*, in
" *Williamſburg*, in the Preſence of ſeveral Gentlemen, the Gov-
" ernor [*Botetourt*] declare that he ſhould write to Lord *Hillſbor-*
" *ough* (who was then ſeventy Years old), who was then in the
" *American* Department of State, and aſſure him that unleſs the
" obnoxious Aƈts of Parliament were repealed, he ſhould deſire
" to be recalled from his Government. . . . "

[218]

Daniel Call, REPORTS OF THE CASES ARGUED AND DECIDED IN THE COURT OF APPEALS OF VIRGINIA (Richmond: Publiſhed by *Robert I. Smith*, 1833), Vol. IV, p. xvi.

[219]

THE VIRGINIA GAZETTE (Williamſburg: Printed by *William Rind*), No. 232, *Oƈtober* 18, 1770.

" *Williamſburg, October* 18 [1770].

" On *Monday* the 15th Inſtant, about one o'Clock in the Morn-
" ing departed this Life, univerſally lamented throughout this
" Colony, his Excellency the Right Honourable *Norborne*
" Baron *de Botetourt*, his Majeſty's Lieutenant, Governor
" General and Commander in Chief of the Colony and Dominion
" of *Virginia*, and Vice Admiral of the ſame. . . . "

[220]

WILLIAM AND MARY COLLEGE QUARTERLY HISTORICAL MAGAZINE, Firſt Series, Vol. V (1897), pp. 169-170.

" *Williamſburg, October* 16, 1770.

" The

" The Gentlemen appointed to conduct the Funeral of his
" Excellency Lord *Botetourt*, prefent their Compliments to all
" Gentlemen and Ladies, and beg the Favour of their Attendance
" at the Palace at two o'Clock on *Friday* next.

" The Proceffion to begin precifely at three, and move to the
" Church, where the ufual Service will be performed; after which
" the Corps will be conducted to the College Chapel, and there
" interred. "

[221]

John Pendleton Kennedy, ed., *JOURNALS OF THE
HOUSE OF BURGESSES OF VIRGINIA, 1770-
1772 (Richmond:* 1906), p. 138.

" *Saturday*, the 20th of *July*. 11 *Geo*. III. 1771. "

" *Refolved, Nemine Contradicente*, That an elegant Statue of
" his late Excellency the Right Honourable *Norborne*, Baron *de
" Botetourt* be erected in Marble at the public Expence, with
" proper Infcriptions, expreffing the grateful Senfe this Houfe
" entertains of his Lordfhip's prudent and wife Adminiftration,
" and their great Solicitude to perpetuate, as far as they are able,
" the Remembrance of thofe many public and focial Virtues
" which adorned his illuftrious Character. That the fame be
" fent for to *Great-Britain* under the Direction of the Honourable
" *William Nelfon, Thomas Nelfon*, and *Peyton Randolph*, Ef-
" quires, *Robert Carter Nicholas, Lewis Burwell*, and *Dudley
" Digges*, Efquires. "

Alfo:

A. G. Bradley, ed., *THE JOURNAL OF NICHOLAS
CRESSWELL, 1774-1777 (New York:* The *Dial Prefs*
1928), pp. 206-208.

" *Williamfburg*, the Capitol of *Virginia*—*Tuefday, April* 29th,
" 1777. . . . This is the fineft Town I have feen in *Virginia*.
" . . . The Capitol is the Place where all public Bufinefs is done,
" the colonial Affembly meets, *&c* . . . In the Capitol is a fine
" Marble Statue of the late Governor *Batitourt* [*fic*], as large as
" Life, in the Attitude of an Orator, a Roll of Parchment in one
" Hand as an Emblem of their Charter, and the Cap of Liberty
" in the other. It is mounted on a Pedeftal and furrounded with
" Iron Baluftrades. On the Front of the Pedeftal is his Excel-
" lency's Arms and this Infcription: . . . "

[222]

[222]

*ACCOUNT BOOK OF HUMPHERY HARWOOD—
LEDGER B.* [Ms. Account Book which has been
depofited with the *Refearch Department, Colonial
Williamfburg* Foundation.]

> " The Commonwelth of *Virginia* Dʳ [Ledger B- 7.]
> > " 1777.   *October* 20. To Cleaning the Statue   12/6 . . .
> > " 1778.   *May 5.* To Cleaning the Statue   20/- . . .
> > " 1778.   *October* 10.   To Cleaning the Statue   20/- . . .
> " The Commonwealth of *Virginia* Dʳ [Ledger B- 31.]
> " 1779. Octobʳ 2 . . .   To Cleening Statue 100/- "

[223]

The Infcription as given here was taken directly from
the Statue.

[224]

THE VIRGINIA GAZETTE (*Williamfburg:* Printed
by *John Dixon & William Hunter*), No. 1252, *Auguft*
5, 1775. Addrefs of the Houfe of Burgeffes of *Virginia* to Governor *Dunmore*, after his Removal from
Williamfburg to the *Fowey*, Man of War.

> " *Williamfburg, Auguft* 5 [1775].

" . . . We will prefume to carry your Attention no further back
" than to the Adminiftration of a Governor immediately preced-
" ing your Lordfhip. Previous to his Coming over to *Virginia*,
" there had arifen fome unhappy Difputes between *Great Britain*
" and the Colonies.   His Majefty was gracioufly pleafed to fend
" over to us, from his immediate Prefence, the truly noble Lord
" *Botetourt*, who told us, that he had received it in Command from
" his Majefty to do Juftice, and maintain the Rights of all his
" Subjects.   He cheerfully entered upon the Duties of his exalted
" Station, in which he acted as a true Reprefentative of his royal
" Mafter, at once fupporting the Dignity of his Crown, difpenfing
" the utmoft Juftice, and diffufing Benevolence throughout the
" Country.   By his exemplary Conduct, in all Refpects, he ac-
" complifhed what he deemed a glorious Work: He gave us
" Tranquillity, and Happinefs.   Indeed he was often heard to
" declare,

" declare, that the Bufinefs of a Governor of *Virginia* was much
" eafier than he could have conceived, as he found that the Gov-
" ernment almoft executed itfelf. Matters were not at that
" Time carried on, and precipitated, with fo high an Hand, on
" the other Side of the Water, as at Prefent. This probably was
" owing to his minutely Examining every Subject to the Bottom
" himfelf, taking Nothing upon Truft; to his Difcountenancing
" Tale-bearers, and malicious Informers; and, at laft, making a
" faithful Reprefentation of Things, as he found them. In a
" fhort, too fhort a Time, for the Happinefs of *Virginia*, it
" pleafed *God* to remove him from us. When we received the
" Account of your Lordfhip's Appointment, we indulged the
" pleafing Hopes that we fhould again be made happy in a Ruler;
" and, when you were pleafed to honour us with your Prefence,
" we vied with each other in endeavouring to make your Admini-
" ftration eafy and agreeable. . . . "

[225]

THE VIRGINIA GAZETTE (*Williamfburg:* Printed
by *Alex. Purdie & John Dixon*), No. 1052, *September*
26, 1771.

" *Williamfburg, September* 26 [1771].

" Yefterday arrived in Town, between ten and eleven o'Clock,
" the Right Honourable the Earl of *Dunmore*, our Governour,
" with Captain *Foy*, his Excellency's Secretary. He came from
" *York* that Morning, accompanied by his Honour the Prefident,
" Mr. Secretary *Nelfon*, and the Honourable *John Page*, Efquire;
" and immediately, with thofe Gentlemen, and the Honourable
" *Robert Carter*, Efquire, repaired to the Palace, where he was
" fworn in to the Adminiftration of Government. They, with
" feveral of the principal Gentlemen in this City, who went to
" pay their Refpects to his Excellency. were invited to dine at
" the Palace, where they fpent the Day. In the Evening there
" were Illuminations, &c. as a Teftimony of our Joy at his Ex-
" cellency's fafe Arrival, and in Gratitude to his Majefty for
" appointing a Nobleman of his Abilities and good Character to
" prefide over us in the Room of our late worthy Governour. "

[226]

*LETTER BOOK OF WILLIAM NELSON OF
YORKTOWN, VIRGINIA* [Ms. Volume, *Virginia
State Library* Archives, *Richmond.*] p. 150.

Letter

Letter from *William Nelfon* to Mr. *John Norton*,
Merchant of *London*, dated " *Virginia, Jan^{ry}* 24th
" 1770. "

[227]

See Page 56 of Text, and Note 206.

[228]

THE SOUTH-CAROLINA GAZETTE (*Charlefton:*
1772), No. 1914, *September* 10, 1772.

" *London, June* 19 [1772]　In *Virginia* their new *Scotch* Governor
" began his Government . . . "　[See Text.]

[229]

Paul Leicefter Ford, ed., *THE WRITINGS OF
THOMAS JEFFERSON* (*New York: G. P. Putnam's*
Sons, 1904), Vol. I, pp. 9-10.

" Nothing of particular Excitement occurring for a confiderable
" Time our Countrymen feemed to fall into a State of Infenfi-
" bility to our Situation.　The Duty on Tea not yet repealed &
" the Declaratory Act of a Right in the *Britifh* Parl to bind us
" by their Laws in all Cafes whatfoever, ftill fufpended over us.
" But a Court of Inquiry held in *R. Ifland* in 1762 [this was the
" famous ' *Gafpee* ' Inquiry, the Date being a Slip for 1772], with
" a Power to fend Perfons to *England* to be tried for Offences
" committed here was confidered at our Seffion of the Spring
" of 1773, as demanding Attention.　Not thinking our old &
" leading Members up to the Point of Forwardnefs & Zeal
" which the Times required, Mr. *Henry*, R. H. *Lee*, *Francis L.*
" *Lee*, Mr. *Carr* & myfelf [*Thomas Jefferfon*] agreed to meet in
" the Evening in a private Room of the *Raleigh* to confult on the
" State of Things.　There may have been a Member or two more
" whom I do not recollect.　We were all fenfible that the moft
" urgent of all Meafures was that of coming to an Underftanding
" with all the other Colonies to confider the *Britifh* Claims as a
" common Caufe to all, & to produce an Unity of Action: and
" for this Purpofe that a Commee of Correfpondce in each Colony
" would be the beft Inftrument for Intercommunication: and
" that their firft Meafure would probably be to propofe a Meet-
" ing of Deputies from every Colony at fome central Place, who
" fhould be charged with the Direction of the Meafures which
" fhould

" fhould be taken by all.   We therefore drew up the Refolutions
" which may be feen in *Wirt* pa 87.   The confulting Members
" propofed to me to move them, but I urged that it fhould be
" done by Mr. *Carr* [*Dabney Carr*, who married *Martha Jefferfon*,]
" my Friend & Brother in Law, then a new Member to whom
" I wifhed an Opportunity fhould be given of making known to
" the Houfe his great Worth & Talents.   It was fo agreed; he
" moved them, they were agreed to *nem. con.* and a Commee of
" Correfpondence appointed of whom *Peyton Randolph*, the
" Speaker, was Chairman.   The Govr. (then Ld. *Dunmore*)
" diffolved us, . . . "

[230]

John Pendleton Kennedy, ed., *JOURNALS OF THE
HOUSE OF BURGESSES OF VIRGINIA, 1773-
1776 (Richmond:* 1905), *p.* 28.

"*Friday*, the 12th of *March*, 13 *Geo.* III. 1773."

" Be it *refolved*, that a ftanding Committee of Correfpondence
" and Inquiry be appointed to confift of eleven Perfons, to wit,
" the Honourable *Peyton Randolph*, Efquire, *Robert Carter*
" *Nicholas*, *Richard Bland*, *Richard Henry Lee*, *Benjamin Harri-*
" *fon*, *Edmund Pendleton*, *Patrick Henry*, *Dudley Digges*, *Dabney*
" *Carr*, *Archibald Cary*, and *Thomas Jefferfon*, Efquires, any fix
" of whom to be a Committee, whofe Bufinefs it fhall be to obtain
" the moft early and authentic Intelligence of all fuch Acts and
" Refolutions of the *Britifh* Parliament, or Proceedings of Ad-
" miniftration, as may relate to or affect the *Britifh* Colonies in
" *America*, and to keep up and maintain a Correfpondence and
" Communication with our Sifter Colonies, refpecting thefe im-
" portant Confiderations; and the Refult of fuch their Proceed-
" ings, from Time to Time, to lay before this Houfe. . . .

" *Refolved*, That the Speaker of this Houfe do tranfmit to the
" Speakers of the different Affemblys of the *Britifh* Colonies, on
" the Continent, Copies of the faid Refolutions, and defire that
" they will lay them before their refpective Affemblies; and re-
" queft them to appoint fome Perfon or Perfons, of their refpec-
" tive Bodies, to communicate, from Time to Time, with the
" faid Committee. "

Alfo:

Ibid., pp. 41-64.

" Minutes of the Committee of Correfpondence " and
" Letters

" Letters received by the Committee of Correfpond-
" ence " from the Committtees of other Provinces.

[231]

Ibid., pp. 36, 69-73.

[232]

*THE VIRGINIA GAZETTE (Williamfburg: Alex.
Purdie & John Dixon)*, No. 1162, *January* 13, 1774.
[In this Iffue there is an interefting Account of the
Deftruction of the Tea at *Bofton*.]

[233]

John Pendleton Kennedy, ed., *JOURNALS OF THE
HOUSE OF BURGESSES OF VIRGINIA, 1773-
1776 (Richmond:* 1905), p. 124.

" *Tuefday*, the 24th of *May*, 14 *Geo.* III.   1774. "

" This Houfe, being deeply impreffed with Apprehenfion of the
" great Dangers, to be derived to *Britifh America*, from the hof-
" tile Invafion of the City of *Bofton*, in our Sifter Colony of
" *Maffachufetts Bay,* whofe Commerce and Harbour are, on the
" firft Day of *June* next, to be ftopped by an armed Force, deem
" it highly neceffary that the faid firft Day of *June* be fet apart,
" by the Members of this Houfe, as a Day of Fafting, Humilia-
" tion, and Prayer, devoutly to implore the Divine Interpofition,
" for averting the heavy Calamity which threatens Deftruction
" to our civil Rights, and the Evils of civil War; to give us one
" Heart and one Mind firmly to oppofe, by all juft and proper
" Means, every Injury to *American* Rights; and that the Minds
" of his Majefty and his Parliament, may be infpired from above
" with Wifdom, Moderation, and Juftice, to remove from the
" loyal People of *America* all Caufe of Danger, from a continued
" Purfuit of Meafures, pregnant with their Ruin.

" Ordered, therefore, that the Members of this Houfe do attend
" in their Places, at the Hour of ten in the Forenoon, on the faid
" firft Day of *June* next, in order to proceed with the Speaker,
" and the Mace, to the Church in this City, for the Purpofes
" aforefaid; and that the Reverend Mr *Price* be appointed to
" read Prayers, and the Reverend Mr *Gwatkin*, to preach a Ser-
" mon, fuitable to the Occafion. "

[234]

[234]

John C. Fitzpatrick, ed., *THE DIARIES OF GEORGE WASHINGTON, 1748-1799 (Boſton & New York: Houghton Mifflin* Co., 1925), Vol. II, 1771-1785, p. 153.

[235]

John Pendleton Kennedy, ed., *JOURNALS OF THE HOUSE OF BURGESSES OF VIRGINIA, 1773-1776 (Richmond:* 1905), p. 132. *May* 26, 1774. Governor *Dunmore* to the Houſe of Burgeſſes:

" I have in my Hand a Paper publiſhed by Order of your
" Houſe, conceived in ſuch Terms as reflect highly upon his
" Majeſty and the Parliament of *Great Britain;* which makes it
" neceſſary for me to diſſolve you; and you are diſſolved ac-
" cordingly."

[236]

Ibid., pp. xiii-xiv, 138.

[237]

THE VIRGINIA GAZETTE (Williamſburg: Printed by *Alex. Purdie & John Dixon*), No. 1192, *Auguſt* 11, 1774.

" Inſtructions for the Deputies appointed to meet in General
" Congreſs on the Part of this Colony. "

[238]

Worthington Chauncey Ford, ed., *JOURNALS OF THE CONTINENTAL CONGRESS (Waſhington:* Government Printing Office, 1904), Vol. I, pp. 13-14.

[239]

Edmund C. Burnett, ed., *LETTERS OF MEMBERS OF THE CONTINENTAL CONGRESS (Waſhington:* The *Carnegie Inſtitution of Waſhington,* 1921), Vol. I, 1774-1776, pp. 12, 14. Notes of Proceedings of the Congreſs by *James Duane.*

" *Tueſday* the 6th *September* [1774]

" The

" The Congrefs met, and the firft Queftion debated was whether
" the Congrefs fhould vote by Colonies and what Weight each
" Colony fhould have in the Determination?

" Mr. *Henry* from *Virginia* infifted that by the Oppreffion of
" Parliament all Government was diffolved, and that we were
" reduced to a State of Nature. That there were no longer any
" fuch Diftinction as Colonies, and that he conceived himfelf not
" a *Virginian* but an *American* . . . "

[240]

THE VIRGINIA GAZETTE (*Williamfburg: Alex. Purdie & John Dixon*), No. 1192, *Auguft* 11, 1774.

" Williamfburg, Auguft 11.

" In Confequence of an Invitation from the Honourable *Pey-*
" *ton Randolph*, Efq; our worthy Reprefentative, there was Yef-
" terday a very full Meeting of the Inhabitants of this City at the
" Courthoufe, when they generally approved of the Affociation
" entered into by the Delegates from the feveral Counties of this
" Colony, and fubfcribed thereto; and, at the fame Time, con-
" tributed moft generoufly for the Relief of our diftreffed Fellow
" Subjects at *Bofton*, both in Cafh and Provifions. "

Alfo:

THE VIRGINIA GAZETTE (*Williamfburg: John Pinckney*), *Thurfday, April* 20, 1775.

" On *Tuefday* laft the Inhabitants of this City met at the
" Court Houfe, and generoufly fubfcribed towards the Relief of
" thofe brave Sons of Liberty, the *Boftonians.*"

[241]

THE VIRGINIA GAZETTE (*Williamfburg: Alex. Purdie & John Dixon*), No. 1169, *March* 3, 1774.

" Williamfburg, March 3.

" Laft *Saturday* Evening the Right Honourable the Countefs
" of *Dunmore*, with Lord *Fincaftle*, the Honourable *Alexander*
" and *John Murray*, and the Ladies *Catharine*, *Augufta*, and
" *Sufan Murray*, accompanied by Captain *Foy* and his Lady,
" arrived at the Palace in this City; to the great Joy of his Excel-
" lency the Governour, and the inexpreffible Pleafure and Satis-
" faction of the Inhabitants, who made a general Illumination
" upon

" upon this happy Occafion, and with repeated Acclamations
" welcomed her Ladyfhip and Family to *Virginia.* "

[242]

Ibid., No. 1218, *December* 8, 1774.

Supplement.

·' *Williamfburg, December* 8.

" Laft *Saturday* Morning the Right Honourable the Countefs
" of *Dunmore* was fafely delivered of a Daughter, at the Palace.
" Her Ladyfhip continues in a very favourable Situation, and the
" young *Virginian* is in perfect Health. "

Alfo:

Ibid., (*Williamfburg: John Dixon & Wm. Hunter*), No.
1224, *January* 21, 1775.

" *Wednefday* laft being the Day for celebrating the Birth of her
" Majefty, his Excellency the Earl of *Dunmore* gave a Ball and
" elegant Entertainment at the Palace to a numerous Company
" of Ladies and Gentlemen. The fame Day his Lordfhip's
" youngeft Daughter was baptifed by the Name of *Virginia.* "

[243]

*THE PROCEEDINGS OF THE CONVENTION
OF DELEGATES FOR THE COUNTIES &
CORPORATIONS IN THE COLONY OF VIR-
GINIA, HELD AT RICHMOND TOWN . . . 1775.
(Richmond: Ritchie, Trueheart & Du-Val, 1816), pp. 3-5.*

" *Thurfday, March* 23, 1775. "

" *Refolved*, That a well regulated Militia, compofed of Gentle-
" men and Yeoman, is the natural Strength, and only Security,
" of a free Government; that fuch a Militia in this Colony would
" forever render it unneceffary for the Mother Country to keep
" among us, for the Purpofe of Defence, any ftanding Army of
" mercenary Forces, always fubverfive of the Quiet, and dan-
" gerous to the Liberties of the People, and would obviate the
" Pretext of taxing us for their Support.

" That the Eftablifhment of fuch a Militia is at this Time pe-
" culiarly neceffary, by the State of our Laws for the Protection
" and Defence of the Country, fome of which are already expired,
" and others will fhortly do fo; and that the known Remiffnefs of
" Government,

" Government, in calling us together in a legiflative Capacity,
" renders it too infecure, in this Time of Danger and Diftrefs, to
" rely, that Opportunity will be given of renewing them in Gen-
" eral Affembly, or making any Provifion to fecure our ineftim-
" able Rights and Liberties from thofe farther Violations with
" which they are threatened.

" *Refolved* therefore, That this Colony be immediately put
" into a Pofture of Defence; and that *Patrick Henry, Richard*
" *Henry Lee, Robert Carter Nicholas, Benjamin Harrifon, Lemuel*
" *Riddick, George Wafhington, Adam Stephen, Andrew Lewis,*
" *William Chriftian, Edmund Pendleton, Thomas Jefferfon,* and
" *Isaac Zane,* Efquires, be a Committee to prepare a Plan for the
" Embodying, Arming, and Difciplining fuch a Number of Men as
" may be fufficient for that Purpofe. "

Alfo:

William Wirt, SKETCHES OF THE LIFE AND
CHARACTER OF PATRICK HENRY (*Hartford:
S. Andrus & Son,* 1847), pp. 134-143.

[244]

Ibid., p. 141.

[245]

PUBLIC RECORD OFFICE, *London.* C. O. 5/1353.
Letter from Lord *Dunmore* to Lord *Dartmouth,
Britifh* Secretary of State, dated " *Williamfburg,*
" 1ft *May* 1775. " [Photoftatic Copy in *Refearch
Department, Colonial Williamfburg* Foundation.]

[246]

A Broadfide printed in *Williamfburg* by *Alexander
Purdie, Saturday, April* 29, 1775. This Broadfide,
evidently haftily prepared, prefents the following
Items with no particular Pretence of Arrangement.

" *Williamfburg, Saturday, April* 29, 1775.

" Late laft Night an Exprefs arrived from *Philadelphia,* with
" the following melancholy Advices from the Province of *Con-
" necticut,* forwarded to the Committee of Correfpondence in
" this City.

" The

" The Blow (fo much dreaded by our noble Friend Lord *Chat-*
" *ham*) is now ftruck, a great Deal of Blood fpilt, and much more,
" it is likely, than the prefent Advices communicate. That
" great Man, in his Speech upon the Neceffity of withdrawing
" the Troops from *Bofton* (delivered in the Houfe of Lords the
" 20th of *January* laft) fays: ' Perhaps, even whilft I am now
" fpeaking, the decifive Blow is ftruck, which may involve Mil-
" lions in the Confequences; and, believe me, the very firft Drop
" of Blood that is fpilled will not be a Wound eafily fkinned over;
" it will be *irritabile vulnus*, a Wound of that rancorous and fefter-
" ing Kind, that, in all Probability, will mortify the whole
" Body. '

" *Philadelphia, April* 24, 1775.

" An Exprefs arrived at five o'Clock this Evening, by which
" we have the following Advices, *viz.*

" *Watertown, Wednefday* Morning, near 10 o'Clock.
" To all *FRIENDS* of *AMERICAN LIBERTY.*

" Be it known, that this Morning, before Break of Day, a Brig-
" ade, confifting of about 1000 or 1200 Men, landed at *Phipps*
" Farm, at *Cambridge*, and marched to *Lexington*, where they
" found a Company of our Colony Militia in Arms, upon whom
" they fired, without any Provocation, and killed fix Men, and
" wounded four Others. By an Exprefs from *Bofton*, we find
" another Brigade is now on its March from *Bofton*, fuppofed to
" confift of 1000 Men. The Bearer, *Trial Briffet*, is charged to
" alarm the Country, quite to *Connecticut;* and all Perfons are
" defired to furnifh him with frefh Horfes, as they may be
" needed. . . .

" *Thurfday*, 3 o'Clock after Noon.
" Sir.

" I am this Moment informed, by an Exprefs from *Woodftock*,
" taken from the Mouth of the Exprefs at two of the Clock after
" Noon, that the Conteft between the firft Brigade that marched
" to *Concord* was ftill continuing this Morning at the Town of
" *Lexington*, to which faid Brigade had retreated; that another
" Brigade, faid to be the fecond mentioned in the Letter of this
" Morning, had landed with a Quantity of Artillery at the Place
" where the firft did. The Provincials were determined to pre-
" vent the two Brigades from joining their Strength, if poffible,
" and remain in great Need of Succour. . . .

" P. S. Mr. *M'Farlane* of *Plainfield*, Merchant, has juft return-
" ed from *Bofton*, by way of *Providence*, who converfed with an
" Exprefs from *Lexington*, who farther informs, that 4000 of our
" Troops

" Troops had furrounded the firft Brigade above mentioned, who
" were on a Hill in *Lexington;* that the Action continued, and
" there were about 50 of our Men killed, and 150 of the Regu-
" lars, as near as they could determine, when the Exprefs came
" away. It will be expedient for every Man to go, who is fit and
" willing.

" The above is a true Coppy, as received by Exprefs from *New-*
" *haven,* and attefted by the Committee of Correfpondence from
" Town to Town. . . .

[Williamfburg]

" This Morning the Committee of Correfpondence met, and
" have determined to fend Expreffes to the fouthward.—It is
" now full Time for us all to be on our Guard, and to prepare
" ourfelves againft every Contingency. The *Sword is now*
" *drawn,* and *God* knows when it will be fheathed. "

[247]

THE VIRGINIA GAZETTE (Williamfburg: John Dixon & Wm. Hunter), No. 1240, *May* 13, 1775.

" At a Committee appointed and held for *Hanover* County, at the
" Courthoufe, on *Tuefday* the 9th of *May,* 1775, . . .

" Agreeable to a Refolution of the Committee held at *New-*
" *caftle* the 2d Inftant, fetting forth, that they, being fully in-
" formed of the violent Hoftilities committed by the King's
" Troops in *America,* and of the Danger arifing to the Colony by
" the Lofs of the public Powder, and of the Conduct of the Gov-
" ernor [*Dunmore*], which threatens altogether Calamities of the
" greateft Magnitude, and moft fatal Confequences to this Col-
" ony, and therefore recommending Reprifals to be made upon
" the King's Property fufficient to replace the Gunpowder taken
" out of the Magazine, it appears to this Committee, that the
" Volunteers who marched from *Newcaftle,* to obtain Satisfaction
" for the public Powder, by Reprifal, or otherwife, proceeded on
" that Bufinefs as follows, to wit: That an Officer with 16 Men
" was detached to feize the King's Receiver General, with Orders
" to detain him; and this, it was fuppofed, might be done with-
" out impeding the Progrefs of the main Body. The faid Re-
" ceiver General not being apprehended, owing to his Abfence
" from Home, the faid Detachment, according to Orders, pro-
" ceeded to join the main Body on its March to *Williamfburg;*
" and the Junction happened the 3d Inftant, at *Doncaftle's* Ordi-
" nary, about Sunfet. A little after Sunrife next Morning, the
" Commanding

' Commanding Officer being aſſured that proper Satisfaction, in
' Money, ſhould be inſtantly made, the Volunteers halted, and
'' the Propoſal being conſidered by them, was judged ſatisfactory
' as to that Point; and the following Receipt was given, to wit:
'' ' *Doncaſtle's* Ordinary, *New Kent, May* 4, 1775, received
'' from the Hon. *Richard Corbin*, Eſq; his Majeſty's Receiver
'' General, £330 as a Compenſation for the Gunpowder lately
'' taken out of the public Magazine by the Governor's Order;
'' which Money I promiſe to convey to the *Virginia* Delegates at
'' the General Congreſs, to be, under their Direction, laid out in
'' Gunpowder for the Colony's Uſe, and to be ſtored as they ſhall
'' direct, until the next Colony Convention, or General Aſſembly,
'' unleſs it ſhall be neceſſary, in the meantime, to uſe the ſame in
'' Defence of this Colony. It is agreed, that in Caſe the next
'' Convention ſhall determine that any Part of the ſaid Money
'' ought to be returned to his Majeſty's ſaid Receiver General,
'' that the ſame ſhall be done accordingly.

"   Teſt,   *Patrick Henry*, Jun. ' "

Alſo:

THE PROCEEDINGS OF THE CONVENTION OF DELEGATES FOR THE COUNTIES AND CORPORATIONS IN THE COLONY OF VIRGINIA, HELD AT RICHMOND TOWN . . . 1775 *(Richmond: Ritchie, Truehart & Du-Val*, 1816), p. 23.

"*Friday, Auguſt* 25, 1775. "

" *Reſolved*, As the Opinion of this Convention, that ſufficient
'' Proof being had of there being only fifteen Half-barrels of
'' Powder ſo taken by Lord *Dunmore's* Order, that no more Money
'' ſhould be retained than one Hundred and twelve Pounds ten
'' Shillings, which we judge fully adequate to the Payment of
'' the ſaid Powder, and that the Reſidue of the ſaid three Hun-
'' dred and thirty Pounds ought to be returned to the ſaid Re-
'' ceiver-general, and it is hereby directed to be paid to him by
'' the Treaſurer of this Colony. "

[248]

John Pendleton Kennedy, ed., *JOURNALS OF THE HOUSE OF BURGESSES OF VIRGINIA, 1773-1776 (Richmond:* 1905), pp. 173-283.

[249]

[249]

THE VIRGINIA GAZETTE (*Williamſburg: Alexander Purdie*), *April* 28, 1775, No. 13, Supplement.

[250]

Frequent Advertiſements appear in the *Virginia Gazettes* for the Years 1775 and 1776, announcing Subſcribers' Intentions of leaving the Colony.

[251]

PUBLIC RECORD OFFICE, London, Colonial Office 5/ 1353. Letter of Lord *Dunmore* to the Earl of *Dartmouth,* dated " *Williamſburg,* 15ᵗʰ *May* 1775. " Nº. 27. [Photoſtatic Copy in *Reſearch Department, Colonial Williamſburg* Foundation.]

" My Lord
    " The Commotion in this Colony, of the Cauſe of which I
" gave your Lordſhip an Account in my Letter Nº. 26 dated the
" 1ſt of *May,* has obliged me to ſhut myſelf in, and make a Garri-
" ſon of my Houſe, expecting every Moment to be attacked
" There is ſcarce a County of the whole Colony wherin Part of
" the People have not taken up Arms and declared their Inten-
" tion of forcing me to make Reſtitution of the Powder; Bodies of
" different Numbers have been in Motion in all Parts of the
" Colony, who have been only diſſuaded from purſuing their
" Attempts, by the Interpoſition of ſome leſs violent People,not
" compelled to lay down their Arms and atone for their Offences
" by the Juſtice of the Country or the Support due from Subjects
" to their lawfull Government.
    " A Party headed by a certain *Patrick Henry,* one of the Dele-
" gates of this Colony, a Man of deſperate Circumſtances, and
" one who has been very active in encouraging Diſobedience and
" exciting a Spirit of Revolt among the People for many Years
" paſt, advanced to within a few Miles of this Place, and there
" encamped with all the Appearances of actual War, ſtoping and
" detaining every Paſſenger on the Road coming this Way for
" Fear of my obtaining Intelligence of their Motions;*Henry*, their
" Leader diſpatching Letters all over the Country to excite the
" People to join him; and he ſent one particularly to direct that
" the People of the County of *York* ſhould prevent, at all Events,
                                                                " any

" any Succour being fent to me from the Man of War lying at
" *York*, or my Retreat to the Man of War. . . ."

[252]

PUBLIC RECORD OFFICE, London, Colonial Office
5/ 1353. Letter of Lord *Dunmore* to the Earl of
Dartmouth, dated " The *Fowey* in *York* River *July*
" the 12ᵗʰ 1775." Nº. 29. [Photoſtatic Copy in *Reſearch
Department, Colonial Williamſburg* Foundation.]

Alſo:

*THE VIRGINIA GAZETTE (Williamſburg: John
Dixon & Wm. Hunter),* No. 1244, *June* 10, 1775.

" *Williamſburg, June* 10."

" Laſt *Thurſday* Morning, about two o'Clock, our Governor
" and his Family decamped from the Palace, and are now on
" Board the *Fowey* Man of War at *York Town.* His Excellency
" left the following Meſſage to be delivered to the Aſſembly.

" ' Mr. Speaker, and Gentlemen of the Houſe of Burgeſſes,
" ' Being now fully perſuaded that my Perſon, and thoſe of my
" Family likewiſe, are in conſtant Danger of falling Sacrifices to
" the blind and unmeaſurable Fury which has ſo unaccountably
" ſeized upon the Minds and Underſtanding of great Numbers of
" the People, and apprehending that at Length ſome among them
" may work themſelves up to that Pitch of Daringneſs and Atro-
" ciouſneſs as to fall upon me in the defenceleſs State in which
" they know I am in the City of *Williamſburg,* and perpetrate
" Acts that would plunge this Country into the moſt horrid Ca-
" lamities, and render the Breach with the Mother Country irre-
" parable; I have thought it prudent for myſelf, and ſerviceable
" for the Country, that I remove to a Place of Safety, conform-
" able to which I have fixed my Reſidence, for the Preſent, on
" Board his Majeſty's Ship the *Fowey,* lying at *York.*

" ' It is not my Intention to give the leaſt Interruption to the
" Sitting of the Aſſembly, but I hope they will proceed in the
" great Buſineſs which they have before them, with Diligence and
" Effect. I ſhall take Care to make the Acceſs to me ſo eaſy and
" ſafe, that the neceſſary Communication between me and the
" Houſe may be attended with the leaſt Inconvenience poſſible;
" and I thought it would be more agreeable to the Houſe to ſend
" to me, from Time to Time, ſome of their Members, as Occaſion
" ſhall

" fhall require, than be put all to the Trouble of moving to be
" nearer me.

" ' I hope the Houfe will fee my Proceedings on this Occafion as
" they were really meant; and I beg them to be affured that I
" fhall now be as ready to attend to all the Duties of my Office
" as I was before, and that I am perfectly difpofed to contribute
" all in my Power, if Opportunity be given me, to reftore that
" Harmony, the Interruption of which is likely to coft fo dear to
" the Repofe, as well as to the Comforts of every Individual.

" *Dunmore.* ' "

Alfo:

Ibid., No. 1247, *July* 1, 1775.

" *Williamfburg, July* 1. "

" We hear from *York*, that Lord *Dunmore*, in the *Fowey*, and
" his Lady and Family, on Board the *Magdalen*, failed from that
" Place laft *Thurfday* Morning. It is faid the *Magdalen* will
" proceed to *England*, and that the *Fowey* is to return to *York*
" *Town* with the Governor, after having convoyed the Schooner
" as far as the Capes. "

[253]

Ibid., No. 1253, *Auguft* 12, 1775.

" *Williamfburg, Auguft* 12.

" . . . it is certain that the Earl of *Dunmore's* Ship is now com-
" pleted for an Expedition, and that his Lordfhip has fitted up
" thirteen Field Pieces for Service. It is apprehended he intends
" to commence Hoftilities upon *York* or *James* River very foon. "

Alfo:

Ibid., From No. 1255, *Auguft* 26, 1775, through No.
1305, *Auguft* 10, 1776.

[254]

Ibid., No. 1305, *Auguft* 10, 1776.

" *Williamfburg, Auguft* 10. "

" A Captain of a Veffel, who is juft arrived with Powder and
" Arms, informs, that he met with Lord *Dunmore's* Fleet off the
" Capes, ftanding out to Sea, in two Divifions, one to the fouth-
" ward, and the other to the northward. They have been fev-
" eral Days lying in *Lynhaven* Bay, and have burnt fome fmall
" Veffels

" Veffels which probably they had not Men to manage, or were
" unfit for a Voyage.—May they never return. "

[255]

THE VIRGINIA GAZETTE (Williamſburg: Alex-ander Purdie), January 3, 1777.

" There is certain Intelligence of our *Quondam* Governour,
" Lord *Dunmore*, that celebrated Chief, having at laſt taken his
" Departure for *England*, to enjoy the Smiles of his Sovereign
" for the many ſignal Services rendered to his auguſt Houſe while
" Commander in Chief in *Virginia*. "

[256]

At the Cloſe of the Meeting of *Saturday*, the 24th of
June, 1775, the Houſe adjourned until *Thurſday*,
the 12th of *October*, 1775, at which Time the
" Houſe met according to the Adjournment; but no
" more than thirty-ſeven Members appearing,
" which was not a ſufficient Number to proceed
" to Buſineſs. The Houſe adjourned til the firſt
" *Thurſday* in *March* next. " On *Thurſday*, the
7th of *March*, 1776, only thirty-two Members
appeared, and the Houſe again adjourned until the
firſt *Monday* in *May*. On *May* 6th " Several
" Members met " for the laſt Time as a Houſe of
Burgeſſes.

[See: *Journals of the Houſe of Burgeſſes of Virginia*,
1773-1776 (*Richmond:* 1905), pp. 280-283.]

[257]

THE PROCEEDINGS OF THE CONVENTION OF DELEGATES FOR THE COUNTIES AND CORPORATIONS IN THE COLONY OF VIR-GINIA, HELD AT RICHMOND TOWN ... on Monday the 17th of July 1775. [July 17—Auguſt 26, 1775.] (Richmond: Ritchie, Trueheart & Du-Val, 1816), pp. 21-22, 44-46.

[258]

[258]

Ibid., pp. 11, 25.

Alſo:

THE VIRGINIA GAZETTE (Williamſburg: Printed by *Alexander Purdie*), No. 34, *September* 22, 1775.

" *Williamſburg, September* 22.

" On *Wedneſday* laſt Col. *Henry* arrived here, to make Choice
" of a proper Spot for an Encampment, and to give Directions for
" laying out the Ground.   The Forces will begin to aſſemble in
" a very ſhort Time, and the Rendezvous, we hear, will be cloſe
" by this City. "

Ibid., No. 35, *September* 29, 1775.

" *Williamſburg, September* 29. "

" A Camp is now marked out, behind the College; Tents, and
" other Camp Equipage, are getting ready with the utmoſt Expe-
" dition; and the Troops, from the different Counties, are on
" their March for this City. "

[259]

John Pendleton Kennedy, ed., *JOURNALS OF THE HOUSE OF BURGESSES OF VIRGINIA, 1773 1776 (Richmond:* 1905), p. 283.

[260]

See Note 114.

[261]

THE PROCEEDINGS OF THE CONVENTION OF DELEGATES HELD AT THE CAPITOL, IN THE CITY OF WILLIAMSBURG. In the COL-ONY OF VIRGINIA, on Monday, the 6th of May, 1776. [From *May* 6 through *July* 5, 1776.] (*Richmond: Ritchie, Trueheart & Du-Val*, 1816.)

[262]

WILLIAM AND MARY COLLEGE QUARTERLY HISTORICAL MAGAZINE, Firſt Series, Vol. II (1893-4), pp. 253-254. " The Inſtructions to the Dele-
" gates

" gates to be chosen for the County of *Cumberland* on
" *Monday*, the 22nd Day of *April*, 1776, to sit in the
" General Convention of this Colony . . ."

" To *John Mayo* and *William Fleming*, Gent. :

" When the King of *Great Britain*, deaf to all the humiliating
" and well intended Petitions from his once loyal Subjects, not
" only of *America*, but of *Great Britain* also, changes his Justice
" into Severity; when he stoops to the low Artifice of bribing to
" carry his despotic Designs into Effect, and his first Dignities are
" Marks of the first Servitude; when he prefers arbitrary Sway
" unknown to the Constitution which placed his Family on the
" Throne to the Love and Happiness of his Subjects; when the
" *British* Parliament so far sunk in Venality and Corruption as to
" sacrifice their most inestimable Privileges, adding Insult to
" Oppression, have given his Majesty the warmest Assurances,
" that they will, with their Lives and Fortunes, support him in
" a ruinous and cruel War against us.   When his Majesty, after
" a wanton Abuse of his Negative on our Acts of Assembly, by
" which he has forced the Slave Trade on us for several Years un-
" mindful of his Coronation Oath, has ordered his Governor
" Lord *Dunmore*, to arm our Slaves against us, in open Violation
" of several Acts of Assembly which have the Royal Sanction;
" when an uniform System through all the Acts of Parliament in
" the present Reign, tending evidently to the total Destruction
" of *American* Liberty, leaves no other Alternative than a base
" Submission to their inhuman, impolitic and oppressive Mea-
" sures, or Independency; actuated by a tender Regard to our-
" selves and to our Posterity we think ourselves indispensably
" obliged to declare boldly for the latter.   We, therefore, your
" Constituents, instruct you positively to declare for Indepen-
" dency; that you solemnly abjure any Allegeance to his *Britan-*
" *nick* Majesty, and bid him a good Night forever; that you pro-
" mote in our Convention an Instruction to our Delegates, now
" sitting in Continental Congress, to do the same; . . ."

[263]

*William Wirt Henry, PATRICK HENRY, LIFE,
CORRESPONDENCE AND SPEECHES (New
York: Charles Scribner's Sons,* 1891*),* Vol. I, pp.
387-401.

[264]

[264]

THE PROCEEDINGS OF THE CONVENTION OF DELEGATES HELD AT THE CAPITOL, IN THE CITY OF WILLIAMSBURG. IN THE COLONY OF VIRGINIA, On Monday, the 6th of May, 1776. [May 6-July 5, 1776] (Richmond: Ritchie, Trueheart & Du-Val, 1816), pp. 15-16.

" *Wednefday, May* 15, 1776. "

" The Convention then, according to the Order of the Day
" refolved itfelf into a Committee on the State of the Colony; and
" after fome Time fpent therein, Mr. Prefident [*Edmund Pendle-*
" *ton*] refumed the Chair, and Mr. [*Archibald*] *Cary* reported, that
" the Committee had, according to Order, had under their Con-
" fideration the State of the Colony, and had come to the follow-
" ing Refolutions thereupon; which he read in his Place, and
" afterwards delivered in at the Clerk's Table, where the fame
" were again twice read, and unanimoufly agreed to, one Hundred
" and twelve Members being prefent.

" Forafmuch as all the Endeavours of the United Colonies, by
" the moft decent Reprefentations and Petitions to the King and
" Parliament of *Great Britain*, to reftore Peace and Security to
" *America* under the *Britifh* Government, and a Re-union with
" that People upon juft and liberal Terms, inftead of a Redrefs of
" Grievances, have produced, from an imperious and vindictive
" Adminiftration, increafed Infult, Oppreffion, and a vigorous
" Attempt to effect our total Deftruction. By a late Act, all
" thefe Colonies are declared to be in Rebellion, and out of the
" Protection of the *Britifh* Crown, our Properties fubjected to
" Confifcation, our People, when captivated, compelled to join
" in the Murder and Plunder of their Relations and Countrymen,
" and all former Rapine and Oppreffion of *Americans* declared
" legal and juft. Fleets and Armies are raifed, and the Aid of
" foreign Troops engaged to affift thefe deftructive Purpofes.
" The King's Reprefentative in this Colony hath not only with-
" held all the Powers of Government from operating for our
" Safety, but, having retired on Board an armed Ship, is carrying
" on a piratical and favage War againft us, tempting our Slaves,
" by every Artifice, to refort to him, and training and employing
" them againft their Mafters. In this State of extreme Danger,
" we have no Alternative left but an abject Submiffion to the
" Will of thofe overbearing Tyrants, or a total Separation from
" the

" the Crown and Government of *Great Britain*, uniting and exert-
" ing the Strength of all *America* for Defence, and forming Al-
" liances with foreign Powers for Commerce and Aid in War:
" Wherefore, appealing to the Searcher of Hearts for the Sincerity
" of former Declarations, expreffing our Defire to preferve the
" Connexion with that Nation, and that we are driven from that
" Inclination by their wicked Councils, and the eternal Laws of
" Self-prefervation;

" *Refolved unanimoufly*, That the Delegates appointed to rep-
" refent this Colony in General Congrefs be inftructed to propofe
" to that refpectable Body to declare the United Colonies free
" and independent States, abfolved from all Allegiance to, or
" Dependence upon, the Crown or Parliament of *Great Britain;*
" and that they give the Affent of this Colony to fuch Declara-
" tion, and to whatever Meafures may be thought proper and
" neceffary by the Congrefs for forming foreign Alliances, and a
" Confederation of the Colonies, at fuch Time, and in the Manner,
" as to them fhall feem beft: Provided, that the Power of forming
" Government for, and the Regulations of the internal Concerns
" of each Colony, be left to the refpective colonial Legiflatures. "

[265]

Ibid., pp. 42-43.

" *Wednefday, June* 12, 1776.

" The Declaration of Rights having been fairly tranfcribed,
" was read a third Time, and paffed as follows, *nem. con.*

" *A Declaration of Rights made by the Reprefentatives of the*
" *good People of* Virginia, *affembled in full and free Convention;*
" *which Rights do pertain to them, and their Pofterity, as the Bafis*
" *and Foundation of Government.*

" 1. That all Men are by Nature equally free and independent,
" and have certain inherent Rights, of which, when they enter
" into a State of Society, they cannot, by any Compact, deprive
" or diveft their Pofterity; namely, the Enjoyment of Life and
" Liberty, with the Means of acquiring and poffeffing Property,
" and purfuing and obtaining Happinefs and Safety.

" 2. That all Power is vefted in, and confequently derived
" from, the People; that Magiftrates are their Truftees and Ser-
" vants, and at all Times amenable to them.

" 3. That Government is, or ought to be, inftituted for the
" common Benefit, Protection, and Security, of the People, Na-
" tion, or Community; of all the various Modes and Forms of
" Government that is beft, which is capable of producing the
" greateft

" greateſt Degree of Happineſs and Safety, and is moſt effectually
" ſecured againſt the Danger of Mal-adminiſtration; and that,
" whenever any Government ſhall be found inadequate or con-
" trary to theſe Purpoſes, a Majority of the Community hath an
" indubitable, unalienable, and indefeaſible Right, to reform,
" alter, or aboliſh it, in ſuch Manner as ſhall be judged moſt con-
" ducive to the public Weal.

" 4. That no Man, or Set of Men, are entitled to excluſive or
" ſeparate Emoluments or Privileges from the Community, but
" in Conſideration of public Services; which, not being deſcen-
" dible, neither ought the Offices of Magiſtrate, Legiſlator, or
" Judge, to be hereditary.

" 5. That the legiſlative and executive Powers of the State
" ſhould be ſeparate and diſtinct from the Judicative; and, that
" the Members of the two firſt may be reſtrained from Oppreſſion,
" by feeling and participating the Burthens of the People, they
" ſhould, at fixed Periods, be reduced to a private Station, return
" into that Body from which they were originally taken, and the
" Vacancies be ſupplied by frequent, certain, and regular Elec-
" tions, in which all, or any Part of the former Members, to be
" again eligible, or ineligible, as the Laws ſhall direct.

" 6. That Elections of Members to ſerve as Repreſentatives of
" the People, in Aſſembly, ought to be free; and that all Men,
" having ſufficient Evidence of permanent common Intereſt with,
" and Attachment to, the Community, have the Right of Suf-
" frage, and cannot be taxed or deprived of their Property for
" public Uſes without their own Conſent or that of their Repre-
" ſentatives ſo elected, nor bound by any Law to which they
" have not, in like Manner, aſſented, for the public Good.

" 7. That all Power of ſuſpending Laws, or the Execution of
" Laws, by any Authority without Conſent of the Repreſenta-
" tives of the People, is injurious to their Rights, and ought not
" to be exerciſed.

" 8. That in all capital or criminal Proſecutions a Man hath a
" Right to demand the Cauſe and Nature of his Accuſation, to
" be confronted with the Accuſers and Witneſſes, to call for Evi-
" dence in his Favour, and to a ſpeedy Trial by an impartial
" Jury of his Vicinage, without whoſe unanimous Conſent he can-
" not be found guilty, nor can he be compelled to give Evidence
" againſt himſelf; that no Man be deprived of his Liberty except
" by the Law of the Land, or the Judgment of his Peers.

" 9 That exceſſive Bail ought not to be required, nor exceſſive
" Fines impoſed; nor cruel and unuſual Puniſhments inflicted.

" 10

" 10. That general Warrants, whereby any Officer or Meff-
" enger may be commanded to fearch fufpected Places without
" Evidence of a Fact committed, or to feize any Perfon or Perfons
" not named, or whofe Offence is not particularly defcribed and
" fupported by Evidence, are grievous and oppreffive, and ought
" not to be granted.

" 11. That in Controverfies refpecting Property, and in Suits
" between Man and Man, the ancient Trial by Jury is preferable
" to any other, and ought to be held facred.

" 12. That the Freedom of the Prefs is one of the greateft
" Bulwarks of Liberty, and can never be reftrained but by
" defpotic Governments.

" 13. That a well regulated Militia, compofed of the Body of
" the People, trained to Arms, is the proper, natural, and fafe
" Defence of a free State; that ftanding Armies, in Time of Peace,
" fhould be avoided, as dangerous to Liberty; and that, in all
" Cafes, the Military fhould be under ftrict Subordination to, and
" governed by, the civil Power.

" 14. That the People have a Right to uniform Government;
" and therefore, that no Government feparate from, or independ-
" ent of, the Government of *Virginia*, ought to be erected or
" eftablifhed within the Limits thereof.

" 15. That no free Government, or the Bleffing of Liberty, can
" be preferved to any People but by a firm Adherence to Juftice,
" Moderation, Temperance, Frugality, and Virtue, and by fre-
" quent Recurrence to fundamental Principles.

" 16. That Religion, or the Duty which we owe to our Creator,
" and the Manner of difcharging it, can be directed only by Rea-
" fon and Conviction, not by Force or Violence; and therefore,
" all Men are equally entitled to the free Exercife of Religion,
" according to the Dictates of Confcience; and that it is the
" mutual Duty of all to practife Chriftian Forbearance, Love,
" and Charity, towards each other. "

Alfo:

*Hugh Blair Grigfby, THE VIRGINIA CONVEN-
TION OF 1776 (Richmond: J. W. Randolph, 1855),
pp. 161-166.*

[266]

*THE PROCEEDINGS OF THE CONVENTION OF
DELEGATES HELD AT THE CAPITOL, IN
THE CITY OF WILLIAMSBURG. . . . On Mon-
day,*

day, the 6th of May, 1776. [*May 6-July 5,* 1776.] (*Rich-mond: Ritchie, Trueheart & Du-Val,* 1816), pp. 66, 78.

Alſo:

ORDINANCES PASSED AT A GENERAL CON-VENTION, OF DELEGATES AND REPRE-SENTATIVES . . . HELD AT THE CAPITOL, IN THE CITY OF WILLIAMSBURG, On Monday, the 6th of May, Anno. Dom. 1776. (*Richmond: Ritchie, Trueheart & Du-Val,* 1816), pp. 4-6.

" The Conſtitution or Form of Government, agreed to and re-
" ſolved upon by the Delegates and Repreſentatives of the
" ſeveral Counties & Corporations of *Virginia.* . . . "

Alſo:

Paul Leiceſter Ford, ed., *THE WORKS OF THOMAS JEFFERSON* (*New York: G. P. Putnam's Sons,* 1905), Vol. XII, pp. 407-408. Letter from *Thomas Jefferſon* to Judge *Auguſtus B. Woodward,* " Monti-
" *cello, April* 3, 1825. "

" . . . The Faſt is unqueſtionable, that the Bill of Rights, and
" the Conſtitution of *Virginia,* were drawn originally by *George*
" *Maſon,* one of our really great Men, and of the firſt Order of
" Greatneſs. The Hiſtory of the Preamble to the latter is this:
" I was then at *Philadelphia* with Congreſs ; and knowing that
" the Convention of *Virginia* was engaged in forming a Plan of
" Government, I turned my mind to the ſame Subjeſt, and drew
" a Sketch or Outline of a Conſtitution, with a Preamble, which
" I ſent to Mr. *Pendleton,* Preſident of the Convention, on the
" mere Poſſibility that it might ſuggeſt Something worth Incor-
" poration into that before the Convention. He informed me
" afterwards by Letter, that he received it on the Day on which
" the Committee of the Whole had reported to the Houſe the
" Plan they had agreed to; that that had been ſo long in Hand, ſo
" diſputed Inch by Inch, . . . that they were worried with the Con-
" tentions it had produced, and could not, from mere Laſſitude,
" have been induced to open the Inſtrument again; but that, be-
" ing pleaſed with the Preamble to mine, they adopted it in the
" Houſe, by Way of Amendment to the Report of the Committe;

"and

" and thus my Preamble became tacked to the Work of *George*
" *Mafon*. The Conftitution, with the Preamble, was paffed on
" the 29th of *June*, . . . "

[267]

*THE PROCEEDINGS OF THE CONVENTION OF
DELEGATES HELD AT THE CAPITOL, IN
THE CITY OF WILLIAMSBURG, . . . On Mon-
day, the 6th of May, 1776. (Richmond: Ritchie, Trueheart & Du-Val, 1816), pp. 78-79.*

" *Saturday, June* 29, 1776. "

" *Refolved*, That the Salary of the Governor of this Common-
" wealth be £1000 per Annum.

" The Convention proceeded, by Ballot, according to the
" Order of the Day, to the Appointment of a Governor for this
" Commonwealth; and the Members having prepared their
" Tickets, and put the fame into the Ballot Box, Mr. *Wythe*,
" Mr. *Curle*, Mr. *Dandridge*, and Mr. *Madifon*, were appointed a
" Committee to examine the fame, and report upon whom the
" Majority falls; and it appearing, from their Report, that the
" Numbers ftood as follows:

" For *PATRICK HENRY*, Jun. Efq.   60
" *THOMAS NELSON*, Efq.   45
" *JOHN PAGE*, Efq.   1

" *Refolved therefore*, That the faid *Patrick Henry*, Jun. Efq. be
" Governor of this Commonweath, to continue in that Office
" until the End of the fucceeding Seffion of Affembly after the
" laft of *March* next; and that Mr. *Mafon*, Mr. *Henry Lee*, Mr.
" *Digges*, Mr. *Blair*, and Mr. *Dandridge*, be a Committee to wait
" upon him, and notify such Appointment. "

[268]

Ibid., p. 80.

" *Monday, July* 1, 1776. "

" *Refolved*, That the former Refolution of this Convention [fee
" *Ibid.*, p. 51] for appropriating the Palace, and as many of the
" Out-buildings as might be neceffary for the Purpofe of a public
" Hofpital, be now refcinded; and that the Committee appointed
" to notify to the Governor his Appointment do alfo inform him,
" the Convention defire he will make the fame his Place of
" Refidence. "

Alfo:

Alſo:

Ibid., p. 84

" *Friday, July* 5, 1776. "

" *Reſolved*, That the Sum of £1000 be laid out in Furniture
" for the Palace in this City, including the Furniture already
" there belonging to the Country, at a reaſonable Appraiſement;
" and that Mr. *Digges*, Mr. *Blair*, Mr. *Everard*, and Mr. *Ran-*
" *dolph*, be deſired to procure the ſame. "

Alſo:

H. R. McIlwaine, ed., *JOURNALS OF THE COUN-
CIL OF THE STATE OF VIRGINIA* (*Richmond:*
1931), Vol. I, pp. 90, 121, 142, 192, 280.

[269]

*THE PROCEEDINGS OF THE CONVENTION OF
DELEGATES HELD AT THE CAPITOL, IN
THE CITY OF WILLIAMSBURG. . . . On
Monday, the 6th of May, 1776* (*Richmond: Ritchie,
Trueheart & Du-Val,*1816), p. 51.

" *Saturday, June* 15, 1776. "

" *Ordered*, That *Thomas Everard*, *Robert Prentis*, *Edmund*
" *Randolph*, *John Blair*, and *James Cocke*, Gentlemen, be, and
" they are hereby appointed Commiſſioners to rent out the
" Lands, and to ſell at public Auction the Slaves and perſonal
" Eſtate, of Lord *Dunmore*, at or in the Neighbourhood of the
" City of *Williamſburg*, on twelve Months Credit, taking Bond,
" with ſufficient Security; . . . and that the Commiſſioners
" aforeſaid do pay the Money thence ariſing into the public
" Treaſury, there to remain till the farther Order of the Con-
" vention. "

Alſo:

THE VIRGINIA GAZETTE (*Williamſburg: Dixon &
Hunter*), No. 1298, *June* 22, 1776.

[270]

See Note 268.

[271]

*William Wirt, SKETCHES OF THE LIFE AND
CHARACTER*

CHARACTER OF PATRICK HENRY (Hartford: S. Andrus & Son, 1847), p. 423.

Alſo:

William Wirt Henry, PATRICK HENRY, LIFE, CORRESPONDENCE AND SPEECHES (New York: Charles Scribner's Sons, 1891), Vol. I, pp. 457-458.

" . . . Governor *Henry*, while retaining his Simplicity and Affa-
" bility of Manner, now aſſumed a Dignity of Demeanor which
" commanded the Admiration of all. He could no longer be re-
" marked on for his Plainneſs in Dreſs. He ſeldom appeared on
" the Streets of *Williamſburg*, and never without a ſcarlet Cloak,
" black Clothes, and a dreſſed Wig. " [From Letter of Judge
" *Roane* to Mr. *Wirt*.]

[272]

THE VIRGINIA GAZETTE (Williamſburg: Dixon & Hunter), No. 1387, October 31, 1777.

" Head Quarters, *Williamſburg*, *October* 30, 1777.
" A *Feu de Joy* this Afternoon at three o'Clock, on the Con-
" firmation of the glorious News of General *Burgoyne* and his
" Army being Priſoners of War, all the Troops are to parade at
" the Barracks, the Artillery with thirteen Diſcharges, the In-
" fantry with three Rounds; from thence they will proceed, in
" marching Order, near to Mr. *Powell's*, where they will be joined
" by the City Militia, from thence the whole will march in Pla-
" toons round the Capitol up the main Street, to the Common
" behind the Court Houſe, there the Battalion will be formed,
" and the Firing begin; thirteen Diſcharges of Cannon will be
" made, under the Command of Captain *De la Porte* of the
" Artillery; and, after a ſhort Interval, three Vollies will be fired
" by the Infantry; the whole Battalion will then give three
" Cheers, in which the Spectators will moſt joyfully join. The
" Officers will ſee that the Men ſhall be clean, ſhaved, their Hats
" cocked, and their Arms and Accoutrements in good Order. A
" general Diſcharge of all Priſoners from the Guards on this
" Occaſion, except Deſerters, who cannot be ranked amongſt the
" Friends of the thirteen *United States*. A Gill of Rum will be
" iſſued for every Soldier, in Evidence of the Governor's hearty
" Congratulation with them on this Occaſion. "

[273]

[273]

AMERICAN PHILOSOPHICAL SOCIETY, Philadelphia. Correſpondence of General *George Weedon*, 1777-1786. Letter from *John Page* to General *Weedon*, dated *October*, 1777.

[274]

H. R. McIlwaine, ed., *OFFICIAL LETTERS OF THE GOVERNORS OF THE STATE OF VIRGINIA.* Vol. I, *The Letters of Patrick Henry* (*Richmond:* 1926), pp. 222-224, 323-325, 338-340, 371, 372.

Alſo:

William Wirt Henry, PATRICK HENRY, LIFE, CORRESPONDENCE AND SPEECHES (*New York: Charles Scribner's* Sons, 1891), Vol. I, pp. 580-605.

[275]

William P. Palmer, ed., *CALENDAR OF VIRGINIA STATE PAPERS* (*Richmond:* 1875), Vol. I, pp. 315-316. Letter of Colonel *George Rogers Clarke* to *Patrick Henry*, Governor of *Virginia*, written from *Kaſkaſkias, Illinois, February* 3, 1779.

" A late Menuvᵣ of the famous Hair Buyer General, *Henry Ham-*
" *ilton* Eſqᵣ Lieut: Governor of *DeTroit*, hath allarmed us much:
" on the 16ᵗʰ of *December* laſt, he with a Body of ſix Hundred
" Men, compoſed of Regulars, *French* Volunteers and *Indians*
" took poſſeſſion of *Sᵗ Vincent* on the *Waubash*, . . . He is influ-
" encing all the *Indians* he poſſibly can to join him . . . "

[276]

THE VIRGINIA GAZETTE (*Williamſburg: Dixon & Nicolſon*), No. 19, *June* 19, 1779; No. 20, *June* 26, 1779.

Alſo:

WIDENER LIBRARY, Harvard Univerſity. Journal of Governor *Henry Hamilton*, 1779.

[277]

[277]

Ibid., " *June* 15, 1779. "

[278]

JOURNAL OF THE HOUSE OF DELEGATES OF THE COMMONWEALTH OF VIRGINIA; Begun and Held at the Capitol, in the City of Williamſburg. On Monday, the third Day of May, . . . 1779 (Richmond: Thomas W. White, 1827), p. 29.

" *Tueſday, June* 1, 1779. . . .

" The Houſe then, according to the Order of the Day, pro-
" ceeded by joint Ballot with the Senate, to the Choice of a Gov-
" ernor or Chief Magiſtrate, in the Room of *Patrick Henry,* Eſq.,
" who hath reſigned; and Meſſrs. *Harvie, Tazewell, Lyne* and
" *Robert W. Carter,* were appointed a Committee, in Conjunction
" with a Committee from the Senate, to examine the joint Ballot
" of both Houſes. And the Committee withdrew.

" The Committee being returned, Mr. *Harvie* reported, that
" they had, according to Order, in Conjunction with a Committee
" from the Senate, examined the joint Ballots of both Houſes,
" and found the Numbers to ſtand as follows:

" For *Thomas Jefferſon,* Eſq.   55
" General *Nelſon,*   32
" For the Hon. *John Page,*   38

" But neither of the Perſons ballotted for having a Majority of
" both Houſes, the Houſe proceeded to ballot between *Thomas*
" *Jefferſon* Eſq., and the Hon. *John Page,* who ſtand foremoſt.

" And Mr. *Harvie* reported the Numbers to ſtand as follows:

" For *Thomas Jefferſon,* Eſq.   67
" For the Hon. *John Page,*   61

" *Reſolved,* That *Thomas Jefferſon,* Eſq. be appointed Gov-
" ernor or Chief Magiſtrate of this Commonwealth. "

[279]

H. R. McIlwaine, ed., *OFFICIAL LETTERS OF THE GOVERNORS OF THE STATE OF VIRGINIA.* Vol. II, *The Letters of Thomas Jefferſon (Richmond:* 1928), p. 5. Letter from *Thomas Jefferſon* to Col. *William Fleming,* " *Williamſburgh June* 8 1779. "

" . . . the

" . . . the Houfe of Delegates have paffed a Bill for removing the
" Seat of Government to *Richmond*. It hefitates with the
" Senate . . . "

[280]

See Note 167.

[281]

Paul Leicefter Ford, ed., *THE WORKS OF THOMAS
JEFFERSON* (*New York: G. P. Putnam's* Sons,
1904), Vol. I, p. 64, Vol. II, pp. 271-276, 375.

[282]

*JOURNAL OF THE HOUSE OF DELEGATES OF
THE COMMONWEALTH OF VIRGINIA; Begun
and Held at the Capitol, in the City of Williamfburg.
On Monday, the third Day of May, . . . 1779* (*Richmond: Thomas W. White*, 1827), p. 44.

" *Saturday, June* 12, 1779. . . .

" A Meffage from the Senate by Mr. *Harrifon:*

" Mr. Speaker,—The Senate . . . have alfo agreed to the Bill
" entitled 'An Act, for the Removal of the Seat of Government, '
" with feveral Amendments; to which they defire the concur-
" rence of this Houfe. And then he withdrew.

" The Houfe proceeded to confider the Amendments made by
" the Senate, to the Bill, entitled ' An Act, for the Removal of the
" Seat of Government; ' and the fame being read, were agreed
" to. "

[283]

*William Waller Hening, THE STATUTES AT
LARGE* (*Richmond: George Cochran*, 1822), Vol. X,
pp. 85-89. "*An Act for the Removal of the Seat of
" Government. "

" I. WHEREAS great Numbers of the Inhabitants of this
"' Commonwealth muft frequently and of neceffity refort to the
" Seat of Government where General Affemblies are convened,
" fuperior Courts are held, and the Governour and Council
" ufually tranfact the executive Bufinefs of Government; and
" the equal Rights of all the faid Inhabitants require that fuch
" Seat of Government fhould be as nearly central to all as may
" be,

" be, having Regard only to Navigation, the Benefits of which
" are neceſſary for promoting the Growth of a Town ſufficient
" for the Accommodation of thoſe who reſort thereto, and able
" to aid the Operations of Government: And it has been alſo
" found inconvenient in the Courſe of the preſent War, where
" Seats of Government have been ſo ſituated as to be expoſed to
" the Inſults and Injuries of the publick Enemy, which Dangers
" may be avoided and equal Juſtice done to all the Citizens of
" this Commonwealth by removing the Seat of Government to
" the Town of *Richmond*, in the County of *Henrico*, which is more
" ſafe and central than any other Town ſituated on navigable
" Water: *Be it therefore enacted by the General Aſſembly*, That
" ſix whole Squares of Ground ſurrounded each of them by four
" Streets, and containing all the Ground within ſuch Streets,
" ſituate in the ſaid Town of *Richmond*, and on an open and airy
" Part thereof, ſhall be appropriated to the Uſe and Purpoſe of
" publick Buildings: . . . "

[284]

*THE VIRGINIA GAZETTE (Williamſburg: Dixon &
Nicolſon)*, No. 59, *March* 25, 1780.

" NOTICE is hereby given, that the Buſineſs of Government,
" in the Executive Department, will ceaſe to be tranſacted at
" *Williamſburg* from the 7th of *April* next, and will commence at
" *Richmond* on the 24th of the ſame Month.   The Governour
" will be in *Richmond* during the Interval, to do ſuch Buſineſs as
" may be done by him, without the Concurrence of the publick
" Boards.

" *Arch: Blair*, C.C. "

[285]

*Jedidiah Morſe, THE AMERICAN UNIVERSAL
GEOGRAPHY (Boſton: Iſaiah Thomas & Ebenezer
T. Andrews*, 1793), pp. 548-551.

" *Williamſburgh,* which till the Year 1780 was the Seat of Govern-
" ment, never contained above 1800 Inhabitants, and *Norfolk*,
" the moſt populous Town they ever had in *Virginia*, contained
" but 6000.   . . .

    " *Alexandria* ſtands on the ſouth Bank of *Patomak* River in
" *Fairfax* County . . . It contains about 400 Houſes, many of
" which are handſomely built, and nearly 3000 Inhabitants. . . .

" *Frederickſburgh*,

"*Frederickſburgh*, in the County of *Spotſylvania*, is ſituated on
"the South Side of *Rappahannock* River . . . and contains
"about 200 Houſes, principally on one Street, which runs nearly
"parallel with the River, and 1500 Inhabitants. . . .

"*Richmond*, in the County of *Henrico*, is the preſent Seat of
"Government, and ſtands on the north Side of *James* River, juſt
"at the Foot of the Falls, and contains between 400 and 500
"Houſes, and nearly 4000 Inhabitants. Part of the Houſes are
"built upon the Margin of the River, convenient for Buſineſs;
"the Reſt are upon a Hill which overlooks the lower Part of the
"Town, . . . A large State Houſe or Capitol, has lately been
"erected on the Hill. . . .

"*Peterſburg*, 25 Miles ſouthward of *Richmond*, ſtands on the
"ſouth Side of *Appamattox* River, and contains upwards of 300
"Houſes in two Diviſions; one is upon a Clay cold Soil, and is very
"dirty, the other upon a Plain of Sand or Loam. There is no
"Regularity and very little Elegance in *Peterſburg*, it is merely
"a Place of Buſineſs. . . .

"*Williamſburgh* is 60 Miles eaſtward of *Richmond*, ſituated be-
"tween two Creeks; one falling into *James*, the other into *York*
"River. . . . It conſiſts of about 200 Houſes, going faſt to
"decay, and has about 1400 Inhabitants. It is regularly laid
"out in parallel Streets, with a Square in the Center, . . .

"*Yorktown*, 13 Miles eaſtward from *Williamſburgh*, and 14
"from *Monday's Point* at the Mouth of the River, is a Place of
"about 100 Houſes, ſituated on the ſouth Side of *York* River,
"and contains about 700 Inhabitants. . . ."

Alſo:

*Thomas Jefferſon, NOTES ON THE STATE OF VIR-
GINIA (Philadelphia:* Printed for *Mathew Carey,*
1794), pp. 152-153.

[286]

*William Gordon, THE HISTORY OF THE RISE,
PROGRESS, AND ESTABLISHMENT, OF THE
INDEPENDENCE OF THE UNITED STATES
OF AMERICA: INCLUDING AN ACCOUNT
OF THE LATE WAR (London:* Printed for the
Author; and ſold by *Charles Dilly,* in the *Poultry,*
1788), Vol. IV, pp. 110-118.

[287]

[287]

William P. Palmer, ed., *CALENDAR OF VIRGINIA STATE PAPERS* (Richmond: R. F. *Walker*, 1875), Vol. I, pp. 523-524. Letter from *Beniamin Harrifon* to General *Wafhington*.

Philadelphia February 16, 1781.

" My dear Sir,

" I arrived at this Place five Days ago, fent by our Affembly " to make Application to Congrefs for immediate Affiftance in " Men, Arms, Ammunition and Cloathing, and was alfo directed " to wait on you on the fame Subject; . . .

" Our Affembly on taking a full and acurate View of the " Southern War, and of our own Situation, on whom very much " of its Succefs depends, are juftly alarmed. They find the " Country greatly exhaufted in the Articles of Provifions, Arms " and military Stores of all Kinds, and that there is but little " Profpect of Affiftance in thefe Particulars from the adjoining " States, except as to Provifions from *N. Carolina*, and even " thefe we have but too much Reafon to fear will be furnifhed " in but fcanty Proportion. The greateft Part of the Ammuni- " tion fent to the South went from *Virg*ᵃ, by which Means weare " left with about 47000ʷᵗ of Powder of all Kinds, and much of " that muft be worked over before it can be ufed. Several " Thoufand Stand of Arms have alfo gone on, but very few of " them have been returned, and thofe in fuch wretched Order " that they are ufelefs to us for Want of Artificers to repair them; " from this fummary State of the Matter, you may eafily con- " clude that our own Safety forbids us to disfurnifh ourfelves any " farther, as from the foregoing Invafions of late, we have abun- " dant Reafon to conclude that the Enemy mean to over-run us " whenever an Opportunity fhall offer; but our Wants and Dif- " treffes do not end here. We have ftill greater which feems to " be almoft infuperable, what Men we have in the Field are fo " naked that they can render but little Service. . . . Every " Method has been tried by the Affembly and Executive to fur- " nifh them, but with very little Succefs. Not more than 300 " Suits of Cloaths and about as many Blankets have been ob- " tained, tho' we have made ufe of Imprefs where it was necef- " fary. The Affembly have paffed a Bill for raifing 3000 Men. " I think we may expect at leaft 2500 from the Law, but without " Cloaths &c they will alfo be ufelefs: next to Congrefs we look

" up

" up to you for Affiſtance, not doubting but you will do Every-
" thing within your Line to forward the Service. "

[288]

B. F. *Stevens*, THE CAMPAIGN IN VIRGINIA,
1781. (*London:* 4 *Trafalgar Square*, 1888), Vol. I,
pp. 65-70. " *An Anſwer to that Part of the Narrative*
" *of Lieutenant-General Sir* Henry Clinton, *K. B.*,
" *which relates to the Conduct of Lieutenant-General Earl*
" Cornwallis, . . . By *Earl* Cornwallis, London: J.
" Debrett, 1783. "

" It is foreign to the preſent Purpoſe, and I ſhall therefore not
" endeavour to enumerate the many Difficulties, which I had to
" ſtruggle with, in my Command of the ſouthern Diſtrict, pre-
" vious to the March into *North Carolina*, in the Beginning of the
" Year 1781 . . . I was principally induced to decide in Favour
" of its Expediency from a clear Conviction, that the Men and
" Treaſures of *Britain* would be laviſhed in Vain upon the
" *American* War, without the moſt active Exertions of the
" Troops allotted for that Service; and, that, while the Enemy
" could draw their Supplies from *North Carolina* and *Virginia*,
" the Defence of the Frontier of *South Carolina*, even againſt an
" inferior Army, would be from its Extent, the Nature of the
" Climate, and the Diſpoſition of the Inhabitants, utterly im-
" practicable. . . . I was likewiſe influenced by having juſt
" received an Account from *Charles-town* of the Arrival of a
" Frigate with Diſpatches from the Commander in Chief, the
" Subſtance of which, then tranſmitted to me, was, that General
" *Phillips* had been detached to the *Cheſapeak*, and put under
" my Orders; which induced me to hope, that ſolid Operations
" might be adopted in that Quarter: and I was moſt firmly per-
" ſuaded, that, until *Virginia* was reduced, we could not hold
" the more ſouthern Provinces; and that, after its Reduction,
" they would fall without much Reſiſtance, and be retained with-
" out much Difficulty.
" With theſe Sentiments, I joined General *Phillips's* Corps at
" *Peterſburgh* on the 20th of *May* [1781] a few Days after his
" Death; . . . "

[289]

John C. Fitzpatrick, ed., THE WRITINGS OF
GEORGE

GEORGE WASHINGTON, 1745-1799 (*Waſhington: Government Printing Office*, 1937), Vol. XXI, p. 52. Letter from General *Waſhington* to Comte *de Rochambeau*, from " Head Quarters, *New Windſor*, " *January* 3, 1781. "

" . . . Since my laſt, which was on the 23rd. of *Decemr*. I have " gained Intelligence through a Channel on which I can depend, " that the Detachment which ſailed from *New York* the 20th. of " laſt Month conſiſted of about 1600 Men and was chiefly com- " poſed of Drafts from the different *Britiſh, German* and Pro- " vincial Regiments. The *Queens Rangers* was the only intire " Corps, that I have heard of. *Arnold* commanded the Detach- " ment. There is little Doubt but they have gone to the " ſouthward. "

Alſo:

H. R. McIlwaine, ed., *OFFICIAL LETTERS OF THE GOVERNORS OF THE STATE OF VIR- GINIA—The Letters of Thomas Jefferſon* (*Richmond: Virginia State Library*, 1928), Vol. II, pp. 266-268. Letter from Governor *Jefferſon* to the Preſident of Congreſs and General *Waſhington*, " *Richmond* " *January* 10. 1781. "

" It may ſeem odd conſidering the important Events which " have taken Place in this State within the Courſe of ten Days " paſt that I ſhould not have tranſmitted an Account of them to " your Excellency; but ſuch has been their extraordinary Rapid- " ity and ſuch the unremitted Exertions they have required from " all concerned in Government that I do not recollect the Por- " tion of Time which I could have taken to commit them to " Paper.

" On the 30th of *December* a Letter from a private Gentleman " to Genl *Nelſon* came to my Hands, notifying that in the Morn- " ing of the preceeding Day 27 Sail of Veſſels had entered the " Capes and from the Tenor of the Letter we had Reaſon to " expect within a few Hours further Intelligence whether they " were Friends or Foes, their Force, & other Circumſtances. " We immediately diſpatched Genl *Nelſon* to the lower Country " with Power to call on the Militia in that Quarter or to act other- " wiſe as Exigencies ſhould require but waited further Intelli- " gence before we would call for Militia from the middle or upper " Counties.

" Counties. No further Intelligence came till the fecond Inft.
" when the former was confirmed, it was afcertained that they
" were Enemies and had advanced up *James* River to *Warra-*
" *fqueak* Bay. All Arrangements were immediately taken for
" calling in a fufficient Body of Militia for Oppofition. In the
" Night of the 3d we received Advice that they were at Anchor
" oppofite *James Town:* We then fuppofed *Williamfburg* to be
" their Object. The Wind however, which had hitherto been
" unfavorable, fhifted fair, and the Tide being alfo in their Favor
" they afcended the River to *Kennon's* that Evening and with
" the next Tide came up to *Weftover*, having on their Way taken
" Poffeffion of fome Works we had at *Hoods*, by which two or
" three of their Veffels had received fome Damage but which
" were of Neceffity abandoned by the fmall Garrifon of 50 Men
" placed there on the Enemy's Landing to inveft the Works. In-
" telligence of their having quitted the Station at *James Town*
" . . . reached us the next Morning at 5 o'Clock and was the
" firft Indication of their Meaning to penetrate towards this
" Place or *Peterfburg*. As the Orders for drawing Militia hither
" had been given but two Days no Oppofition was in Readinefs:
" every Effort was therefore neceffary to withdraw the Arms and
" other military Stores Records &c. from this Place. Every
" Effort was accordingly exerted to convey them to the Foundery
" five Miles, and to a Laboratory fix Miles above this [Place] till
" about Sunfet of that Day when we learnt that the Enemy had
" come to an Anchor at *Weftover* that Morning. . . . They marched
" from *Weftover* at 2 o'Clock in the Afternoon of the 4th and entered
" *Richmond* at 1 o'Clock of the Afternoon of the 5th. A Regiment
" of Infantry and about 30. Horfe continued on without halting
" to the Foundery. They burnt that, the boring Mill, the Maga-
" zine & two other Houfes, and proceeded to *Weftham;* but Noth-
" ing being in their Power there, they retired to *Richmond*. The
" next Morning they burnt fome Buildings of public, and fome
" of private Property, with what Stores remained in them,
" deftroyed a great Quantity of private Stores and about 12
" o'Clock retired towards *Weftover* where they encamped within
" the Neck the next Day. The Lofs fuftained is not yet accu-
" rately known. . . . Their Numbers from the beft Intelligence
" I have had are about 1500 Infantry & as to their Cavalry
" Accounts vary from 50 to 120, the Whole commanded by the
" Parracide *Arnold*. Our Militia difperfed over a large Tract of
" Country can be called in but flowly. . . . "

[290]

[290]

HEADQUARTERS PAPERS OF THE BRITISH ARMY IN AMERICA [Photoſtats in Poſſeſſion of *Colonial Williamſburg* Foundation.] Vol. XXIX, *April* 1-*May* 15, 1781. No. 3436. Letter from General Sir *Henry Clinton* to Lord *George Germain*, " *New* " *York April* 5th 1781. "

" In my Diſpatch marked N° 121 I had the Honor to inform your
" Lordſhip that the Expedition under the Command of Major
" General *Phillips* ſailed for the *Cheſapeak* the 20th Ultimo.
" And a Letter I have this Day received from that General
" Officer affords me the Pleaſure of acquainting you that he
" arrived with the Troops at *Portſmouth* on the 26th . . . "

Alſo:

John C. Fitzpatrick, ed., *THE WRITINGS OF GEORGE WASHINGTON*, 1745-1799 (*Waſhington: Government Printing Office*, 1937), Vol. XXI, pp. 414, 421, 428. [p. 428. General *Waſhington* to Comte de *Rochambeau*, *April* 7, 1781.]

" . . . the Marquis *de la Fayette* writes me from *Virginia* that
" the *Britiſh* Fleet which had left *Lynn Haven* Bay on the 24th:
" had returned again on the 25th. with a Number of Tranſports.
" The Detachment is ſaid to conſiſt of 1500 Men and to be under
" the Command of Major General *Phillips*. "

[291]

Ibid., Vol. XXI, pp. 253-256. General *Waſhington's* Inſtructions to Marquis *de Lafayette*. *February* 20, 1781.

[292]

HEADQUARTERS PAPERS OF THE BRITISH ARMY IN AMERICA. [Photoſtats in Poſſeſſion of *Colonial Williamſburg* Foundation.] Vol. XXX, *May* 16-*June* 30, 1781. Nos. 3518 and 3532. Letters from Earl *Cornwallis* to General Sir *Henry Clinton*, written from *Peterſburg* 20th *May*, 1781, and from *Byrd's Plantation*, 26th *May*, 1781.

See

See alfo Note 288.

[293]

H. R. *McIlwaine*, ed., *OFFICIAL LETTERS OF
THE GOVERNORS OF THE STATE OF VIR-
GINIA*, Vol. II, *The Letters of Thomas Jefferfon
(Richmond: Virginia State Library*, 1928), p. 524.
Letter of Governor *Jefferfon* to *Samuel Huntington*,
Prefident of Congrefs.

" *Charlottefville May* 28ᵗʰ 1781.

" . . . The whole Force of the Enemy within this State from
" the beft Intelligence I have been able to get I think is about
" 7000 Men Infantry and Cavalry including alfo the fmall
" Garrifon left at *Portfmouth*. . . . "

Alfo:

B. F. *Stevens*, *THE CAMPAIGN IN VIRGINIA,
1781. (London:* 4 *Trafalgar* Square, 1888), Vol. I, p. 24.
" *Narrative of Lieutenant-General Sir* Henry Clinton,
" *K. B., relative to his Conduct during Part of his
" Command of the King's Troops in* North America
" (London: J. Debrett, 1783). "

" . . . I recommended the Taking a refpectable defenfive Station
" either at *Williamfburg*, or *York* . . . and left his Lordfhip at
" Liberty to keep all the Troops he had in *Virginia*, (amounting
" to about feven Thoufand Men). But thinking that he might
" well fpare three Thoufand; I defired he would keep all that were
" neceffary for a refpectable Defenfive, and defultory Water
" Movements, and fend me of three Thoufand Men all he
" could. . . . "

[294]

*HEADQUARTERS PAPERS OF THE BRITISH
ARMY IN AMERICA.* [Photoftats in Poffeffion
of *Colonial Williamfburg* Foundation.] Vol. XXX,
May 16-*June* 30, 1781. No. 3582. Letter from
Earl *Cornwallis* to General Sir *Henry Clinton*.

" *Williamfburgh* 30ᵗʰ *June* 1781.

" Sir

" Sir.

" After paſſing *James* River at *Weſtover*, I moved to *Hanover*
" Court Houſe, and croſſed the *South Anna*. The Marquis *de*
" *Lafayette* marched to his left, keeping above me at the Diſtance
" of about twenty Miles.

" By puſhing my light Troops over the *North Anna*, I alarmed
" the Enemy for *Frederickſburgh*, & for the Junction with General
" *Wayne*, who was then marching through *Maryland*. . . . it
" was impoſſible to prevent the Junction between the Marquis &
" *Wayne;* I therefore took the Advantage of the Marquis's paſſing
" the *Rappahanock*, & detached Lieut Colonels *Simcoe & Tarle-*
" *ton* to diſturb the Aſſembly, then ſitting at *Charlotteville*, and
" to deſtroy the Stores there, at Old *Albermarle Court Houſe*, &
" the *Point of Fork*, moving with the Infantry to the Mouth of
" *Bird* Creek, near the *Point of Fork*, to receive thoſe Detach-
" ments. Lieut Colonel *Tarleton* took ſome Members of the
" Aſſembly at *Charlotteville*, & deſtroyed there, & on his Return,
" 1000 Stand of good Arms, ſome Clothing & other Stores, &
" between 4 or 500 Barrels of Powder, without Oppoſition.
" Baron *Steuben* who commanded about 800 Twelvemonth's Men
" & Militia, retired with great Precipitation from the *Point of*
" *Fork*. Lieut Colonel *Simcoe* after uſing every Exertion to
" attack his rear Guard, deſtroyed there, & at Places adjacent,
" about 3300 Stand of Arms, moſt of which unſerviceable, but
" then under Repair, ſome Salt, Harneſs &c. & about 150 Barrells
" of Powder. I then moved by *Richmond*, & arrived in *Will-*
" *iamſburgh*, on the 25th Inſt having in Addition to the Articles
" already mentioned, deſtroyed on this Expedition, at different
" Places above 2000 Hogſheads of Tobacco, & a great Number of
" iron Guns, & brought off 4 braſs 13 inch Mortars, 5 braſs 8
" inch Howitzes, & four long braſs nine Pounders all *French* . . .
" And we found at *Williamſburgh* a conſiderable Quantity of Shot
" & Shells, which are embarked. General *Wayne* joined the
" Marquis about the Middle of the Month, as did Baron *Steuben*
" ſoon after, and their Army has generally kept about twenty
" Miles from us, without any material Attempt by Detachment,
" except in an Attack on Lieut Colonel *Simcoe* on the 26th, as he
" was returning with his Corps & the *Yagers*, from the Deſtruc-
" tion of ſome Boats & Stores on the *Chickahominy*. The
" Enemy tho' much ſuperior in Numbers, were repulſed with
" conſiderable Loſs, . . .

" The Morning after my Arrival here [*Williamſburg*], I was
" honoured with your Excellency's Diſpatches of the 11th & 15th
" Inſt

"Inft. . . . By them I find, that you think if an offenfive Army
"could be fpared, it would not be advifeable to employ it in
"this Province. It is natural for every Officer to turn his
"Thought particularly to the Part of the War, in which he has
"been moft employed. And as the Security at leaft of *South
"Carolina*, if not the Reduction of *North Carolina*, feemed to be
"generally expected from me, both in this Country & in *England*,
"I thought myfelf called upon, after the Experiment I had made,
"had failed, to point out the only Mode in my Opinion of effect-
"ing it, and to declare, that untill *Virginia* was to a Degree fub-
"jected, we could not reduce *North Carolina*, or have any certain
"Hold of the back Country of *South Carolina;* . . . the Men &
"Riches of *Virginia* furnifhing ample Supplies to the Rebel
"Southern Army. . . .

"*Lafayette's* Continentals I believe, confift of about 17 or
"1800 Men, exclufive of fome Twelvemonths Men, collected by
"*Steuben;* he has received confiderable Reinforcements of
"Militia, & about 800 Mountain Rifle Men under *Campbell;*
"he keeps with his main Body about 18 or 20 Miles from us,
"his advanced Corps about 10 or 12, probably with an Intention
"of infulting our Rear Guard, when we pafs *James* River; I
"hope however to put that out of his Power, by croffing at
"*James City* Ifland, and if I can get a favourable Opportunity of
"ftriking a Blow at him without Lofs of Time, I will certainly
"try it. . . ."

[295]

See above Note.

[296]

Ibid., Vol. XXXI, *July* 1-*Auguft* 15, 1781. No. 3601.
Letter from Earl *Cornwallis* to General Sir *Henry
Clinton*, dated " *Cobham* 8th *July* 1781. "

[297]

THE MAGAZINE OF AMERICAN HISTORY, Vol.
VII (1881), pp. 207-208. Letter from *St. George
Tucker* to his Wife, *Frances Bland Randolph Tucker*,
dated "*Williamſburg July* 11[th]1781. "

" . . . Here [*Williamſburg*] they [the *Britiſh* Forces] remained for
"fome Days, and with them Peftilence and Famine took root,
"and Poverty brought up the Rear. Inftead of attempting a
"florid

" florid Defcription of the Horrors of this Place, I will endeavour
" to give you an Account of the Situations of a few Individuals
" with whom you are acquainted. Our Friend *Madifon* and his
" Lady (they have loft their Son) were turned out of their Houfe
" [the Prefident's Houfe] to make Room for Lord *Cornwallis*.
" Happily the College afforded them an Afylum. They were
" refufed the fmall Privilege of drawing Water from their own
" Well. A contemptuous Treatment, with the Danger of ftarving
" were the only Evils he recounted, as none of his Servants
" left him. The Cafe was otherwife with M^r *McClurg*. He has
" one fmall Servant left . . . But that is not all. The Small-
" pox, which the hellifh Polling of thefe infamous Wretches has
" fpread in every Place through which they have paffed has now
" obtained a Crifis throughout the Place fo that there is fcarcely
" a Perfon to be found to nurfe thofe who are moft afflicted by
" it. . . . To add to the Catalogue of Mortifications, they con-
" ftrained all the Inhabitants of the Town to take Paroles.
" After tyranizing ten Days here, they went to *James Town*
" where they were attacked by our advanced Parties. . . .
" The *Britifh* have fince croffed at *Cobham*, and their Ships have
" gone down the River. Our Army is in Motion. . . . Among
" the Plagues the *Britifh* left in *Williamfburg*, that of Flies is in-
" conceivable. It is impoffible to eat, drink, fleep, write, fit ftill
" or even walk about in Peace on Account of their confounded
" Stings. Their Numbers exceed Defcription, unlefs you look
" into the eighth Chapter of *Exodus* for it. . . . "

[298]

HEADQUARTERS PAPERS OF THE BRITISH ARMY IN AMERICA. [Photoftats in Poffeffion of *Colonial Williamfburg* Foundation.] Vol. XXXI, *July* 1-*Auguft* 15, 1781. No. 3601. Letter from Earl *Cornwallis* to Sir *Henry Clinton*, from " *Cobham* " 8th *July* 1781. "

" . . . I marched on the 4th [*July*] from *Williamfburgh*, to a Camp
" which covered a Ford into the Ifland of *James Town*. The
" *Queen's Rangers* paffed the River that Evening, on the 5th I
" fent over all the Wheel Carriages, & on the 6th the Bat Horfes,
" & Baggage of every Kind, intending to pafs with the Army on
" the 7th. About Noon on the 6th Information was brought to me
" of the Approach of the Enemy and about four in the Afternoon
" a large Body attacked our Out-pofts. Concluding, that the
" Enemy

" Enemy would not bring a confiderable Force within our Reach,
" unlefs they fuppofed that Nothing was left but a Rear-guard,
" I took every Means to convince them of my Weaknefs, &
" fuffered my Picquets to be infulted & driven back; Nothing
" however appeared near us, but Rifle Men & Militia 'till near
" Sun-fet, when a Body of Continentals with Artillery began to
" form in the Front of our Camp. I then put the Troops under
" Arms & ordered the Army to advance in two Lines. The
" Attack was began by the firft Line with great Spirit, there
" being Nothing but Militia oppofed to the Light Infantry. The
" Action was foon over on the Right, but Lieut Colonel *Dundas's*
" Brigade confifting of the 43rd 76th, & 80th Regiments which
" formed the left Wing, meeting the *Penfylvania* Line, & a
" Detachment of the Marquis *de Lafayette's* Continentals with
" two fix Pounders, a fmart Action enfued for fome Minutes,
" when the Enemy gave Way, & abandoned their Cannon. The
" Cavalry were perfectly ready to purfue, but the Darknefs of
" the Evening prevented my being able to make ufe of them. I
" cannot fufficiently commend the Spirit & good Behaviour of the
" Officers & Soldiers of the whole Army, but the 76th & 80th
" Regimts on whom the Brunt of the Action fell, had an Oppor-
" tunity of diftinguifhing themfelves particularly, & Lieut
" Colonel *Dundas's* Conduct & Gallantry deferve the higheft
" Praife. The Force of the Enemy in the Field was about two
" Thoufand, & their Lofs, I believe, between two & three
" Hundred, half an Hour more of Day-light would probably have
" given us the greateft Part of the Corps. . . . "

[299]

See Note 298.

[300]

B. F. *Stevens*, THE CAMPAIGN IN VIRGINIA,
1781 (*London:* 4 *Trafalgar* Square, 1888), Vol. II,
pp. 104-108. Letter from Earl *Cornwallis* to his
Exeellency General Sir *Henry Clinton*, dated *Portfmouth, Virginia, July* 27th, 1781.

" . . . You mention *Williamfburgh* and *York* in your Letter of the
" 11th, as defenfive Stations, but only as being fuppofed healthy,
" without deciding on their Safety. *Williamfburgh* having no
" Harbour, and requiring an Army to occupy the Pofition, would
" not have fuited us. I faw that it would require a great Deal
" of

" of Time and Labour to fortify *York* and *Gloucefter*, both of which
" are neceffary to fecure a Harbour for Veffels of any Burthen,
" and to effect it Affiftance would have been wanted from fome
" of the Troops then under Embarkation Orders, which, when
" *New-York* was in Danger, I did not think myfelf at Liberty to
" detain for any other Purpofe than Operations in the upper
" *Chefapeak;* . . . I therefore under thefe Circumftances, . . .
" did not hefitate in deciding to pafs *James* River, and to retire
" to *Portfmouth*, that I might be able to fend you the Troops
" required. . . . "

[301]

Ibid., pp. 107-108.

" Immediately on the Receipt of your cyphered Letter I gave
" Orders to the Engineer to examine and furvey *Point Comfort*,
" and the Channels adjoining to it; . . . I have the Honor to en-
" clofe to you Copies of the Report of the Engineer, . . . From
" all which your Excellency will fee that a Work on *Point Comfort*
" would neither command the Entrance, nor fecure his Majefty's
" Ships at Anchor in *Hampton Road*. This being the Cafe, I
" fhall, in Obedience to the Spirit of your Excellency's Orders,
" take Meafures with as much Difpatch as poffible, to feize and
" fortify *York* and *Gloucefter*, being the only Harbour in which
" we can hope to be able to give effectual Protection to the Line
" of Battle Ships. I fhall likewife ufe all the Expedition in
" my Power to evacuate *Portfmouth* and the Pofts belonging to
" it, but until that is accomplifhed it will be impoffible for me to
" fpare Troops. For *York* and *Gloucefter*, from their Situation,
" command no Country; and a Superiority in the Field will not
" only be neceffary to enable us to draw Forage and other
" Supplies from the Country, but likewife to carry on our Works
" without Interruption. "

Alfo:

*HEADQUARTERS PAPERS OF THE BRITISH
ARMY IN AMERICA.* [Photoftats in Poffeffion
of *Colonial Williamfburg* Foundation.] Vol. XXXII,
Auguft 16-*September* 30, 1781. No. 3689. Copy of
Letter—original in Cypher—from Earl *Cornwallis*
to Sir *Henry Clinton*, dated " *York Town* in *Virginia*
" 16 *Aug*ſ 1781. "

" . . . The Evacuation of *Portfmouth* has employed one Engineer
" &

" & a Number of Labourers & Artificers, & with every Exertion
" by Land & Water, I do not expect that Busineſs to be com-
" pleted before the 21ˢᵗ or 22ᵈ Inſᵗ. Since our Arrival we have
" beſtowed our whole Labour on the *Glouceſter* Side, but I do not
" think the Works there, (after great Fatigue to the Troops) are
" at Preſent, or will be for ſome Time to come, ſafe againſt a
" *Coup de Main* with leſs than one Thouſand Men. After our
" Experience of the Labour & Difficulty of conſtructing Works
" at this Seaſon of the Year, & the Plan for fortifying this Side
" not being entirely ſettled, I cannot at Preſent ſay, whether I
" can ſpare any Troops, or if any, how ſoon; . . . "

[302]

John C. Fitzpatrick, ed., *THE WRITINGS OF
GEORGE WASHINGTON*, 1745-1799 (*Waſhington:
Government Printing Office*, 1937), Vol. XXIII, pp.
26-28. Circular ſent by General *Waſhington* to the
States.

" Head Quarters, *Kings Ferry, Auguſt* 21, 1781.

" I feel myſelf unhappy in being obliged to inform you, that the
" Circumſtances in which I find myſelf at this late Period, have
" induced me to make an Alteration of the main Object which
" was at firſt adopted, and has hitherto been held in View, for
" the Operations of this Campaign. . . .

" The Fleet of the Count *de Graſſe*, with a Body of *French*
" Troops on Board, will make its firſt Appearance in the *Cheſa-*
" *peak;* which, ſhould the Time of the Fleets Arrival prove
" favorable, and ſhould the Enemy under Lord *Cornwallis* hold
" their preſent Poſition in *Virginia*, will give us the faireſt Oppor-
" tunity to reduce the whole *Britiſh* Force in the South, and to
" ruin their boaſted Expectations in that Quarter: to effect this
" deſirable Object, it has been judged expedient, taking into
" Conſideration our own preſent Circumſtances, with the Scitua-
" tion of the Enemy in *New York* and at the ſouthward, to
" abandon the Seige of the former, and to march a Body of
" Troops, confiſting of a Detachment from the *American* Army,
" with the Whole of the *French* Troops, immediately to *Virginia*.
" With this Detachment, which will be very conſiderable, I have
" determined to march myſelf. The *American* Troops are al-
" ready on the weſt Side of the *Hudſon*, and the *French* Army
" will arrive at *Kings Ferry* this Day. When the Whole are
" croſſed,

" croffed, our March will be continued with as much Difpatch
" as Circumftances will admit. . . . "

Alfo:

*HEADQUARTERS PAPERS OF THE BRITISH
ARMY IN AMERICA.* [Photoftats in Poffeffion
of *Colonial Williamfburg* Foundation.] Vol. XXXII,
Auguft 16-*September* 30, 1781.   Nos. 3758 and 3770.
Letters from General Sir *Henry Clinton* to Earl
  Cornwallis, written from *New York*, *September* 2nd
  and *September* 6th, 1781.

[No. 3770] " As I find by your Lordfhip's Letters that *Le*
" *Graffe* has got into the *Chefapeak*, and I can have no Doubt
" that *Wafhington* is moving with at leaft 6000 *French &* Rebel
" Troops againft you, I think the beft Way to relieve you is to
" join you as foon as poffible with all the Force that can be fpared
" from hence, which is about 4000 Men.   They are already em-
" barked, and will proceed the Inftant I receive Information from
" the Admiral that we may venture . . . "

[303]

H. R. McIlwaine, ed., *OFFICIAL LETTERS OF
THE GOVERNORS OF THE STATE OF VIR-
GINIA (Richmond:* 1929), Vol. III, pp. 49-50.   Let-
ters of Governor *Nelfon* written from *Williamfburg*,
September 14, 1781, announcing the Arrival of General
Wafhington in *Williamfburg* " between 4 & 5 o'Clock
" this Afternoon. "

[304]

*HEADQUARTERS PAPERS OF THE BRITISH
ARMY IN AMERICA.* [Photoftats in Poffeffion
of *Colonial Williamfburg* Foundation.] Vol. XXXII,
Auguft 16-*September* 30, 1781.   No. 3784.   Letter
of Earl *Cornwallis* to General Sir *Henry Clinton*,
dated " *York Town Virginia.* 16th *Sept* 1781. "

" . . . The Enemy's Fleet has returned.   Two Line of Battle
" Ships and one Frigate lie at the Mouth of this River, and three
" or four Line of Battle Ships, feveral Frigates and Tranfports
went

" went up the Bay on the 12ᵗʰ & 14ᵗʰ. I hear *Washington*
" arrived at *Williamsburg* on the 14ᵗʰ. . . .

" If I had no Hopes of Relief I would rather risk an Action than
" defend my half finished Works. But as you say Admiral *Digby*
" is hourly expected, and promise every Exertion to assist me, I do
" not think myself justifiable in putting the Fate of the War on
" so desperate an Attempt. . . . I am of Opinion that you can
" do me no effectual Service but by coming directly to this
" Place. . . ."

[305]

WILLIAM AND MARY COLLEGE QUARTERLY HISTORICAL MAGAZINE, First Series, Vol. XVI (1908), pp. 58-59. [Letter from *St. George Tucker* to his Wife, *Frances Bland Randolph Tucker*, written on *September* 15, 1781.]

[306]

William P. Palmer, ed., *CALENDAR OF VIRGINIA STATE PAPERS (Richmond: James E. Goode,* 1881), Vol. II, p. 589. Letter of *Timothy Pickering,* Quartermaster General, to Governor *Nelson, Williamsburg, November* 8th 1781.

" On my Arrival here, I found the *American* Sick in a suffering
" Condition; and I fear it will not be in my Power to yield them
" adequate Releif—Wood & Straw are most wanted at Present,
" and the Means of procuring them are hardly attainable. . . .

" . . . Doct *Treat* informs me that there are three large Rooms
" at the Palace destitute of Fire Places; and the Sick cannot re-
" main in them unless Stoves can be procured—Mr. *Holt* thinks
" those formerly belonging to the Palace were removed to *Rich-*
" *mond*—As I know not where to procure any, and these Rooms
" are essential for our Sick, I request your Excellency will be so
" kind as to cause the Palace Stoves to be sent hither as quick as
" possible, as the Sick have already suffered by the Cold. "

Also:

LIBRARY OF CONGRESS, Division of Manuscripts. Journal of Baron Louis Von Closen, 1780-1782, Vol. II, p. 12.

[*December,*

[*December*, 1781] " The Fire ſtarted at eleven o'Clock in the
" Evening (at the above mentioned) Governor's Houſe which was
" uſed as a Hoſpital for the wounded of the *American* Army.It was
" abſolutely conſumed by the Flames during the Night. . . . "

[307]

John C. Fitzpatrick, ed., *THE WRITINGS OF
GEORGE WASHINGTON, 1745-1799 (Waſhington:
Government Printing Office*, 1937), Vol. XXIII, pp.
234-235. Letter from General *Waſhington* to *John
Blair*, from " Camp before *York*, *October* 17, 1781. "

Alſo:

*LIBRARY OF CONGRESS, Diviſion of Manuſcripts.
Waſhington* Collection. Letter to " His Excellency
" General *Waſhington* " from " *le C*ᵗ *de Rochambeau* "
written from " *Williamſburgh, Dec*ᵉʳ 24ᵗʰ 1781. "

" I have learnt by the common Report, that your Excellency's
" Seat has ſuffered by the Fire. We are likewiſe plagued with it
" in this Town, where we have no Water nor Buckets to put it out,
" tho' we give all the Succours we can, with the greateſt Prompti-
" tude. The Wing of the College where we lodged our wounded
" Officers has begun to be burnt down, we carried away all the
" Sick, and all the Furniture, but could only think about hindering
" the Communication of the Fire with the main Building. Laſt
" Night, the ſame Accident happened to the Palace, in which was
" the *American* Hoſpital, all the Sick were ſaved as well as the
" greateſt Part of the Effects, and we hindered the Fire from com-
" municating to the neighbouring Houſes, to mine ſpecially; it is the
" firſt one occupied by your Excellency, it was covered all the Night
" long with a Rain of red hot Aſhes. We have put all your Sick in the
" Capitol, and to day they have had all which it was poſſible for us
" to furniſh them with. At Colonel *Menzies's* Requiſition, I have
" ordered a Guard to be ſet round it to prevent the ſame Accident,
" and I have cauſed the Precautions to be tripled, for the Police of
" the Eſtabliſhment of our Hoſpital at the College. "

[308]

H. R. McIlwaine, ed., *OFFICIAL LETTERS OF
THE GOVERNORS OF THE STATE OF VIR-
GINIA*

GINIA (Richmond: 1929), Vol. III, pp. 88-89. Letter from Governor *Nelſon* to the Delegates in Congreſs, written from " Camp before *York Oct*[r] 20. " 1781. "

Alſo:

JOURNAL OF ST. GEORGE TUCKER DURING THE SIEGE OF YORKTOWN. [Ms. Journal in *Tucker-Coleman* Papers, *William and Mary* Library.]

" *Wedneſday [October]* 17 [1781]. As we have heard a very ſmart " or rather inceſſant Cannonade laſt Night and this Morning I " take it for granted that all or the greater Part of our Batteries " are opened by this Time. This Forenoon a Flag from *York* " brought a Letter couch'd nearly in the following Terms—

" ' Sir, I propoſe a Ceſſation of Hoſtilities for twenty-four " Hours, and that two Officers be appointed from both Sides to " meet at M[r] *Moores*, and agree on Terms for the Surrender of " the Poſts of *York & Glouceſter.* . . *Cornwallis* '

. . .

" *Thurſday* 18th. Lord *Cornwallis* being allow'd but two Hours " ſent out another Flag to requeſt further Time to digeſt his " Propoſals. . . . It was pleaſing to contraſt the laſt Night with " the preceeding. A ſolemn Stillneſs prevailed—the Night was " remarkably clear & the Sky decorated with ten Thouſand " Stars—numberleſs Meteors gleaming thro' the Atmoſphere " afforded a pleaſing Reſemblance to the Bombs which had ex- " hibited a noble Firework the Night before, but happily diveſted " of all their Horror. At Dawn of Day the *Britiſh* gave us a " Serenade with the Bag Pipe, I believe, & were anſwered by " the *French* with the Band of the Regiment of *Deux Ponts.* As " ſoon as the Sun roſe one of the moſt ſtriking Pictures of War " was diſplay'd that Imagination can paint. From the Point of " *Rock Battery* on one Side our Lines completely mann'd and " our Works crowded with Soldiers were exhibited to View. " Oppoſite theſe at the Diſtance of two Hundred Yards you were " preſented with a Sight of the *Britiſh* Works; their Parapets " crowded with Officers looking at thoſe who were aſſembled at " the Top of our Works. The Secretary's [*Nelſon's*] Houſe with " one of the Corners broke off, & many large Holes thro the " Roof & Walls Part of which ſeem'd tottering with their Weight " afforded a ſtriking Inſtance of the Deſtruction occaſioned by " War. Many other Houſes in the Vicinity contributed to ac- " compliſh

" complifh the Scene. On the Beach of *York* directly under the
" Eye Hundreds of bufy People might be feen moving to & fro.
" At a fmall Diftance from the Shore were feen Ships funk down
" to the Waters Edge. Further out in the Channel the Mafts
" Yards & even the top Gallant Mafts of fome might be feen,
" without any Veftige of the Hulls. . . .

" This was the Scene which ufhered in the Day when the Pride
" of *Britain* was to be humbled in a greater Degree than it had
" ever been before, unlefs at the Surrender of *Burgoyne*. It is
" remarkable that the Propofals for a Surrender of Lord *Corn-*
" *wallis's* Army were made on the Anniverfary of that important
" Event. At two o'Clock the Surrender was agreed on & Com-
" miffioners appointed to draw up the Articles of Capitulation.
" They are now employed on that Bufinefs. . . .

" *Fryday* 19th At two o'Clock today a Detachm[t] of *American*
" Light Infantry and *French* Grenadiers took Poffeffion of the
" Horn-Work on the eaft End of *Yorktown*. Our Army was
" drawn up in a Line on each Side of the Road extending from
" our front Parallel to the Forks of the Road at *Hudfon Allen's*
" the *Americans* on the right, the *French* on the left. Thro'
" thefe Lines the whole *Britifh* Army march'd their Drums in
" Front beating a flow March. Their Colours furl'd and cafed.
" I am told they were reftricted by the Capitulation from beat-
" ing a *French* or *American* March. General *Lincoln* with his
" Aids conducted them. Having paffed thro' our whole Army
" they grounded their Arms & march'd back againt thro' the
" Army a fecond Time into the Town. . . .

" I have not yet been happy enough to fee, or hear of the
" Particulars of the Capitulation.

" Three Thoufand two Hundred & feventy three Men March'd
" out & grounded their Arms on the *York* Side of the River—
" Including the non commiff'd Officers the Garrifon in *York*
" amounted to five Thoufand five Hundred and fixty four Men,
" and two Hundred & fifty four commiffion'd Officers, including
" thirty two Surgeons with their Mates. Lord *Cornwallis* and
" General *O'Hara* are not included. I have not yet heard the
" Strength of the Poft at *Gloucefter*. It is about a Thoufand
" Men I believe. . . . "

[309]

John C. Fitzpatrick, ed., *THE WRITINGS OF GEORGE WASHINGTON*, 1745-1799 (*Wafhington: Government Printing Office*, 1937), Vol. XXIII, p. 311,

311, 360. Letters from General *Washington* to Major General *Nathaniel Greene* and Governor *Jonathan Trumbull*.

[p. 311] " Head Quarters near *York*, *October* 31, 1781." " The Count *de Rochambeau* will eftablifh Winter Quarters for " his Troops at this Place, *Williamfburg* and the Vicinity; . . . "

Alfo:

William P. Palmer, ed., *CALENDAR OF VIRGINIA STATE PAPERS* (*Richmond: James E. Goode*, 1883), Vol. III, pp. 97-98.

[310]

HEADQUARTERS PAPERS OF THE BRITISH ARMY IN AMERICA. [Photoftats in Poffeffion of *Colonial Williamfburg* Foundation.] Vol. LV, *November* 20-30, 1782. No. 6291.

Articles agreed upon and figned at *Paris* on *November* 30, 1782, between *Richard Ofwald*, the Commiffioner of " His *Britannic* Majefty, for treating of " Peace with the Commiffioners of the *United* " *States* of *America* ," and *John Adams*, *Benjamin Franklin*, *John Jay*, and *Henry Laurens*, four of the Commiffioners for the *United States*. This Treaty was " not to be concluded until Terms of a Peace, " fhall be agreed upon, between *Great Britain* and " *France*. "

Alfo:

William Waller Hening, *THE STATUTES AT LARGE* (*Richmond: George Cochran*, 1823), Vol. XI, pp. 549-552.

" By the *United States* of *America* in Congrefs affembled. A " Proclamation declaring the Ceffation of Arms, as well by Sea " as by Land, agreed upon between the *United States* of *America* " and his *Britannic* Majefty; and enjoining the Obfervance " thereof. "

[Proclamation follows.]

" Done

" Done in Congrefs, at *Philadelphia*, this eleventh Day of *April*
" in the Year of our Lord 1783, and of our Sovereignty and
" Independence the feventh. "

[311]

WILLIAM AND MARY COLLEGE *QUARTERLY
HISTORICAL MAGAZINE, Firft Series*, Vol.
XIV (1906), pp. 278-279. " Order of the Proceffion
" on the great Day, *Thurfday, May 1ft* [1783]. "

[312]

See Note 311.

[313]

Jedidiah Morfe, THE AMERICAN UNIVERSAL
GEOGRAPHY (*Bofton: Ifaiah Thomas & Ebenezer T.
Andrews*, 1793), pp. 550-551.

" *Williamfburgh* . . . confifts of about 200 Houfes, going faft to
" Decay, and has about 1400 Inhabitants. . . .
" Every Thing in *Williamfburgh* appears dull, forfaken and
" melancholy—no Trade—no Amufements, but the infamous one
" of Gaming—no Induftry, and very little Appearance of Re-
" ligion. The unprofperous State of the College, but principally
" the Removal of the Seat of Government, have contributed
" much to the Decline of this City. "

[314]

Ifaac Weld, Jr., TRAVELS THROUGH THE
STATES OF NORTH AMERICA (*London:* Printed
for *John Stockdale, Picadilly*, 1799), pp. 94-96.

[*April*, 1796.] " Twelve Miles from *York*, to the weftward,
" ftands *Williamfburgh*, formerly the Seat of Government of
" *Virginia*. . . .
" The Town confifts of one principal Street, and two others
" which run parallel to it. At one End of the main Street ftands
" the College, and at the other End the old Capitol or Statehoufe,
" a capacious Building of Brick, now crumbling to Pieces from
" Negligence. The Houfes around it are moftly uninhabited,
" and prefent a melancholy Picture. . . .
" The College of *William and Mary*, as it is ftill called, ftands
" at

" at the oppofite End of the main Street; it is a heavy Pile which
" bears, as Mr. *Jefferfon*, I think, fays, ' a very clofe Refemb-
" lance to a large Brick Kiln, excepting that it has a Roof.'
" The Students were about thirty in Number when I was there:
" from their Appearance one would imagine that the Seminary
" ought rather to be termed a Grammar School than a College;
" yet I underftand that the Vifiters, fince the prefent Revolution,
" finding it full of young Boys juft learning the Rudiments of
" *Greek* and *Latin*, a Circumftance which confequently deterred
" others more advanced from going there, dropped the Pro-
" fefforfhips of thefe two Languages, and eftablifhed others in
" their Place. . . . The Bifhop of *Virginia* is Prefident of the
" College. . . . Half a Dozen or more of the Students, the
" eldeft about twelve Years old, dined at his Table one Day that
" I was there. . . . A Couple of Difhes of falted Meat, and fome
" Oyfter Soup, formed the Whole of the Dinner. . . .

" The *Epifcopalian* Church, the only one in the Place, ftands
" in the Middle of the main Street; it is much out of Repair. On
" either Side of it is an extenfive Green, furrounded with neat
" looking Houfes, which bring to Mind an *Englifh* Village.

" The Town contains about 1200 Inhabitants & the Society in
" it is thought to be more extenfive and more genteel at the
" fame Time than what is to be met with in any other Place of
" its Size in *America*. No Manufactories are carried on here,
" and fcarcely any Trade. . . . "

Alfo:

*WILLIAM & MARY COLLEGE QUARTERLY
HISTORICAL MAGAZINE, Firft Series,* Vol.
XIII (1904), pp. 107-108. Letter of *William Taylor
Barry* to his Brother, written while a Student of
Law at *William and Mary* College.

" *Williamfburgh, January 30,* 1804.

" . . . I arrived in *Williamfburg* the Day after I wrote you from
" *Richmond*, and met with a very polite Reception from thofe
" Perfons to whom I had Letters. Mr. *Tucker*, in particular,
" treated me with Attention. He is a Man of genuine Clevernefs
" and of the moft exalted Talents. . . .

" I did not find the College of *William and Mary* in fo flourifh-
" ing a Condition as I anticipated. There are not more than
" fifty Students, befides twelve or thirteen Law Students . . .

" I am pretty well pleafed with the Society of *Williamfburg;* it is
" very

" very agreeable. The People are familiar in their Intercourfe
" and free and open in all their Communications. They are re-
" markable for their Hofpitality and familiar Deportment to-
" wards Strangers, which does away with many Embarraffments
" which the odious Formalities of fome Places give rife to. ... "

[315]

Ibid., Firft Series, Vol. IX (1900), p. 22. Letter of
John Brown, Student at College of *William & Mary*,
to his Uncle, *William Prefton*, dated " *W^m & Mary*
" *Decemb^r* 9th 1779."

" . . .

  " *William & Mary* has undergone a very confiderable Revo-
" lution; the Vifitors met on the 4th Inftant & form'd it into a
" Univerfity, annul'd the old Statutes, abolifh'd the Grammar
" School continued Mr *Madifon* Prefident, & Profeffor of Math-
" ematics appointed Mr *Wyth* Profeffor of Law, D^r *McClurg* of
" Phyfick Mr *Andrews* of Moral Philofophy, & Monf^r *Belini* of
" modern Languages. . . . "

See alfo Note 156.

Alfo:

*THE HISTORY OF THE COLLEGE OF WILLIAM
AND MARY (Richmond: J. W. Randolph &
English, 1874), p. 51.*

  " In 1781 the Exercifes of the College were fufpended, and the
" Buildings were alternately occupied the Summer before the
" memorable Siege of *Yorktown* by the *Britifh* and the *French*
" and *American* Troops. . . . It does not appear how long the
" College was clofed—probably the Exercifes were fufpended not
" more than a Year. . . . "

[316]

*COLLEGE OF WILLIAM AND MARY, Faculty
Minutes, 1817-1830, pp. 178-184.*

[*January* 15, 1825. See Reports of the Profeffor of Law
    and the Burfar of the College of *William and Mary*
    in anfwer to Queries propounded by the *Virginia*
                                                Houfe

House of Delegates regarding the Holdings and financial Status of the College.]

[317]

LIBRARY OF CONGRESS, Divifion of Manufcripts. Wafhington Papers, 1781. Vol. 189. [Letter of *F. Mentges* to General *Wafhington.*]

" *Williamfburg* the 26 *Decr* 1781

" It is with the greateft Mortification I am to acquaint your
" Excellency of the Accident happned on the Night of the 22
" Inftant, by a Fire brocke out at the Palace, where the General
" Hofpital was keept, and the whole Building was confumed,
" lukely [luckily] the Sick & Wounded were faved—but one—
" who perifhed by the Flames. It is generaly t[h]ought the Fire
" was laid in to the lower Rooms where no Sick were, by Negroes
" or difaffected Perfons. . . . "

See alfo Note 307.

[318]

Samuel Shepherd, THE STATUTES AT LARGE OF VIRGINIA (Richmond: Samuel Shepherd, 1835), Vol. I, p. 273. " An Act concerning the Capitol in " the City of *Williamfburg.*

(Paffed *December* 9, 1793.)

" 1. Whereas it is reprefented that the Building called the Capi-
" tol, in the City of *Williamfburg*, is in a ruinous Condition, and
" muft foon, if not repaired, be unfit for the public Purpofes, to
" which it has been applied, . . .
" 2. Be it therefore enacted by the General Affembly, that the
" Mayor, Recorder and Aldermen of the City of *Williamfburg*
" fhall be . . . authorized and empowered to fell . . . the
" eaftern Wing of the faid Capitol, in the City of *Williamfburg*,
" and to apply the Money arifing from the Sale, or fo much
" thereof as fhall be neceffary, to the Repairing of the weftern
" or front Wing; and if the Money produced by the Sale fhall be
" more than fufficient for the Purpofe herein before mentioned,
" the faid Mayor, Recorder and Aldermen fhall place out the
" Surplus at Intereft, and the Intereft of the faid Surplus fhall
" be a Fund for keeping the faid Capitol in Repair. . . . "

[319]

[319]

H. W. Flournoy, ed., CALENDAR OF VIRGINIA STATE PAPERS (Richmond: James E. Goode, 1892), Vol. X, pp. 574-575. Letter from A. P. Up-shur to the Governor, dated Williamsburg, April 10, 1832.

" It is my unpleasant Duty to inform you that the former " Capitol in this City was this Day entirely consumed by Fire. " I am happy, however, to be able to add that all the Record " Books and Papers are saved.

" The Term of the Superior Court of Law and Chancery com-" menced on Friday last, and will expire on Friday Night next. " In the meantime it is highly important that the Executive, . . . " should designate some other Place at which the future Sessions " of the Court may be held until Provision shall be made therefor " by the Legislature. The Court House of James City County is " at Present the only suitable Place for this Purpose. "

[320]

Robert D. Ward, AN ACCOUNT OF GENERAL LA FAYETTE'S VISIT TO VIRGINIA, 1824-1825 (Richmond: 1881), p. 42.

" . . . After dining at York, he sat out at 2 o'Clock, Wed-" nesday Afternoon in his Barouche, attended by his Suite, and " others in Carriages. . . . He arrived at Williamsburg at 6 " o'Clock, amidst merry Peals of Bells and the Congratulations " of its Citizens. He was conducted to the Residence of Mrs. " Mary Monroe Peachy, which had been volunteered for his Ac-" commodation by that patriotic Lady, where he was received " by the Mayor and civil Authorities, with an eloquent Address, " delivered by Mr. Robert Anderson, to which he made a neat and " appropriate Address . . .

" After visiting our College, and going to pay his Respects to " Mrs. Page, the Widow of the late Governor Page, he sat down " to Dinner at the Raleigh Tavern, at which Colonel Bassett pre-" sided, assisted by J. A. Smith and Ro. McCandlish, as Vice-" presidents, at which there were many distinguished Gentlemen " —the Governor and Council, Chief-Justice Marshall, John C. " Calhoun, Generals Taylor, Macomb, Jones, Brodnax, and Car-" rington, with their Suites; Captain Elliott, of the Navy; ' Colonels Peyton, Harvie, Mercer, George Hay, Major Gibbons, " John

" *John Tyler*, Dr. *S. S. Griffin*, Dr. *S. Cotton*, *William T. Galt*,
" Judge *Brooke*, *Robert G. Scott*, Dr. *John A. Smith*, Captain *Ro.*
" *McCandliſh*, and others.
" *On Friday* Morning, the General left Williamſburg . . . "

[321]

See Note 320.

[322]

Lyon G. Tyler, ed., *TYLER'S QUARTERLY HIS-
TORICAL AND GENEALOGICAL MAGAZINE*,
Vol. III (1922), pp. 164-165. Letter from *C. De La
Pena*, Profeſſor of Modern Languages at *William
and Mary* College, to *John Adams Smith* of Rich-
mond, dated " *Williamſburg Novr 3rd* 1827. "

[323]

BRUTON PARISH VESTRY BOOK, 1827-1889,
p. 42.

" At a Meeting of the Veſtry of *Bruton* Pariſh in the Church
" on *Tueſday* the 8th *May* 1838 . . .
" By Order of the Ladies of the *Bruton* Pariſh Working Society,
" the Directreſs and Managers of the ſame tender to the Veſtry
" of *Bruton* Pariſh ſeven Hundred Dollars, being the Proceeds of
" the late Fair for the Repairs of the Church. "

[324]

*COLLEGE OF WILLIAM AND MARY. Faculty
Minutes, 1859.* [Dr. *Totten's* Account of the Fire—
February 8, 1859.]

" On the Morning of the 8th of *February* a few Minutes before
" three o'Clock the north Wing of the College Building was dif-
" covered to be on fire. Flames were iſſuing from the Window
" of the lower Story occupied as the Chemical Laboratory. . . .
" The Fire when difcovered had made ſuch Progreſs that there
" could be no Hope of ſaving the Building. From the Wing the
" Flames ſpread with great Rapidity through the Main Building
" and the ſouth Wing taking fire in the Roof, . . . the Country
" was illuminated for Miles in every Direction. . . . In four
" Hours after the Difcovery of the Fire the Woodwork of the
" Building

" Building was entirely confumed, except here and there a blaz-
" ing Beam upon the Walls or Fragments of Timber fmouldering
" in the Ruins.

" The Philofophical and Chemical Apparatus was entirely
" deftroyed, not a fingle Book was faved from the Library, the
" Smoke being too denfe to enter . . .

" The exterior Walls are ftill ftanding though warped and
" cracked by the intenfe Heat, all Chimneys and a Portion of the
" interior Walls have fallen. The Lofs fuftained by the College
" is not eafily eftimated. The Buildings though old were in
" good Repair, the Interior having been almoft entirely renewed
" within the paft few Years . . . The Library contained about
" eight Thoufand Volumes. It contained many rare and curious
" Books, and many that were valued highly on Account of the
" Affociations connected with them. The Philofophical Apparatus
" may be eftimated as worth two Thoufand Dollars. It con-
" tained feveral old Inftruments valuable for their Antiquity . . ."

[325]

See the *Minutes of the Faculty of the College of William
and Mary* for *March* and *April* of the Year 1859.
The Material from thefe Minutes relating to the
Rebuilding of the College has been printed in the
*WILLIAM AND MARY COLLEGE QUAR-
TERLY HISTORICAL MAGAZINE*, *Second
Series*, Vol. VIII, pp. 266-286, in " *Some Notes on
" the Four Forms of the Oldeft Building of* William
" and Mary *College*, " by Dr. *Earl G. Swem.*

[326]

RICHMOND ENQUIRER (*Richmond:* Publifhed by
Ritchie, Dunnavant, Tyler & Wife), Vol. LVI, No. 57,
Friday Morning, *December* 16, 1859.

" On the 11ᵗʰ Inftant, the old *Raleigh* Tavern, at *Williamfburg,*
" was willfully burnt down. The Flames alfo communicated to
" the Store of Meffrs. *Veft & Hansford*, but nearly all their Stock
" of Goods was faved, not, however, without being damaged.
" Total Lofs about $15,000. All Parties are partly infured. "

[327]

[327]

COLLEGE OF WILLIAM AND MARY. *Faculty Minutes,* 1846-1883.

" Called Meeting of the Faculty– *May* 10, 1861. . . .

" *Whereas*– Civil War is imminent, and the State of *Virginia*
" is threatened with an armed Invafion; and whereas the expofed
" Pofition of this Section of the State requires that every Citizen
" fhould be free to enlift in its Defenfe; and whereas, a large Ma-
" jority of the Students have already left College, and thofe who
" ftill remain—moft of whom alfo purpofe to leave—are unable,
" from the excited State of the public Mind, to purfue their colle-
" giate Duties with profit– Therefore–

" *Refolved*– That the Exercifes of the College be fufpended
" from this Day, during the Remainder of the prefent Seffion. . .

" *Whereas*– the Prefident [*Benjamin S. Ewell*] of the College
" has accepted, at the Call of the State, a military Pofition in her
" Service, . . .

" *Refolved*– That the Records and Keys of the College be com-
" mitted to the Care of Profeffor *Morrifon,* . . . "

Alfo:

Herbert B. Adams, THE COLLEGE OF WILLIAM AND MARY (*Wafhington: Government Printing Office,* Circulars of Information, No. 1—1887), p. 61.

" When the Civil War broke out, it was but natural that the
" Profeffors and Students of a thoroughly fouthern Inftitution
" fhould follow the Fortunes of their own Section of the Country.
" The Intenfity of Feeling in thofe Times is feen in the Fact that
" ninety per cent. of the Youth then purfuing a Courfe of Study
" at the College joined the *Confederate* Army. In the War of the
" *American* Revolution only fifty per cent. of the Students from
" *William and Mary* took Arms for the Caufe of Independence. "

[328]

THE WAR OF THE REBELLION: A Compilation of the Official Records of the Union and Confederate Armies (*Washington: Government Printing Office,* 1884), Series I, Vol. XI, pp. 14, 15, 406.

[329]

[329]

Ibid., pp. 405-411.   Letter from Major-General *J. Bankhead Magruder, Lee's Farm, Va.*, *May* 3, 1862, to General *S. Cooper.*

" . . . I have no accurate Data upon which to bafe an exact
" Statement of his Force, but from various Sources of Informa-
" tion I was fatisfied that I had before me the Enemy's Army of
" the *Potomac*, under the Command of General *McClellan*, with
" the Exception of the two *Corps d'armee* of *Banks* and *McDowell*,
" refpectively, forming an aggregate Number of certainly not lefs
" than 100,000, fince afcertained to have been 120,000.   On
" every Portion of my Lines he attacked us with a furious Can-
" nonading and Mufketry, which was refponded to with Effect
" by our Batteries and Troops of the Line.   His Skirmifhers
" were alfo well thrown forward on this and the fucceeding Day
" and energetically felt our whole Line, but were everywhere
" repulfed by the Steadinefs of our Troops.   Thus, with 5,000
" Men, exclufive of the Garrifons, we ftopped and held in check
" over 100,000 of the Enemy.   . . . "

[330]

*David E. Cronin, THE VEST MANSION—Its Hif-
torical and Romantic Affociations as Confederate and
Union Headquarters in the American Civil War*, pp.
8-11. [Typed Copy of Ms. in Poffeffion of *Colonial
Williamfburg* Foundation.   *Cronin* was *Federal*
Provoft Marfhall of *Williamfburg* in 1864.]

" During the firft few Months of its Organization Gen. *Ma-
" gruder's* Army of the Peninfula did not exceed ten Thoufand
" Men, but fhortly before the Battle of *Williamfburg—May* 5,
" 1862—it was reinforced by 8,000 Men under Gen. *Jubal A.
" Early* and when joined fomewhat later by the Divifions of
" Generals *Jones* and *Hill* it numbered 33,000.

" Toward the End of *April* Gen. *Jofeph E. Johnfton*, Chief
" Commander in the Army of *Virginia*, arrived at the Front from
" *Richmond*, eftablifhed his Headquarters in the *Veft* Manfion
" and appointed Gen. *James Longftreet* 'in the immediate Com-
" mand on the Field, ' thus fuperfeding Gen. *Magruder*.   . . .

" In falling back from *Yorktown*, *Johnfton's* Purpofe was to
" take Advantage of the naturally defenfible Pofition of *Wil-
                                                    " liamfburg*

" *liamsburg* and to make a vigorous Resistance there, inflicting
" whatever Damage possible on the Enemy, and trusting to the
" Chances of War for a favorable Outcome; at least in the Matter
" of Delay, . . .

" With this Determination in View, but anticipating the prob-
" able Results of an Encounter with a Force so far superior in
" Numbers to his own, he had already given Orders for the Re-
" tirement of his Baggage Trains farther up the Peninsula and
" they began to leave *Williamsburg* a Day or two before the
" Battle. . . .

" The Evacuation of *Yorktown* by the *Confederates* began on
" the Night of the third of *May*, during heavy Rains. As the
" Troops arrived on the Heights of *Williamsburg*, they were
" aligned under the Direction of Gen. *Longstreet* in Positions cov-
" ering the Line of Intrenchments already described of which
" *Fort Magruder* was the commanding Center. On the Morning
" of the 5th they were ready for Action. The Day was cloudy
" and rainy. "

[331]

See Note 330.

[332]

*THE WAR OF THE REBELLION: A Compilation
of the Official Records of the Union and Confederate
Armies* (*Washington: Government Printing Office*,
1884), Series I, Vol. XI, pp. 447-611. *Union* and
Confederate Reports of the Battle of *Williamsburg*,
fought on *May* 5, 1862.

[333]

Ibid., p. 572. Report of Brig. Gen. *J. E. B. Stuart*,
Commanding Cavalry Brigade of C. S. Army, on
Battle of *Williamsburg*.

" Darkness soon closed upon the Scene, and our Troops
" were withdrawn from the Field of Victory to resume their
" March, not, however, until all the Wounded (for whom we
" had no Transportation) were removed to the Houses of Resi-
" dents of *Williamsburg*. "

Also:

*David E. Cronin, THE VEST MANSION—Its His-
torical*

*torical and Romantic Aſſociations as Confederate and
Union Headquarters in the American Civil War*, p. 14
[Ms. Copy *Colonial Williamſburg* Foundation.]

" *McClellan* ſays he found the Town [*Williamſburg*] ' filled
" with *Confederate* Wounded. ' The College Buildings, the
" Court Houſe, the ſpacious *Baptiſt* Church and many private
" Dwellings, were converted into temporary Hoſpitals. Room
" had to be made for the moſt ſeriouſly wounded of the *Union*
" Soldiers—thoſe whoſe Conditions would not permit Removal to
" Hoſpitals already eſtabliſhed at *Yorktown* and below. As
" uſual, immediately after a heavy Battle, there was a great
" Dearth of Army Surgeons and Nurſes. There were but few
" local Surgeons to lend Aid, but one of them, Doƈtor *R. M.*
" *Garrett*, a Graduate of *Jefferſon Medical College* in *Philadelphia*,
" did noble Work in caring for and treating the Wounded of both
" Sides, impartially, as they were brought to him, on the Lawn
" of his handſome colonial Reſidence not far from the *Veſt*
" Houſe. . . . "

[334]

Ibid., p. 12.

" About Mid-day Gen. *Johnſton* left the *Veſt* Houſe, rode out
" to the Field and joined Gen. *Longſtreet* as a ' Speƈtator ' of the
" Battle, he ſays, for he found everything going ſo well that he
" gave no Orders. He noticed however, that a Brigade of *North*
" *Carolina* Troops had broken its Formation and was retiring.
" He waited until this Brigade was ' colleƈted on its firſt Poſi-
" tion, ' before returning to Headquarters. On his Way, he
" paſſed little Groups of curious, rather than anxious Citizens
" with Umbrellas, who had come a ſhort Way out of Town to
" ſee the Smoke, to hear the Roar and ſmell the Gunpowder of
" the Battle more diſtinƈtly. Apparently, they had no Notion
" of a Retreat and conſidered the Umbrellas ſufficient Pro-
" teƈtion."

[335]

Ibid., pp. 14-17.

" *Williamſburg* was entered the next Morning [*May* 6, 1862]
" by the *Union* Advance compoſed of Cavalry under Gen. *Stone-*
" *man*. The Rain Clouds had paſſed away and the Morning was
" clear, balmy and beautiful. . . .

" The *Union* Advance was ſoon followed by Gen. *McClellan*
" who

" who, after riding about the Town, took Poffeffion of the whole
" of the *Veſt* Manſion for the Uſe of himſelf and Staff, the Pro-
" prietor and his Family having fled with their *Confederate*
" Friends toward *Richmond.* The General inſtalled himſelf in
" the ſumptious Quarters vacated the Evening before by *John-*
" *ſton* and *Longſtreet.* . . .

" The *Union* Lines were eſtabliſhed weſt of the College, while
" a large Reſerve tented on the ſhaded Campus. On Account of
" the almoſt impaſſable Condition of the Roads, due to the
" recent Rains, and for other Reaſons, the principal one being a
" contemplated Change in the Plan of the Campaign, purſuit of
" the Enemy was not vigorouſly preſſed . . .

" One of *McClellan's* firſt Orders iſſued from the *Veſt* Houſe,
" imperatively prohibited Moleſtation of the Inhabitants of the
" Town or of their Property.

" Safe-guards were placed wherever requeſted. Many of the
" Inhabitants had fled precipitately, leaving much valuable port-
" able Property. . . . The General was invariably ſtrict in
" protecting private Property . . . but ſome of the Reſidences
" which had been wholly abandoned, had been more or leſs De-
" ſpoiled before the General's Arrival; . . .

" The Neceſſity of a Departure from the original Plans of
" Campaign, was now generally underſtood and haſtened by a
" Succeſſion of Events. . . . on or about the 10th [*May*],
" *McClellan* himſelf and the Group at Headquarters, departed
" for the new Front, leaving Gen. *Keyes* in Charge to ſuperintend
" the Withdrawal of the Remainder of the Army. "

Alſo:

*THE WAR OF THE REBELLION: A Compilation
of the Official Records of the Union and Confederate
Armies (Waſhington: Government Printing Office,*
1884), Series I, Vol. XI, pp. 564-568. Report of Maj.
Gen. *James Longſtreet,* C. S. Army.

[336]

Ibid., p. 449.

" *Williamſburg, May 6, 1862*

" Hon. *E. M. Stanton,*
" Secretary of War.

" Every Hour proves our Victory more complete. Enemy's
" Loſs

" Lofs great; efpecially in Officers. Have juft heard of five more
" of their Guns captured. Prifoners conftantly arriving.
" —*Geo. B. McClellan*, Major-General, Commanding. "

Alfo:

Ibid., pp. 568-569.

" General Orders, *Hdqrs. Dept. Northern Virginia, May* 6, 1862
" No.——

" The commanding General announces to the Army an im-
" portant Succefs achieved Yefterday in the Repulfe of the
" Enemy's Attacks upon the Pofition of our rear Guard near
" *Williamfburg* and the Driving his Forces to the Woods by the
" Troops of Major-Generals *Longftreet* and *Hill*, and Brigadier-
" General *Stuart*, commanded by the former. He congratulates
" thofe engaged upon the Honors they have won, and offers them
" the Thanks of the Army for their admirable Conduct. .   .

" By Command of General *Johnfton:*
" *Thos. G. Rhett,*
" Affiftant Adjutant-General. "

Alfo:

*David E. Cronin, THE VEST MANSION—Its Hif-
torical and Romantic Affociations as Confederate and
Union Headquarters in the American Civil War*
[Ms. Copy *Colonial Williamfburg* Foundation],
p. 12-13.

" . . . From the Field he [*McClellan*] fent a Difpatch to *Wafh-*
" *ington* announcing the Victory in a few graphic Words . . .

" In Gen. *Johnfton's* official Report of the Engagement, he
" claimed that the Victory, or as he expreffed it ' the Trophy of
" the Battle ' was with the *Confederates:* and impartial Hiftori-
" ans are ftill puzzled about bringing in a Verdict either Way.

" The official Reports of Loffes give:
" *Union.* . . . 468 killed, 1442 wounded, 373 captured or miffing.*
" *Confederate* 288 killed, 975 wounded, 297 captured or miffing. "

[**Note:* In " *The War of the Rebellion* " previoufly referred to, the
Union Cafualties in the Battle of *Williamfburg* are given as follows: 456 killed, 1410 wounded, 373 captured or miffing. (See
p. 450.) The *Confederate* Cafualties in this Record agree with
David Cronin's Account as above ftated.]

[337]

Ibid., pp. 19-27.

" After *McClellan's* Departure, Gen. *Keyes* remained at Head-
" quarters a few Days and then removed to *Yorktown*. No
" Troops of the Army of the *Potomac* now remained at *Williamf-*
" *burg*. A thin Picket Line compofed of Companies of the *Fifth*
" *Pennfylvania* Cavalry, was drawn around the Place and on
" *May* 12th, the Commander of the Regiment—Col. *David*
" *Campbell*—was appointed military Governor. . . .

" By the Appointment of a ' Military Governor, ' afterward
" comprehended in the Title of ' Provoft Marfhal, ' *Williamfburg*
" was formally placed under martial Law and fo remained until
" the End of the Struggle. From the Date of the Removal of
" *McClellan's* Army from *Harrifon's* Landing, *Aug.* 19th 1862,
" to the Occupation of *Bermuda Hundreds* by the Army of the
" *James*, *May* 12th, 1864 . . . *Williamfburg* was the neareft
" Poft to *Richmond* held by *Union* Troops. In confequence, it
" became, during this Period, a falient Point of Obfervation in
" the whole military Line drawn about the *Confederacy;* a prin-
" cipal Channel in fecuring the lateft News from the Southern
" Capital, fometimes of great Value to the War Dept. at *Wafh-*
" *ington,* with which it was connected by Telegraph Lines ftarting
" from *Fort Magruder*. It was an important Terminal for the
" Arrival and Departure of Spies in the employ of the Depart-
" ment, as well as for Scouts belonging to Commands within our
" Lines. . . .

" During Col. *Campbell's* rather brief Adminiftration, his Lines
" were frequently attacked. At Times, the Enemy appeared in
" Force, driving the thin Line of Pickets and few Provoft Guards
" back to the main Line and Referve at *Fort Magruder*. Gen-
" erally, however, the Attacks were made by fmall Bodies of
" Cavalry who dafhed into the Streets at any Hour of the Day
" or Night killing or capturing a Picket or two, or difperfing both
" Pickets and Guards, holding brief Conferences with Groups of
" Citizens and retiring as fuddenly as they came. . . .

" As may be imagined, the Condition of the houfed-up Inhabi-
" tants, under thefe trying Circumftances, was unhappy in the
" extreme and was long continued. . . . As a general Thing
" the Expreffion on the Faces of the People, particularly of the
" Women, whenever they happened to come into View of *Union*
" Officials, was one of undifguifed Hatred and Contempt. . . .

" Though the Colonel was a Man of mature Age, he was like
" the

" the Reſt of us at that early Period, without much Experience as
" a military Commander.   Strongly oppoſed to the Separation
" of the States, he believed that Rebellion could be ſpeedily ſup-
" preſſed by vigorous Action.   To help carry out this View, he
" cauſed the Arreſt of ſeveral of the leading Citizens of the Town
" and ſent them under Guard to the Diſtrict Commander at
" *Norfolk*, . . . who promptly liberated them and returned them
" to their Homes, on the technical Ground that there was no
" material Charge againſt them as peaceful Citizens, and that all
" were exempt from military Duty by Reaſon of Age or Profeſſion
" —one of them being a practicing Phyſician.   The Colonel was
" inſtructed that theſe People were not to be moleſted in any
" Way in the Future.   . . .

    " The Arreſts made by Order of Col. *Campbell* had cauſed pain-
" ful Apprehenſions among the Citizens of *Williamſburg*, gener-
" ally; had arouſed paſſionate Reſentment in *Richmond* and in-
" ſpired Gen. *Wiſe* . . . to attempt the Colonel's Capture, in
" Retaliation.   All the Citizens arreſted were *Wiſe's* perſonal
" Friends.   As a Lawyer, he had long practiced at the Bar in
" *James City* County in which *Williamſburg* is ſituated.   . . .
" Moreover, he now held a ſeparate Command on the Peninſula
" —a ' Legion ' it was called, a Force of eighteen Hundred Men,
" including Infantry, Cavalry and a Battery: and he was free to
" act.

    " Taking with him his Cavalry far in advance, he ſtole upon
" the Town ſhortly after Dawn on the Morning of *Sept.* 9th, 1862,
" knowing the exact Locality of the Pickets and Reſerve.   After
" a few Minutes Skirmiſh near the College, during which the
" Reſerve of 33 Men, ſleeping on the Lawn, was captured, be-
" ſides 6 of the Pickets killed and fifteen of the whole Force
" wounded, including two Officers . . . his Command charged
" into the Town and beyond, towards *Fort Magruder*, eſtabliſhing
" a Line facing and threatening the interior and actual military
" Line.Then for temporary Purpoſes and with ſlight Loſs to the
" *Confederates* the Town was within the Enemy's Lines and ſe-
" curely poſſeſſed.   In Juſtice to the Detachment of the Fifth,
" which had been ſo ſwiftly overcome, it ſhould be mentioned
" that the Men at that Time moſtly were armed with Sabres and
" Revolvers, while their Enemies were armed beſide theſe Weap-
" ons with Carbines.

    " Leading the extreme Advance in the Charge, was an in-
" ſtructed Officer with a few Men,who halted at the *Veſt* Manſion.
" The Colonel, aſleep in the Bedroom in Rear of his Office, was
                                                              " not

" not awakened by the diſtant Firing and was firſt arouſed by
" the Preſence of a *Confederate* Officer who in imperative Tones,
" with pointed Revolver, ordered him to ſurrender and get up
" and dreſs. . . . Juſt as he reached the front Door with his
" Captors, the General [*Wife*] himſelf arrived and ordered him
" back for an Interview which was brief, . . . The General's
" firſt Queſtion was ſingular but explainable when it is remem-
" bered that *Wife* had near Relatives in *Philadelphia* and the
" ſocial Conſequence of the Priſoner might be conſidered in the
" Importance of his Capture. ' To what Family of the *Camp-*
" *bell's* in *Philadelphia,* do you belong? ' he aſked. ' To no
" Family on the Face of the Earth, juſt now, ' was the Colonel's
" bitter Reſponſe. . . . No Queſtions bearing upon the mili-
" tary Situation, were aſked. The Interview was interrupted by
" the Arrival of welcoming Townſpeople and the Colonel was
" ſuavely committed to the Cuſtody of his Guards and taken
" away. For a few Weeks he was confined in *Libby* Priſon and
" then exchanged. . . .

" In the Afternoon of the Day of the *Confederates'* Departure
" —*September* 9th, the College Building of *William and Mary*
" . . . was diſcovered to be on fire. The Flames rapidly de-
" ſtroyed the Interior, and by Evening nothing remained but the
" bare and tottering Walls. . . .

" Many of the Men of the *Fifth Pennſylvania* Cavalry, had
" begun to regard the Building as an Outpoſt of the Enemy: . . .
" They claimed that the *Confederate* Sharpſhooters frequently
" uſed it as a Shelter in Skirmiſhes, . . .

" At all Events, it is now known that it was ſtealthily ſet on fire
" by a few of the Rank and File in a Spirit of Retaliation and
" Revenge, and without the Knowledge or Approval of any com-
" miſſioned Officer. "

Alſo:

*THE WAR OF THE REBELLION: A Compilation
of the Official Records of the Union and Confederate
Armies* (*Waſhington: Government Printing Office,*
1887), Series I, Vol. XVIII, pp. 11-13, 388.

[338]
See Note 337.

[339]
See Note 337.

[340]

[340]
See Note 337.

Also:

COLLEGE OF WILLIAM AND MARY. Faculty Minutes, 1846-1883. [Also printed in *William and Mary College Quarterly*, Second Series, Vol. III, pp. 221-230.] Report of *Benjamin S. Ewell*, President of the College of *William and Mary*, to the Board of Visitors and Governors on *July* 5th, 1865.

" The Town was evacuated by the *Confederate* Forces as early
" as 11 o'Clock A. M. of the same Day [*September* 9, 1862].
" Later in the Day Parties of the Regiment of Cavalry (the 5th
" *Pa.*) which constituted the Garrison entered the Town, as I
" have been credibly informed, and under the Excitement pro-
" duced by their Defeat and the Use of a Quantity of Whiskey,
" which they found, fired the College Building. This was con-
" sumed with the Chemicals & Chemical Apparatus, a small
" Portion of the Philosophical Apparatus the Furniture and a
" Part of the Library. Most of the Books were saved by the
" strenuous Exertions of the Citizens, the Ladies being conspicu-
" ous in the good Work. The Fire did not reach the upper Floor
' & Roof of the southern Tower . . . Subsequent to this all
" the Out-houses in the College Yard excepting Portions of the
" Brick Kitchens of the *Brafferton* and President's House were
" pulled down and carried off; the House occupied by the late
" Professor *Morrison* was burned; and the Wood-work of the
" *Brafferton* with the Exception of the Roof, and the Floor of one
" Room and the lower Passage was carried off. . . . "

[341]
John S. Charles, RECOLLECTIONS OF WILLIAMS-BURG, AS IT APPEARED AT THE BEGINNING OF THE CIVIL WAR, AND JUST PREVIOUS THERETO. [Manuscript in Possession of the *Research Department, Colonial Williamsburg* Foundation.] pp. 1, 55, 62.

Also:

Victoria Lee, WILLIAMSBURG IN 1861. [Manuscript

ſcript in Poſſeſſion of the *Reſearch Department, Colonial Williamſburg* Foundation.] pp. 25, 27.

[342]

MAGAZINE OF WESTERN HISTORY, Vol. II (1885), pp. 522-523. [An Article on *Williamſburg* by *James Drew Sweet.*]

Alſo:

Lyon Gardiner Tyler, WILLIAMSBURG, THE OLD COLONIAL CAPITAL (Richmond: Whittet & Shepperſon: 1907), p. 218.

" The two Brick Houſes at the Side [Offices of the Governor's
" Palace] ſtood till the War of 1861-1865, when they were pulled
" down by *Federal* Troops to furniſh Chimneys for the Huts of
" the Officers at *Fort Magruder.* . . . "

[343]

David E. Cronin, THE VEST MANSION—Its Hiſtorical and Romantic Aſſociations as Confederate and Union Headquarters in the American Civil War. [Ms. in *Reſearch Department, Colonial Williamſburg* Foundation.] pp. 37, 39.

[344]

Victoria Lee, WILLIAMSBURG IN 1861. [Manuſcript in Poſſeſſion of the *Reſearch Department, Colonial Williamſburg* Foundation.] p. 28.

[345]

THE WAR OF THE REBELLION: A Compilation of the Official Records of the Union and Confederate Armies (Waſhington: Government Printing Office. 1894), Series I, Vol. XLVI, Part III, pp. 663-686, 744,

[346]

*COLLEGE OF WILLIAM AND MARY—Faculty Minutes—*1846-1883.

" Seſſion—1865-66.

" The

" The Seffion was opened one Week after the Time prefcribed
" by Law—the Buildings not being in Condition fooner . . ."

Alfo:

HISTORY OF THE COLLEGE OF WILLIAM AND MARY (Richmond: J. W. Randolph & Englifh, 1874), pp. 64-66.

" At a Convocation of the Board of Vifitors and Governors
" held during the Month of *Auguft*, 1865, in *Richmond*, it was
" determined to re-open the College at the ufual Time, to repair
" fome of the College Buildings for Recitation Rooms, and to
" provide other Accommodations neceffary for the Students.
" This was done, and fufficient temporary Arrangements made.

" At the fame Time, a Grammar School was eftablifhed, to be
" under the Care and Supervifion of the Faculty.

" The Wifdom of this Action is abundantly confirmed by the
" Refult. At this Time, *January* 15th, 1866, there is a Grammar
" School in fuccefsful operation. The Numbers compofing the
" College Claffes exceed the Anticipations of the moft fanguine;
" nearly fixty attend the academic Exercifes.

" In 1867, to continue this hiftorical Sketch to the prefent
" Time [1874], the Vifitors and Governors encouraged by the
" Intereft manifefted in the Reftoration of the College by dif-
" tinguifhed Perfons in every Part of the Country, and the fub-
" ftantial Aid furnifhed by *W. W. Corcoran*, of *Wafhington* City,
" *A. T. Stewart*, *James T. Soutter*, Hon. *A. E. Borie*, and other
" prominent Gentlemen of *New York*, *Philadelphia* and *Balti-*
" *more*, and the Decree of the *Englifh* Courts giving the ' *Matty*
" *Fund* ' ' in Truft ' to the College, took the neceffary Steps to
" rebuild and reorganize the Inftitution.

" In *July*, 1869, the main Building being fubftantially reftored,
" the Faculty was reorganized with a fufficient Corps of academic
" Profeffors; the Courfe of Studies revifed and modified; and the
" College ordered to be regularly opened for Students, for the
" firft Time with a full Faculty fince 1861. "

[347]

BULLETIN. THE COLLEGE OF WILLIAM AND MARY IN VIRGINIA. Catalogue of the Alumni and Alumnae for the Years 1866-1932, Vol. XXVI, No. 2, p. 38.

" During

"During the fix Seffions between *June*, 1881, and *September*,
"1888, the Fortunes of the College were very low. In thofe
"Years, Prefident *Ewell*, fometimes with Affiftants and fome-
"times as the foleTeacher, kept theCollege in partial Operation.
"The only Students were young Men of *Williamfburg* and Vi-
"cinity. No Catalogues were publifhed and if any Records
"were kept, they have fince difappeared. . . ."

[348]

COLLEGE OF WILLIAM AND MARY—*Faculty Minutes*—1903-1911, pp. 134-139.

"An Act to amend and re-enact an Act entitled: An Act to
"eftablifh a Normal School at *William and Mary* College in
"Connection with its collegiateCourfe, approved *March* 5th,1888,
"and to transfer the Ownerfhip of the real Eftate and perfonal
"Property of the faid College to the State. Approved *March* 7,
"1906. . . ."

Alfo:

Lyon G. Tyler, WILLIAMSBURG, THE OLD COLONIAL CAPITAL (Richmond: Whittet & Shepperfon, 1907), pp. 192-193.

[349]

PROCEEDINGS AT THE OPENING OF RALEIGH TAVERN *as an Exhibition Building in the Reftoration of Colonial Williamfburg (Williamfburg: Whittet & Shepperfon,* 1932), p. 15. Speech made by Mayor *George P. Coleman,* on *September* 16, 1932, at the Opening of the *Raleigh Tavern* as an Exhibition Building by *Colonial Williamfburg,* Incorporated.

[350]

Rev. *William A. R. Goodwin, BRUTON PARISH CHURCH RESTORED (Peterfburg:* The *Franklin Prefs,* 1907), pp. 83-92. "*Notes relative to the Refto-*
"*ration of* Bruton Parifh *Church.*"

[351]

BRUTON PARISH VESTRY BOOK, *1913-1937,* pp. 89,

89, 91-92, 95-97, 100-101, 103, 104, 105 [*April* 13, 1926—*March* 18, 1927.]

[352]

YEAR BOOK FOR THE ASSOCIATION FOR THE PRESERVATION OF VIRGINIA ANTIQUI-TIES (*Richmond: Wm. Ellis Jones*) 1896-7, pp. 3, 35-38, 49; 1898, pp. 31-33.

Also:

Jeannette S. Kelly, THE FIRST RESTORATION IN WILLIAMSBURG (*Richmond:* Printed for the *Association for the Preservation of Virginia Antiquities*, by *Whittet & Shepperson*, 1933), pp. 7-13.

[353]

Arthur Kyle Davis, ed., *VIRGINIA COMMUNITIES IN WAR TIME* (*Richmond:* Publications of the *Virginia War History Commission*, Source Volume VI, 1926), p. 575.

" The geographical Position of the County [*Warwick* County],
" with its great Port of Embarkation at *Newport News*, necessi-
" tated the Passing through it of Thousands of Boys from all
" Parts of *America*. The County was the Base of military
" Activities on the Peninsula. Military Camps and Lines and
" Lines of Warehouses were rapidly constructed, . . . Five
" Camps were established—*Eustis, Morrison, Hill, Alexander* and
" *Stuart*. Boys were trained in the Aviation and Balloon
" Schools, in Infantry, heavy Artillery, and all Branches of the
" Service, to be sent later to Camp *Stuart*, the Port of Embarka-
" tion. Camp *Eustis* is said to have been the only School of
" Railway Artillery in the World."

Note: The above Reference pertains to a single neighboring County. In *York* County were the Navy Mine Depot and a large Naval Fuel Oil Station. Substantial Portions of the Fleet were anchored in the *York* River and the great Naval Operating Base was located across the Bay, near *Norfolk*. *Fortress Monroe* and *Langley Field* were situated in *Elizabeth City* County, at the Foot of the Peninsula.

[354]

[354]

Ibid., pp. 611-613.

" In the Fall of 1915 a Rumor to the Effect that the *Du Ponts*
" were trying to purchafe *Jameftown* for the Purpofe of erecting
" a black Powder Plant thereon caufed much Excitement.
" Nothing further was heard from this Rumor . . . By Spring a
" credited Report went out that the *Du Pont Powder* Company
" would erect on the *York* River a large black Powder Plant.
" Another Report was to the Effect that a fteam and electric
" Railway was to be built between *Williamfburg* and this Plant.
" By this Time real Eftate Men from all over the County began
" to pour into the Town of *Williamfburg*. The Town was on a
" Boom, Options were taken on nearly every other Piece of
" Property in the Town, and fuburban Sites were being laid out
" and big Land Sales were on.

" Along with the Confirmation of the Eftablifhment of a Dyna-
" mite Plant, came an authorized Report from the *C. & O. Rail-*
" *way* Company that they would build a Spur Track from *Will-*
" *iamfburg* to the *York* River Site, the *C. & O.* Depot to be ufed
" for the *Du Pont* Station. . . .

" On *June* 1, 1916, the new Branch Line of the *C. & O.* Rail-
" road to the *Du Pont* Plant was formally opened, an Employment
" Department eftablifhed, the Conftruction Work ftarted, and in
" the Fall of 1916, the firft Unit of the Plant at *Penniman* was
" completed. . . .

" In the Beginning it was reported from the Publicity Depart-
" ment of the *Du Pont Powder* Company, *Wilmington, Delaware,*
" that there would poffibly be about 200 Men employed at the
" new Powder Plant. As early as *July*, 1916, the *Williamfburg*
" *Chamber of Commerce* requefted the *C. & O. Railway* Company
" to put on a regular Paffenger Train between the City and
" *Penniman*. By the Fall of 1918, *Penniman* was a Town of
" about fifteen Thoufand Inhabitants, the Plant large enough to
" take care of about ten Thoufand Employees, and there were
" three Paffenger Trains a Day each Way between *Williamfburg*
" and *Penniman*. Even though every Facility was provided at
" *Penniman* to take care of the People employed, many refided
" in *Williamfburg* and Hundreds of *Williamfburg* People worked
" at the Munition Plant. While the Hiftory of *Penniman* be-
" longs to that of a fifter County, it would be impoffible not to
" refer to it in Connection with the War-time Activities of *James*
" *City* County, as *Williamfburg* was the Bafe of Supplies for the
" Shell

"Shell manufacturing Town and its Railroad Station the
"Junction for all *Penniman* Travel. . . ."

[355]

JAMES CITY COUNTY RECORDS, *Plat Book II*,
p. 38; *Plat Book III*, p. 10.

YORK COUNTY RECORDS, *Plat Book II*, pp. 45,
54-56, 58, 60, 62, 63, 64, 69, 72, 74, 78-83.

[Eighteen Subdivifions in and around *Williamfburg*
are recorded in this Plat Book.]

See alfo Note 354

[356]

For Photographs of *Williamfburg* juft prior to its Reftoration, fee Archives of *Colonial Williamfburg*
Foundation.

[357]

THE PHI BETA KAPPA KEY, Vol. VII, No. 8
(*May*, 1930), pp. 514-520. "*The Reftoration of Colo-*
"*nial* Williamfburg," by Dr. *W. A. R. Goodwin.*

Alfo:

THE NATIONAL GEOGRAPHIC MAGAZINE,
Vol. LXXI, No. 4, *April*, 1937), pp. 401-443. "*The*
"*Genefis of the* Williamfburg *Reftoration,*" by Mr.
John D. Rockefeller, Jr.; "*The Reftoration of Colonial*
"Williamfburg," by Dr. *W. A. R. Goodwin.*

[*Note:* It will be found that the Date of the *Phi Beta Kappa* Banquet is given as 1924 in the firft Publication cited above, whereas
1925 is given in the fecond. The correct Date is 1924 and, inaf-
much as the incorrect Date has been ufed inadvertantly in numerous Publications, this Emphafis is given here.]

[358]

[358]
See Note 357

[359]
*THE WILLIAMSBURG RESTORATION—A Brief
Review of the Plan, Purpofe, and Policy of the Williamfburg Reftoration* (Colonial Williamfburg, Incorporated, 1933), p. 5.

> [*Note:* In the firft Edition of *Williamfburg in Virginia*
> the Word "typical" in the Definition referred to
> above was officially changed to the Word " im-
> " portant. "]

[360]
WILLIAMSBURG—Paft, Prefent, Future, 1699-1921
(*Williamfburg:* The Bufinefs Men's Affociation, 1921)

> " *Williamfburg* is well equipped with Bufinefs Houfes, there
> " being two profperous Banks; three Hotels; one Reftaurant;
> " numerous up-to-date Stores; one Bakery; four public Garages;
> " electric Light and Power Plant, furnifhing 24-hour Service; a
> " Steam Laundry; flouring Mill; Ice Plant; one Moving-Picture
> " Theatre; commercial Job Printing and Stationery Eftablifh-
> " ment; and one Newfpaper, the *Virginia Gazette*, eftablifhed in
> " 1736. "

[361]
In a Senfe, this Statement may be fpecious, in that it
hinges upon *Williamfburg's* legal Claffification as a *City*.
It is poffible that certain *Towns* may have preferved a
greater Proportion of colonial Structures in Relation to
their original Size than were to be found in *Williamfburg* at the Time of its Reftoration. It is extremely
doubtful, however, that this would be true of *Englifh-
American* colonial *Cities*. Within the Area with which
the *Reftoration* is concerned, approximately four Hundred Buildings are fhown on the *Frenchman's Map* of
1782.   Ninety of thefe Buildings were ftill ftanding in
1928.

[362]

[362]

WILLIAMSBURG RESTORATION ARCHIVES.
See Photographs of *Williamſburg* Buildings and their
Surroundings before Reſtoration Work began. Alſo
Motion-picture Film of the City, made in 1930 for
Purpoſes of Record.

[363]

WILLIAMSBURG RESTORATION ARCHIVES.
(Private). Memorandum of Conference between Mr.
John D. Rockefeller, Jr., Dr. *W. A. R. Goodwin*, and
Mr. *Charles O. Heydt*, held in *New York, November* 21,
1927, and Letter from Mr. *Rockefeller* to Colonel
Arthur Woods, November 30, 1927, outlining Mr.
Rockefeller's Underſtanding with Dr. *Goodwin* con-
cerning Purchaſe of *Williamſburg* Properties.

[364]

*RECORDS OF CLERK'S OFFICE, CITY OF
WILLIAMSBURG AND COUNTY OF JAMES
CITY.*

[365]

WILLIAMSBURG RESTORATION ARCHIVES.
Certificates of Incorporation iſſued to *Colonial
Williamſburg,* Incorporated and *Williamſburg Holding Corporation* by *Virginia State Corporation Commiſſion, February* 27, 1928. Amendment to Certificate
of Incorporation of the *Williamſburg Holding Corporation* changing Name to *Williamſburg Reſtoration,*
Incorporated, dated *February* 15, 1934.

[366]

WILLIAMSBURG RESTORATION ARCHIVES.
(Private). " Contract for Building and Reſtoration of
" *Williamſburg, Virginia,*" made between *Williamſburg Holding Corporation* and *Perry, Shaw & Hepburn,*

burn, Architects, of *Boston*, *Massachusetts*, *February* 2, 1929. Prior to that Date, in 1927, Mr. *William G. Perry* had been authorized to prepare Studies and Plans for the Restoration of certain *Williamsburg* Buildings.

[367]

WILLIAMSBURG RESTORATION ARCHIVES. (Private). Agreement with Mr. *Arthur A. Shurcliff*, Landscape Architect, *Boston*, *Massachusetts*, outlined in following Letters: Mr. *Shurcliff* to Dr. *W. A. R. Goodwin*, *March* 6, 1928; Dr. *Goodwin* to Colonel *Arthur Woods*, *March* 8, 1928; Colonel *Woods* to Dr. *Goodwin*, *March* 15, 1928.

[368]

WILLIAMSBURG RESTORATION ARCHIVES. (Private). " Contract for Building and Restoration " of *Williamsburg*, *Virginia*," made between *Williamsburg Holding Corporation* and *Todd Robertson*, *Todd Engineering Corporation*, of *New York*, *June* 6, 1928. *Todd & Brown*, Incorporated, was formed as a Subsidiary of *Todd, Robertson, Todd* to carry on structural and engineering Work at *Williamsburg*.

[369]

WILLIAMSBURG RESTORATION ARCHIVES. See " *Map of Williamsburg*, *Virginia—Restoration* " *Survey for Williamsburg Holding Corporation*," prepared by *J. Temple Waddill*, Civil Engineer, of *Richmond*, *Virginia*, in 1928.

[370]

WILLIAMSBURG RESTORATION ARCHIVES. Report of *Metcalf & Eddy*, Engineers, of *Boston*, *Massachusetts*, *August* 17, 1928, on " Sewerage and " Sewage Treatment."

[371]

[371]

WILLIAMSBURG RESTORATION ARCHIVES.
General File on "Underground Wiring"; alfo
Contracts made between *Reftoration* Organizations
and *Virginia Electric & Power Company* and *Chefapeake & Potomac Telephone Company of Virginia*

[372]

WILLIAMSBURG RESTORATION ARCHIVES.
Report on Zoning and Town Planning made by Mr.
John P. Fox of *Murray Hill Affociation*, Incorpor-
ated, of *New York, December* 17, 1930.

[373]

WILLIAMSBURG RESTORATION ARCHIVES.
Underwood Brothers, of *Richmond, Virginia*, em-
ployed in 1928 to care for Trees and Boxwood on
Reftoration Property.

[374]

WILLIAMSBURG RESTORATION ARCHIVES.
Building Code of *Williamfburg*—1930.

[375]

WILLIAMSBURG RESTORATION ARCHIVES.
Minutes of firft Meeting of Advifory Committee of
Architects, held in *Williamfburg* on *November* 25–26,
1928, and of fubfequent Meetings.

[376]

WILLIAMSBURG RESTORATION ARCHIVES.
Minutes of firft Meeting of Committee from the
American Society of Landfcape Architects, held in
Williamfburg on *June* 7–9, 1929, and of fubfequent
Meetings.

[377]

WILLIAMSBURG RESTORATION ARCHIVES.
Minutes

Minutes of Meeting of firſt Committee of Hiſtorians, held in *Williamſburg* on *October* 21–22, 1932, and of Meetings of ſubſequent Committees.

[378]

WILLIAMSBURG RESTORATION ARCHIVES. Minutes of Meeting of firſt Ladies' Advisory Committees on Decoration and Furniſhings, held in *Williamſburg* on *November* 25, 1930, and of ſubſequent Committees.

[379]

WILLIAMSBURG RESTORATION ARCHIVES. (Private). Letter of Mr. *William G. Perry* to Mr. *Harold R. Shurtleff*, *March* 29, 1930, regarding Mr. *Shurtleff's* Appointment as Architectural Recorder; alſo Memorandum of a Conference, *July* 16, 1930, regarding Coordination of this Work with hiſtorical Reſearch and archaeological Endeavors under Mr. *Shurtleff's* Direction.

[380]

THE WILLIAMSBURG RESTORATION—A Brief Review of the Plan, Purpoſe and Policy of the Williamſburg Reſtoration (Williamſburg Holding Corporation: Whittet & Shepperſon, 1931), p. 9.

[381]

WILLIAMSBURG RESTORATION ARCHIVES. An Authorization Report of September, 1940, liſts 591 ſuch Structures, large and ſmall, diſpoſed of at that Time, and 188 of colonial Date reconſtructed on their original Sites. Whereas the firſt Figure has grown little ſince then, the ſecond has more than doubled. Preciſe Numbers, however, have not been currently aſſembled.

[382]

WILLIAMSBURG RESTORATION ARCHIVES. Architectural Records and Reports on individual Buildings

Buildings reftored or reconftructed cite original Features retained or duplicated, as well as documentary, archaeological, and pictorial Evidences employed; alfo Precedents followed where fpecific Evidences were lacking or obfcure.

[383]

Eighty-eight colonial and early nineteenth-Century Buildings are located in and adjacent to the Hiftoric Area.

[384]

WILLIAMSBURG RESTORATION ARCHIVES. Reports and Records refulting from fuch Refearch now in the Keeping of Department of Refearch & Record.

[385]

WILLIAMSBURG RESTORATION ARCHIVES. The following Quotation clofes a Letter from the Librarian of the *Bodleian* Library, *Oxford, England,* to Mr. *John D. Rockefeller,* Jr., prefenting him with the Copperplate.

" My Curators recognize that in reconftructing this important
" Piece of colonial Hiftory in *Williamfburg* you have carried
" through a notable Achievement from which Pofterity will per-
" manently benefit. In Appreciation they would like to prefent
" to you this Copper-plate of the old Buildings, perhaps as an
" Addition to the Archives of the *Reftoration,* but at all Events
" as a Mark of their great Regard for the Service you have thus
" rendered to hiftorical Education."

[386]

Photographs of *Thomas Jefferfon's* Floor Plan of the Governor's Palace are in the Archives of the *Williamf-burg Reftoration.* The original Drawing is in Poffeffion of the *Maffachufetts Hiftorical Society.*

[387]

WILLIAMSBURG RESTORATION ARCHIVES. Archaeological Reports and Drawings of excavated colonial

colonial Foundations are at Prefent in the Keeping of the architectural refearch Office.

[388]

WILLIAMSBURG RESTORATION ARCHIVES. The Palace Foundations were excavated in 1930 and 1931. Reports and Drawings of the archaeological Findings are at Prefent in the Keeping of the architectural refearch Office.

[389]

See Note 381.

[390]

WILLIAMSBURG RESTORATION ARCHIVES. Refearch Information and Reports on Paint Colors are now in the Keeping of the Divifion of Aₗchitecture, Conftruction & Maintenance.

[391]

YORK COUNTY RECORDS, Wills, Inventories, Book XXII, pp. 83-99. Inventory of the Eftate of *Francis Fauquier*, 1768.

VIRGINIA STATE LIBRARY ARCHIVES, *Botetourt Papers*. Inventory of the perfonal Eftate of Lord *Botetourt*, *October*, 1770.

[This Inventory lifts the Furniture in the Governor's Palace Room by Room.]

[392]

VIRGINIA STATE LIBRARY ARCHIVES, *Botetourt Papers*.

[In the Inventory of the perfonal Eftate of Lord *Botetourt*, *October*, 1770, the " Standing Furniture " at the Palace " is lifted alfo.]

[393]

H. R. McIlwaine, ed., *JOURNALS OF THE HOUSE OF*

OF BURGESSES OF VIRGINIA, 1702-1712.
(Richmond: 1912), pp. 29-30.

" *Friday.* 9th *April* 1703

. . .

" Agreed That the Overseer of the Works of ye Capitoll and
" Prison take Care and see that the same be forthwith done and
" finished according to the following Directions (*vizt.*)

" That the Footsteps of the Generall Court House be rais'd two
" Feet from the Floor, and the Seats or Benches whereon the
" Court is to sit rais'd a convenient Highth above that.

" That the circular Part thereof be rais'd from the Seat up to
" the Windows.

" That there be a Seat rais'd one Step above ye Bench in the
" Middle of the circular End of ye Court made Chairwise

" That the Queens Arm's be provided to set over it

" That the Rest of ye Court be fitted with a Table for the Clerk
" and such Barrs and Benches as shall be found requisite and
" necessary.

" That there be two Galeries made one at the lower End of the
" Room, and the other on the east Side.

" That the Fitting and Furnishing the Room appropriated for
" the Secretaries Office with Partitions Boxes &c for keeping and
" preserving the Records belonging be left to the Direction of
" Mr Secretary.

" That there be provided to be set in ye Councill Chamber one
" oval Table fourteen Foot long and six Foot broad with two
" Doz: arm'd Cain Chairs, one larger ditto, twenty five green
" Cushions for ye said Chairs stuft with Hair, and a large *Turky*
" Work Carpet for ye Table

" That ye Room appropriated for ye Councill Office be fitted
" and furnished with Boxes or Presses for preserving and keeping
" ye Records and Papers thereto belonging according to ye
" Direction of the Clerk of ye Councill.

" That ye Barr of ye Burgesses Room be set off even with the
" Jamns of the Wall next the Door.

" That that Part of the Floor without ye Barr and from ye
" Footsteps within be pav'd with Stone, and from ye Barr to the
" Setting off of ye Circle on each Side of the House a Platform a
" Foot from ye Floor four Foot and a half broad with a Seat next
" ye Wall of a suteable Highth, and the Wall to be wainscotted
" three Foot above that, and one other Seat within the Barr
" round ye Room of a suitable Hight above ye Floor, and that a
" Break to pass through next the Barr, and in the Middle of ye
" lower

" lower Side Seats, be left open, and that the Queens Arm's be
" provided to be fet up in the Affembly Room.

" That the back Part of that Seat within the Circle be wain-
" fcotted three Foot high on yᵉ Wall above the Seat, and the
" lower Seat without the Circle two Foot above that.

" That yᵉ circular End be raifed one Step above the outward
" Floor and laid with Plank.

" That the Room be furnifhed with a large armed Chair for yᵉ
" Speaker to fit in, and a Cufhion ftuft with Hair fuitable to it,
" and a Table eight Foot long and five Foot broad.

" That yᵉ Room appropriated for the Affembly Office be fitted
" and furnifhed with Boxes &c for keeping and preferving the
" Records and Papers thereto belonging and according to yᵉ
" Direction of yᵉ Clerk of the Houfe of Burgeffes.

" That the Room over the Burgeffes Room be divided by a
" Partition Wall to be ftudded lathed and plaifter'd.

" That the Room over the Clerk of yᵉ Houfe of Burgeffes
" Office be furnifhed with a long fquare Table eight Foot long
" and four Foot broad

" That the Conference Room be furnifhed with an oval Table
" fourteen Foot long and fix Foot broad

" That the two Rooms over the Burgeffes Room be furnifhed
" with three oval Tables each nine Foot long and fix Foot broad.

" That a fufficient Quantity of green Cloth be provided to
" make Carpets off for all the Tables.

" That feven Doz: of *Ruffia* Leather Chairs be provided for
" furnifhing the Rooms above-ftairs, and one Doz: of large high
" Brafs Candlefticks one Doz: of fflatt ditto one Doz pe Brafs
" Snuffers & Half a Doz: Snuffdifhes, four Doz: large ftrong
" Brafs Sconces.

" That all the Seats in yᵉ Generall Court and Affembly Room
" be cover'd with green Serge and ftuft with Hair, and that
" there be provided Serge Hair red Tape and Brafs burnifhed
" Nails fufficient for doing the fame (to wit) one Hundred Yards
" of three Yrs wide green Serge, twelve Peices of fine narrow red
" Tape five Thoufand Brafs burnifhed Nailes and feventy Yards
" of ftrong green Cloth for Carpets

" That yᵉ Roomes in yᵉ Roofe of yᵉ Building not being yet
" appropriated to any particular Ufe, the Furnifhing the fame
" be referr'd till there fhall be Occafion of them.

" That the Records and Papers in yᵉ Secretaries Office remain
" where they now are till yᵉ Place in yᵉ Capitoll, appropriated
" for

" for yᵉ Secretaries Office be ffurnifhed and made fufficient to
" fecure them from Danger.

" That *John Redwood* is yᵉ moft fit Perfon of the feverall
" Petitioners to be imployed to look after and take Care of the
" Capitol & yᵉ Furniture and to be Goaler of yᵉ Country Prifon
" when they fhall be ffinifhed. "

Alfo

Ibid., pp. 96, 217, 219, 232-233; *1712-1726*, pp. 340, 350-351, 369.

H. R. McIlwaine, ed., *EXECUTIVE JOURNALS OF THE COUNCIL OF COLONIAL VIRGINIA* (*Richmond:* 1927), Vol. II, pp. 365-366.

H. R. McIlwaine, ed., *LEGISLATIVE JOURNALS OF THE COUNCIL OF COLONIAL VIRGINIA* (*Richmond:* 1918), Vol. I, pp. 416, 485; Vol. II, p. 681.

[394]

YORK COUNTY RECORDS, *Wills*, *Inventories*, Book XXI, pp. 36-43.

[Inventory of *Henry Wetherburn*, Tavernkeeper, 1760. Although *Wetherburn* was not Keeper of the *Raleigh* Tavern in 1760, it is conceivable that some of this Furniture was at the *Raleigh* when he was its Keeper, c. 1742.]

Ibid., Book XXII.

[Inventory of *Anthony Hay*, Keeper of the *Raleigh*, dated 1771.]

[395]

In the Archives of the *Williamfburg Reftoration* there are numerous Studies, Reports, Drawings, and Photographs compiled by Mr. *Arthur A. Shurcliff* as a Bafis for his Landfcape Work. See alfo Articles by Mr. *Shurcliff* on the Landfcape Work in *Williamfburg* in the following Periodicals:

THE

THE ARCHITECTURAL RECORD, Vol. LXXVIII, No. 6, *December,* 1935.

LANDSCAPE ARCHITECTURE, Vol. XXVII, No. 2, *January,* 1937; and Vol. XXVIII, No. 2, *January,* 1938.

[396]

LANDSCAPE ARCHITECTURE, Vol. XXVIII, No. 2, *January,* 1938, pp. 87-107.

" The Ancient Plan of *Williamsburg,* " by *Arthur A. Shurcliff.*

[397]

A BRIEF & TRUE REPORT FOR THE TRAVELLER CONCERNING WILLIAMSBURG IN VIRGINIA (Richmond: Dietz Prefs, Firft Edition, *April,* 1935),* pp. 136-141.

[398]

A HANDBOOK FOR THE EXHIBITION BUILDINGS OF COLONIAL WILLIAMSBURG, INCORPORATED (Williamsburg: 1936), p. 23.

" On *February* 24, 1934, the reconftructed Capitol was opened
" by the Houfe of Delegates and the Senate of the Common-
" wealth of *Virginia,* meeting in joint Seffion . . . The Af-
" fembly was addreffed by Governor *George C. Peery,* and by Mr.
" *John D. Rockefeller,* Jr., whofe Addrefs clofed with the follow-
" ing Words:—

" ' What a Temptation to fit in Silence and let
" the Paft fpeak to us of thofe great Patriots
" whofe Voices once refounded in thefe great
" Halls, and whofe far-feeing Wifdom, high
" Courage and unfelfifh Devotion to the com-
" mon Good will ever be an Infpiration to
" noble Living. To their Memory the Rebirth
" of this Building is dedicated . . . ' "

[399]

THE VIRGINIA GAZETTE (Williamsburg, Va.), New

New Series, Vol. V, No. 16, *Friday, April* 20, 1934. [Announcement of Opening of reconſtructed Governor's Palace to the Public on *April* 23, 1934].

[400]

PROCEEDINGS AT THE OPENING OF RALEIGH TAVERN AS AN EXHIBITION BUILDING IN THE RESTORATION OF COLONIAL WILL-IAMSBURG (*Williamſburg:* 1932)

[The *Raleigh* Tavern was opened to the Public on *September* 16, 1932.]

[401]

WILLIAMSBURG RESTORATION ARCHIVES.

The Court Houſe of 1770, newly reſtored and containing a Diſplay of excavated Material recovered in the Courſe of archaeological Inveſtigation in *Williamſburg*, was opened to the Public on *Monday, April* 24, 1933.

[402]

THE VIRGINIA GAZETTE (*Williamſburg, Va.*)
New Series, Vol. VI, No. 14, *Friday, April* 5, 1935.

" A Group of two Hundred and fifty Examples of *American*
" Folk Art, collected by Mrs. *John D. Rockefeller,* Jr., over a
" Period of Years, has been loaned to *Colonial Williamſburg,*
" Incorporated. The Collection, which is one of the moſt im-
" portant of its Kind, has been aſſembled in the reſtored *Ludwell-*
" *Paradiſe* Houſe, one of the hiſtoric Buildings in the Reſtoration
" of *Williamſburg* . . . It will be placed on public Exhibition
" beginning *April* 1ſt [1935]. "

[*Note:* This Collection has ſince been enlarged and preſented by Mrs. *Rockefeller* to *Colonial Williamſburg,* Incorporated.]

[403]

THE VIRGINIA GAZETTE (*Williamſburg, Va.*),
New Series, Vol. V, No. 41, *Friday, October* 19, 1934.

" Ancient *Duke of Glouceſter* Street, reconſtructed by the
" *Rockefeller*

" *Rockefeller* Reſtoration and to be formally dedicated tomorrow
" —*October* 20th—by Preſident *Rooſevelt*, has a Hiſtory that is a
" Part of the City of *Williamſburg* itſelf, dating from the
" Eſtabliſhment of the colonial Capital here in 1699 . . . "

[404]

WILLIAMSBURG RESTORATION ARCHIVES.
Announcement dated *June* 12, 1928, concerning a
Speech made by Dr. *W. A. R. Goodwin* at a *Will-
iamſburg* Town Meeting on that Date.

" Buildings in that Part of the City which is to be reſtored, and
" which do not harmonize with the Plan of colonial Reſtoration
" will probably be taken away or rebuilt. Some of the notable
" old Buildings deſtroyed by Fire will be rebuilt according to the
" Details and Deſcriptions gathered from many Sources. Theſe
" will include the Palace where the royal Governors lived, the
" Houſe of Burgeſſes [Capitol] in which the Aſſembly met and
" the *Raleigh* Tavern, where the *Phi Beta Kappa* was formed.

" The public Greens and Gardens will be reſtored to their
" original Condition of 150 and more Years ago. Every Effort
" will be made to recreate the ſimple and beautiful Atmoſphere
" which characterized *Williamſburg* in the Years before the
" *American* Revolution.

" The City reſtored will be a perpetual Example of the Lives
" of the Founders of the *American* Republic, dedicated to the
" Preſervation and Enrichment of the Spirit which animated our
" Fathers. We believe that it will be a powerful Influence to
" keep alive the Dignity and Simplicity of the old Coloniſts,
" exemplified in their Architecture and their Conduct. "

[405]

THE ARCHITECTURAL RECORD, Vol. LXXVIII,
No. 6, *December*, 1935, p. 359. " The Reſtoration of
Colonial*Williamſburg* in *Virginia*, " by *Fiſke Kimball*

[406]

THE VIRGINIA GAZETTE (*Williamſburg, Va.*),
New Series, Vol. VII, No. 13, *Friday, March* 27, 1936.

" *Williamſburg's* reſtored Public Gaol, Part of which has ſur-
" vived

" vived for more than 200 Years, will be opened to the Public as
" one of the Exhibition Buildings of *Colonial Williamſburg*,
" beginning *Wedneſday, April* 1ſt. . . ."

[407]

Ibid., New Series, Vol. XI, No. 13, *Friday, March* 22 to
Friday, March 29, 1940.

" The Home of *George Wythe*, fully reſtored, on *Palace Green*,
" will be open to the Public on *Saturday, March* 30th . . ."

[408]

Ibid., New Series, Vol. XXIII, No. 3, *Friday, January*
11 to *Friday, January* 18, 1952.

" The *Bruſh-Everard* Houſe which will become the eighth exhi-
" bition Building on *Monday* has an unuſual and romantic
" Hiſtory. It has been reſtored as an Example of the leſs
" Pretentious Type of colonial Town Dwelling . . ."

[409]

Ibid., New Series, Vol. XXXIX, No. 26, *Friday, June*
21 to *Friday, June* 28, 1968, Sec. B. pp. 1-2.

[410]

WILLIAMSBURG RESTORATION ARCHIVES.
Preſs Releaſes and other Records of Shop Openings
as follows: Apothecary—*Paſteur-Galt*, Shop, *Octo-
ber*, 1950; Dr. *McKenzie* Shop (ſeaſonal) *July*, 1968.
Baker at *Raleigh* Tavern, *October*, 1953. Barber &
Perukemaker at *King's Arms* Barber Shop, 1950.
Basket-Maker at *Wythe* South Office, *May*, 1967.
Blacksmith at *Deane* Forge, *October*, 1937. Boot
& Shoemaker at *Repiton* Shop, *April*, 1940. Cabi-
netmaker at *Anthony Hay's* Shop, *January*, 1966.
Cooper at *Taliaferro-Cole* Shop, *July*, 1968. Jew-
eler & Clock-Maker at *Golden Ball*, *July*, 1955.
Gunsmith at *Ayſcough* Houſe, *January*, 1966, Har-
ness-Maker at *Deane* Shop, *April*, 1966. Metal
Founder at *James Geddy* Foundry, *July*, 1968.
Miller

MILLER at *Robertſon's* Windmill, *May,* 1957. MILLI-
NER at *Margaret Hunter* Shop, *January,* 1954. PRINT-
ER & BOOKBINDER at Printing Office, *May,* 1958.
SILVERSMITH at *James Geddy* Shop, *July,* 1968.
SPINNER & WEAVER at *Greenhow* Lumber Houſe,
April, 1957. MUSICK TEACHER at *Mary Stith* Shop,
July, 1970.

[411]

In 1939-40 the Reſtoration of *Bruton Pariſh* Church
was completed. Mr. *John D. Rockefeller,* Jr. was the
principal Donor, although ſome five Hundred Others
contributed Funds to the Undertaking. [*THE VIRGI-
NIA GAZETTE,* New Series, Vol. XI, No. 14, *Friday,
March* 29 to *Friday, April* 5, 1940, p. 8; and No. 15,
Friday, April 5, to *Friday, April* 12, 1940, p. 3.]

[412]

The Powder Magazine, which for many years had
been owned and preſerved by the *Aſſociation for the
Preſervation of Virginia Antiquities,* was in *December,*
1946, leaſed by that Aſſociation to *Colonial Williamſburg.* The Magazine and the reconſtructed Guard-
houſe near it were opened to the Publick by the latter
Organization on *July* 4, 1949. [*Ibid.,* New Series, Vol.
XX, No. 26, *Friday, June* 24 to *Friday, July* 1, 1949,
SUPPLEMENT, Section 3, pp. 65, 91.]

[413]

THE VIRGINIA GAZETTE, (*Williamſburg, Va.*),
New Series, Vol. II, No. 37, *Friday, September* 11,
1931.

" The College of *William & Mary* will occupy the reſtored
" *Wren* Building at the Opening of the preſent Fall Term.
" Since *June* 1, 1928, the Building has been in Courſe of Recon-
" ſtruction through the Generoſity of Mr. *John D. Rockefeller,*
" Jr. . . . "

Alſo:

Alſo:

Ibid., New Series, Vol. II, No. 38, *Friday, September* 18, 1931.

[414]

Ibid., New Series, Vol. VIII, No. 44, *Friday, October* 22, 1937.

" Opening of the Craft Houſe and the firſt three Craft Shops
" in *Williamſburg* repreſents a major Step in the *Reſtoration's*
" Program of reviving ſelected Handicrafts of the eighteenth
" Century in Harmony with the eſtabliſhed educational Ob-
" jectives of the *Reſtoration*. . . . "

[415]

*HANDBOOK. THE INSTITUTE OF EARLY
AMERICAN HISTORY AND CULTURE (Williamſburg: The Inſtitute of Early American Hiſtory
and Culture,* 1957), pp. 3-4.

" . . in 1943 the *Inſtitute of Early American History and Culture*
" was organized under the joint Sponſorſhip of the College of
" *William and Mary* and *Colonial Williamſburg*. "

[416]

THE VIRGINIA GAZETTE (Williamſburg, Va.)
New Series, Vol. XXVIII, No. 14, *Friday, March*
29, to *Friday, April 5, 1957.*

" The State of *Virginia* has developed a major new Economy
" baſed upon the Accommodation of its Viſitors, Governor
" *Thomas B. Stanley* ſaid *Sunday* Morning at dedication Cere-
" monies of *Colonial Williamſburg's* new *Information Center*. "

[417]

Ibid., New Series Vol. XXVIII, No. 11 *Friday, March*
8, to *Friday, March* 15, 1957.

" A preview Showing of the *Abby Aldrich Rockefeller Folk*
" *Art Collection* for Reſidents of the *Williamſburg* Area will
" be held tomorrow from 4 to 6 P.M.

" The

" The Collection, houfed in a new, fpecially defigned Build-
" ing facing the *Williamfburg* Inn Golf Courfe, will be placed
" on difplay daily, ftarting *Sunday*, from noon until 9 P.M."

[418]

The firft of the *Williamfburg Reftoration Hiftorical
Studies* publifhed under the Aufpices of the Department of Refearch & Record of *Colonial Williamfburg*,
Incorporated, was *THE PRESENT STATE OF
VIRGINIA, AND THE COLLEGE* (by *Henry Hart-
well*, *James Blair*, and *Edward Chilton*, firft publifhed
in 1727), edited, with an Introduction, by the late
Hunter Dickinfon Farifh, former Director of the Department of Refearch & Record.

[419]

WILLIAMSBURG RESTORATION ARCHIVES.
See " Announcement for the Year 1940-41 " made
by the Department of Refearch & Record regarding
Fellowfhips.

APPENDIX.

APPENDIX.

PART II.

1. The Acts directing the Building the Capitol and the City of *Williamsburg.*

2. The Charter of the City.

Act XIV — *April - June* 1699.

" *AN ACT DIRECTING THE BUILDING THE*
" *CAPITOLL AND THE CITY OF WILLIAMS-*
" *BURGH.* "

[*Note:* This Act was passed on *June* 7th by a
" Generall Assembly, begun at *James City* " the
27th Day of *April,* 1699. It is here copied from
a Manuscript Volume entitled " *ACTS OF THE*
" *VIRGINIA ASSEMBLY 1662-1702,*" Pages
399-401, in the *Jefferson Collection, Division of
Manuscripts, Library of Congress.*]

" WHEREAS the State House where the Generall Assemblys
" and Generall Courts for yᵉ his Maᵗⁱᵉˢ Colony & Dominion of
" *Virginia* were kept and held hath been unhappily burnt downe
" and it being of absolute Necessity yᵗ another Building be
" erected wᵗʰ all the Expedition possible for the convenient Siting
" and Holding of the Generall Assemblyes and Courts at a
" healthy proper & comodius Place suitable for the Reception of
" a considerable Number and Concourse of People yᵗ of Neces-
" sity must resort to yᵉ Place where the Generall Assemblys will
" be

" be convened and where the Councill and Supream Courts of
" Juftice of yᵉ his Maᵗⁱᵉˢ Colony and Dominion will be held and
" kept and forafmuch as the Place commonly called and knowne
" by the Name of yᵉ *Middleplantation* hath been found by conftᵗ
" Experience to be healthy and agreeable to the Conftitutions of
" yᵉ Inhabitants of yᵉ his Majeftyes Colony and Dominion have-
" ing the naturall Advantage of a ferene and temperate Aire dry
" and champaign Land and plentifully ftored with wholefome
" Springs and the Conveniency of two navigable and pleaſᵗ
" Creeks that run out of *James* and *York* Rivers neceffary for
" the Supplying the Place with Provifions and other Things of
" Neceffity. *Be it therefore enacted by the Governer Councill and*
" *Burgeſſes of yᵉ preſᵗ Generall Aſſembly and the Authority thereof*
" *and it is hereby enacted* that four Hundᵈ & feventy-five Foot
" fquare of Land lying and being at the fᵈ *Middleplantation* wᶜʰ
" hath been already agreed upon by his Excelency the Governer
" Councill and Burgeffes of this preſᵗ Generall Affembly to be
" taken up and furveyed as a convenient Place for fuch Ufes be
" the Ground appropriated to the onely and fole Ufe of a Build-
" ing for the Generall Affemblys and Courts to be held and kept
" in and yᵗ the fᵈ Building fhall for ever hereafter be caled and
" knowne by the Name of the *Capitoll* of yᵉ his Matᵉˢ Colony
" and Dominion of *Virgᵃ* and yᵗ the Space of two Hundᵈ Foot
" of Ground every Way from the fᵈ Capitol fhall not be built
" upon planted or occupied for ever but fhall be wholy and folely
" appropriated and kept for the fᵈ Ufe and to no other Ufe or
" Purpofe wᵗfoever. *And be it further enacted by the Authority*
" *aforeſᵈ and it is hereby enacted* yᵗ the fᵈ Capitoll fhall be
" erected and built in Manner and Forme according to the
" Rules & Dimentions following (*viz*) yᵗ the fᵈ Building fhall be
" made in yᵉ Forme and Figure H yᵗ the Foundation of the fᵈ
" Building fhall be four Bricks thick up to or near the Surface
" of the Ground and yᵗ the Walls of the fᵈ Building from thence
" fhall be three Bricks and a halfe Brick thick to the Water Table
" and from the Water Table to the Top of the firft Story three
" Bricks thick and from thence to the Top of the fecond Story two
" Bricks and a halfe Brick thick the Length of each Side or Parte
" of wᶜʰ Building fhall be feventy five Foot from Infide to Infide
" the Breadth thereof twenty five Foot from Infide to Infide and
" the firft Story of each Part or Side fhall be fifteen Foot Pitch
" one End of each Pᵗ or Side of wᶜʰ fhall be femicircular and the
" lower Rooms at the fᵈ End fifty Foot long and fhall be parted
" by a Wall from the Reft of the Building on each Side or Part

" wᶜʰ

" wch other Part fhall be divided into four Divifions whereof one
" to be for a large and handfome Staire Cafe that the Midle [of
" the Front *] on each Side of the f{d} Building fhall have a cir-
" cular Porch wth an Iron Belcony upon the firft Floor over it &
" great folding Gates to each Porch of fix Foot Breadth both and
" that four Galleryes fhall be in the Room below that fhall be
" caled the Generall Court Houfe the upper Story of each Side
" to be tenn Foot Pitch and be divided as fhall be directed by
" the Comitees appointed to revife the Laws yt the two Parts of
" the Building fhall be joyned by a crofs Gallery of thirty Foot
" long and fifteen Foot wide each Way according to the Figure
" herein before fpeecified raifed upon Piazzas and built as high
" as the other Parts of the Building and in the Middle thereof a
" Cupulo to furmount the Reft of the Building wch fhall have a
" Clock placed in it and on the Top of the f{d} Cupulo fhall be put
" a Flag upon Occafion yt the Windows to each Story of the f{d}
" Building fhall be Safh Windows and yt the Roofe fhall be a Hip
" Roof with Dormand Windows and fhall be well fhingled with
" Cyprefs Shingles and that the great Roomes below of each
" Building fhall be laid with Flag-ftone one P{t} or Side of which
" Building fhall be and is hereby appropriated to the Ufe of the
" Generall Court & Councill for the Holding and Keeping of
" the f{d} Generall Court and Councill therein and the feverall
" Offices thereto belonging the other Part or Side of the f{d} Build-
" ing fhall be and is hereby appropriated to the Ufe of the Houfe
" of Burgiffes and the Offices thereof and to no other Ufe or Ufes
" w{t}foever. *And be it further enacted by the Authority aforef{d} and*
" *it is hereby enacted* that the Comitee appointed for the Revifall
" of the Laws are hereby impowered and required from Time to
" Time to infpect and overfee the f{d} Building untill it fhall be
" finifhed and to covenant and agree with fuch and fo many
" Undertakers or Overfeers of the f{d} Building as they fhall think
" fitt and to give fuch neceffary Orders and Directions therein
" 'from Time to Time as they fhall fee Caufe for the Carrying on
" Furtherance and Finifhing of the f{d} Work according to the
" aforef{d} Rules and Dimenfions and yt the f{d} Comitee be likewife
" impowered by Virtue of y{s} Act on the Publick Account and
" Rifque to fend for out of *England* Iron Work Glafs Paint Stone
" and all other Materialls as they fhall think neceffary for and
" towards ye Carrying on and Finifhing of the f{d} Building. *And*
" *be it further enacted by the Authority aforef{d} and it is hereby en-*
" *acted* yt the f{d} Comitee as often as they fhall have Occafion for
                                                        " Money

---

* Manufcript torn.

" Money for the Ufes aforef⁴ ſhall from Time to Time apply
" themſelves to the Governer or Commander in Cheif for the
" Time being to iſſue out his Warrant to the Treaſurer of yᵉ his
" Majeſtyes Colony and Dominion requireing him to pay ſoe
" much Money as they ſhall have Occaſion for not exceeding the
" Sume of two Thouſand Pᵈˢ Ster: who is hereby impowered and
" required to deliver and pay the ſame to the ſᵈ Comitee upon
" ſuch Warrᵗ wᶜʰ ſᵈ Sume or Sumes the ſᵈ Comitee ſhall account
" for to the next Meeting of Aſſembly and alſo make Report of
" their Proceedings in the Building the ſᵈ Capitoll And foraſmuch
" as the Generall Aſſembly and Generall Courts of yᵉ his Maᵗⁱᵉˢ
" Colony and Dominion cannot poſſibly be held and kept at the
" ſᵈ Capitoll unleſs a good Towne be built and ſettled adjacent
" to the ſᵈ Capitoll ſuitable for the Accomodation and Enter-
" tainmᵗ of a conſiderable Number of Perſons that of Neceſſity
" muſt reſort thither and whereas in all Propability it will prove
" highly advantageous and beneficiall to his Maᵗⁱᵉˢ Royall
" Colledge of *Wᵐ & Mary* to have the Conveniences of a Towne
" near the ſame *Be it therefore enacted by the Authority aforeſ⁴*
" *and it is hereby enacted* that two Hundᵈ eighty three Acres
" thirty five Poles and a halfe of Land ſcituate lying and being
" at the *Middleplantation* in *James Citye* and *York* Countyes
" bounded according to a Draught Plott or Survey made by
" Order of the Governer Councill and Burgeſſes of yᵉ preſᵗ
" Generall Aſſembly and now lying in the Aſſembly Office of yᵉ
" his Maᵗⁱᵉˢ Colony and Dominion ſhall be and is hereby reſerved
" and appropriated for the onely and ſole Uſe of a City to be
" there built and erected and to no other [Uſe*] Intent or Purpoſe
" whatſoever *And [be it*] further enacted by the Authority aforeſ⁴*
" *and it is hereby enacted* yᵗ two Hundᵈ & twenty Acres of the ſᵈ
" Land according [to the *] Bounds of the aforeſᵈ Draught or
" Plott ſhall be and is hereby appointed and ſett a part for
" Ground on wᶜʰ the ſᵈ City ſhall be built and erected according
" to the Form and Manner laid downe in the ſᵈ Draught or
" Plott wᶜʰ ſᵈ City in Honour of our moſt gratious & glorious
" King *Wᵐ* ſhall be for ever hereafter called and known by the
" Name of the City of *Williamſburgh* and fifteen Acres forty four
" Poles and a quartʳ of Land according to the aforeſᵈ Draught
" or Plott ſhall be and is hereby appointed and ſett a part for
" a Road or Way from the ſᵈ City to the Creek commonly
" caled and knowne by the Name of *Queens* Creek runing into
" *York* River and fourteen Acres ſeventy one Poles and a
                                                    " quartʳ

* Manuſcript torn.

" quart^r of Land according to the afore^{fd} Draught or Plott lying
" on the f^d *Queens* Creek fhall be and is hereby appointed and
" fett a part for a Port or Landing Place in Comemoracon of
" the late Queen *Mary* of blefed Memory for the f^d City of
" *Williams Burgh* on the f^d Creek w^{eh} f^d Port or Landing Place
" fhall for ever hereafter be called and knowne by the Name of
" *Queen Marys* Port and the aforementioned Road or Way
" leading thereto fhall be caled *Queen's* Road and ten Acres
" forty two Poles and a halfe of Land according to the afore^{fd}
" Draught or Plott fhall be and is hereby appointed & fet a part.
" for a Road or Way from the f^d City of *Williamfburgh* to the
" Creek commonly called and knowne by the Name of *Archers*
" *Hope* Creek runing into *James* River w^{eh} f^d Creek fhall for ever
" hereafter be caled and knowne by the Name of *Princefs* Creek
" & twenty three Acres thirty feven Poles and a halfe of Land
" according to the afore^{fd} Draught or Plott lying upon the f^d
" *Princefs* Creek fhall be and is hereby appointed and fett a part
" for a Port or Landing Place for the f^d City of *W^{ms}burgh* on the
" f^d Creek w^{eh} f^d Port or Landing Place in Honour of her Royall
" Highnefs the Princifs *Ann* of *Denmark* fhall be called and
" known by the Name of *Princifs Ann* Port for ever hereafter
" and the aforementioned Road or Way leading thereto fhall be
" caled *Princes* Road *And be it further enacted by the Authority*
" *aforef^d and it is hereby enacted* that the Ground or Land by
" Virtue of this Act fett a part for the Ufe of the faid City of
" *Williamfburgh* fhall be laid out and proportioned into halfe
" Acres every of which halfe Acre fhall be a diftinct Lott of
" Ground to be built upon in Manner and Forme as is hereafter
" exprefled that is to fay that whofoever fhall build in the maine
" Street of the f^d City of *Williamfburgh* as laid out in the afore-
" faid Draught or Plott fhall not build a Houfe lefs than tenn
" Foot Pitch and the Front of each Houfe fhall come within
" fix Foot of the Street and not nearer and that the Houfes in
" the feverall Lots in the faid main Street fhall front a like which
" faid Street in Honour of his Highnefs *William* Duke of
" *Gloceter* fhall for ever hereafter be called and knowne by the
" Name of *Duke of Gloceter* Street and that the other Streets
" or Lanes fhall be built in fuch Manner and according to fuch
" Rules and Orders as fhall be given and made by the Directors
" by Virtue of this Act hearafter appointed or by the Incorpora-
" tion of the Mayor Alderman and Comonalty of the City of
" *Williamfburgh* And to the End reafonable Satisfaction may
" be paid allowed and given for all fuch Land and Ground as
                                                              " by

" by Virtue of this Act is taken up and appropriated to the
" Ufes aforefaid *Be it enacted by the Authority aforefaid and it is*
" *hereby enacted* that his Excellency the Governer or the Govern·
" or Commander in Cheife for the Time being is hereby im-
" powered and defired to iffue out his Warrants to the feverall
" Sherrifs of *James City York* and *New Kent* Countyes comanding
" them refpectively [to *] impanell four of the moft [able
" and *] difcreet Freeholders in each of their Bailywicks no
" Wayes conferned in Intereft in the faid Land or any Wayes
" related to the Owners or Proprietors thereof to meet at fuch
" Time as he fhall think fitt who fhall be fworne by fuch Perfon
" or Perfons as he fhall appoint and fhall upon their Oaths
" vallue and appraife the faid Land or Ground in fo many
" feverall and diftinct Parts and Parcels as fhall be owned and
" claimed therein by feverall and diftinct Owners Proprietors
" and Claimers thereof and after fuch Valluation and Appraif-
" ment fo made the fᵈ Jury fhall forthwith returne the fame
" under their Hands and Seals to the Secretaryes Office of this
" his Majeftyes Colony and Dominion and after fuch Vallue-
" ation and Returne made as aforefaid the Feofees or Truftees
" by Virtue of this Act hereafter appointed fhall enter and
" imediatly upon fuch Entry made the faid Feofees and Truftees
" and every of them fhall be vefted wᵗʰ and feized of and in a
" pure abfolute perfect and indefefible Eftate of Inheritance
" in Fee in Truft to and for yᵉ Intents Ufes and Purpofes
" hereafter mentioned and fhall be binding and effectuall in Law
" without further or other Act or Acts to all Intents and Pur-
" pofes againft all and every the faid Owners Claimers or
" Proprietors whither they be capeable of confenting thereto
" or difabled by Nonage Coverture Entaile or other Impedi-
" ments and all and every their Heirs Executors Adminif-
" trators and Affignes for ever or any Claimer or Pretender
" thereto *PROVIDED alwayes and be it further enacted by the*
" *Authority aforefaid and it is hereby enacted* that the faid Jury
" in the faid Valluation fhall have due Regard to the refpective
" Interefts and Eftates in the fame and fhall make a Valluation
" and Eftimation thereof accordingly *And be it further enacted*
" *by the Authority aforefaid and it is hereby enacted* that *Lewis*
" *Burwell Phill: Ludwell* Junʳ, *Benjamin Harrifon* Junʳ, *James*
" *Whaley, Hugh Norwell,* and *Mongo Ingles,* Gentlemen fhall be
" and are hereby nominated and appointed Feofees or Truftees
" for the Land appropriated to the Ufes aforefaid which faid
" Feofees

---

* Manufcript torn.

" Feofees or Truſtees in Manner aforeſaid ſhall have hold and
" enjoy a good pure abſolute and indefeaſible Eſtate in Fee of
" in and to the aforeſaid two Hundred eighty three Acres thirty
" five Poles and a halfe of Land in ſpeciall Truſt and Confidence
" and to and for the Uſes herein after mentioned that is to ſay
" to the Uſes Intents and Purpoſes that the ſaid Feofees and
" Truſtees or any two or more of them ſhall out of two Hundred
" and twenty Acres of the ſaid Land hereby appropriated for
" the Uſe of the ſaid City of *Williamſburgh* convey and aſſure in
" Fee unto any Perſon requeſting the ſame and paying unto the
" ſaid Feofees or Truſtees the firſt Coſt of the Purchaſe thereof
" and fifty Percent Advance one or more halfe Acre or halfe
" Acres of the ſaid Land or Ground by ſuch good and ſufficient
" Deed and Aſſurance in the Law unto ſuch Perſon or Perſons
" their Heirs and Aſſignes for ever as by ſuch Perſon or Perſons
" or their Councill learned in the Law ſhall be required—
" *Provided alwayes and be it further enacted by the Authority*
" *aforeſaid and it is hereby enacted* that if ſuch Grantee his Heirs
" or Aſſignes ſhall not within the Space of twenty four Months
" next enſuing the Date of ſuch Grant begin to build and finiſh
" on each halfe Acre or Lott ſo granted one good Dweling Houſe
" containing twenty Foot in Width and thirty Foot in Length
" at the leaſt if in the maine Street caled *Duke of Gloceter* Street
" of tenn Foot Pitch and within ſix Foot of the Street if in any
" other Place according to the Rules and Directions that ſhall
" be given by the Directors hereafter appointed that then ſuch
" [Grant and Con *]-veyance ſo made ſhall be utterly void
" and null in Law and the Lands therein granted lyable to the
" Choice and [Pur *]-chaſe of any other Perſon or Perſons
" and ſhall be imediatly reinveſted in the ſaid Truſtees or
" Feofees to the Uſes aforeſaid in as full and ample Manner as
" if the ſame had never been diſpoſed of *And be it further enacted*
" *by the Authority aforeſaid and it is hereby enacted* that the
" Coſts and Charges of the Purchaſe of the ſaid two Hundred
" eighty three Acres thirty five Poles and a halfe of Land ſhall
" be paid and ſatisfyed by the Publick at the next Seſſion of
" Aſſembly to the ſeverall and reſpective Proprietors and Owners
" thereof according to the Valuacon and Appraiſment made in
" Manner as is afore expreſed and alſo that the aforeſaid Feofees
" and Truſtees ſhall render an Account of the Produce and
" Profits of the ſeverall halfe Acres or Lots of Land by them
" ſold in Manner aforeſaid to the next Generall Aſſembly which
                                                      " ſhall

---

* Manuſcript torn.

" fhall be then allowed and difpofed of for the Reimburfement
" of the Publick in the firft Purchafe of the faid Land & untill
" the fame be fully paid and reimburf'd and to no other Ufe
" Intent or Purpofe whatfoever *Provided alwayes and be it further*
" *enacted by the Authority aforefaid and it is hereby enacted* that in
" Cafe of the Death Removall out of the Country or into remote
" Partes or other legal Difability of one or more of the faid
" Feofees or Truftees his Exelency the Governer or the Govern'
" or Commander in Cheif for the Time being is hereby impow-
" ered and defired to nominate fuch and fo many Feofees or
" Truftees as fhall from Time to Time be under the Number of
" fix which faid Feofees or Truftees fo nominated and appointed
" fhall be imediatly vefted with equall Right and Title to the
" aforefaid Land and Ground to the Ufes aforefaid as the
" Feofees or Truftees appointed by Virtue of this Act might or
" could have or as if they were by this Act particularly nomi-
" nated and appointed *Provided likewife and be it further enacted*
" *by the Authority aforefaid and it is hereby enacted* that the Lots
" at the aforementioned Ports or Landings fhall be proportioned
" at the Difcretion of the Directors hearafter mentioned, pro-
" vided that each Lott fhall not exceed fixty Foot fquare which
" faid Lott fhall be difpofed of in Manner aforefaid and the
" Produce thereof to be accounted for by the faid Feofees or
" Truftees in Manner as is before exprefed any Thing in this
" Act to the Contrary in any Wife notwithftanding *Provided*
" *alfo*—that a fufficient Quantity of Land at each Port or
" Landing Place fhall be left in comon at the Difcretion of the
" Directors hearafter appointed *And be it further enacted by the*
" *Authority aforefaid and it is hereby enacted* that it fhall and
" may be lawfull to and for his Exelency the Governer and to
" and for his Majeftys Governour or Commander in Cheife of
" this his Majeftyes Colony and Dominion for the Time being
" by Letters Patents under the Seale of this his Majeftyes
" Colony and Dominion to incorporate all and every Perfon
" & Perfons who from Time to Time and at any Times hearafter
" fhall have any Intereft Freehold or Habitation in the faid
" City to be one Body politick and corporall by the Name of
" the Mayor Alderman and Comonalty of the City of *Williamf-*
" *burgh* and by that Name to have perpetuall Succeffion and a
" common Seale and that they and their Succeffors by the
" Name aforefaid fhall be able and capable in Law to have pur-
" chafe receive enjoy poffes and retaine to them and their Suc-
" ceffors for ever any Lands Rents Tenements & Hereditaments
" of

" of what Kind Nature or Quallity foever and alfo to fell grant
" demife alien or difpofe of the fame and by the fame Name to fue
" and implead be fued and impleaded anfwer and be anfwered in
" all Courts of Record and any other Place whatfoever and from
" Time to Time under their common Seale to make and eftablifh
" fuch by Laws Rules and Ordinances not contrary to the Laws
" and Conftitutions of *England* and this his Majeftyes Colony
" and Dominion as fhall by them be thought requifite and necef-
" fary for the gcod Ordering and Government of fuch Perfons as
" fhall from Time to Time refide within the Limits of the fᵈ City
" and Corporation or fhall be concerned in Intereft therein and
" by the Name aforefaid to do and execute all and fingular other
" Matters and Things that to them fhall or may appertaine to do
" And that there may not be any Defeét in the good Order-
" ing or Management of the faid Land appropriated by this Aét
" for the Building of the fᵈ [City *] and in provideing for the
" better Regulation thereof untill the next Meeting of Affembly
" *be it enaéted by the Authority aforefaid and it is hereby enaéted* that
" his Exelency *Francis Nicholfon* Efqʳ his Majeftyes Lieutenant
" and Governer Generall of *Virginia Edmund Jenings* Efqʳ of his
" Majeftyes honerable Councill *Phill: Ludwell* Efqʳ and
" *Thomas Ballard* Gent: Members of the right worfhipfull Houfe
" of Burgeffes of this prefent Generall Affembly *Lewis Burrell*
" *Phill: Ludwell* Junʳ *John Page   Henry Tylor James Whaley*
" and *Benjamin Harrifon* Junʳ Gent. or any five or more of them
" fhall be and are hereby nominated authorized and impowered
" by the Name of the Direétors appointed for the Settlement
" and Encouragment of the City of *Williamfburgh* to make fuch
" Rules and Orders and to give fuch Direétions in the Building
" of the faid City and Portes not already provided for by this
" Aét as to them fhall feem beft and moft convenient *And be it*
" *further enaéted by the Authority aforefaid and it is hereby enaéted*
" that his Exelency the Governer or the Governer or Commander
" in Cheife of this his Majeftyes Colony and Dominion for the
" Time being is hereby impowered and defired by Letters Pat-
" tents under the Seale of this his Majeftyes Colony and Domin-
" ion to grant unto the faid City of *Williamfburgh* the Liberty
" and Priviledge of holding and keeping fuch and fo many
" Markets and Faires at fuch Time and Times and upon fuch
" Conditions and under fuch Limitations as he fhall think fitt
" *Provided alwayes and be it further enaéted by the Authority afore-*
" *faid and it is hereby enaéted* that no Lott or Lotts of any half
"   " Acre

---

* Manufcript torn.

" Acre or halfe Acres of Land fhall be fold or difpofed of to any
" Perfon or Perfons whatfoever before the twentieth Day of
" *October* next enfuing the Date of this Act to the End that the
" whole Country may have timely Notice of this Act and equall
" Liberty in the Choice of the Lots."

Act VI—*August* 1701.

" *AN ACT GIVEING FURTHER DIRECTIONS*
" *IN BUILDING THE* CAPITOLL *AND FOR*
" *BUILDING A PUBLICK* PRISON. "

[*Note:* This Act was paffed by a " Generall Affembly,
" begun at His Majeftyes Royall Colledge of
" *William & Mary* " on *December* 5, 1700, and
thence continued by feveral Prorogations to *August*
6, 1701. The Act is here copied from a Manufcript
Volume entitled " *ACTS OF THE VIRGINIA*
" *ASSEMBLY 1662-1702,* " Pages 412-413, in the
*Jefferfon Collection, Divifion of Manufcripts, Li-
brary of Congrefs.*]

" WHEREAS it is concluded to be more fuitable and como-
" dius for the uniforme Carrying on and Finifhing the Capitoll
" now erecting in the City of *Williamfburgh* that fome Altera-
" tions be made in the Modell of the faid Capitoll laid downe and
" exprefed in an Act of Affembly made at *James City* the 27ᵗʰ
" Day of *Aprill Aº Domini:* 1699 *Be it therefore enacted by the*
" *Governer Councill and Burgeffes of this prefent Generall Affembly*
" *and the Authority thereof and it is hereby enacted* that the follow-
" ing Directions be obferved *vizᵗ.*
" That the Porches of the faid Capitoll be built circular fifteen
" Foot in Breadth from Outfide to Outfide and that they ftand
" upon Cedar Collums (if to be had) if not the fame to be fett
" upon other good lafting and fubftanciall Wood; that the crofs
" Building betwixt the two main Buildings be of the fame
" Breadth with the maine Buildings that all the great Doors be
" arched and that it be left to the Comitee which now is or hear-
" after fhall be appointed to overfee the Building of the Capitoll
" to direct what other Doors fhall be made therein that the
" Placeing

" Placeing the four Galleryes be left to the Commitee that now
" is or hearafter fhall be appointed to overfee the Building of the
" Capitoll and that they have Liberty to take fo much Room out
" of the adjacent Rooms as in their Defcretion they fhall think
" fitt for the Carrying up a fuitable Pair of Staires—

" That the Windows in the lower Story be arched and that the
" lower Floors be raifed two Foot from the Ground and that the
" Comitee appointed to overfee the Building of the fᵈ Capitoll
" have Power and they are hereby impowered to fend to *England*
" for all fuch Materialls as are yet wanting to finifh the faid
" Worke

" AND WHEREAS it is abfolutely neceffary that a Publick
" Prifon be built near and convenient to the Siting of the Generall
" Court for the Reception of Criminals of both Sexes *Be it en-*
" *acted [by the Authority *] aforefaid and it is hereby enacted* that
" there be forthwith built convenient to the Capitoll a [good *]
" and fubftanciall Brick Prifon thirty Foot long in the Clear and
" twenty Foot wide in the Clear [- - - *] three Rooms on the
" lower Floor *viz*ᵗ one with the Chambers above for the Goalers or
" Prifon Keepers owne Ufe and for Confinement of fmall Offend-
" ers and the other two fmaler on the lower Floor for Goals for
" the Criminals of both Sexes to be underlaid with Timbers
" under Ground to the Foundations to prevent Undermining
" and that at one End thereof there be waled in with a fubftan-
" tiall Wall tenn Foot high twenty Foot fquare of Ground for the
" Prifoners to be let into to aire them as Occafion fhall require for
" Prefervation of their Life and Health till Tryall whereby it will
" be a convenient Reception for all Criminals upon their Com-
" mitments and fave the Charge which neceffarily acrews in each
" County by keeping continuall Guards upon them and that the
" Comitee for overfeing the Building the Capitoll have Power
" and they are hereby impowered to fend to *England* for Iron
" Barrs Bolts and all fuch Materialls as fhall be thought neceffary
" for the fame and direct the Building thereof both in thefe and
" in all other Things neceffary thereunto.

" AND WHEREAS the former Law for building the Capitoll
" gave Power to the Comitee to make Ufe only of two Thoufand
" Pounds Ster: which Sume is well nigh expended *Be it therefore*
" *enacted by the Authority aforefaid and it is hereby enacted* that
" the faid Comitee as often as they fhall have Occafion for Money
" for the Ufes of the Capitoll or Prifon fhall from Time to Time
" apply themfelves to the Governor or Commander in Cheife
" for

* Manufcript torn.

" for the Time being to iffue out his Warrant to the Treafurer of
" this his Majeftyes Colony and Dominion requireing him to pay
" fo much Money as they fhall have Occafion for, any former
" Law to the Contrary in any Wife notwithftanding.

" Signed by *Francis Nicholfon*, Efq⠂ Gov
"   *Peter Beverley*, Speaker"

October 1705.

" *AN ACT CONTINUEING Yᵉ ACT DIRECTING*
" *Yᵉ BUILDING Yᵉ CAPITOL AND Yᵉ CITY OF*
" WILLIAMSBURGH *WITH ADDITIONS.*

[*Note:* This Act was paffed at a " General Affembly,
" begun at the Capitol, in the City of *Williamf-*
" *burg,* " on *October* 23, 1705. It is here copied
from Manufcript Volume entitled " *Acts of Vir-*
" *ginia Affembly, 1705. Second Seffion—Chap.*
" *2-53* " from *Charles City* County Clerk's Office.
This Volume is in the *Jefferfon Collection, Divifion*
of Manufcripts, Library of Congrefs.]

" WHEREAS By an Act made at a Genˡˡ Affembly begun at
" *James City* yᵉ 27ᵗʰ Day of *Aprill* and in yᵉ eleventh Year of his
" late Majefty's Reign entituled *An Act Directing yᵉ Building yᵉ*
" *Capitol and yᵉ City of Williamfburgh* it is enacted that
" . . .

[*Note:* At this Point, the Act of 1699, entitled
" *An Act directing the Building the Capitoll and the*
" *City of Williamfburgh* " was re-enacted with Additions. To print the full Act here would be to
reprint verbatim the Act of 1699 as it appears on
Pages 335-344 of this Volume. In Confequence,
only the Additions made in 1705 are given here
as follows:]

" Now forafmuch as feverall Parts and Claufes recited in yᵉ
" aforefaid Act are not executed others neceffary to remain in
" Force and for confirming every Thing already done by any Per-
"   " fon

" fon or Perfons whatfoever by Virtue of and purfuant to yᵉafore-
" faid Act. *Be it enacted by yᵉ Governor Councill & Burgeſſes of this*
" *prefent Genˡˡ Aſſembly and it is hereby enacted by yᵉ Authority of*
" *yᵉfame* that yᵉ aforerecited Act and every Part & Claufe thereof
" be and are hereby declared to be in full Force. *And be it fur-*
" *ther enacted* if any Perfon fhall hereafter take a Grant of two
" Lotts or half Acres of Land upon yᵉ great Street of yᵉ faid City
" comonly called *Duke of Glouceſter* Street and within yᵉ Space of
" four and twenty Months next enfuing fuch Grant upon yᵉ faid
" Lotts or half Acres or either of them fhall build & finifh one
" Houfe fifty Foot long and twenty Foot broad or within yᵉ Space
" aforefᵈ upon yᵉ faid Lotts or half Acres or either of them fhall
" build and finifh one Brick Houfe or framed Houfe with two
" Stacks of Brick Chimney's & Cellers under yᵉ whole Houfe
" bricked forty Foot long & twenty Foot broad either of yᵉ faid
" Performances fhall be fufficient to fave yᵉ Grant of both yᵉ fᵈ
" Lotts or half Acres from becomeing void and fhall be fo adjudg-
" ed deemed and taken any Law Ufage or Cuftome heretofore to
" yᵉ Contrary notwithftanding. And if any Perfon fhall hereafter
" take a Grant of two Lotts or half Acres of Land upon yᵉ great
" Street of yᵉ faid City and one or more Lotts or half Acres back-
" ward & within yᵉ Space of four & twenty Months next enfuing
" fuch Grant upon yᵉ Lotts or half Acres contiguous to yᵉ great
" Street or either of them fhall build and finifh in ordinary ffram-
" ed Work as much Dwelling Houfing as will make five Hundred
" fquare Feet fuperficiall Meafure on yᵉ Ground Plat for every
" Lott or half Acre taken up or within yᵉ Space aforefaid upon yᵉ
" faid two Lotts or half Acres or either of them fhall build and
" finifh in Brick Work or fframed Work with Brick Cellars under
" yᵉ whole and Brick Chimney's as much Dwelling Houfing as
" will make four Hundred fquare Feet fuperficiall Meafure on yᵉ
" Ground Plat for every Lot or half Acre taken up either of yᵉfaid
" Performances fhall be fufficient to fave yᵉ Grant of all & every
" of yᵉ faid Lotts or half Acres from becomeing void and fhall be
" fo adjudged deemed and taken any Law Ufage or Cuftome here-
" tofore to yᵉ Contrary notwithftanding. PROVIDED always
" that yᵉ Building of one Houfe be yᵉ Dimenfions thereof never fo
" large fhall not fave more than two Lotts or half Acres on yᵉ
" great Street and that whatever Lotts or half Acres more yᵉ
" Builder is willing to take a Grant of fhall be taken backward.
" *And be it further enacted* that every Perfon having any Lotts or
" half Acres of Land contiguous to yᵉ great Street fhall inclofe yᵉ
" faid Lotts or half Acres with a Wall Pales or Poft and Rails within

" fix

" fix Months after y° Building which y° Law requires to be erected
" thereupon fhall be finifhed upon Penalty of forfeiting & paying
" five Shillings a Month for every Lot or half Acre fo long as y°
" fame fhall remaine without a Wall Pales or Rails as aforefaid to
" be recovered before any Juftice of Peace of *York* or *James City*
" County upon y°Complaint of any one of y° Truftees or Directors
" and to be difpofed off by y° Directors as they fhall think ffit for
" y° Ufe and Benefit of y° faid City & Ports thereunto belonging
" *And be it further enacted by y° Authority aforef* and it is hereby*
" *enacted* that none of y° Lotts or half Acres of Land in y° City of
" *Williamfburgh* whereon any Houfes were ftanding at y° Laying
" out of y° faid City fhall veft in y° faid Feoffees and Truftees of y°
" faid City to be difpofed off as y° Reft of y° Lotts and half Acres
" may be by Virtue of y° faid Act made at a Gen¹¹ Affembly begun
" at *James City* y° twenty feventh Day of *Aprill* one Thoufand fix
" Hundred ninety nine entituled *An Act directing y° Building y°*
" *Capitol and y° City of Williamfburgh* but that all and every of y°
" faid Lotts and half Acres fhall remain and continue y° proper
" Eftate of y° refpective Proprietors unaltered by y° faid Act and
" fhall be fo adjudged deemed and taken any Thing in y° faid Act
" to y° Contrary or feeming to y° Contrary notwithftanding. *And*
" *be it alfo enacted* that y° four Lotts or half Acres which at y° firft
" Laying out of y° Land for y° faid City were laid out and appro-
" priated for y° Buildings then erected on y° fame by *Benjamin*
" *Harrifon* Junior Efq ʳ fhall remaine & continue to y° Ufe of y° faid
" *Benjamin Harrifon* his Heirs and Affigns and fhall not lapfe for
" Want of other Building thereon any Thing in this Act to y°
" Contrary notwithftanding. AND WHEREAS by y° Death Re-
" movall out of y° Country or into remote Parts of feverall of y°
" Perfons nominated Directors in y° aforerecited Act and y° re-
" fufall of others to concern themfelves therein y° Powers and
" Authority's to them granted have not been fo fully executed as
" was intended and it being neceffary for y° better Regulating and
" Ordering y° Building of y° faid City of *Williamfburgh* that a
" competent Number of Directors be appointed and continued to
" infpect y° fame. *Be it therefore enacted by y° Authority afore-*
" *faid and it is hereby enacted* that his Excly: *Edward Nott* Efq ʳ
" her Majeftys Lieuᵗ and Governor Gen¹¹ of *Virginia Edmund*
" *Jenings Philip Ludwell William Byrd*, and *Benjamin Harrifon*
" Junʳ Efq ʳˢ *Henry Tyler, David Bray, Frederick Jones, Archibald*
" *Blair, Chichley Corbin Thacker,* & *William Robertfon* Gentlemen
" or any five or more of them be & they are hereby authorifed and
" impowered by y° Name of y° Directors for y° Settlement & En-
" couragement

" couragement of y⁰ City of *Williamſburgh* from Time to Time
" and at all Times hereafter untill y⁰ ſaid City ſhall be erected
" into a Corporacon in Manner aforementioned to direct and
" order y⁰ Laying out y⁰ Lotts & Streets of y⁰ ſaid City where y⁰
" Bounds & Marks thereof are worne out to lay out a convenient
" Space of Ground for y⁰ Churchyard to enlarge y⁰ Market Place
" and to alter any of y⁰ Streets or Lands thereof where y⁰ ſame are
" found inconvenient & alſo to ſettle & eſtabliſh ſuch Rules and
" Orders for y⁰ more regular and orderly Building of y⁰ Houſes in
" y⁰ ſaid City as to them ſhall ſeem beſt and moſt convenient
" PROVIDED alway's that y⁰ main Street called *Duke of Glou-*
" *ceſter* Street extending from y⁰ Capitol to y⁰ utmoſt Limitts of
" y⁰ City weſtward till it joyn's on y⁰ Land belonging to y⁰ College
" ſhall not hereafter be altered either in y⁰ Courſe or Dimenſions
" thereof. AND *be it further enacted* that in Caſe of y⁰ Death Re-
" movall out of y⁰ Country or other legall Diſability of any one or
" more of y⁰ Directors before named it ſhall and may be lawfull
" for y⁰ ſurviving or remaining Directors from Time to Time to
" elect and chooſe ſo many other Perſons in y⁰ Room of thoſe ſo
" dead or removed as ſhall make up y⁰ Number of ten which Di-
" rectors ſo choſen ſhall be to all Intents and Purpoſes veſted
" with y⁰ ſame Power as any other in this Act particularly nom-
" inated and appointed."

CHARTER

CHARTER *of* WILLIAMSBURG

[Taken from a Copy by the firſt Town Clerk, *Joſeph Davenport*, now preſerved in the Library of the College of *William & Mary*.]

" Geo. I. [1722, *July* 28.]

" GEORGE by the Grace of *God* of *Great Britain*, *France*, *Ire-*
" *land*, and the Dominions thereunto belonging, King, Defender
" of the Faith &c. TO ALL and ſingular our faithfull Subjeċts,
" *Greeting*. Whereas a healthfull, pleaſant, & commodious
" Place by Aċt of the General Aſſembly of our Colony & Domin-
" ion of *Virginia*, hath been appointed & laid out for a Town, in
" Honor to our royal Predeceſſor, King *William* the Third,
" called *Williamſburg*, and for two Ports thereto adjoining,
" where our Capitol for the Reception of our General Aſſembly
" and Courts of Judicature and a commodious Houſe for the Re-
" ception of our Governor [- - - *] which ſaid Town and Ports,
" of late Years, eſpecially during the Adminiſtration of our truſty
" and wellbeloved *Alexander Spotſwood* Eſq ᵗ, our Lieutenant Gov-
" ernor and Commander in Chief of our ſaid Colony, have very
" greatly increaſed in the Number of Inhabitants and of public
" and private Buildings; KNOW YEE that we being willing to
" encourage all our good and faithfull Subjeċts, as well at preſent
" reſiding and inhabiting, as which ſhall or may hereafter reſide
" and inhabit within the ſaid Town of *Williamſburg*, and the
" ſaid Ports, at the Inſtance and Petition of our dutifull and
" ſocial Subjeċts the Burgeſſes of our preſent General Aſſembly,
" of our royal Grace, good Will, certain Knowledge and meer
" Motion, with the Advice of our Council of our ſaid Colony,
" HAVE

* Manuſcript torn.

" HAVE conftituted and erected, and by thefe our Letters Pat-
" ents, do conftitute and erect the faid Town of *Williamfburg*, and
" the faid Ports thereto adjoining, including the Lands heretofore
" laid out for the faid Town and Ports a City by the Name of the
" City of *WILLIAMSBURG;* and for us, our Heirs, and Suc-
" ceffors do, by thefe Prefents, grant to the Inhabitants of the
" faid City, that the faid City fhall be a City incorporate, con-
" fifting of a Mayor, one Perfon learned in the Law, ftiled and
" bearing the Office of Recorder of the faid City, fix Aldermen
" and twelve other Perfons to be Common Council Men of the
" faid City: Which faid Mayor, Recorder, Aldermen and Com-
" mon Council-men, fhall be a Body incorporate, and one Com-
" munity, for ever, in Right, in Fact, and by the Name of
" Mayor, Recorder, Aldermen, and Common Council, of the
" City of *Williamfburg*, and as fuch fhall be Perfons able and
" capable in Law to acquire, purchafe and receive Manors, Lands,
" Tenements and Hereditaments, not exceeding two Thoufand
" Pounds Sterling per Annum; and all Goods and Chattels what-
" foever to have, hold, and enjoy to them and their Succeffors
" for ever; AND ALSO that they the faid Mayor, Recorder,
" Aldermen & Common Council, by the fame Name may plead
" and be impleaded, profecute and defend, anfwer and be an-
" fwered, in all and fingular Caufes, Complaints, Actions, real,
" perfonal and mixt, of what Kind or Nature foever, in all Courts
" and Places, and before all Judges and Juftices whatfoever.
" AND ALSO that the faid Mayor, Recorder, Aldermen and
" Common Council and their Succeffors, fhall have one common
" Seal, to be ufed for their Caufes and Bufineffes, and that it
" fhall be lawfull for them, the faid Mayor, Recorder, Aldermen,
" and Common Council and their Succeffors, their faid Seal, at
" their Pleafure, to break, change, and to make anew, from Time
" to Time as to them fhall feem expedient. AND we will, and
" by thefe Prefents declare, name and appoint, *John Holloway*,
" Efquire, to be Mayor of the faid City for the Year enfuing, and
" afterwards, untill the Day for the Electing a Mayor herein
" after appointed: And *John Clayton* Efquire, to be Recorder of
" the faid City, and *John Randolph, John Cuftis, James Bray*,
" *Archibald Blair, William Robertfon* and *Thomas Jones*, Gentle-
" men, Inhabitants of the faid City, to be Aldermen thereof, for
" fo long Time as they fhall well behave themfelves in their
" refpective Offices & Places. AND WE do further order and
" direct that the faid Mayor, Recorder, Aldermen, & Common
" Council before they fhall enter into and upon the Execution of
" their

" their faid Offices fhall take the feveral Oaths by Law appointed
" for the Security of our Perfon and Government and the Oath
" by our faid Lieutenant Governor, appointed to be taken by the
" Mayor, Recorder, & Aldermen of the faid City and fubfcribe
" the Teft: Which Oath fhall be adminiftered to them by our
" faid Lieutenant Governer, or by fuch Perfon or Perfons as he
" fhall authorize and appoint to adminifter the fame. AND we
" grant that the faid Mayor, Recorder, and Aldermen or the
" major Part of them fhall elect and chufe other of the moft fuffi-
" cient of the Inhabitants of the faid City, being free Men
" thereof to be of the Common-Council of the faid City, for fo
" long a Time as they fhall well behave themfelves in their refpec-
" tive Places. AND, to perpetuate the Succeffion of the faid
" Mayor, Recorder, Aldermen and Common Council Men, in all
" Time to come, we do grant that for the Future they fhall af-
" femble in fome convenient Place in the faid City, upon the
" Feaft Day of *Saint Andrew*, in every Year, and fhall elect and
" chufe by the major Vote of fuch of them as fhall be then prefent,
" one other of the Aldermen of the faid City for the Time being
" to be Mayor of the faid City for the enfuing Year: And upon
" the Death or Removal of the faid Mayor of the faid City for
" the Time being, or upon the Death or Removal of the faid Re-
" corder or Aldermen, or the Refignation of any of them, or
" within one Month after fuch refpective Death or Deaths, Re-
" moval or Removals, or Refignation or Refignations, the reft of
" the faid Aldermen, together with the faid Mayor and Recorder
" (if they fhall be living) and Common Council or the major Part
" of them fhall at a Time by them to be appointed, meet within
" the faid City, and elect and nominate fome other Perfon and
" Perfons to be Mayor, Recorder, Alderman and Aldermen of the
" faid City, in Place and Places of fuch Perfon or Perfons fo
" deceafed or removed, as the Cafe fhall require; fo as the faid
" Mayor fo to be elected and nominated be at the Time of fuch
" Election and Nomination be actually one of the Aldermen of
" the faid City, and fo as the faid Recorder fo to be elected and
" nominated, be a Perfon learned in the Law, fo as the faid Alder-
" man and Aldermen fo to be elected and nominated at the Time
" of fuch Election and Nomination be actually of the Common
" Council of the faid City, the faid Mayor, Recorder, Alderman
" and Aldermen fo elected and nominated, fhall at the Time and
" Place of Election, take the feveral Oaths abovementioned, and
" fubfcribe the Teft: Which Oaths the faid Mayor, Recorder
" or any one of the Aldermen may and is hereby required to ad-
                                                    " minifter

" minifter; and fhall then likewife, or on the faid Feaft of *Saint*
" *Andrew*, out of, and from among the Inhabitants and Free-
" holders of the faid City, elect and nominate fo many Perfons to
" be of the Common Council, as fhall be wanting to make the full
" Number of twelve Perfons, AND THAT the Perfons hereby ap-
" pointed and named, or hereafter to be elected and nominated,
" Mayor, Recorder, and Aldermen, be Juftices of the Peace
" within the faid City, the Precincts and Liberties thereof, and
" Directors of the Buildings and Streets in the faid City, and
" that they or any three of them, whereof the Mayor or Recorder,
" for the Time being, fhall be always one, fhall have within the
" faid City and the Precincts thereof, full Power and Authority,
" to make Conftables, Surveyors of the Highways, and other
" neceffary Officers, and to rule, order, and govern the Inhabi-
" tants and Buildings and the Streets thereof, as Juftices of the
" Peace and Directors are, or fhall be authorized to do: And
" fhall have Power and may execute all the Laws, Ordinances &
" Statutes in that Behalf: made as fully and amply as if they
" were authorized thereto by exprefs Commiffion; willing and
" commanding that no other Juftice of the Peace or Quorum,
" within our faid Colony, do at any Time hereafter, take upon
" them, or any of them to execute the Office of a Juftice of the
" Peace within the faid City, or Precincts thereof, in any Caufe,
" Matter, or Thing, hereby declared to be cognizable by the faid
" Mayor, Recorder, and Aldermen; notwithftanding any Com-
" miffion at large authorizing them thereto, SAVING AL-
" WAYS the Authority and Jurifdiction of our Judges of the
" General Court, our Juftices of Oyer and Terminer, and Goal
" Delivery, and our Juftices of the Peace of our County of *James*
" *City*, now or at any Time hereafter to be affigned, during the
" Time of their holding their feveral and refpective Courts in the
" faid City. SAVING ALSO to all and every other Judges,
" Juftices, and Officers all fuch Rights, Powers, Jurifdictions and
" Authorities granted or which fhall be granted to them or any of
" them by any Statute or Act of Affembly of this Colony; PRO-
" VIDED ALSO that Nothing herein contained fhall be con-
" ftrued, deemed or taken to give any Power, Jurifdiction or
" Authority to the faid Mayor, Recorder, or Aldermen, or any
" Officer by them appointed to hold Plea of any Matter or Thing
" arifing within the Bounds of the Land appropriated for the
" Governor's Houfe, or to ferve any Procefs or Execution on any
" Perfon or Perfons being within the Governor's Houfe, or of his
" Family without the Licence of fuch Governor for the Time
                                                          " being;

" being; AND FURTHER WE WILL AND GRANT the said
" Mayor, Recorder, Aldermen, and Common Council for the
" Time being full Power and Authority to erect Work Houses
" and Houses of Correction and Prisons within the said City, and
" to make, order, and appoint such By Laws, Rules and Ordi-
" nances for the Regulation and good Government of the Trade,
" and other Matters, Exigencies and Things within the said City
" and Precincts as to them or the major Part of them shall seem
" most to be consonant to Reason and Justice, and not contrary
" but as near as conveniently may be agreable to the Laws, Acts
" of Assembly and Statutes now in force; which said By-Laws,
" Rules and Ordinances shall be observed, kept, and performed,
" by all Manner of Persons, trading or residing within the said
" City, under such reasonable Pains, Penalties, and Forfeitures as
" shall be imposed by the said Mayor, Recorder, Aldermen and
" Common Council Men, or the major Part, of them then assem-
" bled from Time to Time, not exceeding forty Shillings current
" Money of *Virginia*, which said Pains, Penalties, and Forfei-
" tures shall be levied by Distress, and Sales of the Land of the
" Person offending, and be imployed for the public Benefit of the
" said City [- - - *] Discretion; and further we have given and
" granted to the said Mayor, Recorder, Aldermen, & Common
" Council, of the said City, and to their Successors, for ever, and
" to all Freeholders of the said City, owning one whole Lott of
" Land, with an House built thereon according to Law, and to
" all Persons actually residing and inhabiting in the said City,
" having a visible Estate, of the Value of fifty Pounds current
" Money at the least, and to all Persons, who hereafter shall
" serve five Years, to any Trade within the said City, and shall
" after the Expiration of their Time of Service, be actually House-
" keepers and Inhabitants in the said City and for us, and our
" Successors, by these Presents, do give and grant to them full
" Power and absolute Authority to name, elect, and send one
" Citizen out of the Inhabitants actually residing and being
" within the said City; which Citizen elected, shall have a Free-
" hold or visible Estate within the said City, of the Value of two
" Hundred Pounds Sterling, and if such Person so elected, be not
" actually residing in the said City, then he shall have a Freehold
" or other visible Estate of the Value of five Hundred Pounds
" Sterling, to be present, sit, and vote in the House of Burgesses
" of our said Colony of *Virginia* and there to do and consent to
" those Things, which by the Common Council of our said Colony
" shall

* Manuscript torn.

" fhall happen to be ordained. And we do hereby grant and
" order that Writ or Writs of Election of a Citizen for the faid
" City fhall be iffued and fent to the faid Mayor, Recorder, and
" Aldermen, for the Time being, when and fo often as a General
" Affembly fhall be called, or Occafion fhall require. PRO-
" VIDED always that all fuch Electors and Voters, fhall and do,
" before they be admitted to give their Vote at fuch Election,
" make Oath of their Freehold, and of the Value of their perfonal
" Eftate if the Candidates or other Elector fhall require the fame
" to be done. AND FURTHER WE OF OUR ESPECIAL
" GRACE, certain Knowledge, and meer Motion, for us, our
" Heirs and Succeffors by thefs Prefents, give, and grant, to the
" faid Mayor, Recorder, Aldermen and Common Council Men, of
" the faid City, and to their Succeffors, for ever, full and free
" Licence, Power & Authority to have, hold, and keep, two
" Markets weekly in fome convenient Place in the faid City, to
" be by them appointed (that is to fay) on every *Wednefday* and
" every *Saturday*, in the Week; and alfo two Fairs yearly to be
" held and kept on the twelfth Day of *December*, and on the
" twenty third Day of *April*, commonly called *Saint George*, his
" Day in every Year, or on the Day next following, each or either
" of them, in Cafe they fhall happen to fall on a *Sunday* for the
" Sale and Vending all, and all Manner of Cattle, Victuals, Pro-
" vifions, Goods, Wares and Merchandizes, whatfoever. On
" which Fair Days, and on two Days next before, and on two
" Days next after, each of the faid Fair Days, all Perfons coming
" to or being at the faid Fairs, together with their Cattle, Goods,
" and Merchandizes, fhall be exempt and priviledged from all
" Arrefts, Attachments or Executions, except for Toll and Pro-
" cefs from the Court of Pipowder. AND that the faid Mayor,
" Recorder, Aldermen and Common Council and their Suc-
" ceffors, for ever, fhall have Power to fett fuch reafonable Tole
" upon all fuch Cattle, Goods, Wares and Merchandizes and
" other Commodities as fhall be fold in the faid Markets and
" Fairs refpectively, as fhall be by them thought reafonable, not
" exceeding fix Pence on every Beaft and three Pence on every
" Hogg and the twentieth Part of the Value of any fuch Com-
" modity fold therein. PROVIDED ALWAYS THAT THE
" TOLL to be rated and affeffed on the Cattle and Goods, fo
" fold, which fhall be belonging to the Freemen Inhabitants of
" the faid City fhall be but one Half of the faid Tole, which fhall
" be rated on other Perfons not Freemen of the faid City, AND
" that the faid Mayor, Recorder and Aldermen or any three of
" them,

" them, of which the Mayor, and Recorder fhall be one, fhall
" and may hold a Court of Pipowder, during the Time of the faid
" Fairs for the Hearing and Determining all Controverfies, Suits
" and Quarrels that may arife and happen therein, according to
" the ufual and legal Courfe in the like Cafes in *England*. AND
" WE do for us and our Succeffors give and grant to the faid
" Mayor, Recorder, Aldermen, and Common Council and to
" their Succeffors for ever, all and every the Tole, Profits, and
" Perquifites, arifing, due or incident from or to the faid Markets,
" Fairs and Court of Pipowder, to be by them or the major Part
" of them ufed, laid out and expended for the Benefit, and Ad-
" vantage of the faid City. AND FURTHER WE DO GRANT
" for us and our Succeffors, that the faid Mayor, Recorder and
" Aldermen and their Succeffors or any four or more of them, of
" which the faid Mayor, Recorder or the laft preceeding Mayor
" fhall be one, fhall hold a Court of Huftings once in every Month
" within the faid City, of which Court they are hereby impow-
" ered to appoint and make Clerks and other proper Officers
" [- - - - *] the Fees now fettled and allowed in the County
" Courts of our faid Colony, and fhall have Jurifdiction and
" hold Plea of Trefpafs and Ejectment and of all Writs of Dower
" for any Lands and Tenements within the faid City, and of all
" other Actions perfonal and mixt arifing within the faid City
" and Ports thereof; and as a Court of Record give Judgment,
" and award Execution thereon, according to the Laws and
" Statutes of *England* and of the faid Colony. PROVIDED
" the Demand in the faid Action perfonal or mixt do not exceed
" twenty Pounds current Money, or four Thoufand Pounds of
" Tobacco. AND PROVIDED neverthelefs, that any Party
" or Parties, Plaintiff or Defendant fhall be at Liberty to appeal
" from the Judgment of the faid Court of Huftings to the
" General Court, or to obtain a Supercedeas to fuch Judgm͏ͭ
" returnable to the faid General Court, under fuch Limitations,
" Rules and Orders, as are already prefcribed and fett down
" by the Acts of Affembly of the faid Colony, for obtaining
" and profecuting Appeals and Writs of Supercedeas from
" the Judgment of the County Court, to the General Court.
" PROVIDED ALWAYS that no Perfon hereafter elected Alder-
" man fhall take upon him to act as a Juftice of the Peace or fit
" as fuch in the Court of Huftings, unlefs he be a Juftice named
" in fome Commiffion of the Peace within this Colony. AND
" FURTHER we will and by thefe Prefents, name, conftitute
" and

* Manucript torn.

" and appoint *Joseph Davenport* Gent: Town Clerk of the said
" City to hold and enjoy the said Office of Town Clerk with all
" [- - - - *] and Perquisites which shall be due or arising there-
" from, for so long a Time as the said *Joseph Davenport* shall well
" behave himself in the said Office. IN WITNESS whereof we
" have caused these our Letters to be made Patents. WITNESS
" our Trusty and well beloved *Alexander Spotswood* Esq[r] our
" Lieutenant Governor of our said Colony and Dominion of
" *Virginia*, the twenty eighth Day of *July* in the eighth Year of
" our Reign.
"   *ALEXANDER SPOTSWOOD*

" Truly recorded and examined with the Original by *Joseph*
" *Davenport* Town Cl. A.D. 1722"

* Manuscript torn.

APPENDIX.

PART III.

1. The Presidents of The Colonial Williamsburg Foundation.

2. The Chairmen of the Board of The Colonial Williamsburg Foundation.

Presidents

VERNON M. GEDDY
> February 27, 1928–April 6, 1928

ARTHUR WOODS
> April 6, 1928–October 11, 1935

KENNETH CHORLEY
> October 11, 1935–May 21, 1958

CARLISLE H. HUMELSINE
> May 21, 1958–November 12, 1977

CHARLES R. LONGSWORTH
> November 12, 1977–

Chairmen of the Board

ARTHUR WOODS
> October 11, 1935–November 10, 1939

JOHN D. ROCKEFELLER 3RD
> November 10, 1939–April 20, 1953

WINTHROP ROCKEFELLER
> April 20, 1953–February 22, 1973

LEWIS F. POWELL, JR.
> May 19, 1973–November 12, 1977

CARLISLE H. HUMELSINE
> November 12, 1977–

The
INDEX.

Auctions

(College

(Richmond,